W. J. Bristol

DR. E. K. KANE.
FROM AN AMBROTYPE BY BRADY.

THE ADVANCE AND RESCUE IN WINTER QUARTERS.

ARCTIC

EXPLORATIONS AND DISCOVERIES

DURING THE NINETEENTH CENTURY.

BEING DETAILED ACCOUNTS OF

THE SEVERAL EXPEDITIONS TO THE NORTH SEAS,

BOTH ENGLISH AND AMERICAN, CONDUCTED BY

ROSS, PARRY, BACK, FRANKLIN, M'CLURE AND OTHERS.

INCLUDING

THE FIRST GRINNELL EXPEDITION,

UNDER LIEUTENANT DE HAVEN, AND THE

FINAL EFFORT OF DR. E. K. KANE

IN

SEARCH OF SIR JOHN FRANKLIN.

EDITED AND COMPLETED

BY

SAMUEL M. SMUCKER, A. M.,

AUTHOR OF "COURT AMD REIGN OF CATHERINE II.," "NICHOLAS I.," "MEMORABLE SCENES IN FRENCH HISTORY," "HISTORY OF THE MORMONS," ETC.

NEW YORK AND AUBURN:
MILLER, ORTON & CO.,
New York: 25 Park Row—Auburn: 107 Genesee-st.
1857.

PREFACE.

THE records of maritime adventure and discovery constitute one of the most attractive pages in literature. Nearly three thousand years before the birth of Christ, the bold Tyrians and Phœnicians deserted the confines of their native continent to explore new realms, and to obtain from the then unknown land of Spain, the means of augmented splendor, luxury, and wealth. From that remote period, down through succeeding ages until the present, the most enterprising and dauntless of human spirits have found their congenial field of labor and activity in adventuring into untrodden and unfamiliar re gions in search of riches, celebrity, and conquest.

It was this spirit which has in the past given birth to many great states and empires. It was this spirit which planted Carthage on the northern shores of Africa, and eventually rendered her the dangerous and not unworthy rival of Rome. It was this spirit which built Marseilles, Arles, Nismes, and many of the most important cities of

France, which contain to this day impressive monuments of Roman origin and supremacy. It was this spirit which made England pass successively under the resistless sway of her Roman, Saxon, Danish, and Norman conquerors. But more especially was it this restless and insatiable genius of adventure which created the greatness of the chief maritime cities of modern Italy, of Genoa and Venice, as well as that of the kingdom of Portugal and Spain. To this same desire for discovery the world is indebted for the glorious achievements of Columbus, Vespucius, and De Soto; and for the revelation of the magnificent novelties and unparalleled beauties of these western continents, ladened with the most valuable treasures and products of the earth, which they threw open to the knowledge and the possession of mankind.

After the discovery of the American continents, and after the thorough exploration of the Southern and Pacific oceans, it was generally supposed that the materials for further adventures of this description had all been exhausted. The whole habitable globe seemed then to have been made accessible and familiar to men, both as apostles of science and as emissaries of commerce. It was thought that the era of maritime discovery, the days of Vasco de Gama, of Marco Polo, and of Sydney, had ended forever. But this supposition was erroneous. One additional field of this description yet remained. It was indeed a gloomy and repulsive one. It was totally devoid of the attractive and romantic splendors which in other days had allured men to sail through tranquil oceans to fragrant islands, which bloomed like gardens on the bosom of summer seas; or to continents which were covered with the richness of tropical vegetation and luxu riance, and were stored with spices, gold, and gems. But it was a field which demanded greater heroism, greater endurance, and was fraught with greater perils, than any other department of discovery. This region lay far up toward the Northern Pole. It was the vast frozen land of everlasting snow-fields, of stupendous ice-bergs, of hyperborean storms, of the long, cheerless nights of the Arctic Zone. To navigate and explore these dismal realms, men of extreme daring, of sublime fortitude, of unconquerable perseverance, were absolutely necessary. And such men possessed one great element of distinguishing greatness, of which the explorers of more genial and inviting climes were destitute. Their investigations were made entirely without the prospect of rich reward, and chiefly for the promotion of the magnificent ends of science. The discovery of a north-western passage was indeed not forgotten; but it must be conceded that other less mercenary and more philanthropic motives have given rise to the larger portion of the expeditions which, during the progress of the nineteenth century, have invaded the cheerless solitudes of that dangerous and repulsive portion of the globe.

The following pages contain a narrative of the chief adventures and discoveries of Arctic explorers during this century. No expedition of any importance has been omitted; and the work has been brought down in its details to the present time, so as to include a satisfactory account of the labors, sufferings, and triumphs of that prince of Arctic explorers and philanthropists, Dr. Kane; whose adventures, and whose able narrative of them, entitle him to fadeless celebrity, both as a hero in the field, and as a man of high genius and scholarship.

Every reader who carefully peruses the following pages must be convinced that the Arctic hemisphere has now been thoroughly explored. Every accessible spot has been visited and examined by some one or other of the various expeditions which have been sent out; and that vast extent of countries and of seas which intervene from Smith's Sound and Wolstenholme Sound in the extreme east, being the remotest northern limits of Greenland, to the westward as far as to Behring's Straits, which divide America from Asia, has been examined. These limits inclose an area of about four thousand miles, every attainable portion of which has been subjected to the scrutiny of recent Arctic explorers. It can scarcely be expected that any traces of the existence and fate of Sir John Franklin still remain on the globe, which further perseverance and research could possibly reveal. Even if the great chapter of Arctic discovery and adventure should now be closed, it will constitute one of the most remarkable and entertaining departments of human heroism, enterprise, and endurance, which biography or history presents.

CONTENTS.

THE ADVANCE AMONG HUMMOCKS.

THE PROGRESS

OF

ARCTIC DISCOVERY

IN THE

NINETEENTH CENTURY.

If we examine a map of Northern, or Arctic, America, showing what was known of the countries around the North Pole in the commencement of the present century, we shall find that all within the Arctic circle was a complete blank. Mr. Hearne had, indeed, seen the Arctic Sea in the year 1771; and Mr. Mackenzie had traced the river which now bears his name to its junction with the sea; but not a single line of the coast from Icy Cape to Baffin's Bay was known. The eastern and western shores of Greenland, to about 75° latitude, were tolerably well defined, from the visits of whaling vessels; Hudson's Bay and Strait were partially known; but Baffin's Bay, according to the statement of Mr. Baffin, in 1616, was bounded by land on the west, running parallel with the 90th meridian of longitude, or across what is now known to us as Barrow's Strait, and probably this relation led to the subsequently formed hasty opinion of Captain Sir John Ross, as to his visionary Croker Mountains, of which I shall have occasion to speak hereafter.

As early as the year 1527, the idea of a passage to the East Indies by the North Pole was suggested by a

Bristol merchant to Henry VIII., but no voyage seems to have been undertaken for the purpose of navigating the Polar seas, till the commencement of the following century, when an expedition was fitted out at the expense of certain merchants of London. To this attempt several others succeeded at different periods, and all of them were projected and carried into execution by private individuals. The adventurers did not indeed accomplish the object they exclusively sought, that of reaching India by a nearer route than doubling the Cape of Good Hope, but though they failed in that respect, the fortitude, perseverance, and skill which they manifested, exhibited the most irrefragable proofs of the early existence of that superiority in naval affairs, which has elevated this country to her present eminence among the nations of Europe.

At length, after the lapse of above a century and a half, this interesting question became an object of Royal patronage, and the expedition which was commanded by Captain Phipps (afterward Lord Mulgrave,) in 1773, was fitted out at the charge of Government. The first proposer of this voyage was the Hon. Daines Barrington, F. R. S., who, with indefatigable assiduity, began to collect every fact tending to establish the practicability of circumnavigating the Pole, and as he accumulated his materials, he read them to the Royal Society, who, in consequence of these representations, made that application to Lord Sandwich, then First Lord of the Admiralty, which led to the appointment of this first official voyage. Captain Phipps, however, found it impossible to penetrate the wall of ice which extended for many degrees between the latitude of 80° and 81°, to the north of Spitzbergen. His vessels were the Racehorse and Carcass; Captain Lutwidge being his second in command, in the latter vessel, and having with him, then a mere boy, Nelson, the future hero of England.

From the year 1648, when the famous Russian navigator, Senor Deshnew, penetrated from the river Kolyma through the Polar into the Pacific Ocean, the

Russians have been as arduous in their attempts to discover a northeast passage to the north of Cape Shelatskoi, as the English have been to sail to the northwest of the American continent, through Baffin's Bay and Lancaster Sound. On the side of the Pacific, many efforts, have, within the last century, been made to further this object. In 1741, the celebrated Captain Behring discovered the straits which bear his name, as we are informed by Muller, the chronicler of Russian discoveries, and several subsequent commanders of that nation seconded his endeavors to penetrate from the American continent to the northeast. From the period when Deshnew sailed on his expedition, to the year 1764, when Admiral Tchitschagof, an indefatigable and active officer, endeavored to force a passage round Spitzbergen, (which, although he attempted with a resolution and skill which would fall to the lot of few, he was unable to effect,) and thence to the present times, including the arduous efforts of Captain Billings and Vancouver, and the more recent one of M. Von Wrangell, the Russians have been untiring in *their* attempts to discover a passage eastward, to the north of Cape Taimur and Cape Shelatskoi. And certainly, if skill, perseverance, and courage, could have opened this passage, it would have been accomplished.

Soon after the general peace of Europe, when war's alarms had given way to the high pursuits of science, the government recommenced the long-suspended work of prosecuting discoveries within the Arctic circle.

An expedition was dispatched under the command of Sir John Ross, in order to explore the scene of the former labors of Frobisher and Baffin. Still haunted with the golden dreams of a northwest passage, which Barrington and Beaufoy had in the last age so enthusiastically advocated, our nautical adventurers by no means relinquished the long-cherished chimera.

It must be admitted, however, that the testimony of Parry and Franklin pass for much on the other side of the question. Both these officers, whose researches in the cause of scientific discovery entitle them to very high respect, have declared it as their opinion that such a passage does not exist to the north of the 75th degree of latitude.

Captain Parry, in the concluding remarks of his first voyage, (vol. ii. p. 241,) says—" Of the existence of a northwest passage to the Pacific, it is now scarcely possible to doubt, and from the success which attended our efforts in 1819, after passing through Sir James Lancaster's Sound, we were not unreasonable in anticipating its complete accomplishment," &c. And Franklin, in the eleventh chapter of his work, is of the same opinion, as to the practicability of such a passage

But in no subsequent attempt, either by themselves or others, has this long sought desideratum been accomplished; impediments and barriers seem as thickly thrown in its way as ever.*

An expedition was at length undertaken for the sole purpose of reaching the North Pole, with a view to the ascertainment of philosophical questions. It was planned and placed under the command of Sir Edward Parry, and here first the elucidation of phenomena connected with this imaginary axis of our planet formed the primary object of investigation.

My space and purpose in this work will not permit me to go into detail by examining what Barrow justly terms "those brilliant periods of early English enterprise, so conspicuously displayed in every quarter of the globe, but in none, probably, to greater advantage than in those bold and persevering efforts to pierce through frozen seas, in their little slender barks, of the most miserable description, ill provided with the means either of comfort or safety, without charts or instruments, or any previous knowledge of the cold and inhospitable region through which they had to force and to feel their way; their vessels oft beset amidst endless fields of ice, and threatened to be overwhelmed with instant destruction from the rapid whirling and bursting of those huge floating masses, known by the

* Colonial Magazine, vol. xiii, p. 340

name of icebergs. Yet so powerfully infused into the minds of Britons was the spirit of enterprise, that some of the ablest, the most learned, and most respectable men of the times, not only lent their countenance and support to expeditions fitted out for the discovery of new lands, but strove eagerly, in their own persons, to share in the glory and the danger of every daring adventure."

To the late Sir John Barrow, F. R. S., for so long a period secretary of the Admiralty, and who, in early life, himself visited the Spitzbergen seas, as high as the 80th parallel, we are mainly indebted for the advocacy and promotion of the several expeditions, and the investigations and inquiries set on foot in the present century, and to the voyages which have been hitherto so successfully carried out as regards the interests of science and our knowledge of the Polar regions.

Although it is absurd to impute the direct responsibility for these expeditions to any other quarter than the several administrations during which they were undertaken, there can be no question but that these enterprises originated in Sir John Barrow's able and zealous exhibition, to our naval authorities, of the several facts and arguments upon which they might best be justified and prosecuted as national objects. The general anxiety now prevailing respecting the fate of Sir John Franklin and his gallant companions, throws at this moment somewhat of a gloom on the subject, but it ought to be remembered that, up to the present period, our successive Polar voyages have, without exception, given occupation to the energies and gallantry of British seamen, and have extended the realms of magnetic and general science, at an expense of lives and money quite insignificant, compared with the ordinary dangers and casualties of such expeditions, and that it must be a very narrow spirit and view of the subject which can raise the cry of "*Cui bono*," and counsel us to relinquish the honor and peril of such enterprises to Russia and the United States of America!

It can scarcely be deemed out of place to give here a short notice of the literary labors of this excellent and talented man, as I am not aware that such an outline has appeared before.

Sir John Barrow was one of the chief writers for the Quarterly Review, and his articles in that journal amount to nearly 200 in number, forming, when bound up, twelve separate volumes. All those relating to the Arctic Expeditions, &c., which created the greatest interest at the period they were published, were from his pen, and consist chiefly of the following papers, commencing from the 18th volume;—On Polar Ice; On Behring's Straits and the Polar Basin; On Ross's Voyage to Baffin's Bay; On Parry's First Voyage; Kotzebue's Voyage; Franklin's First Expedition; Parry's Second and Third Voyages, and Attempt to Reach the Pole; Franklin's Second Expedition; Lyon's Voyage to Repulse Bay; Back's Arctic Land Expedition, and his Voyage of the Terror. Besides these he published "A Chronological History of Voyages to the Arctic Seas," and afterward a second volume, "On the Voyages of Discovery and Research within the Arctic Regions."

He also wrote lives of Lord Macartney, 2 vols. 4to; of Lord Anson and Howe, each 1 vol. 8vo; of Peter the Great; and an Account of the Mutiny of the Bounty, (in the "Family Library;") "Travels in Southern Africa," 2 vols, 4to; and "Travels in China aud Cochin China," each 1 vol. 4to.

In the "Encyclopedia Britannica" are ten or twelve of his articles, and he wrote one in the Edinburgh Review by special request.

In addition to these Sir John Barrow prepared for the press innumerable MSS. of travelers in all parts of the globe, the study of geography being his great delight, as is evidenced by his having founded the Royal Geographical Society of London, which now holds so high and influential a position in the learned and scientific world, and has advanced so materially the progress of discovery and research in all parts of the globe. Lastly, Sir John Barrow, not long before his death, published his own autobiography, in which he records the labors, the toil, and adventure, of a long and honorable public life.

Sir John Barrow has described, with voluminous care and minute research, the arduous services of all the chief Arctic voyagers by sea and land, and to his volume I must refer those who wish to obtain more extensive details and particulars of the voyages of preceding centuries. He has also graphically set forth, to use his own words, "their several characters and conduct, so uniformly displayed in their unflinching perseverance in difficulties of no ordinary description, their patient endurance of extreme suffering, borne without murmuring, and with an equanimity and fortitude of mind under the most appalling distress, rarely, if ever, equaled, and such as could only be supported by a superior degree of moral courage and resignation to the Divine will—displaying virtues like those of no ordinary caste, and such as will not fail to excite the sympathy, and challenge the admiration of every right-feeling reader."

Hakluyt, in his "Chronicle of Voyages," justly observes, that we should use much care in preserving the memories of the worthy acts of our nation.

The different sea voyages and land journeys of the present century toward the North Pole have redounded to the honor of our country, as well as reflected credit on the characters and reputation of the officers engaged in them; and it is to these I confine my observations.

The progress of discovery in the Arctic regions has been slow but progressive, and much still within the limits of practical navigation remains yet unexplored. As Englishmen, we must naturally wish that discoveries which were first attempted by the adventurous spirit and maritime skill of our countrymen, should be finally achieved by the same means.

"Wil it not," says the worthy 'preacher,' Hakluyt, "in all posteritie be as great a renown vnto our English natione, to have beene the first discouerers of a sea beyond the North Cape, (neuer certainely knowen before,) and of a conuenient passage into the huge empire of Russia by the Baie of St. Nicholas and of the Riuer of Duina, as for the Portugales, to have found a sea beyond the Cape of Buona Esperanza, and so consequently a passage by sea into the East Indies?"

I cordially agree with the Quarterly Review, that "neither the country nor the naval service will ever believe they have any cause to regret voyages which, in the eyes of foreigners and posterity, must confer lasting honor upon both."

The cost of these voyages has not been great, while the consequences will be permanent; for it has been well remarked, by a late writer, that "the record of enterprising hardihood, physical endurance, and steady perseverance, displayed in overcoming elements the most adverse, will long remain among the worthiest memorials of human enterprise."

"How shall I admire," says Purchas, "your heroic courage, ye marine worthies, beyond all names of worthiness! that neyther dread so long eyther the presence or absence of the sunne; nor those foggy mysts, tempestuous winds, cold blasts, snowe and hayle in the ayre; nor the unequall seas, which might amaze the hearer, and amate the beholder, when the Tritons and Neptune's selfe would quake with chilling feare to behold such monstrous icie ilands, renting themselves with terror of their own massines, and disdayning otherwise both the sea's sovereigntie and the sunne's hottest violence, mustering themselves in those watery plaines where they hold a continual civill warre, and rushing one upon another, make windes and waves give backe; seeming to rent the eares of others, while they rent themselves with crashing and splitting their congealed armors."

So thickly are the Polar seas of the northern hemisphere clustered with lands, that the long winter months serve to accumulate filed ice to a prodigious extent, so as to form an almost impenetrable barrier of hyperborean frost—

> "A crystal pavement by the breath of Heaven
> Cemented firm."

Although there are now no new continents left to discover, our intrepid British adventurers are but too eager to achieve the bubble reputation, to hand down their names to future ages for patient endurance, zeal, and enterprise, by explorations of the hidden mysteries of —

> "the frigid zone,
> Where, for relentless months, continual night
> Holds o'er the glittering waste her starry light;"

by undergoing perils, and enduring privations and dangers which the mind, in its reflective moments, shudders to contemplate.

It is fair to conjecture that, so intense is the cold, and so limited the summer, and consequently so short the time allowed for a transit within the Arctic circle, from Baffin's Bay to Behring's Straits, that a passage, even if discovered, will never be of any use as a channel. It is not likely that these expeditions would ever have been persevered in with so much obstinacy, had the prospects now opening on the world of more practicable connections with the East been known forty years ago. Hereafter, when the sacred demands of humanity have been answered, very little more will be heard about the northwest passage to Asia; which, if ever found, must be always hazardous and protracted, when a short and quick one can be accomplished by railroads through America, or canals across the Isthmus.

A thorough knowledge of the relative boundaries of land and ocean on this our globe has, in all ages and by all countries, been considered one of the most important desiderata, and one of the chief features of popular information.

But to no country is this knowledge of such practical utility and of such essential importance, as to a maritime nation like Great Britain, whose mercantile marine visits every port, whose insular position renders her completely dependent upon distant quarters for half the necessary supplies, whether of food or luxury, which her native population consume, or which the arts and manufactures, of which she is the emporium, require.

With a vast and yearly increasing dominion, covering almost every region of the habitable globe, — the chart of our colonies being a chart of the world in outline, for we sweep the globe and touch every shore, — it becomes necessary that we should keep pace with the progress of colonization, by enlarging, wherever possible, our maritime discoveries, completing and verifying our nautical surveys, improving our meteorological researches, opening up new and speedier perodical pathways over the oceans which were formerly traversed with so much danger, doubt, and difficulty, and maintaining our superiority as the greatest of maritime nations, by sustaining that high and distinguished rank for naval eminence which has ever attached to the British name.

The arduous achievements, however, of our nautical discoverers have seldom been appreciated or rewarded as they deserved. We load our naval and military heroes — the men who guard our wooden walls and successfully fight our battles — with titles and pensions; we heap upon these, and deservedly so, princely remuneration and all manner of distinctions; but for the heroes whose patient toil and protracted endurance far surpass the turmoil of war, who peril their lives in the cause of science, many of whom fall victims to pestilential climates, famine, and the host of dangers which environ the voyager and traveler in unexplored lands and unknown seas, we have only a place in the niche of fame.

What honors did England, as a maritime nation, confer on Cook, the foremost of her naval heroes, — a man whose life was sacrificed for his country? His widow had an annuity of 200*l*., and his surviving children 25*l*. each per annum. And this is the reward paid to the most eminent of our naval discoverers, before whom Cabot, Drake, Frobisher, Magellan, Anson, and the arctic adventurers, Hudson and Baffin, — although all eminent for their discoveries and the important services they rendered to the cause of nautical science, — sink into insignificance! If we glance at the results of Cook's voyages we find that to him we are indebted for the innumerable discoveries of islands and colonies planted in the Pacific; that he determined the conformation, and surveyed the numerous bays and inlets, of New Holland; established the geographical position of the northwestern shores of America; ascertained the trending of the ice and frozen shores to the north of Behring's Straits; approached nearer the South Pole, and made more discoveries in the Australian regions, than all the navigators who had preceded him. On the very shores of their vast empire, at the extremity of Kamtschatka, his active genius first taught the Russians to examine the devious trendings of the lands which border the Frozen Ocean, in the neighborhood of the Arctic circle. He explored both the eastern and western coasts above Behring's Straits to so high a latitude as to decide, beyond doubt, the question as to the existence of a passage round the two continents. He showed the Russians how to navigate the dangerous seas between the old and the new world; for, as Coxe has remarked, "before his time, every thing was uncertain and confused, and though they had undoubtedly reached the continent of America, yet they had not ascertained the line of coast, nor the separation or vicinity of the two continents of Asia and America." Coxe, certainly, does no more than justice to his illustrious countryman when he adds, "the solution of this important problem was reserved for our great navigator, and every Englishman must exult that the discoveries of Cook were extended further in a single expedition, and at the distance of half the globe, than the Russians accomplished in a long series of years, and in a region contiguous to their own empire."

Look at Weddell, again, a private trader in sealskins, who, in a frail bark of 160 tons, made important discoveries in the Antarctic circle, and a voyage of greater length and peril, through a thousand miles of ice, than had previously been performed by any navigator, paving the way for the more expensively fitted expedition under Sir James Ross. Was Weddell remunerated on a scale commensurate with his important services?

Half a century ago the celebrated Bruce of Kinnaird, by a series of soundings and observations taken in the Red Sea, now the great highway of overland eastern traffic, rendered its navigation more secure and punctual. How was he rewarded by the then existing ministry?

Take a more recent instance in the indefatigable energy of Lieutenant Waghorn, R. N., the enterprising pioneer of the overland route to India. What does not the commerce, the character, the reputation, of this country owe to his indefatigable exertions, in bringing the metropolis into closer connection with our vast and important Indian empire? And what was the reward he received for the sacrifices he made of time, money, health and life? A paltry annuity to himself of 100*l*., and a pension to his widow of 25*l*. per annum!

Is it creditable to us, as the first naval power of the world, that we should thus dole out miserable pittances, or entirely overlook the successful patriotic exertions and scientific enterprises and discoveries of private adventurers, or public commanders?

The attractions of a summer voyage along the bays and seas where the sun shines for four months at a time, exploring the bare rocks and everlasting ice, with no companion but the white bear or the Arctic fox, may be all very romantic at a distance; but the mere thought of a winter residence there, frozen fast in some solid ocean, with snow a dozen feet deep, the thermometer ranging from 40° to 50° below zero, and not a glimpse of the blessed sun from November to February, is enough to give a chill to all adventurous notions. But the officers and men engaged in the searching expeditions after Sir John Franklin have calmly weighed all these difficulties, and boldly gone forth to encounter the perils and dangers of these icy seas for the sake of their noble fellow-sailor, whose fate has been so long a painful mystery to the world.

It has been truly observed, that "this is a service for which all officers, however brave and intelligent they may be, are not equally qualified; it requires a peculiar tact, an inquisitive and persevering pursuit after details of fact, not always interesting, a contempt of danger, and an enthusiasm not to be damped by ordinary difficulties."

The records which I shall have to give in these pages of voyages and travels, unparalleled in their perils, their duration, and the protracted sufferings which many of them entailed on the adventurers, will bring out in bold relief the prominent characters who have figured in Arctic Discovery, and whose names will descend to posterity, emblazoned on the scroll of fame, for their bravery, their patient endurance, their skill, and, above all, their firm trust and reliance on that Almighty Being who, although He may have tried them sorely, has never utterly forsaken them.

Capt. John Ross's Voyage, 1818.

In 1818, His Royal Highness the Prince Regent having signified his pleasure that an attempt should be made to find a passage by sea between the Atlantic and Pacific Oceans, the Lords Commissioners of the Admiralty were pleased to fit out four vessels to proceed toward the North Pole, under the command of Captain John Ross. No former expedition had been fitted out on so extensive a scale, or so completely equipped in every respect as this one. The circumstance which mainly led to the sending out of these vessels, was the open character of the bays and seas in those regions, it having been observed for the previous three years that very unusual quantities of the polar ice had floated down into the Atlantic. In the year 1817, Sir John Barrow relates that the eastern coast of Greenland, which had been shut up with ice for four centuries, was found to be accessible from the 70th to the 80th degree of latitude, and the intermediate sea between it and Spitzbergen was so entirely open in the latter parallel, that a Hamburgh ship had actually sailed along this track.

On the 15th of January, 1818, the four ships were put in commission — the Isabella, 385 tons, and the Alexander, 252 tons — under Captain Ross, to proceed up the middle of Davis' Strait, to a high northern latitude, and then to stretch across to the westward, in the hope of being able to pass the northern extremity of America, and reach Behring's Strait by that route. Those destined for the Polar sea were, the Dorothea, 382 tons, and the Trent, 249 tons, which were ordered to proceed between Greenland and Spitzbergen, and seek a passage through an open Polar sea, if such should be found in that direction.

I shall take these voyages in the order of their publication, Ross having given to the world the account of his voyage shortly after his return in 1819: while the narrative of the voyage of the Dorothea and Trent was only published in 1843, by Captain Beechey, who served as Lieutenant of the Trent, during the voyage.

The following were the officers, &c., of the ships under Captain Ross: —

Isabella.

Captain — John Ross.
Lieutenant — W. Robertson.
Purser — W. Thom.
Surgeon — John Edwards.
Assistant Surgeon — C. J. Beverley.
Admiralty Midshipmen — A. M. Skene and James Clark Ross.
Midshipman and Clerk — J. Bushnan.
Greenland Pilots — B. Lewis, master; T. Wilcox, mate.
Captain (now Colonel) Sabine, R. A.

45 petty officers, seamen, and marines.
Whole complement, 57.

Alexander.

Lieutenant and Commander — William Edward Parry, (now Captain Sir Edward.)
Lieutenant — H. H. Hoopner, (a first rate artist.)
Purser — W. H. Hooper.
Greenland Pilots — J. Allison, master; J. Philips, mate.
Admiralty Midshipmen — P. Bisson and J. Nius.
Assistant Surgeon — A. Fisher.
Clerk — J. Halse.
28 petty officers, seamen, &c.
Whole complement, 37.

On the 2d of May, the four vessels being reported fit for sea, rendezvoused in Brassa Sound, Shetland, and the two expeditions parted company on the following day for their respective destinations.

On the 26th, the Isabella fell in with the first iceberg, which appeared to be about forty feet high and a thousand feet long. It is hardly possible to imagine any thing more exquisite than the variety of tints which these icebergs display; by night as well as by day they glitter with a vividness of color beyond the power of art to represent. While the white portions have the brilliancy of silver, their colors are as various and splendid as those of the rainbow; their ever-changing disposition producing effects as singular as they are new and interesting to those who have not seen them before.

On the 17th of June, they reached Waygatt Sound, beyond Disco Island, where they found forty-five whalers detained by the ice. Waygatt Island, from observations taken on shore, was found to be 5° longitude and 30 miles of latitude from the situation as laid down in the Admiralty Charts.

They were not able to get away from here till the 20th, when the ice began to break. By cutting passages through the ice, and by dint of towing and warping, a slow progress was made with the ships until the 17th of July, when two ice-floes closing in upon them, threatened inevitable destruction, and it was only by the greatest exertions that they hove through into open water. The labors of warping, towing, and tracking were subsequently very severe. This tracking, although hard work, afforded great amusement to the men, giving frequent occasion for the exercise of their wit, when some of the men occasionally fell in through holes covered with snow or weak parts of the ice.

Very high mountains of land and ice were seen to the north side of the bay, which he named Melville's Bay, forming an impassable barrier, the precipices next the sea being from 1000 to 2000 feet high.

On the 29th of June, the Esquimaux, John Sacheuse, who had accompanied the expedition from England as interpreter, was sent on shore to communicate with the natives. About a dozen came off to visit the ship, and, after being treated with coffee and biscuit in the cabin, and having their portraits taken, they set to dancing Scotch reels on the deck of the Isabella with the sailors.

Captain Ross gives a pleasant description of this scene —" Sacheuse's mirth and joy exceeded all bounds; and with a good-humored officiousness, justified by the important distinction which his superior knowledge now gave him, he performed the office of master of the ceremonies. An Esquimaux M. C. to a ball on the deck of one of H. M. ships in the icy seas of Greenland, was an office somewhat new, but Nash himself could not have performed his functions in a manner more appropriate. It did not belong even to Nash to combine in his own person, like Jack, the discordant qualifications of seaman, interpreter, draughtsman, and master of ceremonies to a ball, with those of an active fisher of seals and a hunter of white bears. A daughter of the Danish resident (by in Esquimaux woman,) about eighteen years of age, and by far the best looking of the half-caste group, was the object of

Jack's particular attentions; which being observed by one of our officers, he gave him a lady's shawl, ornamented with spangles, as an offering for her acceptance. He presented it in a most respectful, and not ungraceful manner to the damsel, who bashfully took a pewter ring from her finger and gave it to him in return, rewarding him, at the same time, with an eloquent smile, which could leave no doubt on our Esquimaux's mind that he had made an impression on her heart."* On the 5th of August the little auks (Mergulfus alle,) were exceedingly abundant, and many were shot for food, as was also a large gull, two feet five inches in length, which, when killed, disgorged one of these little birds entire.

A fortnight later, on two boats being sent from the Isabella to procure as many of these birds as possible, for the purpose of preserving them in ice, they returned at midnight with a boat-load of about 1500, having on an average, killed fifteen at each shot. The boats of the Alexander were nearly as successful. These birds were afterward served daily to each man, and, among other ways of dressing them, they were found to make excellent soup — not inferior to hare soup. Not less than two hundred auks were shot on the 6th of August, and served out to the ships' companies, among whose victuals they proved an agreeable variety, not having the fishy flavor that might be expected from their food, which consists of crustacea, small fishes, mollusca, or marine vegetables.

On the 7th of August the ships were placed in a most critical situation by a gale of wind. The Isabella was lifted by the pressure of ice floes on each side of her, and it was doubted whether the vessel could long withstand the grips and concussions she sustained; "every support threatened to give way, the beams in the hold began to bend, and the iron water-tanks settled together. The two vessels were thrown with violent concussion against each other, the ice-anchors

* Vol. I, p. 67, 68.

and cables broke one after the other, a boat at the stern was smashed in the collision, and the masts were hourly expected to go by the board; but at this juncture, when certain destruction was momentarily looked for, by the merciful interposition of Providence the fields of ice suddenly opened and formed a clear passage for the ships."

A singular physical feature was noticed on the part of the coast near Cape Dudley Digges:—"We have discovered, (says Ross,) that the snow on the face of the cliffs presents an appearance both novel and interesting, being apparently stained or covered by some substance which gave it a deep crimson color. This snow was penetrated in many places to a depth of ten or twelve feet by the coloring matter." There is nothing new, however, according to Barrow, in the discovery of red snow. Pliny, and other writers of his time mention it. Saussure found it in various parts of the Alps; Martin found it in Spitzbergen, and no doubt it is to be met with in most alpine regions.

In the course of this tedious, and often laborious progress through the ice, it became necessary to keep the whole of the crew at the most fatiguing work, sometimes for several days and nights without intermission. When this was the case, an extra meal was served to them at midnight, generally of preserved meat; and it was found that this nourishment, when the mind and body were both occupied, and the sun continually present, rendered them capable of remaining without sleep, so that they often passed three days in this manner without any visible inconvenience, returning after a meal to their labor on the ice or in the boats quite refreshed, and continuing at it without a murmur.

After making hasty and very cursory examinations of Smith's and Jones' Sounds, Ross arrived, on the 30th of August, off the extensive inlet, named by Baffin, Lancaster Sound. The entrance was perfectly clear, and the soundings ranged from 650 to 1000 fathoms. I shall now quote Ross's own observations on this subject, because from his unfortunate report of a range called the Croker mountains, stretching across this Strait, has resulted much of the ridicule and discredit which has attached to his accounts, and clouded his early reputation — "On the 31st (he says) we discovered, for the first time, that the land extended from the south two-thirds across this apparent Strait; but the fog which continually occupied that quarter, obscured its real figure. During the day much interest was excited on board by the appearance of this Strait. The general opinion, however, was, that it was only an inlet. The land was partially seen extending across; the yellow sky was perceptible. At a little before four o'clock A. M., the land was seen at the bottom of the inlet by the officers of the watch, but before I got on deck a space of about seven degrees of the compass was obscured by the fog. The land which I then saw was a high ridge of mountains extending directly across the bottom of the inlet. This chain appeared extremely high in the center. Although a passage in this direction appeared hopeless, I was determined to explore it completely. I therefore continued all sail. Mr. Beverly, the surgeon, who was the most sanguine, went up to the crow's nest, and at twelve reported to me that before it became thick he had seen the land across the bay, except for a very short space.

"At three, I went on deck; it completely cleared for ten minutes, when I distinctly saw the land round the bottom of the bay, forming a chain of mountains connected with those which extended along the north and south side. This land appeared to be at the distance of eight leagues, and Mr. Lewis, the master, and James Haig, leading man, being sent for, they took its bearings, which were inserted in the log. At this moment I also saw a continuity of ice at the distance of seven miles, extending from one side of the bay to the other, between the nearest cape to the north, which I named after Sir George Warrender, and that to the south, which was named after Viscount Castlereagh. The mountains, which occupied the center, in a north and south direction, were named Croker's Mountains, after the Secretary to the Admiralty."*

They next proceeded to Possession Bay, at the entrance of the Strait, where a great many animals were observed. Deer, fox, ermine, bears, and hares, were either seen, or proved to be in abundance by their tracks, and the skeleton of a whale was found stranded about 500 yards beyond high-water-mark. Finding, as Ross supposed, no outlet through Lancaster Strait, the vessels continued their progress to the southward, exploring the western coast of Baffin's Bay to Pond's Bay, and Booth's Inlet, discovering the trending of the land, which he named North Galloway, and North Ayr to Cape Adair, and Scott's Bay.

On September the 10th, they landed on an island near Cape Eglington, which was named Agnes' Monument. A flag-staff and a bottle, with an account of their proceedings was set up. The remains of a temporary habitation of some of the Esquimaux were here observed, with a fire-place, part of a human skull, a broken stone vessel, some bones of a seal, burnt wood, part of a sledge, and tracks of dogs, &c.

While the boat was absent, two large bears swam off to the ships, which were at the distance of six miles from the land. They reached the Alexander, and were immediately attacked by the boats of that ship, and killed. One, which was shot through the head, unfortunately sank; the other, on being wounded, attacked the boats, and showed considerable play, but was at length secured and towed to the Isabella by the boats of both ships. The animal weighed 1131½ lbs., besides the blood it had lost, which was estimated at 30 lbs more.

On the following day, Lieut. Parry was sent on shore to examine an iceberg, which was found to be 4169 yards long, 3869 yards broad, and 51 feet high, being aground in 61 fathoms. When they had ascended to the top, which was perfectly flat, they found a huge

* Vol. I, p. 241-46, 8vo. ed.

white bear in quiet possession of the mass, who, much to their mortification and astonishment, plunged without hesitation into the sea from the edge of the precipice, which was fifty feet high.

From careful observation it was found that there was no such land in the center of Davis' Strait as James' Island, which was laid down in most of the charts. Nothing deserving of notice occurred in the subsequent course of the vessels past Cape Walsingham to Cumberland Strait.

The 1st of October having arrived, the limit to which his instructions permitted him to remain out, Ross shaped his course homeward, and after encountering a severe gale off Cape Farewell, arrived in Grimsby Roads on the 14th of November. As respects the purpose of Arctic discovery, this voyage may be considered almost a blank, none of the important inlets and sounds of Baffin's Bay having been explored, and all that was done was to define more clearly the land-bounds of Davis' Strait and Baffin's Bay, if we except the valuable magnetic and other observations made by Captain Sabine. The commander of the expedition was promoted to the rank of captain on paying off the ships in December, 1818.

The account of his voyage, published by Capt. Ross, is of the most meager and uninteresting description, and more than half filled with dry details of the outfit, copies of his instructions, of his routine letters and orders to his officers, &c.

Buchan and Franklin.

Dorothea and Trent to Pole, 1818.

In conjunction with the expedition of Captain John Ross, was that sent out to the coast of Spitzbergen, and of which Captain Beechy has published a most interesting account, embellished with some very elegant illustrations from his pencil. The charge of it was given to Captain D. Buchan, who had, a few years previously, conducted a very interesting expedition into the interior of Newfoundland. The first and most important object of this expedition was the discovery of a passage over or as near the Pole, as might be possible, and through Behring's Straits into the Pacific. But it was also hoped that it might at the same time be the means of improving the geography and hydrography of the Arctic regions, of which so little was at that time known, and contribute to the advancement of science and natural knowledge. The objects to which attention was specially pointed in the Admiralty instructions, were the variation and inclination of the magnetic needle, the intensity of the magnetic force, and how far it is affected by atmospherical electricity; the temperature of the air, the dip of the horizon, refraction, height of the tides, set and velocity of the currents, depths and soundings of the sea. Collections of specimens to illustrate the animal, mineral and vegetable kingdoms, were also directed to be made.

The officers and crew appointed to these vessels were:

Dorothea, 382 tons.

Captain — David Buchan.
Lieutenant — A. Morell.
Surgeon — John Duke.
Assistant Surgeon — W. G. Borland.
Purser — John Jermain.
Astronomer — George Fisher.
Admiralty Mates — C. Palmer and W. J. Dealy.
Greenland Pilots — P. Bruce, master; G. Crawfurd, mate.
45 petty officers, seamen, &c.

Total complement, 55.

Trent, 249 tons.

Lieutenant and Commander — John Franklin.
Lieutenant — Fred. W. Beechy, (artist.)
Purser — W. Barrett.
Assistant Surgeon — A. Gilfillan.
Admiralty Mates — A. Reid and George Back.
Greenland Pilots — G. Fife, master; G. Kirby, mate.
30 petty officers and seamen.

Total complement, 38.

Having been properly fitted for the service, and taken on board two years' provisions, the ships sailed on the 25th of April. The Trent had hardly got clear of the river before she sprang a leak, and was detained in the port of Lerwick nearly a fortnight undergoing repairs.

On the 18th of May, the ships encountered a severe gale, and under even storm stay-sails were buried gunwale deep in the waves. On the 24th they sighted Cherie Island, situated in lat. 74° 33′ N., and long. 17° 40′ E., formerly so noted for its fishery, being much frequented by walrusses, and for many years the Muscovy Company carried on a lucrative trade by sending ships to the island for oil, as many as a thousand animals being often captured by the crew of a single ship in the course of six or seven hours.

The progress of the discovery ships through the small floes and huge masses of ice which floated in succession past, was slow, and these, from their novelty, were regarded with peculiar attention from the grotesque shapes they assume. The progress of a vessel through such a labyrinth of frozen masses is one of the most interesting sights that offer in the Arctic seas, and kept the officers and crew out of their beds till a late hour watching the scene. Capt. Beechey, the graphic narrator of the voyage, thus describes the general impression created :—"There was besides, on this occasion, an additional motive for remaining up; very few of us had ever seen the sun at midnight, and this night happening to be particularly clear, his broad red disc, curiously distorted by refraction, and sweeping majestically along the northern horizon, was an object of imposing grandeur, which riveted to the deck some of our crew, who would perhaps have beheld with indifference the less imposing effect of the icebergs; or it might have been a combination of both these phenomena; for it cannot be denied that the novelty, occasioned by the floating masses, was materially heightened by the singular effect produced by the very low altitude at which the sun cast his fiery beams over the icy surface of the sea. The rays were too oblique to illuminate more than the inequalities of the floes, and falling thus partially on the grotesque shapes, either really assumed by the ice or distorted by the unequal refraction of the atmosphere, so betrayed the imagination that it required no great exertion of fancy to trace in various directions architectural edifices, grottos and caves here and there glittering as if with precious metals. So generally, indeed, was the deception admitted, that, in directing the route of the vessel from aloft, we for awhile deviated from our nautical phraseology, and shaped our course for a church, a tower, a bridge, or some similar structure, instead of for lumps of ice, which were usually designated by less elegant appellations."

The increasing difficulties of this ice navigation soon, however, directed their attention from romance to the reality of their position, the perils of which soon became alarmingly apparent.

"The streams of ice, between which we at first pursued our serpentine course with comparative ease, gradually became more narrow, and at length so impeded the navigation, that it became necessary to run the ships against some of these imaginary edifices, in order to turn them aside. Even this did not always succeed, as some were so substantial and immoveable, that the vessels glanced off to the opposite bank of the channel, and then became for a time embedded in the ice. Thus circumstanced, a vessel has no other resource than that of patiently awaiting the change of position in the ice, of which she must take every advantage, or she will settle bodily to leeward, and become completely entangled."

On the 26th the ships sighted the southern promontory of Spitzbergen, and on the 28th, while plying to windward on the western side, were overtaken by a violent gale at southwest, in which they parted company. The weather was very severe. "The snow fell in heavy showers, and several tons weight of ice accumulated about the sides of the brig, (the Trent,) and formed a complete casing to the planks, which received an additional layer at each plunge of the vessel. So great indeed, was the accumulation about the bows, that we were obliged to cut it away repeatedly with axes to relieve the bow-sprit from the enormous weight that was attached to it; and the ropes were so thickly covered with ice, that it was necessary to beat them with large sticks to keep them in a state of readiness for any evolution that might be rendered necessary, either by the appearance of ice to leeward, or by a change of wind."

On the gale abating, Lieutenant Franklin found himself surrounded by the main body of ice in lat. 80° N., and had much difficulty in extricating the vessel.—Had this formidable body been encountered in thick weather, while scudding before a gale of wind, there would have been very little chance of saving either the vessels or the crews. The Trent fortunately fell in with her consort, the Dorothea, previous to entering the appointed rendezvous at Magdalena Bay, on the 3d of June. This commodious inlet being the first port they had anchored at in the polar regions, possessed many objects to engage attention. What particularly struck them was the brilliancy of the atmosphere, the peaceful novelty of the scene, and the grandeur of the various objects with which nature has stored these unfrequented regions. The anchorage is formed by rugged mountains, which rise precipitously to the height of about 3000 feet. Deep valleys and glens occur between the ranges, the greater part of which are either filled with immense beds of snow, or with glaciers, sloping from the summits of the mountainous margin to the very edge of the sea.

The bay is rendered conspicuous by four huge glaciers, of which the most remarkable, though the smallest in size, is situated 200 feet above the sea, on the slope of a mountain. From its peculiar appearance this glacier has been termed the Hanging Iceberg.

Its position is such that it seems as if a very small matter would detach it from the mountain, and precipitate it into the sea. And, indeed, large portions of its front do occasionally break away and fall with headlong impetuosity upon the beach, to the great hazard of any boat that may chance to be near. The largest of these glaciers occupies the head of the bay, and, according to Captain Beechey's account, extends from two to three miles inland. Numerous large rents in its upper surface have caused it to bear a resemblance to the ruts left by a wagon; hence it was named by the voyagers the "Wagon Way." The frontage of this glacier presents a perpendicular surface of 300 feet in height, by 7000 feet in length. Mountain masses—

"Whose blocks of sapphire seem to mortal eye
Hewn from cerulean quarries in the sky,
With glacier battlements that crowd the spheres,
The slow creation of six thousand years,
Amidst immensity they tower sublime,
Winter's eternal palace, built by Time."

At the head of the bay there is a high pyramidal mountain of granite, termed Rotge Hill, from the myriads of small birds of that name which frequent its base, and appear to prefer its environs to every other part of the harbor. "They are so numerous that we have frequently seen an uninterrupted line of them extending full half way over the bay, or to a distance of more than three miles, and so close together that thirty have fallen at one shot. This living column, on an average, might have been about six yards broad, and as many deep; so that, allowing sixteen birds to a cubic yard, there must have been nearly four millions of birds on the wing at one time. The number I have given certainly seems large; yet when it is told that the little rotges rise in such numbers as completely to darken the air, and that their chorus is distinctly audible at a distance of four miles, the estimate will not be thought to bear any reduction."

One of their earliest excursions in this bay was an attempt to ascend the peak of Rotge Hill, "upon which," says Captain Beechey, "may now, perhaps, be seen at the height of about 2000 feet, a staff that once carried a red flag, which was planted there to mark the greatest height we were able to attain, partly in consequence of the steepness of the ascent, but mainly on account of the detached masses of rock which a very slight matter would displace and hurl down the precipitous declivity, to the utter destruction of him who depended upon their support, or who might happen to be in their path below. The latter part of our ascent was, indeed, much against our inclination; but we found it impossible to descend by the way we had come up, and were compelled to gain a ledge, which promised the only secure resting-place we could find at that height. This we were able to effect by sticking the tomahawks with which we were provided, into crevices in the rock, as a support for our feet; and some of these instruments we were obliged to leave where they were driven, in consequence of the danger that attended their recovery." During the vessel's detention in this harbor, the bay and anchorage were completely surveyed.

When the first party rowed into this bay, it was in quiet possession of herds of walruses, who were so unaccustomed to the sight of a boat that they assembled about her, apparently highly incensed at the intrusion, and swam toward her as though they would have torn the planks asunder with their tusks. Their hides were so tough that nothing but a bayonet would pierce them. The wounds that were inflicted only served to increase their rage, and it was with much difficulty they were kept off with fire-arms. Subsequently the boats went better prepared and more strongly supported, and many of these monsters were killed; some were fourteen feet in length, and nine feet girth, and of such prodigious weight, that the boat's crew could scarcely turn them.

The ships had not been many days at their anchorage when they were truly astonished at the sight of a strange boat pulling toward the ships, which was found to belong to some Russian adventurers, who were engaged in the collection of peltry and morse' teeth. This is the last remaining establishment at Spitzbergen still upheld by the merchants of Archangel.

Although equally surprised at the sight of the vessels, the boat's crew took courage, and after a careful scrutiny, went on board the Dorothea; Captain Buchan gave them a kind reception, and supplied them with whatever they wanted; in return for which they sent on board, the following day, a side of venison in excellent condition. Wishing to gain some further information of these people, an officer accompanied them to their dwelling at the head of a small cove, about four miles distant from the bay, where he found a comfortable wooden hut, well lined with moss, and stored with venison, wild ducks, &c.

It is related by Captain Beechey that it was with extreme pleasure they noticed in this retired spot, probably the most northern and most desolate habitation of our globe, a spirit of gratitude and devotion to the Almighty rarely exercised in civilized countries. "On landing from the boat and approaching their residence, these people knelt upon its threshold, and offered up a prayer with fervor and evident sincerity. The exact nature of the prayer we did not learn, but it was no doubt one of thanksgiving, and we concluded it was a custom which these recluses were in the habit of observing on their safe return to their habitation. It may, at all events, be regarded as an instance of the beneficial effects which seclusion from the busy world, and a contemplation of the works of nature, almost invariably produce upon the hearts of even the most uneducated part of mankind."

On the 7th of June the expedition left the anchorage to renew the examination of the ice, and after steering a few leagues to the northward, found it precisely in the same state as it had been left on the 2d. In spite of all their endeavors, by towing and otherwise, the vessels were driven in a calm by the heavy swell into the packed ice, and the increasing peril of their situation may be imagined from the following graphic description:—

"The pieces at the edge of the pack were at one time wholly immersed in the sea, and at the next raised far above their natural line of flotation, while those further in, being more extensive, were alternately depressed or elevated at either extremity as the advancing wave forced its way along.

"The see-saw motion which was thus produced was alarming, not merely in appearance, but in fact, and must have proved fatal to any vessel that had encountered it; as floes of ice, several yards in thickness, were continually crashing and breaking in pieces, and the sea for miles was covered with fragments ground so small that they actually formed a thick, pasty substance — in nautical language termed, '*brash* ice' — which extended to the depth of five feet. Amidst this giddy element, our whole attention was occupied in endeavoring to place the bow of the vessel, the strongest part of her frame, in the direction of the most formidable pieces of ice — a maneuver which, though likely to be attended with the loss of the bowsprit, was yet preferable to encountering the still greater risk of having the broadside of the vessel in contact with it; for this would have subjected her to the chance of dipping her gunwale under the floes as she rolled, an accident which, had it occurred, would either have laid open her side, or have overset the vessel at once. In either case, the event would probably have proved fatal to all on board, as it would have been next to impossible to rescue any person from the confused moving mass of brash ice which covered the sea in every direction."

The attention of the seamen was in some degree diverted from the contemplation of this scene of difficulty by the necessity of employing all hands at the pump, the leak having gained upon them. But, fortunately, toward morning, they got quite clear of the ice.

Steering to the westward to reconnoiter, they fell in, in longitude 4° 30′ E., with several whale ships, and were informed by them that the ice was quite compact to the westward, and that fifteen vessels were beset in it. Proceeding to the northward, the ships passed, on the 11th of June, Cloven Cliff, a remarkable isolated rock, which marks the northwestern boundary of Spitzbergen, and steered along an intricate channel between the land and ice; but, next morning, their further advance was stopped, and the channel by which the vessels had entered became so completely closed up as to preclude the possibility also of retreating. Lieutenant Beechey proceeds to state —

"The ice soon began to press heavily upon us, and, to add to our difficulties, we found the water so shallow that the rocks were plainly discovered under the bottoms of the ships. It was impossible, however, by any exertion on our part, to improve the situations of the vessels. They were as firmly fixed in the ice as if they had formed part of the pack, and we could only hope that the current would not drift them into still shallower water, and damage them against the ground."

The ships were here hemmed in in almost the same position where Baffin, Hudson, Poole, Captain Phipps, and all the early voyagers to this quarter had been stopped.

As the tide turned, the pieces of ice immediately around the ships began to separate, and some of them to twist round with a loud grinding noise, urging the vessels, which were less than a mile from the land, still nearer and nearer to the beach.

By great exertions the ships were hauled into small bays in the floe, and secured there by ropes fixed to the ice by means of large iron hooks, called ice anchors. Shifting the ships from one part of this floe to the other, they remained attached to the ice thirteen days. As this change of position could only be effected by main force, the crew were so constantly engaged in this harassing duty, that their time was divided almost entirely between the windlass and the pump, until the men at length became so fatigued that the sick-list was seriously augmented. During this period, however, the situation of the leak was fortunately discovered, and the damage repaired.

An officer and a party of men who left the Dorothea to pay a visit to the shore, about three or four miles distant, lost themselves in the fog and snow, and wandered about for sixteen hours, until, quite overcome with wet, cold and fatigue, they sat down in a state of despondency, upon a piece of ice, determined to submit their fate to Providence. Their troubles are thus told:

"To travel over ragged pieces of ice, upon which there were two feet of snow, and often more, springing from one slippery piece to the other, or, when the channels between them were too wide for this purpose, ferrying themselves upon detached fragments, was a work which it required no ordinary exertion to execute.

"Some fell into the water, and were with difficulty preserved from drowning by their companions; while others, afraid to make any hazardous attempt whatever, were left upon pieces of ice, and drifted about at the mercy of the winds and tides. Foreseeing the probability of a separation, they took the first opportunity of dividing, in equal shares, the small quantity of provision which they had remaining, as also their stock of powder and ammunition. They also took it in turns to fire muskets, in the hope of being heard from the ships."

The reports of the fire-arms were heard by their shipmates, and Messrs. Fife and Kirby, the Greenland ice-masters, ventured out with poles and lines to their assistance, and had the good fortune to fall in with the party, and bring them safely on board, after eighteen hours' absence. They determined in future to rest satisfied with the view of the shore which was afforded them from the ship, having not the slightest desire to attempt to approach it again by means of the ice.

The pressure of the ice against the vessels now became very great.

"At one time, when the Trent appeared to be so closely wedged up that it did not seem possible for her to be moved, she was suddenly lifted four feet by an enormous mass of ice getting under her keel; at another, the fragments of the crumbling floe were piled up under the bows, to the great danger of the bowsprit.

"The Dorothea was in no less imminent danger, especially from the point of a floe, which came in contact with her side, where it remained a short time, and then glanced off, and became checked by the field to which she was moored. The enormous pressure to which the ship had been subjected was now apparent by the field being *rent*, and its point broken into fragments, which were speedily heaped up in a pyramid, thirty-five feet in height, upon the very summit of which there appeared a huge mass, bearing the impression of the planks and bolts of the vessel's bottom."

Availing themselves of a break in the ice, the ships were moved to an anchorage between the islands contiguous to the Cloven Cliff; and on the 28th of June, anchored in fifteen fathoms water, near Vogel Sang. On the islands they found plenty of game, and eider-ducks.

The island of Vogel Sang alone supplied the crews with forty reindeer, which were in such high condition that the fat upon the loins of some measured from four to six inches, and a carcass, ready for being dressed, weighed 285 pounds. Later in the season, the deer were, however, so lean that it was rare to meet with any fat upon them at all.

On the 6th of July, finding the ice had been driven to the northward, the ships again put to sea, and Capt. Buchan determined to prove, by a desperate effort, what advance it was possible to make by dragging the vessels through the ice whenever the smallest opening occurred. This laborious experiment was performed by fixing large ropes to iron hooks driven into the ice, and by heaving upon them with the windlass, a party removing obstructions in the channel with saws. But in spite of all their exertions, the most northerly position attained was 80° 37′ N. Although fastened to the ice, the ships were now drifted bodily to the southward by the prevailing current. They were also much injured by the pressure of hummocks and fields of ice.

On the 10th of July, Captain Beechey tells us, the Trent sustained a squeeze which made her rise four feet, and heel over five streaks; and on the 15th and 16th, both vessels suffered considerable damage. "On that occasion," he says, "we observed a field fifteen feet in thickness break up, and the pieces pile upon each other to a great height, until they upset, when they rolled over with a tremendous crash. The ice near the ships was piled up above their bulwarks. Fortunately, the vessels rose to the pressure, or they must have had their sides forced in. The Trent received her greatest damage upon the quarters, and was so twisted that the doors of all the cabins flew open, and the panels of some started in the frames, while her false stern-post was moved three inches, and her timbers cracked to a most serious extent. The Dorothea suffered still more: some of her beams were sprung, and two planks on the lower deck were split fore and aft, and doubled up, and she otherwise sustained serious injury in her hull. It was in vain that we attempted any relief; our puny efforts were not even felt, though continued for eight hours with unabated zeal; and it was not until the tide changed that the smallest effect was produced. When, however, that occurred, the vessels righted and settled in the water to their proper draught."

From the 12th to the 19th, they were closely beset with ice. For nine successive days following this the crews were occupied, night and day, in endeavoring to extricate the ships, and regain the open sea. Thinking he had given the ice a fair trial here, the commander determined upon examining its condition toward the eastern coast of Greenland, and in the event of finding it equally impenetrable there, to proceed round the south cape of Spitzbergen, and make an attempt between that island and Nova Zembla.

On the 30th of July, a sudden gale came on, and brought down the main body of the ice upon them, so that the ships were in such imminent danger that their only means of safety was to take refuge among it — a practice which has been resorted to by whalers in extreme cases — as their only chance of escaping destruction.

The following is a description of the preparation made to withstand the terrible encounter, and the hair-breadth escape from the dangers: —

"In order to avert the effects of this as much as possible, a cable was cut up into thirty-feet lengths, and these, with plates of iron four feet square, which had been supplied to us as fenders, together with some walrus' hides, were hung round the vessels, especially about the bows. The masts, at the same time, were secured with additional ropes, and the hatches were battened and nailed down. By the time these precautions had been taken, our approach to the breakers only left us the alternative of either permitting the ships to be drifted broadside against the ice, and so to take their chance, or of endeavoring to force fairly into it by putting before the wind. At length, the hopeless state of a vessel placed broadside against so formidable a body became apparent to all, and we resolved to attempt the latter expedient."

Eagerly, but in vain, was the general line of the pack scanned, to find one place more open than the other. All parts appeared to be equally impenetrable, and to present one unbroken line of furious breakers, in which immense pieces of ice were heaving and subsiding with the waves, and dashing together with a violence which nothing apparently but a solid body could withstand, occasioning such a noise that it was with the greatest difficulty the officers could make their orders heard by the crew.

The fearful aspect of this appalling scene is thus sketched by Captain Beechey:—

"No language, I am convinced, can convey an adequate idea of the terrific grandeur of the effect now produced by the collision of the ice and the tempestuous ocean. The sea, violently agitated and rolling its mountainous waves against an opposing body, is at all times a sublime and awful sight: but when, in addition, it encounters immense masses, which it has set in motion with a violence equal to its own, its effect is prodigiously increased. At one moment it bursts upon these icy fragments and buries them many feet beneath its wave, and the next, as the buoyancy of the depressed body struggles for reascendancy, the water rushes in foaming cataracts over its edges; while every individual mass, rocking and laboring in its bed, grinds against and contends with its opponent, until one is either split with the shock or upheaved upon the surface of the other. Nor is this collision confined to any particular spot; it is going on as far as the sight can reach; and when from this convulsive scene below, the eye is turned to the extraordinary appearance of the blink in the sky above, where the unnatural clearness of a calm and silvery atmosphere presents itself, bounded by a dark, hard line of stormy clouds, such as at this moment lowered over our masts, as if to mark the confines within which the efforts of man would be of no avail. The reader may imagine the sensation of awe which must accompany that of grandeur in the mind of the beholder."

"If ever," continues the narrator, "the fortitude of seamen was fairly tried, it was assuredly not less so on this occasion; and I will not conceal the pride I felt in witnessing the bold and decisive tone in which the orders were issued by the commander (the present Captain Sir John Franklin) of our little vessel, and the promptitude and steadiness with which they were executed by the crew."

As the laboring vessel flew before the gale, she soon neared the scene of danger.

"Each person instinctively secured his own hold, and with his eyes fixed upon the masts, awaited in breathless anxiety the moment of concussion.

"It soon arrived,—the brig, (Trent) cutting her way through the light ice, came in violent contact with the main body. In an instant we all lost our footing; the masts bent with the impetus, and the cracking timbers from below bespoke a pressure which was calculated to awaken our serious apprehensions. The vessel staggered under the shock, and for a moment seemed to recoil; but the next wave, curling up under her counter, drove her about her own length within the margin of the ice, where she gave one roll, and was immediately thrown broadside to the wind by the succeeding wave, which beat furiously against her stern, and brought her lee-side in contact with the main body, leaving her weather-side exposed at the same time to a piece of ice about twice her own dimensions. This unfortunate occurrence prevented the vessel penetrating sufficiently far into the ice to escape the effect of the gale, and placed her in a situation where she was assailed on all sides by battering-rams, if I may use the expression, every one of which contested the small space which she occupied, and dealt such unrelenting blows, that there appeared to be scarcely any possibility of saving her from foundering. Literally tossed from piece to piece, we had nothing left but patiently to abide the issue; for we could scarcely keep our feet, much less render any assistance to the vessel. The motion, indeed, was so great, that the ship's bell, which, in the heaviest gale of wind, had never struck of itself, now tolled so continually, that it was ordered to be muffled, for the purpose of escaping the unpleasant association it was calculated to produce.

"In anticipation of the worst, we determined to attempt placing the launch upon the ice under the lee, and hurried into her such provisions and stores as could at the moment be got at. Serious doubts were reasonably entertained of the boat being able to live among the confused mass by which we were encompassed; yet as this appeared to be our only refuge, we clung to it with all the eagerness of a last resource."

From the injury the vessel repeatedly received, it became very evident that if subjected to this concussion for any time, she could not hold together long; the only chance of escape, therefore, appeared to depend upon getting before the wind, and penetrating further into the ice.

To effect this with any probability of success, it became necessary to set more head-sail, though at the risk of the masts, already tottering with the pressure of that which was spread. By the expertness of the seamen, more sail was spread, and under this additional pressure of canvass, the ship came into the desired position, and with the aid of an enormous mass under the stern, she split a small field of ice, fourteen feet in thickness, which had hitherto impeded her progress, and effected a passage for herself between the pieces.

In this improved position, by carefully placing the protecting fenders between the ice and the ship's sides, the strokes were much diminished, and she managed to weather out the gale, but lost sight of her consort in the clouds of spray which were tossed about, and the huge intervening masses of ice among which they were embayed. On the gale moderating, the ships were fortunately got once more into an open sea, although both disabled, and one at least, the Dorothea, which had sustained the heavy shocks, in a foundering condition. For the main object of the expedition they were now useless, and, both being in a leaky state, they bore up for Fair Haven, in Spitzbergen. In approaching the anchorage in South Gat, the Trent bounded over a sunken rock, and struck hard, but this, after their recent danger, was thought comparatively light of.

On examining the hulls of the vessels, it was found they had sustained frightful injuries. The intermediate lining of felt between the timbers and planks seems to have aided greatly in enabling the vessels to sustain the repeated powerful shocks they had encountered. Upon consulting with his officers, Captain Buchan came to the opinion that the most prudent course, was to patch up the vessels for their return voyage. Lieutenant Franklin preferred an urgent request that he might be allowed to proceed in his own vessel upon the interesting service still unexecuted; but this could not be complied with, in consequence of the hazard to the crew of proceeding home singly in a vessel so shattered and unsafe as the Dorothea. After refitting, they put to sea at the end of August, and reached England by the middle of October.

Franklin's First Land Expedition, 1819–21.

In 1819, on the recommendation of the Lords of the Admiralty, Capt. Franklin was appointed to command an overland expedition from Hudson's Bay to the northern shores of America, for the purpose of determining the latitudes and longitudes, and exploring the coast of the continent eastward from the Coppermine River. Dr. John Richardson, R. N., and two Admiralty Midshipmen, Mr. George Back, (who had been out on the polar expedition, in the previous year, in H. M. S. Trent,) and Mr. Robert Hood, were placed under his orders. Previous to his departure from London, Capt. Franklin obtained all the information and advice possible from Sir Alex. Mackenzie, one of the only two persons who had yet explored those shores. On the 23d of May, the party embarked at Gravesend, in the Prince of Wales, belonging to the Hudson's Bay Company, which immediately got under weigh in company with her consorts, the Eddystone and Wear. Mr. Back, who was left on shore by accident in Yarmouth, succeeded in catching the ship at Stromness. On the 4th of August, in lat. 59° 58′ N., and long. 59° 53′ W., they first fell in with large icebergs. On the following day, the height of one was ascertained to be 149 feet. After a stormy and perilous voyage they reached the anchorage at York Flats on the 30th of August.

On the 9th of September, Capt. Franklin and his party left York Factory in a boat by the way of the rivers and lakes for Cumberland House, another of the Company's posts, which they reached on the 22d of October.

On the 19th of January, Franklin set out in company with Mr. Back and a seaman named Hepburn, with provisions for fifteen days, stowed in two sledges, on their journey to Fort Chipewyan. Dr. Richardson, Mr. Hood and Mr. Conolly accompanied them a short distance. After touching at different posts of the Company, they reached their destination safely on the 26th of March, after a winter's journey of 857 miles. The greatest difficulty experienced by the travelers was the labor of walking in snow shoes, a weight of between two and three pounds being constantly attached to galled feet and swelled ankles.

On the 13th of July, they were joined by Dr. Richardson and Mr. Hood, who had made a very expeditious journey from Cumberland House; they had only one day's provisions left, the pemmican they had received at the posts being so mouldy that they were obliged to leave it behind. Arrangements were now made for their journey northward. Sixteen Canadian voyageurs were engaged, and a Chipewyan woman and two interpreters were to be taken on from Great Slave Lake. The whole stock of provisions they could obtain before starting was only sufficient for one day's supply, exclusive of two barrels of flour, three cases of preserved meats, some chocolate, arrow-root and portable soup, which had been brought from England, and were kept as a reserve for the journey to the coast in the following season; seventy pounds of deer's flesh and a little barley were all that the Company's officers could give them. The provisions were distributed among three canoes, and the party set off in good spirits on the 18th of July. They had to make an inroad very soon on their preserved meats, for they were very unfortunate in their fishing. On the 24th of July, however, they were successful in shooting a buffalo in the Salt River, after giving him fourteen balls. At Moose Deer Island they got supplies from the Hudson's Bay and North West Companies' officers, and on the 27th set out again on their journey, reaching Fort Providence by the 29th.

Shortly after they had an interview with a celebrated and influential Indian chief, named Akaitcho, who was to furnish them with guides. Another Canadian voyageur was there engaged, and the party now consisted of the officers already named, Mr. Fred. Wentzel, clerk of the N. W. Fur Company, who joined them here, John Hepburn, the English seaman, seventeen Canadian voyageurs, (one of whom, named Michel, was an Iroquois,) and three Indian-interpreters, besides the wives of three of the voyageurs who had been brought on for the purpose of making clothes and shoes for the men at the winter establishment. The whole number were twenty-nine, exclusive of three children. I give the list of those whose names occur most frequently in the narrative:

J. B. Belanger, Peltier, Solomon Belanger, Samandre, Benoit, Perrault, Antonio Fontano, Beauparlant, Vaillant, Credit, Adam St. Germain, interpreter; Augustus and Junius, Esquimaux interpreters. They had provisions for ten days' consumption, besides a little chocolate and tea, viz: two casks of flour, 200 dried reindeer tongues, some dried moose meat, portable soup, and a little arrow-root. A small extra canoe was provided for the women, and the journey for the Coppermine River was commenced on the 2d of August. The party met with many hardships—were placed on short diet—and some of the Canadians broke out into open rebellion, refusing to proceed farther. However, they were at last calmed, and arrived on the 20th of August at Fort Enterprise, on Winter Lake, which, by the advice of their Indian guides, they determined on making their winter quarters. The total length of the voyage from Chipewyan was 552 miles; and after leaving Fort Providence, they had 21 miles of portage to pass over. As the men had to traverse each portage with a load of 180 lbs., and return three times light, they walked, in the whole, upward of 150 miles.

In consequence of the refusal of Akaitcho and his party of Indians to guide and accompany them to the sea, because, as they alledged, of the approach of winter, and the imminent danger, Captain Franklin was obliged to abandon proceeding that season down the river, and contented himself with dispatching, on the 29th, Mr. Back and Mr. Hood, in a light canoe, with St. Germain as interpreter, eight Canadians, and one Indian, furnished with eight days' provisions — all that could be spared.

They returned on the 10th of September, after having reached and coasted Point Lake. In the mean time, Franklin and Richardson, accompanied by J. Hepburn and two Indians, also made a pedestrian excursion toward the same quarter, leaving on the 9th of September, and returning on the fourteenth. The whole party spent a long winter of ten months at Fort Enterprise, depending upon the fish they could catch, and the success of their Indian hunters, for food.

On the 6th of October, the officers quitted their tents for a good log house which had been built. The clay with which the walls and roof were plastered, had to be tempered before the fire with water, and froze as it was daubed on ; but afterward cracked in such a manner, as to admit the wind from every quarter. Still the new abode, with a good fire of fagots in the capacious clay-built chimney, was considered quite comfortable when compared with the chilly tents.

The reindeer are found on the banks of the Coppermine River early in May, as they then go to the seacoast to bring forth their young. They usually retire from the coast in July and August, rut in October, and shelter themselves in the woods during winter. Before the middle of October, the carcasses of one hundred deer had been secured in their store-house, together with one thousand pounds of suet, and some dried meat ; and eighty deer were stowed away at various distances from their house, *en cache.* This placing provisions "en cache," is merely burying and protecting it from wolves and other depredators, by heavy loads of wood or stone.

On the 18th of October, Mr. Back and Mr. Wentzel, accompanied by two Canadian voyageurs, two Indians and their wives, set out for Fort Providence to make the necessary arrangements for transporting the stores they expected from Cumberland House, and to see if some further supplies might not be obtained from the establishments on Slave Lake. Dispatches for England were also forwarded by them, detailing the progress of the expedition up to this date. By the end of the month the men had also completed a house for themselves, 34 feet by 18. On the 26th of October, Akaitcho, and his Indian party of hunters, amounting with women and children to forty souls, came in, owing to the deer having migrated southward. This added to the daily number to be provided for, and by this time their ammunition was nearly expended.

The fishing failed as the weather became more severe, and was given up on the 5th of November. About

1200 white fish, of from two to three pounds, had been procured during the season. The fish froze as they were taken from the nets, becoming in a short time a solid mass of ice, so that a blow or two of the hatchet would easily split them open, when the intestines might be removed in one lump. If thawed before the fire, even after being frozen for nearly two days, the fish would recover their animation.

On the 23d of November, they were gratified by the appearance of one of the Canadian voyageurs who had set out with Mr. Back. His locks were matted with snow, and he was so encrusted with ice from head to foot, that they could scarcely recognize him. He reported that they had had a tedious and fatiguing journey to Fort Providence, and for some days were destitute of provisions. Letters were brought from England to the preceding April, and quickly was the packet thawed to get at the contents. The newspapers conveyed the intelligence of the death of George III. The advices as to the expected stores were disheartening; of ten bales of ninety pounds each, five had been left, by some mismanagement at the Grand Rapid on the Sattkatchawan. On the 28th of November, St. Germain the interpreter, with eight Canadian voyageurs, and four Indian hunters, were sent off to bring up the stores from Fort Providence.

On the 10th of December, Franklin managed to get rid of Akaitcho and his Indian party, by representing to them the impossibility of maintaining them. The leader, however, left them his mother and two female attendants; and old Kaskarrah, the guide, with his wife and daughter, remained behind. This daughter, who was designated "Green Stockings," from her dress, was considered a great beauty by her tribe, and although but sixteen, had belonged successively to two husbands, and would probably have been the wife of many more, if her mother had not required her services as a nurse.

Mr. Hood took a good likeness of the young lady, but her mother was somewhat averse to her sitting for it, fearing that "her daughter's likeness would induce the Great Chief who resided in England to send for the original!"

The diet of the party in their winter abode consisted almost entirely of reindeer meat, varied twice a week by fish, and occasionally by a little flour, but they had no vegetables of any kind. On Sunday morning they had a cup of chocolate ; but their greatest luxury was tea, which they regularly had twice a day, although without sugar. Candles were formed of reindeer fat and strips of cotton shirts; and Hepburn acquired considerable skill in the manufacture of soap from the wood ashes, fat and salt. The stores were anxiously looked for, and it was hoped they would have arrived by New Year's Day, (1821,) so as to have kept the festival. As it was, they could only receive a little flour and fat, both of which were considered great luxuries.

On the 15th, seven of the men arrived with two kegs of rum, one barrel of powder, sixty pounds of ball, two rolls of tobacco, and some clothing.

"They had been twenty-one days on their march from Slave Lake, and the labor they underwent was sufficiently evinced by their sledge collars having worn out the shoulders of their coats. Their loads weighed from sixty to ninety pounds each, exclusive of their bedding and provisions, which at starting must have been at least as much more. We were much rejoiced at their arrival, and proceeded forthwith to pierce the spirit cask, and issue to each of the household the portion of rum which had been promised on the first day of the year. The spirits, which were proof, were frozen; but after standing at the fire for some time they flowed out, of the consistence of honey. The temperature of the liquid, even in this state, was so low as instantly to convert into ice the moisture which condensed on the surface of the dram-glass. The fingers also adhered to the glass, and would doubtless have been speedily frozen had they been kept in contact with it ; yet each of the voyageurs swallowed his dram without experiencing the slightest inconvenience, or complaining of toothache."

It appeared that the Canadians had tapped the rum-cask on their journey, and helped themselves rather freely.

On the 27th, Mr. Wentzel and St. Germain arrived, with two Esquimaux interpreters who had been engaged, possessed of euphonious names, representing the belly and the ear, but which had been Anglicised into Augustus and Junius, being the months they had respectively arrived at Fort Churchill. The former spoke English. They brought four dogs with them, which proved of great use during the season in drawing in wood for fuel.

Mr. Back, at this time, the 24th of December, had gone on to Chipewyan to procure stores. On the 12th of February, another party of six men was sent to Fort Providence to bring up the remaining supplies, and these returned on the 5th of March. Many of the *caches* of meat which had been buried early in the winter were found destroyed by the wolves; and some of these animals prowled nightly about the dwellings, even venturing upon the roof of their kitchen. The rations were reduced from eight to the short allowance of five ounces of animal food per day.

On the 17th of March, Mr. Back returned from Fort Chipewyan, after an absence of nearly five months, during which he had performed a journey on foot of more than eleven hundred miles on snow shoes, with only the slight shelter at night of a blanket and a deer skin, with the thermometer frequently at 40° and once at 57°, and very often passing several days without food.

Some very interesting traits of generosity on the part of the Indians are recorded by Mr. Back. Often they gave up and would not taste of fish or birds which they caught, with the touching remark, "We are accustomed to starvation, and you are not."

Such passages as the following often occur in his narrative:—"One of our men caught a fish, which, with the assistance of some weed scraped from the rocks, (*tripe de roche*) which forms a glutinous substance, made us a tolerable supper; it was not of the most choice kind, yet good enough for hungry men. While we were eating it, I perceived one of the women busily employed scraping an old skin, the contents of which her husband presented us with. They consisted of pounded meat, fat, and a greater proportion of Indian's and deer's hair than either; and, though such a mixture may not appear very alluring to an English stomach, it was thought a great luxury after three days' privation in these cheerless regions of America."

To return to the proceedings of Fort Enterprise. On the 23d of March, the last of the winter's stock of deer's meat was expended, and the party were compelled to consume a little pounded meat, which had been saved for making pemmican. The nets scarcely produced any fish, and their meals, which had hitherto been scanty enough, were now restricted to one in the day.

The poor Indian families about the house, consisting principally of sick and infirm women and children, suffered even more privation. They cleared away the snow on the site of the Autumn encampment to look for bones, deer's feet, bits of hide, and other offal. "When (says Franklin) we beheld them gnawing the pieces of hide, and pounding the bones for the purpose of extracting some nourishment from them by boiling, we regretted our inability to relieve them, but little thought that we should ourselves be afterward driven to the necessity of eagerly collecting these same bones, a second time from the dung-hill."

On the 4th of June, 1821, a first party set off from the winter quarters for Point Lake, and the Coppermine River, under the charge of Dr. Richardson, consisting, in all, voyageurs and Indians, of twenty-three, exclusive of children. Each of the men carried about 80 lbs., besides his own personal baggage, weighing nearly as much more. Some of the party dragged their loads on sledges, others preferred carrying their burden on their backs. On the 13th, Dr. Richardson sent back most of the men; and on the 14th Franklin dispatched Mr. Wentzel and a party with the canoes, which had been repaired. Following the water-course as far as practicable to Winter Lake, Franklin followed himself with Hepburn, three Canadians, two Indian hunters, and the two Esquimaux, and joined Dr. Richardson on the 22d. On the 25th they all resumed their journey, and, as they proceeded down the river, were fortunate in killing, occasionally, several musk oxen.

On the 15th they got a distinct view of the sea from the summit of a hill; it appeared choked with ice and full of islands. About this time they fell in with small parties of Esquimaux.

On the 19th Mr. Wentzel departed on his return for Slave Lake, taking with him four Canadians, who had been discharged for the purpose of reducing the expenditure of provisions as much as possible, and dispatches to be forwarded to England. He was also instructed to cause the Indians to deposit a relay of provisions at Fort Enterprise, ready for the party should they return that way. The remainder of the party, including officers, amounted to twenty persons. The distance that had been traversed from Fort Enterprise to the mouth of the river was about 334 miles, and the canoes had to be dragged 120 miles of this.

Two conspicuous capes were named by Franklin after Hearne and Mackenzie; and a river which falls into the sea, to the westward of the Coppermine, he called after his companion, Richardson.

On the 21st of July, Franklin and his party embarked in their two canoes to navigate the Polar Sea, to the eastward, having with them provisions for fifteen days.

On the 25th they doubled a bluff cape, which was named after Mr. Barrow, of the Admiralty. An opening on its eastern side received the appellation of Inman Harbor, and a group of islands were called after Professor Jameson. Within the next fortnight, additions were made to their stock of food by a few deer and one or two bears, which were shot. Being less fortunate afterward, and with no prospect of increasing their supply of provision, the daily allowance to each man was limited to a handful of pemmican and a small portion of portable soup.

On the morning of the 5th of August they came to the mouth of a river blocked up with shoals, which Franklin named after his friend and companion Back.

The time spent in exploring Arctic and Melville Sounds and Bathurst Inlet, and the failure of meeting with Esquimaux from whom provisions could be obtained, precluded any possibility of reaching Repulse Bay, and therefore having but a day or two's provisions left, Franklin considered it prudent to turn back after reaching Point Turnagain, having sailed nearly 600 geographical miles in tracing the deeply indented coast of Coronation Gulf from the Coppermine River. On the 22d August, the return voyage was commenced, the boats making for Hood's River by the way of the Arctic Sound, and being taken as far up the stream as possible. On the 31st it was found impossible to proceed with them farther, and smaller canoes were made, suitable for crossing any of the rivers that might obstruct their progress. The weight carried by each man was about 90 lbs., and with this they progressed at the rate of a mile an hour, including rests.

On the 5th of September, having nothing to eat, the last piece of pemmican and a little arrow-root having formed a scanty supper, and being without the means of making a fire, they remained in bed all day. A severe snow-storm lasted two days, and the snow even drifted into their tents, covering their blankets several inches. "Our suffering (says Franklin) from cold, in a comfortless canvass tent in such weather, with the temperature at 20°, and without fire, will easily be imagined; it was, however, less than that which we felt from hunger."

Weak from fasting, and their garments stiffened with the frost, after packing their frozen tents and bedclothes the poor travelers again set out on the 7th.

After feeding almost exclusively on several species of Gyrophora, a lichen known as *tripe de roche*, which scarcely allayed the pangs of hunger, on the 10th "they got a good meal by killing a musk ox. To skin and cut up the animal was the work of a few minutes. The contents of its stomach were devoured upon the spot, and the raw intestines, which were next attacked, were pronounced by the most delicate amongst us to be excellent."

Wearied and worn out with toil and suffering, many of the party got careless and indifferent. One of the canoes was broken and abandoned. With an improvidence scarcely to be credited, three of the fishing-nets were also thrown away, and the floats burnt.

On the 17th they managed to allay the pangs of hunger by eating pieces of singed hide, and a little *tripe de roche.* This and some mosses, with an occasional solitary partridge, formed their invariable food; on very many days even this scanty supply could not be obtained, and their appetites became ravenous.

Occasionally they picked up pieces of skin, and a few bones of deer which had been devoured by the wolves in the previous spring. The bones were rendered friable by burning, and now and then their old shoes were added to the repast.

On the 26th they reached a bend of the Coppermine, which terminated in Point Lake. The second canoe had been demolished and abandoned by the bearers on the 23d, and they were thus left without any means of water transport across the lakes and river.

On this day the carcass of a deer was discovered in the cleft of a rock, into which it had fallen in the spring. It was putrid, but little less acceptable to the poor starving travelers on that account; and a fire being kindled a large portion was devoured on the spot, affording an unexpected breakfast.

On the first of October one of the party, who had been out hunting, brought in the antlers and backbone of another deer, which had been killed in the summer. The wolves and birds of prey had picked them clean, but there still remained a quantity of the spinal marrow, which they had not been able to extract. This, although putrid, was esteemed a valuable prize, and the spine being divided into portions was distributed equally. "After eating the marrow, (says Franklin,) which was so acrid as to excoriate the lips, we rendered the bones friable by burning, and ate them also."

The strength of the whole party now began to fail, from the privation and fatigue which they endured.— Franklin was in a dreadfully debilitated state. Mr. Hood was also reduced to a perfect shadow, from the severe bowel-complaints which the *tripe de roche* never failed to give him. Back was so feeble as to require the support of a stick in walking, and Dr. Richardson had lameness superadded to weakness.

A rude canoe was constructed of willows, covered with canvass, in which the party, one by one, managed to reach in safety the southern bank of the river on the 4th of October, and went supperless to bed. On the following morning, previous to setting out, the whole party ate the remains of their old shoes, and whatever scraps of leather they had, to strengthen their stomachs for the fatigue of the day's journey.

Mr. Hood now broke down, as did two or three more of the party, and Dr. Richardson kindly volunteered to remain with them, while the rest pushed on to Fort Enterprise for succor. Not being able to find any *tripe de roche*, they drank an infusion of the Labrador tea-plant (*Ledrum palustre*, var. *decumbens*,) and ate a few morsels of burnt leather for supper. This continued to be a frequent occurrence.

Others of the party continued to drop down with fatigue and weakness, until they were reduced to five persons, besides Franklin. When they had no food or nourishment of any kind, they crept under their blankets, to drown, if possible, the gnawing pangs of hunger and fatigue by sleep. At length they reached Fort Enterprise, and to their disappointment and grief found it a perfectly desolate habitation. There was no deposit of provision, no trace of the Indians, no letter from Mr. Wentzel to point out where the Indians might be found. "It would be impossible (says Franklin,) to describe our sensations after entering this miserable abode, and discovering how we had been neglected: the whole party shed tears, not so much for our own fate as for that of our friends in the rear, whose lives depended entirely on our sending immediate relief from this place." A note, however, was found here from Mr. Back, stating that he had reached the house by another route two days before, and was going in search of the Indians. If he was unsuccessful in finding them, he proposed walking to Fort Providence, and sending succor from thence, but he doubted whether he or his party could perform the journey to that place in their present debilitated state. Franklin and his small party now looked round for some means of present subsistence, and fortunately discovered several deer skins, which had been thrown away during their former residence here. The bones were gathered from the heap of ashes; these, with the skins and the addition of *tripe de roche*, they considered would support life tolerably well for a short time. The bones were quite acrid, and the soup extracted from them, quite putrid, excoriated the mouth if taken alone, but it was somewhat milder when boiled with the lichen, and the mixture was even deemed palatable with a little salt, of which a cask had been left here in the spring. They procured fuel by pulling up the flooring of the rooms, and water for cooking by melting the snow.

Augustus arrived safe after them, just as they were sitting round the fire eating their supper of singed skin.

Late on the 13th, Belanger also reached the house, with a note from Mr. Back, stating that he had yet found no trace of the Indians. The poor messenger was almost speechless, being covered with ice and nearly frozen to death, having fallen into a rapid, and for the third time since the party left the coast, narrowly escaped drowning. After being well rubbed, having had his dress changed, and some warm soup given him, he recovered sufficiently to answer the questions put to him.

Under the impression that the Indians must be on their way to Fort Providence, and that it would be possible to overtake them, as they usually traveled slowly with their families, and there being likewise a prospect of killing deer about Reindeer Lake, where they had been usually found abundant, Franklin determined to take the route for that post, and sent word to Mr. Back by Belanger to that effect on the 18th.

On the 20th of October, Franklin set out in company with Benoit and Augustus to seek relief, having patched three pairs of snow shoes, and taken some singed skin for their support. Poltier and Samandre had volunteered to remain at the house with Adam, who was too ill to proceed. They were so feeble as scarcely to be able to move. Augustus, the Esquimaux, tried for fish without success, so that their only fare was skin and tea. At night, composing themselves to rest, they lay close to each other for warmth, but found the night bitterly cold, and the wind pierced through their famished frames.

On resuming the journey next morning, Franklin had the misfortune to break his snow-shoes, by falling between two rocks. This accident prevented him from keeping pace with the others, and in the attempt he became quite exhausted; unwilling to delay their progress, as the safety of all behind depended on their obtaining early assistance and immediate supplies, Franklin resolved to turn back, while the others pushed on to meet Mr. Back, or, missing him, they were directed to proceed to Fort Providence. Franklin found the two Canadians he had left at the house dreadfully weak and reduced, and so low spirited that he had great difficulty in rallying them to any exertion. As the insides of their mouths had become sore from eating the bone-soup, they now relinquished the use of it, and boiled the skin, which mode of dressing was found more palatable than frying it. They had pulled down nearly all their dwelling for fuel, to warm themselves and cook their scanty meals. The *tripe de roche*, on which they had depended, now became entirely frozen; and what was more tantalizing to their perishing frames, was the sight of food within their reach, which they could not procure. "We saw (says Franklin) a herd of reindeer sporting on the river, about half a mile from the house; they remained there a long time, but none of the party felt themselves strong enough to go after them, nor was there one of us who could have fired a gun without resting it."

While they were seated round the fire this evening, discoursing about the anticipated relief, the sound of voices was heard, which was thought with joy to be that of the Indians, but, to their bitter disappointment, the debilitated frames and emaciated countenances of Dr. Richardson and Hepburn presented themselves at the door. They were of course gladly received, although each marked the ravages which famine, care and fatigue had made on the other. The Doctor particularly remarked the sepulchral tone of the voices of his friends, which he requested them to make more cheerful if possible, unconscious that his own partook of the same key.

Hepburn having shot a partridge, which was brought to the house, Dr. Richardson tore out the feathers, and having held it to the fire a few minutes, divided it into six portions. Franklin and his three companions ravenously devoured their shares, as it was the first morsel of flesh any of them had tasted for thirty-one days, unless, indeed, the small gristly particles which they found adhering to the pounded bones may be termed flesh. Their spirits were revived by this small supply, and the Doctor endeavored to raise them still higher by the prospect of Hepburn's being able to kill a deer next day, as they had seen, and even fired at, several near the house. He endeavored, too, to rouse them into some attention to the comfort of their apartment. Having brought his Prayer-book and Testament, some prayers, psalms, and portions of scripture, appropriate to their situation, were read out by Dr. Richardson, and they retired to their blankets.

Early next morning, the Doctor and Hepburn went out in search of game; but though they saw several herds of deer, and fired some shots, they were not so fortunate as to kill any, being too weak to hold their guns steadily. The cold compelled the former to return soon, but Hepburn perseveringly persisted until late in the evening.

"My occupation, (continues Franklin) was to search for skins under the snow, it being now our object immediately to get all that we could; but I had not strength to drag in more than two of those which were within twenty yards of the house, until the Doctor came and assisted me. We made up our stock to twenty-six; but several of them were putrid, and scarcely eatable, even by men suffering the extremity of famine. Peltier and Samandre continued very weak and dispirited, and they were unable to cut firewood. Hepburn had, in consequence, that laborious task to perform after he came back late from hunting." To the exertions, honesty, kindness, and consideration of this worthy man, the safety of most of the party is to be attributed. And I may here mention that Sir John Franklin, when he became governor of Van Diemen's Land, obtained for him a good civil appointment. This deserving man, I am informed by Mr. Barrow, is now in England, having lost his office, which, I believe, has been abolished. It is to be hoped something will be done for him by the government.

After their usual supper of singed skin and bone soup, Dr. Richardson acquainted Franklin with the events that had transpired since their parting, particularly with the afflicting circumstances attending the death of Mr. Hood, and Michel, the Iroquois; the particulars of which I shall now proceed to condense from his narrative.

After Captain Franklin had bidden them farewell, having no *tripe de roche* they drank an infusion of the country tea-plant, which was grateful from its warmth, although it afforded no sustenance. They then retired to bed, and kept to their blankets all next day, as the snow drift was so heavy as to prevent their lighting a fire with the green and frozen willows, which were their only fuel.

Through the extreme kindness and forethought of a lady, the party, previous to leaving London, had been furnished with a small collection of religious books, of which, (says Richardson,) we still retained two or three of the most portable, and they proved of incalculable benefit to us.

"We read portions of them to each other as we lay in bed, in addition to the morning and evening service, and found that they inspired us on each perusal with so strong a sense of the omnipresence of a beneficent God, that our situation, even in these wilds, appeared no longer destitute; and we conversed not only with calmness, but with cheerfulness, detailing with unrestrained confidence the past events of our lives, and dwelling with hope on our future prospects." How beautiful a picture have we here represented, of true piety and resignation to the divine will inducing patience and submission under an unexampled load of misery and privation.

Michel, the Iroquois, joined them on the 9th of October, having, there is strong reason to believe, murdered two of the Canadians who were with him, Jean Baptiste Belanger and Perrault, as they were never seen afterward, and he gave so many rambling and contradictory statements of his proceedings, that no credit could be attached to his story.

The travelers proceeded on their tedious journey by slow stages. Mr. Hood was much affected with dim ness of sight, giddiness, and other symptoms of ex treme debility, which caused them to move slowly and to make frequent halts. Michel absented himself all day of the 10th, and only arrived at their encampment near the pines late on the 11th.

He reported that he had been in chase of some deer which passed near his sleeping place in the morning, and although he did not come up with them, yet he found a wolf which had been killed by the stroke of a deer's horn, and had brought a part of it.

Richardson adds — "We implicitly believed this story then, but afterward became aware — from circumstances, the details of which may be spared—that it must have been a portion of the body of Belanger, or Perrault. A question of moment here presents itself — namely, whether he actually murdered these men, or either of them, or whether he found the bodies in the snow. Captain Franklin, who is the best able to judge of this matter, from knowing their situation when he parted from them, suggested the former idea, and that both these men had been sacrificed ; that Michel, having already destroyed Belanger, completed his crime by Perrault's death, in order to screen himself from detection."

Although this opinion is founded only on circumstances, and is unsupported by direct evidence, it has been judged proper to mention it, especially as the subsequent conduct of the man showed that he was capable of committing such a deed. It is not easy to assign any other adequate motive for his concealing from Richardson that Perrault had turned back; while his request, over-night, that they would leave him the hatchet, and his cumbering himself with it when he went out in the morning, unlike a hunter, who makes use only of his knife when he kills a deer, seem to indicate that he took it for the purpose of cutting up something that he knew to be frozen.

Michel left them early next day, refusing Dr. Richardson's offer to accompany him, and remained out all day. He would not sleep in the tent with the other two at night. On the 13th, there being a heavy gale, they passed the day by their fire, without food. Next day, at noon, Michel set out, as he said, to hunt, but returned unexpectedly in a short time. This conduct surprised his companions, and his contradictory and evasive answers to their questions excited their suspicions still further. He subsequently refused either to hunt or cut wood, spoke in a very surly manner, and threatened to leave them. When reasoned with by Mr. Hood, his anger was excited, and he replied it was no use hunting — there were no animals, and they had better kill and eat him.

"At this period," observes Dr. Richardson, "we avoided, as much as possible, conversing upon the hopelessness of our situation, and generally endeavored to lead the conversation toward our future prospects in life. The fact is, that with the decay of our strength, our minds decayed, and we were no longer able to bear the contemplation of the horrors that surrounded us. Yet we were calm and resigned to our fate; not a murmur escaped us, and we were punctual and fervent in our addresses to the Supreme Being."

On the morning of the 20th, they again urged Michel to go a-hunting, that he might, if possible, leave them some provision, as he intended quitting them next day, but he showed great unwillingness to go out, and lingered about the fire under the pretense of cleaning his gun. After the morning service had been read, Dr. Richardson went out to gather some *tripe de roche*, leaving Mr. Hood sitting before the tent at the fireside, arguing with Michel; Hepburn was employed cutting fire-wood. While they were thus engaged, the treacherous Iroquois took the opportunity to place his gun close to Mr. Hood, and shoot him through the head. He represented to his companions that the deceased had killed himself. On examination of the body, it was found that the shot had entered the back part of the head and passed out at the forehead, and that the muzzle of the gun had been applied so close as to set fire to the nightcap behind. Michel protested his innocence of the crime, and Hepburn and Dr. Richardson dared not openly evince their suspicion of his guilt.

Next day, Dr. Richardson determined on going straight to the Fort. They singed the hair off a part of the buffalo robe that belonged to their ill-fated companion, and boiled and ate it. In the course of their march, Michel alarmed them much by his gestures and conduct, was constantly muttering to himself, expressed an unwillingness to go to the Fort, and tried to persuade them to go southward to the woods, where he said he could maintain himself all the winter by killing deer. "In consequence of this behavior, and the expression of his countenance, I requested him (says Richardson) to leave us, and to go to the southward by himself. This proposal increased his ill-nature; he threw out some obscure hints of freeing himself from all restraint on the morrow; and I overheard him muttering threats against Hepburn, whom he openly accused of having told stories against him. He also, for the first time, assumed such a tone of superiority in addressing me, as evinced that he considered us to be completely in his power; and he gave vent to several expressions of hatred toward the white people, some of whom, he said, had killed and eaten his uncle and two of his relations. In short, taking every circumstance of his conduct into consideration, I came to the conclusion that he would attempt to destroy us on the first opportunity that offered, and that he had hitherto abstained from doing so from his ignorance of his way to the Fort, but that he would never suffer us to go thither in company with him. Hepburn and I were not in a condition to resist even an open attack, nor could we by any device escape from him — our united strength was far inferior to his; and, beside his gun, he was armed with two pistols, an Indian bayonet, and a knife.

"In the afternoon, coming to a rock on which there was some *tripe de roche*, he halted, and said he would gather it while we went on, and that he would soon overtake us.

"Hepburn and I were now left together for the first time since Mr. Hood's death, and he acquainted me with several material circumstances, which he had observed of Michel's behavior, and which confirmed me in the opinion that there was no safety for us except in his death, and he offered to be the instrument of it. I determined, however, as I was thoroughly convinced of the necessity of such a dreadful act, to take the whole responsibility upon myself; and immediately upon Michel's coming up, I put an end to his life by shooting him through the head with a pistol. Had my own life alone been threatened," observes Richardson, in conclusion, "I would not have purchased it by such a measure, but I considered myself as intrusted also with the protection of Hepburn's, a man who, by his humane attentions and devotedness, had so endeared himself to me, that I felt more anxiety for his safety than for my own.

"Michel had gathered no *tripe de roche*, and it was evident to us that he had halted for the purpose of putting his gun in order with the intention of attacking us — perhaps while we were in the act of encamping."

Persevering onward in their journey as well as the snow storms and their feeble limbs would permit, they saw several herds of deer; but Hepburn, who used to be a good marksman, was now unable to hold the gun straight. Following the track of a wolverine which had been dragging something, he however found the spine of a deer which it had dropped. It was clean picked, and at least one season old, but they extracted the spinal marrow from it.

A species of *cornicularia*, a kind of lichen, was also met with, that was found good to eat when moistened and toasted over the fire. They had still some pieces of singed buffalo hide remaining, and Hepburn, on one occasion, killed a partridge, after firing several times at a flock. About dusk of the 29th they reached the Fort.

"Upon entering the desolate dwelling, we had the satisfaction of embracing Capt. Franklin, but no words can convey an idea of the filth and wretchedness that met our eyes on looking around. Our own misery had stolen upon us by degrees, and we were accustomed to the contemplation of each other's emaciated figures; but the ghastly countenances, dilated eye-balls, and sepulchral voices of Captain Franklin and those with him were more than we could at first bear."

Thus ends the narrative of Richardson's journey.

To resume the detail of proceedings at the Fort. On the 1st of November two of the Canadians, Peltier and Samandre, died from sheer exhaustion.

On the 7th of November they were relieved from their privations and sufferings by the arrival of three Indians, bringing a supply of dried meat, some fat, and a few tongues, which had been sent off by Back with all haste from Akaitcho's encampment on the 5th. These Indians nursed and attended them with the greatest care, cleansed the house, collected fire-wood, and studied every means for their general comfort. Their sufferings were now at an end. On the 26th of November they arrived at the encampment of the Indian chief, Akaitcho. On the 6th of December Belanger and another Canadian arrived, bringing further supplies, and letters from England, from Mr. Back, and their former companion, Mr. Wentzel.

The dispatches from England announced the successful termination of Captain Parry's voyage, and the promotion of Captain Franklin, Mr. Back, and of poor Mr. Hood.

On the 18th they reached the Hudson's Bay Company's establishment at Moose Deer Island, where they joined their friend Mr. Back. They remained at Fort Chipewyan until June of the following year.

It is now necessary to relate the story of Mr. Back's journey, which, like the rest, is a sad tale of suffering and privation.

Having been directed, on the 4th of October, 1821, to proceed with St. Germain, Belanger, and Beauparlant to Fort Enterprise, in the hopes of obtaining relief for the party, he set out. Up to the 7th they met with a little *tripe de roche*, but this failing them they were compelled to satisfy, or rather allay, the cravings of hunger, by eating a gun-cover and a pair of old shoes. The grievous disappointment experienced on arriving at the house, and finding it a deserted ruin, cannot be told.

"Without the assistance of the Indians, bereft of every resource, we felt ourselves," says Mr. Back, "reduced to the most miserable state, which was rendered still worse from the recollection that our friends in the rear were as miserable as ourselves. For the moment, however, hunger prevailed, and each began to gnaw the scraps of putrid and frozen meat and skin that were lying about, without waiting to prepare them." A fire was, however, afterward made, and the neck and bones of a deer found in the house were boiled and devoured.

After resting a day at the house, Mr. Back pushed on with his companions in search of the Indians, leaving a note for Captain Franklin, informing him if he failed in meeting with the Indians, he intended to push on for the first trading establishment — distant about 130 miles — and send us succor from thence. On the 11th he set out on the journey, a few old skins having been first collected to serve as food.

On the 13th and 14th of October they had nothing whatever to eat. Belanger was sent off with a note to Franklin. On the 15th they were fortunate enough to fall in with a partridge, the bones of which were eaten, and the remainder reserved for bait to fish with. Enough *tripe de roche* was, however, gathered to make a meal. Beauparlant now lingered behind, worn out by extreme weakness. On the 17th a number of crows, perched on some high pines, led them to believe that some carrion was near; and on searching, several heads of deer, half buried in the snow and ice, without eyes or tongues, were found. An expression of "Oh, merciful God, we are saved," broke from them both and with feelings more easily imagined than described, they shook hands, not knowing what to say for joy.

St. Germain was sent back, to bring up Beauparlant, for whose safety Back became very anxious, but he found the poor fellow frozen to death.

The night of the 17th was cold and clear, but they could get no sleep. "From the pains of having eaten, we suffered (observes Back) the most excruciating torments, though I in particular did not eat a quarter of what would have satisfied me; it might have been from having eaten a quantity of raw or frozen sinews of the legs of deer, which neither of us could avoid doing, so great was our hunger."

On the following day Belanger returned famishing

with hunger, and told of the pitiable state of Franklin and his reduced party. Back, both this day and the next, tried to urge on his companions toward the object of their journey, but he could not conquer their stubborn determinations. They said they were unable to proceed from weakness ; knew not the way ; that Back wanted to expose them again to death, and in fact loitered greedily about the remnants of the deer till the end of the month. "It was not without the greatest difficulty that I could restrain the men from eating every scrap they found ; though they were well aware of the necessity there was of being economical in our present situation, and to save whatever they could for our journey, yet they could not resist the temptation ; and whenever my back was turned they seldom failed to snatch at the nearest piece to them, whether cooked or raw. Having collected with great care, and by self-denial, two small packets of dried meat or sinews sufficient (for men who knew what it was to fast) to last for eight days, at the rate of one indifferent meal per day, they set out on the 30th. On the 3d of November they came on the track of Indians, and soon reached the tents of Akaitcho and his followers, when food was obtained, and assistance sent off to Franklin.

In July they reached York Factory, from whence they had started three years before, and thus terminated a journey of 5550 miles, during which human courage and patience were exposed to trials such as few can bear with fortitude, unless, as is seen in Franklin's interesting narrative, arising out of reliance on the ever-sustaining care of an Almighty Providence.

Parry's First Voyage, 1819 – 1820.

The Admiralty having determined to continue the progress of discovery in the Arctic seas, Lieut. W. E. Parry, who had been second in command under Capt. Ross, in the voyage of the previous year, was selected to take charge of a new expedition, consisting of the Hecla and Griper. The chief object of this voyage was to pursue the survey of Lancaster Sound, and decide on the probability of a northwest passage in that direction; failing in which, Smith's and Jones' Sounds were to be explored, with the same purpose in view.

The respective officers appointed to the ships, were —

Hecla, 375 tons:

Lieut. and Commander — W. E. Parry.
Lieutenant — Fred. W. Beechey.
Captain — E. Sabine, R. A., Astronomer.
Purser — W. H. Hooper.
Surgeon — John Edwards.
Assistant Surgeon — Alexander Fisher.
Midshipmen — James Clarke Ross, J. Nias, W. J Dealy, Charles Palmer, John Bushnan.
Greenland Pilots — J. Allison, master; G. Crawfurd, mate.
44 Petty Officers, Seamen, &c.
Total complement, 58.

Griper, 180 tons:

Lieutenant and Commander — Matthew Liddon.
Lieutenant — H. P. Hoppner.
Assistant Surgeon — C. J. Beverley.
Midshipmen — A. Reid, A. M. Skene, W. N Griffiths.
Greenland Pilots — George Fyfe, master; A. Eld mate.
28 Petty Officers, Seamen, &c.
Total complement, 36.

The ships were raised upon, strengthened, and well found in stores and provisions for two years. On the 11th of May, 1819, they got away from the Thames, and after a fair passage fell in with a considerable quantity of ice in the middle of Davis' Straits about the 20th of June; it consisted chiefly of fragments of icebergs, on the outskirts of the glaciers that form along the shore. After a tedious passage through the floes of ice, effected chiefly by heaving and warping, they arrived at Possession Bay on the morning of the 31st of July, being just a month earlier than they were here on the previous year. As many as fifty whales were seen here in the course of a few hours. On landing, they were not a little astonished to find their own footprints of the previous year, still distinctly visible in the snow. During an excursion of three or four miles into the interior, a fox, a raven, several ring-plovers and snow-buntings, were seen, as also a bee, from which it may be inferred that honey can be procured even in these wild regions. Vegetation flourishes remarkably well here, considering the high latitude, for wherever there was moisture, tufts and various ground plants grew in considerable abundance.

Proceeding on from hence into the Sound, they verified the opinion which had previously been entertained by many of the officers, that the *Croker Mountains* had no existence, for on the 4th of August, the ships were in long. 86° 56′ W., three degrees to the westward of where land had been laid down by Ross in the previous year. The strait was named after Sir John Barrow, and was found to be pretty clear; but on reaching Leopold Island, the ice extended in a compact body to the north, through which it was impossible to penetrate. Rather than remain inactive, waiting for the dissolution of the ice, Parry determined to try what could be done by shaping his course to the southward, through the magnificent inlet now named Regent Inlet. About the 6th of August, in consequence of the local attraction, the ordinary compasses became useless from their great variation, and the binnacles were removed from the deck to the carpenter's store-room as useless lumber, the azimuth compasses alone remaining; and these became so sluggish in their motions, that they required to be very nicely leveled, and frequently tapped before the card traversed. The local attraction was very great, and a mass of iron-stone found on shore attracted the magnet powerfully. The ships proceeded 120 miles from the entrance.

On the 8th of August, in lat. 72° 13′ N., and long. 90° 29′ W., (his extreme point of view Parry named

Cape Kater,) the Hecla came to a compact barrier of ice extending across the inlet, which rendered one of two alternatives necessary, either to remain here until an opening took place, or to return again to the northward. The latter course was determined on. Making, therefore, for the northern shore of Barrow's Strait, on the 20th a narrow channel was discovered between the ice and the land. On the 22d, proceeding due west, after passing several bays and headlands, they noticed two large openings or passages, the first of which, more than eight leagues in width, he named Wellington Channel. To various capes, inlets, and groups of islands passed, Parry assigned the names of Hotham, Barlow, Cornwallis, Bowen, Byam Martin, Griffith, Lowther, Bathurst, &c. On the 28th a boat was sent on shore at Byam Martin Island with Capt. Sabine, Mr. J. C. Ross, and the surgeons, to make observations, and collect specimens of natural history. The vegetation was rather luxuriant for these regions; moss in particular grew in abundance in the moist valleys and along the banks of the streams that flowed from the hills. The ruins of six Esquimaux huts were observed. Tracks of reindeer, bears, and musk oxen were noticed, and the skeletons, skulls, and horns of some of these animals were found.

On the 1st of September, they discovered the large and fine island, to which Parry has given the name of Melville Island after the First Lord of the Admiralty of that day. On the following day, two boats with a party of officers were dispatched to examine its shores. Some reindeer and musk oxen were seen on landing, but being startled by the sight of a dog, it was found impossible to get near them. There seemed here to be a great quantity of the animal tribe, for the tracks of bears, oxen, and deer were numerous, and the horns, skin, and skulls were also found. The burrows of foxes and field-mice were observed; several ptarmigan were shot, and flocks of snow-bunting, geese, and ducks, were noticed, probably commencing their migration to a milder climate. Along the beach there was an immense number of small shrimps, and various kinds of shells.

On the 4th of September, Parry had the satisfaction of crossing the meridian of 110° W., in the latitude of 74° 44′ 20″, by which the expedition became entitled to the reward of £5000, granted by an order in Council upon the Act 58 Geo. III., cap. 20, entitled, "An Act for more effectually discovering the longitude at sea, and encouraging attempts to find a northern passage between the Atlantic and Pacific Oceans, and to approach the North Pole." This fact was not announced to the crews until the following day; to celebrate the event they gave to a bold cape of the island then lying in sight the name of Bounty Cape; and so anxious were they now to press forward, that they began to calculate the time when they should reach the longitude of 130° W., the second place specified by the order in Council for reward. On the afternoon of the 5th, the compactness of the ice stopped them, and therefore, for the first time since leaving England, the anchor was let go, and that in 110° W. longitude.

A boat was sent on shore on the 6th to procure turf or peat for fuel, and, strangely enough, some small pieces of tolerably good coal were found in various places scattered over the surface. A party of officers that went on shore on the 8th killed several grouse on the island, and a white hare; a fox, some field-mice, several snow-bunting, a snowy owl, and four musk oxen were seen. Ducks, in small flocks, were seen along the shore, as well as several glaucous gulls and tern, and a solitary seal was observed.

As the ships were coasting along on the 7th, two herds of musk oxen were seen grazing, at the distance of about three-quarters of a mile from the beach: one herd consisted of nine, and the other of five of these cattle. They had also a distant view of two reindeer.

The average weight of the hares here is about eight pounds. Mr. Fisher, the surgeon, from whose interesting journal I quote, states that it is very evident that this island must be frequented, if not constantly inhabited, by musk oxen in great numbers, for their bones and horns are found scattered about in all directions, and the greatest part of the carcass of one was discovered on one occasion. The skulls of two carnivorous animals, a wolf and a lynx, were also picked up here. A party sent to gather coals brought on board about half a bushel—all they could obtain.

On the morning of the 10th, Mr. George Fyfe, the master pilot, with a party of six men belonging to the Griper, landed with a view of making an exploring trip of some fifteen or twenty miles into the interior. They only took provisions for a day with them. Great uneasiness was felt that they did not return; and when two days elapsed, fears began to be entertained for their safety, and it was thought they must have lost their way.

Messrs. Reid, (midshipman) Beverly, (assistant surgeon) and Wakeman (clerk) volunteered to go in search of their missing messmates, but themselves lost their way; guided by the rockets, fires, and lights exhibited, they returned by ten at night, almost exhausted with cold and fatigue, but without intelligence of their friends. Four relief parties were therefore organized, and sent out on the morning of the 13th to prosecute the search, and one of them fell in with and brought back four of the wanderers, and another the remaining three before nightfall.

The feet of most of them were much frost-bitten, and they were all wearied and worn out with their wanderings. It appears they had all lost their way the evening of the day they went out. With regard to food, they were by no means badly off, for they managed to kill as many grouse as they could eat.

They found fertile valleys and level plains in the interior, abounding with grass and moss; also a lake of fresh water, about two miles long by one broad, in which were several species of trout. They saw several herds of reindeer on the plains, and two elk; also many hares, but no musk oxen. Some of those, however, who had been in search of the stray party, noticed herds of these cattle.

The winter now began to set in, and the packed ice was so thick, that fears were entertained of being locked up in an exposed position on the coast; it was, therefore, thought most prudent to put back, and endeavor to reach the harbor which had been passed some days before. The vessels now got seriously buffeted among the floes and hummocks of ice. The Griper was forced aground on the beach, and for some time was in a very critical position. Lieutenant Liddon having been confined to his cabin by a rheumatic complaint, was pressed at this juncture by Commander Parry to allow himself to be removed to the Hecla, but he nobly refused, stating that he should be the last to leave the ship, and continued giving orders. The beach being sand, the Griper was got off without injury.

On the 23d of September they anchored off the mouth of the harbor, and the thermometer now fell to 1°. The crew were set to work to cut a channel through the ice to the shore, and in the course of three days, a canal, two and a half miles in length, was completed, through which the vessel was tracked. The ice was eight or nine inches thick. An extra allowance of preserved meat was served out to the men, in consideration of their hard labor. The vessels were unrigged, and every thing made snug and secure for passing the winter. Captain Parry gave the name of the North Georgian Islands to this group, after his Majesty, King George III., but this has since been changed to the Parry Islands.

Two reindeer were killed on the 1st of October, and several white bears were seen. On the 6th a deer was killed, which weighed 170 pounds. Seven were seen on the 10th, one of which was killed, and another severely wounded. Following after this animal, night overtook several of the sportsmen, and the usual signals of rockets, lights, &c. were exhibited, to guide them back. One, John Pearson, a marine, had his hands so frost-bitten that he was obliged, on the 2d of November, to have the four fingers of his left hand amputated. A wolf and four reindeer were seen on the

14th. A herd of fifteen deer were seen on the 15th; but those who saw them could not bring down any, as their fowling-pieces missed fire, from the moisture freezing on the locks. On the 17th and 18th herds of eleven and twenty respectively, were seen, and a small one was shot. A fox was caught on the 29th, which is described as equally cunning with his brethren of the temperate regions.

To make the long winter pass as cheerfully as possible, plays were acted, a school established, and a newspaper set on foot, certainly the first periodical publication that had ever issued from the Arctic regions. The title of this journal, the editorial duties of which were undertaken by Captain Sabine, was "The Winter Chronicle, or New Georgia Gazette." The first number appeared on the 1st of November.

On the evening of the 5th of November the farce of "Miss in her Teens" was brought out, to the great amusement of the ships' companies, and, considering the local difficulties and disadvantages under which the performers labored, their first essay, according to the officers' report, did them infinite credit. Two hours were spent very happily in their theater on the quarter-deck, notwithstanding the thermometer outside the ship stood at zero, and within as low as the freezing point, except close to the stoves, where it was a little higher. Another play was performed on the 24th, and so on every fortnight. The men were employed during the day in banking up the ships with snow.

On the 23d of December, the officers performed "The Mayor of Garrett," which was followed by an after-piece, written by Captain Parry, entitled the "North-West Passage, or the Voyage Finished." The sun having long since departed, the twilight at noon was so clear that books in the smallest print could be distinctly read.

On the 6th of January, the farce of "Bon Ton" was performed, with the thermometer at 27° below zero.— The cold became more and more intense. On the 12th it was 51° below zero, in the open air; brandy froze to the consistency of honey; when tasted in this state it left a smarting on the tongue. The greatest cold experienced was on the 14th of January, when the thermometer fell to 52° below zero. On the 3d of February, the sun was first visible above the horizon, after eighty-four days' absence. It was seen from the maintop of the ships, a height of about fifty-one feet above the sea.

On the forenoon of the 24th a fire broke out at the storehouse, which was used as an observatory. All hands proceeded to the spot to endeavor to subdue the flames, but having only snow to throw on it, and the mats with which the interior was lined being very dry, it was found impossible to extinguish it. The snow, however, covered the astronomical instruments and secured them from the fire, and when the roof had been pulled down the fire had burned itself out. Considerable as the fire was, its influence or heat extended but a very short distance, for several of the officers and men were frost-bitten, and confined from their efforts for several weeks. John Smith, of the Artillery, who was Captain Sabine's servant, and who, together with Sergeant Martin, happened to be in the house at the time the fire broke out, suffered much more severely. In their anxiety to save the dipping needle, which was standing close to the stove, and of which they knew the value, they immediately ran out with it; and Smith not having time to put on his gloves, had his fingers in half an hour so benumbed, and the animation so completely suspended, that on his being taken on board by Mr. Edwards, and having his hands plunged into a basin of cold water, the surface of the water was immediately frozen by the intense cold thus suddenly communicated to it; and notwithstanding the most humane and unremitting attention paid him by the medical gentlemen, it was found necessary, some time after, to resort to the amputation of a part of four fingers on one hand, and three on the other.

Parry adds, "the appearance which our faces presented at the fire was a curious one; almost every nose and cheek having become quite white with frost bites, in five minutes after being exposed to the weather, so that it was deemed necessary for the medical gentlemen, together with some others appointed to assist them, to go constantly round while the men were working at the fire, and to rub with snow the parts affected, in order to restore animation."

The weather got considerably milder in March; on the 6th the thermometer got up to zero for the first time since the 17th of December. The observatory house on shore was now rebuilt.

The vapor, which had been in a solid state on the ship's sides, now thawed below, and the crew, scraping off the coating of ice, removed on the 8th of March, above a hundred bucketsfull each, containing from five to six gallons, which had accumulated in less than a month, occasioned principally from the men's breath, and the steam of victuals at meals.

The scurvy now broke out among the crew, and prompt measures were taken to remedy it. Captain Parry took great pains to raise mustard and cress in his cabin for the men's use.

On the 30th of April, the thermometer stood at the freezing point, which it had not done since the 12th of September last. On the 1st of May, the sun was seen at midnight for the first time that season.

A survey was now taken of the provisions, fuel, and stores; much of the lemon juice was found destroyed from the bursting in the bottles by the frost. Having been only victualed for two years, and half that period having expired, Captain Parry, as a matter of prudence reduced all hands to two-thirds allowance of all sorts of provisions, except meat and sugar.

The crew were now set to work in cutting away the ice round the ships: the average thickness was found to be seven feet. Many of the men who had been out on excursions began to suffer much from snow blindness. The sensation when first experienced, is described as like that felt when dust or sand gets into the eyes. They were, however, cured in the course of two or three days by keeping the eyes covered, and bathing them occasionally with sugar of lead, or some other cooling lotion.

To prevent the recurrence of the complaint, the men were ordered to wear a piece of crape or some substitute for it over the eyes.

The channel round the ships was completed by the 17th of May, and they rose nearly two feet, having been kept down by the pressure of the ice round them, although lightened during the winter by the consumption of food and fuel. On the 24th, they were astonished by two showers of rain, a most extraordinary phenomenon in these regions. Symptoms of scurvy again appeared among the crew; one of the seamen who had been recently cured, having imprudently been in the habit of eating the fat skimmings, or "slush," in which salt meat had been boiled, and which was served out for their lamps. As the hills in many places now became exposed and vegetation commenced, two or three pieces of ground were dug up and sown with seeds of radishes, onions, and other vegetables. Captain Parry determined before leaving to make an excursion across the island for the purpose of examining its size, boundaries, productions, &c. Accordingly on the 1st of June, an expedition was organized, consisting of the commander, Captain Sabine, Mr. Fisher, the assistant-surgeon, Mr. John Nias, midshipman of the Hecla, and Mr. Reid, midshipman of the Griper, with two sergeants, and five seamen and marines. Three weeks provisions were taken, which, together with two tents, wood for fuel, and other articles, weighing in all about 800 lbs., was drawn on a cart prepared for the purpose by the men.

Each of the officers carried a knapsack with his own private baggage, weighing from 18 to 24 lbs., also his gun and ammunition. The party started in high glee, under three hearty cheers from their comrades, sixteen of whom accompanied them for five miles, carrying their knapsacks and drawing the cart for them.

They traveled by night, taking rest by day, as it was

found to be warmer for sleep, and they had only a covering of a single blanket each, beside the clothes they had on.

On the 2d, they came to a small lake, about half a mile long, and met with eider-ducks and ptarmigan; seven of the latter were shot. From the top of a range of hills at which they now arrived, they could see the masts of the ships in Winter Harbor with the naked eye, at about ten or eleven miles distant. A vast plain was also seen extending to the northward and westward.

The party breakfasted on biscuit and a pint of gruel each, made of salep powder, which was found to be a very palatable diet. Reindeer with their fawns were met with.

They derived great assistance in dragging their cart by rigging upon it one of the tent-blankets as a sail, a truly nautical contrivance, and the wind favoring them, they made great progress in this way. Captain Sabine being taken ill with a bowel complaint, had to be conveyed on this novel sail carriage. They, however, had some ugly ravines to pass, the crossings of which were very tedious and troublesome. On the 7th the party came to a large bay, which was named after their ships, Hecla and Griper Bay. The blue ice was cut through by hard work with boarding pikes, the only instruments they had, and after digging fourteen and a half feet, the water rushed up; it was not very salt, but sufficient to satisfy them that it was the ocean. An island seen in the distance was named after Captain Sabine; some of the various points and capes were also named after others of the party. Although this shore was found blocked up with such heavy ice, there appear to be times when there is open water here, for a piece of fir wood seven and a half feet long, and about the thickness of a man's arm, was found about eighty yards inland from the hummocks of the beach, and about thirty feet above the level of the sea. Before leaving the shore, a monument of stones, twelve feet high, was erected, in which were deposited, in a tin cylinder, an account of their proceedings, a few coins, and several naval buttons. The expedition now turned back, shaping its course in a more westerly direction, toward some high blue hills, which had long been in sight. On many days several ptarmigans were shot. The horns and tracks of deer were very numerous.

On the 11th they came in sight of a deep gulf, to which Lieutenant Liddon's name was given; the two capes at its entrance being called after Beechey and Hoppner. In the center was an island about three-quarters of a mile in length, and rising abruptly to the height of 700 feet. The shores of the gulf were very rugged and precipitant, and in descending a steep hill, the axle-tree of their cart broke, and they had to leave it behind, taking the body with them, however, for fuel. The wheels, which were left on the spot, may astonish some future adventurer who discovers them. The stores, &c., were divided among the officers and men.

Making their way on the ice in the gulf, the island in the center was explored, and named after Mr. Hooper, the purser of the Hecla. It was found to be of sandstone, and very barren, rising perpendicularly from the west side. Four fat geese were killed here, and a great many animals were seen around the gulf; some attention being paid to examining its shores, &c., a fine open valley was discovered, and the tracks of oxen and deer were very numerous; the pasturage appeared to be excellent.

On the 13th, a few ptarmigan and golden plover were killed. No less than thirteen deer in one herd were seen, and a musk ox for the first time in this season.

The remains of six Esquimaux huts were discovered about 300 yards from the beach. Vegetation now began to flourish, the sorrel was found far advanced, and a species of saxifrage was met with in blossom. They reached the ships on the evening of the 15th, after a journey of about 180 miles.

The ships' crews, during their absence, had been occupied in getting ballast in and re-stowing the hold.

Shooting parties were now sent out in various directions to procure game. Dr. Fisher gives an interesting account of his ten days' excursion with a couple of men. The deer were not so numerous as they expected to find them. About thirty were seen, of which his party killed but two, which were very lean, weighing only, when skinned and cleaned, 50 to 60 lbs. A couple of wolves were seen, and some foxes, with a great many hares, four of which were killed, weighing from 7 to 8 lbs. The aquatic birds seen were — brent geese, king ducks, long-tailed ducks, and arctic and glaucous gulls. The land birds were ptarmigans, plovers, sanderlings and snow buntings. The geese were pretty numerous for the first few days, but got wild and wary on being disturbed, keeping in the middle of lakes out of gun-shot. About a dozen were, however, killed, and fifteen ptarmigans. These birds are represented to be so stupid, that all seen may be shot. Dr. Fisher was surprised on his return on the 29th of June, after his ten days' absence, to find how much vegetation had advanced; the land being now completely clear of snow, was covered with the purple-colored saxifrage in blossom, with mosses, and with sorrel, and the grass was two to three inches long. The men were sent out twice a week to collect the sorrel, and in a few minutes enough could be procured to make a salad for dinner. After being mixed with vinegar it was regularly served out to the men. The English garden seeds that had been sown got on but slowly, and did not yield any produce in time to be used.

On the 30th of June Wm. Scott, a boatswain's mate, who had been afflicted with scurvy, diarrhœa, &c., died, and was buried on the 2d of July — a slab of sandstone bearing an inscription carved by Dr. Fisher, being erected over his grave.

From observations made on the tide during two months, it appears that the greatest rise and fall here is four feet four inches. A large pile of stones was erected on the 14th of July, upon the most conspicuous hill, containing the usual notices, coins, &c., and on a large stone an inscription was left, notifying the wintering of the ships here.

On the 1st of August, the ships, which had been previously warped out, got clear of the harbor, and found a channel, both eastward and westward, clear of ice, about three or four miles in breadth along the land.

On the 6th they landed on the island, and in the course of the night killed fourteen hares and a number of glaucous gulls, which were found with their young on the top of a precipitous, insulated rock.

On the 9th the voyagers had an opportunity of observing an instance of the violent pressure that takes place occasionally by the collision of heavy ice. "Two pieces," says Dr. Fisher, "that happened to come in contact close to us, pressed so forcibly against one another that one of them, although forty-two feet thick, and at least three times that in length and breadth, was forced up on its edge on the top of another piece of ice. But even this is nothing when compared with the pressure that must have existed to produce the effects that we see along the shore, for not only heaps of earth and stones several tons weight are forced up, but hummocks of ice, from fifty to sixty feet thick, are piled up on the beach. It is unnecessary to remark that a ship, although fortified as well as wood and iron could make her, would have but little chance of withstanding such overwhelming force."

This day a musk-ox was shot, which weighed more than 700 lbs.; the carcass, when skinned and cleaned, yielding 421 lbs. of meat. The flesh did not taste so very strong of musk as had been represented.

The ships made but slow progress, being still thickly beset with floes of ice, 40 or 50 feet thick, and had to make fast for security to hummocks of ice on the beach.

On the 15th and 16th they were off the southwest point of the island, but a survey of the locality from the precipitous cliff of Cape Dundas, presented the same interminable barrier of ice, as far as the eye could reach. A bold high coast was sighted to the southwest, to which the name of Bank's Land was given.

Captain Parry states that on the 23d the ships received by far the heaviest shocks they had experienced during the voyage, and performed six miles of the most difficult navigation he had ever known among ice.

Two musk bulls were shot on the 24th by parties who landed, out of a herd of seven which were seen. They were lighter than the first one shot — weighing only about 360 lbs. From the number of skulls and skeletons of these animals met with, and their capabilities of enduring the rigor of the climate, it seems probable that they do not migrate southward, but winter on this island.

Attempts were still made to work to the eastward, but on the 25th, from want of wind, and the closeness of the ice, the ships were obliged to make fast again, without having gained above a mile after several hours' labor. A fresh breeze springing up on the 26th opened a passage along shore, and the ships made sail to the eastward, and in the evening were off their old quarters in Winter Harbor. On the following evening, after a fine run, they were off the east end of Melville Island. Lieut. Parry, this day, announced to the officers and crew that after due consideration and consultation, it had been found useless to prosecute their researches farther westward, and therefore endeavors would be made in a more southerly direction, failing in which, the expedition would return to England. Regent Inlet and the southern shores generally, were found so blocked up with ice, that the return to England was on the 30th of August publicly announced. This day, Navy Board and Admiralty Inlets were passed, and on the 1st of September the vessels got clear of Barrow's Strait, and reached Baffin's Bay on the 5th. They fell in with a whaler belonging to Hull, from whom they learned the news of the death of George the Third and the Duke of Kent, and that eleven vessels having been lost in the ice last year, fears were entertained for their safety. The Friendship, another Hull whaler, informed them that in company with the Truelove, she had looked into Smith's Sound that summer. The Alexander, of Aberdeen, one of the ships employed on the former voyage of discovery to these seas, had also entered Lancaster

Sound. After touching at Clyde's River, where they met a good-natured tribe of Esquimaux, the ships made the best of their way across the Atlantic, and after a somewhat boisterous passage, Commodore Parry landed at Peterhead on the 30th of October, and, accompanied by Capt. Sabine and Mr. Hooper, posted to London.

PARRY'S SECOND VOYAGE, 1821—1823.

THE experience which Capt. Parry had formed in his previous voyage, led him to entertain the opinion that a communication might be found between Regent Inlet and Roe's Welcome, or through Repulse Bay, and thence to the northwestern shores. The following are his remarks :—"On an inspection of the charts I think it will also appear probable that a communication will one day be found to exist between this inlet (Prince Regent's) and Hudson's Bay, either through the broad and unexplored channel called Sir Thomas Roe's Welcome, or through Repulse Bay, which has not yet been satisfactorily examined. It is also probable that a channel will be found to exist between the western land and the northern coast of America." Again, in another place, he says:—"Of the existence of a northwest passage to the Pacific it is now scarcely possible to doubt, and from the success which attended our efforts in 1819, after passing through Sir James Lancaster's Sound, we were not unreasonable in anticipating its complete accomplishment. But the season in which it is practicable to navigate the Polar Seas does not exceed seven weeks. From all that we observed it seems desirable that ships endeavoring to reach the Pacific Ocean by this route should keep if possible on the coast of America, and the lower in latitude that coast may be found, the more favorable will it prove for the purpose; hence Cumberland Strait, Sir Thomas Roe's Welcome, and Repulse Bay appear to be the points most worthy of attention. I cannot, therefore, but consider that any expedition equipped by Great Britain with this view ought to employ its best energies in attempting to penetrate from the eastern coast of America along its northern shore. In consequence of the partial success which has hitherto attended our attempts, the whalers have already extended their views, and a new field has been opened for one of the most lucrative branches of our commerce, and what is scarcely of less importance, one of the most valuable nurseries for seamen which Great Britain possesses."*

Pleased with his former zeal and enterprise, and in order to give him an opportunity of testing the truth of his observations, a few months after he returned home, the Admiralty gave Parry the command of another expedition, with instructions to proceed to Hudson's Strait, and penetrate to the westward, until in Repulse Bay, or on some other part of the shores of Hudson's Bay to the north of Wager River, he should reach the western coast of the continent. Failing in these quarters, he was to keep along the coast, carefully examining every bend or inlet, which should appear likely to afford a practicable passage to the westward.

The vessels commissioned, with their officers and crews, were the following. Several of the officers of the former expedition were promoted, and those who had been on the last voyage with Parry I have marked with an asterisk:—

Fury.

Commander —*W. E. Parry.
Chaplain and Astronomer — Rev. Geo. Fisher, (was in the Dorothea, under Capt. Buchan, in 1818.)
Lieutenants —*J. Nias and *A. Reid.
Surgeon —*J. Edwards.
Purser —*W. H. Hooper.
Assistant-Surgeon — J. Skeoch.
Midshipmen —*J. C. Ross, *J. Bushnan, J. Henderson, F. R. M. Crozier.

*Parry's First Voyage, vol. ii, p. 240.

Greenland Pilots—*J. Allison, master; G. Crawfurd, mate.
47 Petty Officers, Seamen, &c.
Total complement, 60.

Hecla.

Commander—G. F. Lyon.
Lieutenants—*H. P. Hoppner and *C. Palmer.
Surgeon—*A. Fisher.
Purser—J. Germain.
Assistant-Surgeon—A. M'Laren.
Midshipmen—*W. N. Griffiths, J. Sherer, C. Richards, E. J. Bird.
Greenland Pilots—*G. Fife, master; *A. Elder, mate.
46 Petty Officers, seamen, &c.
Total complement, 58.

Lieutenant Lyon, the second in command, had ob tained some reputation from his travels in Tripoli, Mourzouk, and other parts of Northern Africa, and was raised to the rank of Commander, on his appointment to the Hecla, and received his promotion as Captain, when the expedition returned.

The ships were accompanied as far as the ice by the Nautilus transport, freighted with provisions and stores, which were to be transhipped as soon as room was found for them.

The vessels got away from the little Nore early on the 8th of May, 1821, but meeting with strong gales off the Greenland coast, and a boisterous passage, did not fall in with the ice until the middle of June.

On the 17th of June, in a heavy gale from the southward, the sea stove and carried away one of the quarter boats of the Hecla. On the following day, in lat. 60° 53′ N., long. 61° 39′ W., they made the pack or main body of ice, having many large bergs in and near it. On the 19th, Resolution Island, at the entrance of Hudson's Strait, was seen distant sixty-four miles. Capt. Lyon states, that during one of the watches, a large fragment was observed to fall from an iceberg near the Hecla, which threw up the water to a great height, sending forth at the same time a noise like the report of a great gun. From this period to the 1st of July, the ships were occupied in clearing the Nautilus of her stores, preparatory to her return home, occasionally made fast to a berg, or driven out to sea by gales. On the 2d, after running through heavy ice, they again made Resolution Island, and shaping their course for the Strait, were soon introduced to the company of some unusually large icebergs. The altitude of one was 258 feet above the surface of the sea; its total height, therefore, allowing one-seventh only to be visible, must have been about 1806 feet! This however, is supposing the base under water not to spread beyond the mass above water The vessels had scarcely drifted past this floating mountain, when the eddy tide carried them with great rapidity among a cluster of eleven bergs of huge size, and having a beautiful diversity of form. The largest of these was 210 feet above the water. The floe ice was running wildly at the rate of three miles an hour, sweeping the vessels past the bergs, against any one of which, they might have received incalculable injury. An endeavor was made to make the ships fast to one of them, (for all of them were aground,) in order to ride out the tide, but it proved unsuccessful, and the Fury had much difficulty in sending a boat for some men who were on a small berg, making holes for her ice anchors. They were therefore swept past and soon beset. Fifty-four icebergs were counted from the mast-head.

On the 3d, they made some progress through very heavy floes; but on the tide turning, the loose ice flew together with such rapidity and noise, that there was barely time to secure the ships in a natural dock, before the two streams met, and even then they received some heavy shocks. Water was procured for use from the pools in the floe to which the ships were made fast; and this being the first time of doing so, afforded great amusement to the novices, who, even when it was their period of rest, preferred pelting each other with snow-balls, to going to bed. Buffeting with eddies, strong currents, and dangerous bergs, they were kept in a state of anxiety and danger, for a week or ten days. On one occasion, with the prospect of being driven on shore, the pressure they experienced was so great, that five hawsers, six inches thick, were carried away, and the best bower anchor of the Hecla was wrenched from the bows, and broke off at the head of the shank, with as much ease as if, instead of weighing upward of a ton, it had been of crockery ware. For a week they were embayed by the ice, and during this period they saw three strange ships, also beset, under Resolution Island, which they contrived to join on the 16th of July, making fast to a floe near them. They proved to be the Hudson's Bay Company's traders, Prince of Wales, and Eddystone, with the Lord Wellington, chartered to convey 160 natives of Holland, who were proceeding to settle on Lord Selkirk's estate, at the Red River. "While nearing these vessels, (says Lyon,) we observed the settlers waltzing on deck, for above two hours, the men in old-fashioned gray jackets, and the women wearing long-eared mob caps, like those used by the Swiss peasants. As we were surrounded by ice, and the thermometer was at the freezing point, it may be supposed that this ball, *al vero fresco*, afforded us much amusement." The Hudson's Bay ships had left England twenty days after the expedition.

The emigrant ship had been hampered nineteen days among the ice before she joined the others; and as this navigation was new to her captain and crew, they almost despaired of ever getting to their journey's end, so varied and constant had been their impediments. The Dutchmen had, however, behaved very philosophically during this period, and seemed determined on being merry, in spite of the weather and the dangers. Several marriages had taken place, the surgeon, who was accompanying them to the colony, officiating as clergyman,) and many more were in agitation; each happy couple always deferring the ceremony until a fine day allowed of an evening ball, which was only terminated by a fresh breeze, or a fall of snow.* On the 17th, the ships were separated by the ice, and they saw no more of their visitors. On the 21st, they were only off the Lower Savage Islands. In the evening they saw a very large bear lying on a piece of ice, and two boats were instantly sent off in chase. They approached very close before he took to the water, when he swam rapidly, and made long springs, turning boldly to face his pursuers. It was with difficulty he was captured. As these animals, although very fat and bulky, sink the instant they die, he was lashed to a boat, and brought alongside the ship. On hoisting him in, they were astonished to find that his weight exceeded sixteen hundred pounds, being one of the largest ever killed. Two instances, only, of larger bears being shot are recorded, and these were by Barentz's crew, in his third voyage, at Cherie Island, to which they gave the name of Bear Island. The two bears killed then, measured twelve and thirteen feet, while this one only measured eight feet eight inches, from the snout to the insertion of the tail. The seamen ate the flesh without experiencing any of those baneful effects which old navigators attribute to it, and which are stated to have made three of Barentz's people "so sick that we expected they would have died, and their skins peeled off from head to foot." Bruin was very fat, and having procured a tub of blubber from the carcass, it was thrown over board, and the smell soon attracted a couple of walruses, the first that had been yet seen.

They here fell in with a numerous body of the Esquimaux, who visited them from the shore. In less than an hour the ships were beset with thirty "kayaks," or men's canoes, and five of the women's large boats, or "oomiaks." Some of the latter held upward of twenty women. A most noisy but merry barter instantly took place, the crew being as anxious

* Lyon's Private Journal, p. 11.

to purchase Esquimaux curiosities, as the natives were to procure iron and European toys.

"It is quite out of my power, (observes Captain Lyon,) to describe the shouts, yells, and laughter of the savages, or the confusion which existed for two or three hours. The females were at first very shy, and unwilling to come on the ice, but bartered every thing from their boats. This timidity, however, soon wore off, and they, in the end, became as noisy and boisterous as the men." "It is scarcely possible, (he adds) to conceive any thing more ugly or disgusting than the countenances of the old women, who had inflamed eyes, wrinkled skin, black teeth, and, in fact, such a forbidding set of features as scarcely could be called human; to which might be added their dress, which was such as gave them the appearance of aged ourang-outangs. Frobisher's crew may be pardoned for having, in such superstitious times as A. D. 1576, taken one of these ladies for a witch, of whom it is said, 'The old wretch whom our sailors supposed to be a witch, had her buskins pulled off, to see if she was cloven-footed; and being very ugly and deformed, we let her go.' "

In bartering they have a singular custom of ratifying the bargain, by licking the article all over before it is put away in security. Captain Lyon says he frequently shuddered at seeing the children draw a razor over their tongue, as unconcernedly as if it had been an ivory paper-knife. I cannot forbear quoting here some humorous passages from his journal, which stand out in relief to the scientific and nautical parts of the narrative.

"The strangers were so well pleased in our society, that they showed no wish to leave us, and when the market had quite ceased, they began dancing and playing with our people, on the ice alongside. This exercise set many of their noses bleeding, and discovered to us a most nasty custom, which accounted for their gory faces, and which was, that as fast as the blood ran down, they scraped it with the fingers into their mouths, appearing to consider it as a refreshment, or dainty, if we might judge by the zest with which they smacked their lips at each supply."

* * * * * * * *

"In order to amuse our new acquaintances as much as possible, the fiddler was sent on the ice, where he instantly found a most delightful set of dancers, of whom some of the women kept pretty good time. Their only figure consisted in stamping and jumping with all their might. Our musician, who was a lively fellow, soon caught the infection, and began cutting capers also. In a short time every one on the floe, officers, men, and savages, were dancing together, and exhibited one of the most extraordinary sights I ever witnessed. One of our seamen, of a fresh, ruddy complexion, excited the admiration of all the young females, who patted his face, and danced around him wherever he went.

"The exertion of dancing so exhilarated the Esquimaux, that they had the appearance of being boisterously drunk, and played many extraordinary pranks. Among others, it was a favorite joke to run slily behind the seamen, and shouting loudly in one ear, to give them at the same time a very smart slap on the other. While looking on, I was sharply saluted in this manner, and, of course, was quite startled, to the great amusement of the bystanders: our cook, who was a most active and unwearied jumper, became so great a favorite, that every one boxed his ears so soundly, as to oblige the poor man to retire from such boisterous marks of approbation. Among other sports, some of the Esquimaux rather roughly, but with great good humor, challenged our people to wrestle. One man, in particular, who had thrown several of his countrymen, attacked an officer of a very strong make, but the poor savage was instantly thrown, and with no very easy fall; yet, although every one was laughing at him, he bore it with exemplary good humor. The same officer afforded us much diversion by teaching a large party of women to bow. courtesy, shake hands, turn their toes out, and perform sundry other polite accomplishments; the whole party master and pupils, preserving the strictest gravity.

"Toward midnight all our men, except the watch on deck, turned in to their beds, and the fatigued and hungry Esquimaux returned to their boats to take their supper, which consisted of lumps of raw flesh and blubber of seals, birds, entrails, &c.; licking their fingers with great zest, and with knives or fingers scraping the blood and grease which ran down their chins into their mouths."

Many other parties of the natives were fallen in with during the slow progress of the ships, between Salisbury and Nottingham Islands, who were equally as eager to beg, barter, or thieve; and the mouth was the general repository of most of the treasures they received; needles, pins, nails, buttons, beads, and other small etceteras, being indiscriminately stowed there, but detracting in nowise from their volubility of speech. On the 13th of August the weather being calm and fine, norwhals or sea-unicorns, were very numerous about the ships, and boats were sent, but without success, to strike one. There were sometimes as many as twenty of these beautiful fish in a shoal, lifting at times their immense horn above the water, and at others showing their glossy backs, which were spotted in the manner of coach dogs in England. The length of these fish is about fifteen feet, exclusive of the horn, which averages five or six more.

Captain Parry landed and slept on Southampton Island. His boat's crew caught in holes on the beach sufficient sillocks, or young coal-fish, to serve for two meals for the whole ship's company. During the night white whales were seen lying in hundreds close to the rocks, probably feeding on the sillocks. After carefully examining Duke of York Bay, the ships got into the Frozen Strait of Middleton on the morning of the 20th, and an anxious day was closed by passing an opening to the southward, which was found to be Sir Thomas Roe's Welcome, and heaving to for the night off a bay to the northwest. The ships got well in to Repulse Bay on the 22d, and a careful examination of its shores was made by the boats.

Captains Parry and Lyon, with several officers from each ship, landed and explored the northern shores, while a boat examined the head of the bay. The waters of a long cove are described by Captain Lyon as being absolutely hidden by the quantities of young eider-ducks, which, under the direction of their mothers, were making their first essays in swimming.

Captain Lyon with a boat's crew made a trip of a couple of days along some of the indents of the bay, and discovered an inlet, which, however, on being entered subsequently by the ships, proved only to be the dividing channel between an island and the main-land, about six miles in length by one in breadth. Proceeding to the northward by Hurd's channel, they experienced a long rolling ground swell setting against them. On the 28th, ascending a steep mountain, Captain Lyon discovered a noble bay, subsequently named Gore Bay, in which lay a few islands, and toward this they directed their course.

Captain Parry, who had been two days absent with boats exploring the channel and shores of the strait, returned on the 29th, but set off again on the same day with six boats to sound and examine more minutely. When Parry returned at night, Mr. Griffiths, of the Hecla, brought on board a large doe, which he had killed while swimming (among large masses of ice) from isle to isle; two others and a fawn were procured on shore by the Fury's people. The game laws, as they were laid down on the former voyage while wintering at Melville Island, were once more put in force. These "enacted that for the purpose of economizing the ship's provisions, all deer or musk-oxen killed should be served out in lieu of the usual allowance of meat. Hares, ducks, and other birds were not at this time to be included. As an encouragement to sportsmen, the head, legs, and offal of the larger animals were to be the perquisites of those who procured the carcasses for the general good." "In the animals of this day (observes Lyon) we were convinced that our sportsmen had not forgotten the latitude to which their perquisites might legally extend, for the necks were made so long as to encroach considerably on the vertebræ of the back; a manner of amputating the heads which had been learned during the former voyage, and, no doubt. would be strictly acted up to in the present one."

While the ships on the 30th were proceeding through this strait, having to contend with heavy wind and wild ice, which with an impetuous tide ran against the rocks with loud crashes, at the rate of five knots in the center stream; four boats towing astern were torn away by the ice, and, with the men in them, were for some time in great danger. The vessels anchored for the night in a small nook, and weighing at daylight on the 31st, they stood to the eastward, but Gore Bay was found closely packed with ice, and most of the inlets they passed were also beset.

A prevalence of fog, northerly wind, and heavy ice in floes of some miles in circumference, now carried the ships, in spite of constant labor and exertions, in three days, back to the very spot in Fox's Channel, where a month ago they had commenced their operations. It was not till the 5th of September, that they could again get forward, and then by one of the usual changes in the navigation of these seas, the ships ran well to the northeast unimpeded, at the rate of six knots an hour, anchoring for the night at the mouth of a large opening, which was named Lyon Inlet. The next day they proceeded about twenty-five miles up this inlet, which appeared to be about eight miles broad. Captain Parry pushed on with two boats to examine the head of the inlet, taking provisions for a week. He returned on the 14th, having failed in finding any outlet to the place he had been examining, which was very extensive, full of fiords and rapid overfalls of the tide. He had procured a sufficiency of game to afford his people a hot supper every evening, which, after the constant labor of the day, was highly acceptable. He fell in also with a small party of natives who displayed the usual thieving propensities.

Animal food of all kinds was found to be very plentiful in this locality. A fine salmon trout was brought down by one of the officers from a lake in the mountains. The crew of the Hecla killed in a fortnight four deer, forty hares, eighty-two ptarmigan, fifty ducks, three divers, three foxes, three ravens, four seals, ermines, marmottes, mice, &c. Two of the seals killed were immense animals of the bearded species (*Phoca barbata*,) very fat, weighing about eight or nine cwt.; the others were the common species, (*P. vitulina*.)

Captain Parry again left in boats, on the 15th, to examine more carefully the land that had been passed so rapidly on the 5th and 6th. Not finding him return on the 24th, Captain Lyon ran down the coast to meet him, and by burning blue lights, fell in with him at ten that night. It appeared he had been frozen up for two days on the second evening after leaving. When he got clear he ran down to, and sailed round, Gore Bay, at that time perfectly clear of ice, but by the next morning it was quite filled with heavy pieces, which much impeded his return. Once more he was frozen up in a small bay, where he was detained three days; when, finding there was no chance of getting out, in consequence of the rapid formation of young ice, by ten hours' severe labor, the boats were carried over a low point of land, a mile and a half wide, and once more launched.

On the 6th of October, the impediments of ice continuing to increase, being met with in all its formations of sludges or young ice, pancake ice and bay ice, a small open bay within a cape of land, forming the southeast extremity of an island off Lyon Inlet, was sounded, and being found to be safe anchorage the ships were brought in, and, from the indications which were setting in, it was finally determined to secure them there for the winter; by means of a canal half a mile long, which was cut, they were taken further into the bay. The island was named Winter Isle.

Preparations were now made for occupation and

amusement, so as to pass away pleasantly the period of detention. A good stock of theatrical dresses and properties having been laid in by the officers before leaving England, arrangements were made for performing plays fortnightly, as on their last winter residence, as a means of amusing the seamen, and in some degree to break the tedious monotony of their confinement. As there could be no desire or hope of excelling, every officer's name was readily entered on the list of *dramatis personæ*, Captain Lyon kindly undertaking the difficult office of manager. Those *ladies* (says Lyon) who had cherished the growth of their beards and whiskers, as a defense against the inclemency of the climate, now generously agreed to do away with such unfeminine ornaments, and every thing bade fair for a most stylish theater.

As a curiosity, I may here put on record the play bill for the evening. I have added the ship to which each officer belonged.

THEATER ROYAL,

WINTER ISLE.

The Public are respectfully informed that this little, yet elegant Theater, will open for the season on Friday next, the 9th of November, 1821, when will be performed Sheridan's celebrated Comedy of

THE RIVALS.

Sir Anthony Absolute	Captain Parry, (*Fury.*)
Captain Absolute - -	Captain Lyon, (*Hecla.*)
Sir Lucius O'Trigger,	Mr. Crozier, (*Fury.*)
Faulkland, - - - -	Mr. J. Edwards, (*Fury.*)
Acres, - - - - - -	Mr. J. Henderson, (*Fury.*)
Fay, - - - - - -	Lieut. Hoppner, (*Hecla.*)
David, - - - - - -	Lieut. Reid, (*Fury.*)
Mrs. Malaprop, - -	Mr. C. Richards, (*Hecla.*)
Julia, - - - - - -	Mr. W. H. Hooper, (*Fury.*)
Lydia Languish, - -	Mr. J. Sherer, (*Hecla.*)
Lucy, - - - - - -	Mr. W. Mogg, (*cl'k of Hecla.*)

Songs by Messrs. C. Palmer, (Hecla,) and J. Henderson, will be introduced in the course of the evening.

On the 17th of December, a shivering set of actors performed to a great-coated, yet very cold audience, the comedy of the "Poor Gentleman." A burst of true English feeling was exhibited during the performance of this play. In the scene where *Lieut. Worthington* and *Corporal Foss* recount in so animated a manner their former achievements, advancing at the same time, and huzzaing for "Old England," the whole audience, with one accord, rose and gave three most hearty cheers. They then sat down, and the play continued uninterrupted.

On Christmas Eve, in order to keep the people quiet and sober, two farces were performed, and the phantasmagoria, (which had been kindly presented anonymously to the ships before leaving, by a lady,) exhibited, so that the night passed merrily away.

The coldness of the weather proved no bar to the performance of a play at the appointed time. If it amused the seamen, the purpose was answered, but it was a cruel task to performers. "In our green-room, (says Lyon,) which was as much warmed as any other part of the Theater, the thermometer stood at 16°, and on a table which was placed over a stove, and about six inches above it, the coffee froze in the cups. For my sins, I was obliged to be dressed in the height of the fashion, as *Dick Dowlas*, in the "Heir at Law," and went through the last scene of the play with two of my fingers frost-bitten! Let those who have witnessed and admired the performances of a Young, answer if he could possibly have stood so cold a reception."

Captain Parry also states in his Journal, "Among the recreations which afforded the highest gratification to several among us, I may mention the musical parties we were enabled to muster, and which assembled on stated evenings throughout the winter, alter nately in Commander Lyon's cabin, and in my own. More skillful amateurs in music might well have smiled at these, our humble concerts, but it will not incline them to think less of the science they admire, to be assured that, in these remote and desolate regions of the globe, it has often furnished us with the most pleasurable sensations which our situation was capable of affording; for, independently of the mere gratification afforded to the ear by music, there is, perhaps, scarcely a person in the world really fond of it, in whose mind its sound is not more or less connected with 'his far distant home.' There are always some remembrances which render them inseparable, and those associations are not to be despised, which, while we are engaged in the performance of our duty, can still occasionally transport us into the social circle of our friends at home, in spite of the oceans that roll between us." But their attention was not confined to mere amusements. Much to the credit of the seamen, an application was made in each ship for permission to open an evening school, which was willingly acceded to. Almost every man could read, and some could write a little, but several found that, from long disuse, it was requisite to begin again.

Mr. Halse volunteered to superintend the classes in the Fury; while Benjamin White, a seaman, who had been educated at Christ's Hospital, officiated as schoolmaster in the Hecla, and those best qualified to assist aided in the instruction of their shipmates, who made rapid progress under their tuition. On Christmas Day, Capt. Lyon states that he received sixteen copies from men, who, two months before, scarcely knew their letters. These little specimens were all well written, and sent with as much pride as if the writers had been good little schoolboys, instead of stout and excellent seamen.

An observatory was erected on shore, for carrying on magnetical, astronomical, and other scientific operations. Foxes were very plentiful about the ships; fifteen were caught in one trap in four hours on the night of the 25th of October, and above one hundred were either trapped or killed in the course of three months, and yet there seemed but little diminution in their numbers. Captain Lyon says he found them not bad eating, the flesh much resembling that of kid. A pack of thirteen wolves came occasionally to have a look at the ships, and on one occasion broke into a snow-house alongside, and walked off with a couple of Esquimaux dogs confined there. Bears now and then also made their appearance.

A very beautiful ermine walked on board the Hecla one day, and was caught in a small trap placed on the deck, certainly the first of these animals which was ever taken alive on board a ship 400 yards from the land. The ravenous propensities of even some of the smallest members of the animal kingdom are exemplified by the following extract : —

"We had for some time observed that in the fire-hole, which was kept open in the ice alongside, a countless multitude of small shrimps were constantly rising near the surface, and we soon found that in twenty-four hours they would clean, in the most beautiful manner, the skeletons."

After attending divine service on Christmas day, the officers and crews sat down to the luxury of joints of English roast beef, which had been kept untainted by being frozen, and the outside rubbed with salt. Cranberry pies and puddings, of every shape and size, with a full allowance of spirits, followed, and, probably the natural attendance of headaches succeeded, for the next morning it was deemed expedient to send all the people for a run on the ice, in order to put them to rights ; but thick weather coming on, it became necessary to recall them, and, postponing the dinner hour, they were all danced sober by one o'clock, the fiddler being, fortunately, quite as he should be. During this curious ball, a witty fellow attended as an old cake woman, with lumps of frozen snow in a bucket ; and such was the demand for his pies on this occasion, that he was obliged to replenish pretty frequently. The year had now drawn to a close, and all enjoyed excellent health, and were blessed with good spirits, and zeal for the renewal of their arduous exertions in the summer.

No signs of scurvy, the usual plague of such voyages, had occurred, and by the plans of Captain Parry, as carried out on the former voyage, a sufficiency of mustard and cress was raised between decks to afford all hands a salad once, and sometimes twice a week. The cold now became intense. Wine froze in the bottles. Port was congealed into thin pink laminæ, which lay loosely, and occupied the whole length of the bottle. White wine, on the contrary, froze into a solid and perfectly transparent mass, resembling amber.

On the 1st of February the monotony of their life was varied by the arrival of a large party of Esquimaux, and an interchange of visits thenceforward took place with this tribe, which, singularly enough, were proverbial for their honesty. Ultimately, however, they began to display some thievish propensities, for on one evening in March a most shocking theft was committed, which was no less than the last piece of English corned beef from the midshipmen's mess. Had it been an 18lb. carronade, or even one of the anchors, the thieves would have been welcome to it; but to purloin English beef in such a country was unpardonable.

On the 15th of March Captain Lyon, Lieutenant Palmer, and a party of men, left the ship, with provisions, tents, &c., in a large sledge, for an excursion of three or four days, to examine the land in the neighborhood of the ships.

The first night's encampment was anything but comfortable. Their tent they found so cold, that it was determined to make a cavern in the snow to sleep in; and digging this afforded so good an opportunity of warming themselves, that the only shovel was lent from one to the other as a particular favor. After digging it of sufficient size to contain them all in a sitting posture, by means of the smoke of a fire they managed to raise the temperature to 20°, and, closing the entrance with blocks of snow, crept into their blanket bags and tried to sleep, with the pleasant reflection that their roof might fall in and bury them all, and that their one spade was the only means of liberation after a night's drift of snow.

They woke next morning to encounter a heavy gale and drift, and found their sledge so embedded in the snow that they could not get at it, and in the attempt their faces and extremities were most painfully frost-bitten. The thermometer was at 32° below zero; they could not, moreover, see a yard of the road; yet to remain appeared worse than to go forward — the last plan was, therefore, decided on. The tent, sledge, and luggage were left behind, and with only a few pounds of bread, a little rum, and a spade, the party again set out; and in order to depict their sufferings, I must take up the narrative as related by the commander himself:

"Not knowing where to go, we wandered among the heavy hummocks of ice, and suffering from cold, fatigue and anxiety, were soon completely bewildered. Several of our party now began to exhibit symptoms of that horrid kind of insensibility which is the prelude to sleep. They all professed extreme willingness to do what they were told in order to keep in exercise, but none obeyed; on the contrary, they reeled about like drunken men. The faces of several were severely frost-bitten, and some had for a considerable time lost sensation in their fingers and toes; yet they made not the slightest exertion to rub the parts affected, and even discontinued their general custom of warming each other on observing a discoloration of the skin. Mr. Palmer employed the people in building a snow wall, ostensibly as a shelter from the wind, but in fact to give them exercise, when standing still must have proved fatal to men in our circumstances. My attention was exclusively directed to Sergeant Speckman, who, having been repeatedly warned that his nose was frozen, had paid no attention to it, owing to the state of stupefaction into which he had fallen. The frost-bite had now extended over one side of his face, which was frozen as hard as a mask; the eyelids were stiff, and one corner of the upper lip so drawn up as to expose the teeth and gums. My hands being still warm, I had the happiness of restoring the circulation, after which I used all my endeavors to keep the poor fellow in motion; but he complained sadly of giddiness and dimness of sight, and was so weak as to be unable to walk without assistance. His case was so alarming, that I expected every moment he would lie down, never to rise again.

"Our prospect now became every moment more gloomy, and it was but too probable that four of our party would be unable to survive another hour. Mr. Palmer, however, endeavored, as well as myself, to cheer the people up, but it was a faint attempt, as we had not a single hope to give them. Every piece of ice, or even of small rock or stone, was now supposed to be the ships, and we had great difficulty in preventing the men from running to the different objects which attracted them, and consequently losing themselves in the drift. In this state, while Mr. Palmer was running round us to warm himself, he suddenly pitched on a new beaten track, and as exercise was indispensable, we determined on following it, wherever it might lead us. Having taken the Sergeant under my coat, he recovered a little, and we moved onward, when to our infinite joy we found that the path led to the ships."

As the result of this exposure, one man had two of his fingers so badly frost-bitten as to lose a good deal of the flesh of the upper ends, and for many days it was feared that he would be obliged to have them amputated. Quarter-master Carr, one of those who had been the most hardy while in the air, fainted twice on getting below, and every one had severe frost-bites in different parts of the body, which recovered after the usual loss of skin in these cases.

One of the Esquimaux females, by name Igloolik, who plays a conspicuous part in the narrative, was a general favorite, being possessed of a large fund of useful information, having a good voice and ear for music, being an excellent seamstress, and having such a good idea of the hydrography and bearings of the neighboring sea-coasts, as to draw charts which guided Parry much in his future operations, for he found her sketches to be in the main correct. She connected the land from their winter quarters to the northwest sea, rounding and terminating the northern extremity of this part of America, by a large island, and a strait of sufficient magnitude to afford a safe passage for the ships. This little northwest passage, observes Lyon, set us all castle-building, and we already fancied the worst part of our voyage over ; or, at all events, that before half the ensuing summer was past, we should arrive at Akkoolee, the Esquimaux settlement on the western shore. Half-way between that coast and Re pulse Bay, Igloolik drew on her chart a lake of considerable size, having small streams running from it to the sea, on each side ; and the correctness of this information was fully proved by Rae in his recent expedition in 1846.

On the 13th of April their Esquimaux friends took their departure for other quarters ; towards the end of the month the crews completed the cutting of trenches round the vessels, in order that they might rise to their proper bearings previous to working in the holds, and the ships floated like corks on their native element, after their long imprisonment of 191 days. As the season appeared to be improving, another land expedition was determined on, and Captain Lyon and Lieutenant Palmer, attended by a party of eight men, set off on the 8th of May, taking with them twenty days' provisions. Each man drew on a sledge 126 lbs., and the officers 95 lbs. a-piece.

"Loaded as we were," says the leader, "it was with the greatest difficulty we made our way among and over the hummocks, ourselves and sledges taking some very unpleasant tumbles. It required two and a half hours to cross the ice, although the distance was not two miles, and we then landed on a small island, where we passed the night."

Several islands and shoals in the strait were named Bird's Isles. At noon on the 11th, they camped at the head of a fine bay, to which the name of Blake was given. In spite of all the care which had been taken by using crape shades, and other coverings for the eyes, five of the party became severely afflicted with snow blindness. Before evening two of the sufferers were quite blinded by the inflammation. Their faces, eyes, and even heads, being much swollen, and very red. Bathing would have afforded relief, but the sun did not produce a drop of water, and their stock of fuel being limited, they could only spare enough wood to thaw snow for their midday draught.

As the morning of the 12th brought no change in the invalids, another day was lost. Toward evening, by breaking pieces of ice, and placing them in the full glare of the sun, sufficient water was obtained, both for drinking and for the sick to bathe their faces, which afforded them amazing relief, and on the morrow they were enabled to resume their journey. At noon the sun was sufficiently powerful to afford the travelers a draught of water, without having to thaw it, as had hitherto been the case.

For nearly three days after this, they were imprisoned in their low tent by a snow-storm, but on the morning of the 18th, they were enabled to sally out to stretch their legs, and catch a glimpse of the sun. After examining many bays and indentations of the coast, the party returned to the ships on the evening of the 21st. A canal was now cut through the ice, to get the ships to the open water, in length 2400 feet, and varying in breadth from 60 to 197 feet. The average thickness of the ice was four feet, but in some places it was as much as twelve feet. This truly arduous task had occupied the crews for fifteen days, from six in the morning to eight in the evening; but they labored at it with the greatest spirit and good humor, and it was concluded on the 18th of June, when the officers and men began to take leave of their several haunts and promenades, particularly the "garden" of each ship, which had become favorite lounges during their nine months' detention. A few ill-fated bunting came near enough to be shot, and were instantly roasted for a farewell supper, and bright visions of active exertions on the water on the morrow were universally entertained. But the night dispelled all these airy castles, for with the morning's dawn they found that the whole body of ice astern of the ships had broke adrift, filled up the hard-wrought canal, and imprisoned them as firm as ever.

Death now for the first time visited the crews. James Pringle, a seaman of the Hecla, fell from the mast-head to the deck, and was killed on the 18th of May. Wm. Souter, quarter-master, and John Reid, Carpenter's mate, belonging to the Fury, died on the 26th and 27th, of natural causes. Toward the end of June, the sea began to clear rapidly to the eastward, and the bay ice soon gave way as far as where the ships were lying, and on the 2d of July they put to sea with a fresh breeze, after having been frozen in for 267 days.

In making their way to the northward, they were frequently in much danger. On the 3d, the ice came down on the Hecla with such force as to carry her on board the Fury, by which the Hecla broke her best bower anchor, and cut her waist-boat in two. On the 4th, the pressure of the ice was so great as to break the Hecla adrift from three hawsers. Four or five men were each on separate pieces of ice, parted from the ships in the endeavor to run out a hawser. A heavy pressure closing the loose ice unexpectedly gave them a road on board again, or they must have been carried away by the stream to certain destruction. On the 8th, the Hecla had got her stream-cable out, in addition to the other hawsers, and made fast to the land ice, when a very heavy and extensive floe took the ship on her broad side, and being backed by another large body of ice, gradually lifted her stem as if by the action of a wedge.

"The weight every moment increasing, obliged us," says Captain Lyon, "to veer on the hawsers, whose friction was so great as nearly to cut through the bitt-heads, and ultimately to set them on fire, so that it became requisite for people to attend with buckets of water. The pressure was at length too powerful for resistance, and the stream-cable, with two six and one five-inch hawsers, all gave way at the same moment, three others soon following them. The sea was too full of ice to allow the ship to drive, and the only way in which she could yield to the enormous weight which oppressed her, was by leaning over on the land ice, while her stem at the same time was entirely lifted to above the height of five feet out of the water. The lower deck beams now complained very much, and the whole frame of the ship underwent a trial which would have proved fatal to any less strengthened vessel. At the same moment, the rudder was unhung with a sudden jerk, which broke up the rudder-case, and struck the driver-boom with great force."

From this perilous position she was released almost by a miracle, and the rudder re-hung.

The ships at last reached the island which had been so accurately described to them by the Esquimaux lady — Iglolik, where they came upon an encampment of 120 Esquimaux, in tents. Captains Parry and Lyon and other officers made frequent exploring excursions along the shores of the Fury and Hecla strait, and inland. On the 26th of August the ships entered this strait, which was found blocked up with flat ice. The season had also now assumed so wintry an aspect that there seemed but little probability of getting much farther west: knowing of no harbor to protect the ships, unless a favorable change took place, they had the gloomy prospect before them of wintering in or near this frozen strait. Boating and land parties were dispatched in several directions, to report upon the different localities.

On the 4th of September, Captain Lyon landed on an island of slate formation, about six miles to the westward of the ships, which he named Amherst Island. The result of these expeditions proved that it was impracticable, either by boats or water conveyance, to examine any part of the land southwest of Iglolik, in consequence of the ice. 8

Mr. Reid and a boat-party traveled about sixty miles to the westward of Amherst Island, and ascertained the termination of the strait. On a consultation with the officers, Captain Parry determined to seek a berth near to Iglolik, in which to secure the ships for the winter. They had now been sixty-five days struggling to get forward, but had only in that time reached forty miles to the westward of Iglolik. The vessels made the best of their way to the natural channel between this island and the land, but were for some time drifted with the ice, losing several anchors, and it was only by hard work in cutting channels that they were brought into safer quarters, near the land. Some fine teams of dogs were here purchased from the Esquimaux, which were found very serviceable in making excursions on sledges.

Their second Christmas day in this region had now arrived, and Lyon informs us —

"Captain Parry dined with me, and was treated with a superb display of mustard and cress, with about fifty onions, rivaling a fine needle in size, which I had reared in boxes round my cabin stove. All our messes in either ship were supplied with an extra pound of real English fresh beef, which had been hanging at our quarter for eighteen months. We could not afford to leave it for a farther trial of keeping, but I have no doubt that double the period would not have quite spoiled its flavor."

This winter proved much more severe than the former. Additional clothing was found necessary. The stove funnels collected a quantity of ice within them, notwithstanding fires were kept up night and day, so that it was frequently requisite to take them down in order to break and melt the ice out of them.

Nothing was seen of the sun for forty-two days.

On the 15th of April, Mr. A. Elder, Greenland mate of the Hecla, died of dropsy: he had been leading man with Parry on Ross's voyage, and for his good conduct was made mate of the Griper, on the last expedition.

On the 6th of September, 1823, Mr. George Fife, the pilot, also died of scurvy.

After taking a review of their provisions, and the probability of having to pass a third winter here, Capt. Parry determined to send the Hecla home, taking from her all the provision that could be spared. Little or no hopes could be entertained of any passage being found to the westward, otherwise than by the strait now so firmly closed with ice; but Parry trusted that some interesting additions might be made to the geography of these dreary regions, by attempting a passage to the northward or eastward, in hopes of finding an outlet to Lancaster Sound, or Prince Regent's Inlet.

On the 21st of April, 1823, they began transshipping the provisions; the teams of dogs being found most useful for this purpose. Even two anchors of 22 cwt. each, were drawn by these noble animals at a quick trot.

Upon admitting daylight at the stern windows of the Hecla, on the 22d, the gloomy, sooty cabin showed to no great advantage; no less than ten buckets of ice were taken from the sashes and out of the stern lockers, from which latter some spare flannels and instruments were only liberated by chopping.

On the 7th of June, Captain Lyon, with a party of men, set off across the Melville Peninsula, to endeavor to get a sight of the western sea, of which they had received descriptive accounts from the natives, but owing to the difficulties of traveling, and the ranges of mountains they met with, they returned unsuccessful, after being out twenty days. Another inland trip of a fortnight followed.

On the 1st of August, the Hecla was reported ready for sea. Some symptoms of scurvy having again made their appearance in the ships, and the surgeons reporting that it would not be prudent to continue longer, Captain Parry reluctantly determined to proceed home with both ships. After being 319 days in their winter quarters, the ships got away on the 9th of August.

A conspicuous landmark, with dispatches, was set up on the main-land, for the information of Franklin, should he reach this quarter.

On reaching Winter Island, and visiting their las year's garden, radishes, mustard and cress, and onions were brought off, which had survived the winter and were still alive, seventeen months from the time they were planted, a very remarkable proof of their having been preserved by the warm covering of snow.

The ships, during the whole of this passage, were driven by the current more than three degrees, entirely at the mercy of the ice, being carried into every bight, and swept over each point, without the power of helping themselves.

On the 1st of September, they were driven up Lyon Inlet, where they were confined high up till the 6th, when a breeze sprung up, which took them down to within three miles of Winter Island; still it was not until the 12th, that they got thoroughly clear of the indraught. The danger and suspense of these twelve days were horrible, and Lyon justly observes, that he would prefer being frozen up during another eleven months' winter, to again passing so anxious a period of time.

"Ten of the twelve nights were passed on deck, in expectation, each tide, of some decided change in our affairs, either by being left on the rocks, or grounding in such shoal water, that the whole body of the ice must have slid over us. But, as that good old seaman Baffin expresses himself, 'God, who is greater than either ice or tide, always delivered us!'"

For thirty-five days the ships had been beset, and in that period had driven with the ice above 300 miles, without any exertion on their part, and also without a possibility of extricating themselves. On the 23d of September, they once more got into the swell of the Atlantic, and on the 10th of October, arrived at Lerwick, in Shetland.

Clavering's Voyage to Spitzbergen and Greenland, 1823.

In 1823, Capt. Sabine, R. A., who had been for some time engaged in magnetic observations, and also in experiments to determine the configuration of the earth, by means of pendulum vibrations in different latitudes, having perfected his observations at different points, from the Equator to the Arctic Circle, suggested to the Royal Society, through Sir Humphry Davy, the importance of extending similar experiments into higher latitudes toward the Pole. Accordingly, the government placed at his disposal H. M. S. Griper, 120 tons, Commander Clavering, which was to convey him to Spitzbergen, and thence to the east coast of Greenland.

The Griper sailed from the Nore, on the 11th of May, and proceeded to Hammerfest, or Whale Island, near the North Cape, in Norway, which she reached on the 4th of June, and Capt. Sabine having finished his shore observations by the 23d, the vessel set sail for Spitzbergen. She fell in with ice off Cherry Island, in lat. 75° 5′, on the 27th, and on the 30th disembarked the tents and instruments on one of the small islands round Hakluyt's Headland, near the eightieth parallel. Capt. Clavering, meanwhile, sailed in the Griper due north, and reached the latitude of 80° 20′, where being stopped by close packed ice, he was obliged to return.

On the 24th of July, they again put to sea, directing their course for the highest known point of the eastern coast of Greenland. They met with many fields of ice, and made the land, which had a most miserable, desolate appearance, at a point which was named Cape Borlase Warren. Two islands were discovered, and as Capt. Sabine here landed and carried on his observations, they were called Pendulum Islands. From an island situate in lat. 75° 12′, to which he gave the name of Shannon Island, Clavering saw high land, stretching due north as far as lat. 76°.

On the 16th of August, Clavering landed with a party of three officers, and sixteen men on the mainland, to examine the shores. The temperature did not sink below 23°, and they slept for nearly a fortnight they were on shore with only a boat-cloak and blanket for a covering, without feeling any inconvenience from the cold. A tribe of twelve Esquimaux was met with here. They reached in their journey a magnificent inlet, about fifty miles in circumference, which was supposed to be the same which Gale Hamkes discovered in 1654, and which bears his name. The mountains round its sides were 4000 to 5000 feet high. On the 29th of August, they returned on board, and having embarked the tents and instruments, the ship again set sail on the 31st, keeping the coast in view to Cape Parry, lat. 72½°. The cliffs were observed to be several thousand feet high. On the 13th of September, as the ice in shore began to get very troublesome, the ship stood out to sea, and after encountering a very heavy gale, which drove them with great fury to the southward, and it not being thought prudent to make for Ireland, a station in about the same latitude on the Norway coast was chosen instead by Capt. Sabine. They made the land about the latitude of Christiansound. On the 1st of October, the Griper struck hard on a sunken rock, but got off undamaged.

On the 6th, they anchored in Drontheim Fiord, where they were received with much kindness and hospitality, and after the necessary observations had been completed the ship proceeded homeward, and reached Deptford on the 19th of December, 1823.

Lyon's Voyage in the Griper.

In 1824, three expeditions were ordered out, to carry on simultaneous operations in Arctic discovery. To Capt. Lyon was committed the task of examining and completing the survey of the Melville Peninsula, the adjoining straits, and the shores of Arctic America, if possible as far as Franklin's turning point. Capt. Lyon was therefore gazetted to the Griper gun-brig, which had taken out Capt. Sabine to Spitzbergen, in the previous year. The following officers and crew were also appointed to her :—

Griper.

Captain — G. F. Lyon.
Lieutenants — P. Manico and F. Harding.

Assistant-Surveyor — E. N. Kendal.
Purser — J. Evans.
Assistant-Surgeon — W. Leyson.
Midshipman — J. Tom.
34 Petty Officers, Seamen, &c.
Total complement, 41.

It was not till the 20th of June, that the Griper got away from England, being a full month later than the usual period of departure, and the vessel was at the best but an old tub in her sailing propensities. A small tender, called the *Snap*, was ordered to accompany her with stores, as far as the ice, and having been relieved of her supplies, she was sent home on reaching Hudson's Straits.

The Griper made but slow progress in her deeply laden state, her crowded decks being continually swept by heavy seas, and it was not until the end of August, that she rounded the southern head of Southampton Island, and stood up toward Sir Thomas Roe's Wel come. On reaching the entrance of this channel they encountered a terrific gale, which for a long time threatened the destruction of both ship and crew. Drifting with this, they brought up the ship with four anchors, in a bay with five fathoms and a half water, in the momentary expectation that with the ebb tide the ship would take the ground, as the sea broke fearfully on a low sandy beach just astern, and had the anchors parted, nothing could have saved the vessel. Neither commander nor crew had been in bed for three nights, and although little hope was entertained of surviving the gale, and no boat could live in such a sea, the officers and crew performed their several duties with their accustomed coolness. Each man was ordered to put on his warmest clothing, and to take charge of some useful instrument. The scene is best described in the words of the gallant commander :—

"Each, therefore, brought his bag on deck, and dressed himself; and in the fine athletic forms which stood exposed before me, I did not see one muscle quiver, nor the slightest sign of alarm. Prayers were read, and they then all sat down in groups, sheltered from the wash of the sea by whatever they could find, and some endeavored to obtain a little sleep. Never, perhaps was witnessed a finer scene than on the deck of my little ship, when all hope of life had left us. Noble as the character of the British sailor is always allowed to be in cases of danger, yet I did not believe it to be possible that among forty-one persons not one repining word should have been uttered. Each was at peace with his neighbor and all the world; and I am firmly persuaded that the resignation which was then shown to the will of the Almighty, was the means of obtaining His mercy. God was merciful to us, and the tide, almost miraculously, fell no lower." The appropriate name of the Bay of God's Mercy has been given to this spot on the charts by Captain Lyon.

Proceeding onward up the Welcome, they encountered, about a fortnight later, another fearful storm. On the 12th of September, when off the entrance of Wager Inlet, it blew so hard for two days, that on the 13th the ship was driven from her anchors, and carried away by the fury of the gale, with every prospect of being momentarily dashed to pieces against any hidden rock; but the same good Providence which had so recently befriended them, again stood their protector. On consulting with his officers, it was unanimously resolved, that in the crippled state of the ship, without any anchor, and with her compasses worse than useless, it would be madness to continue the voyage, and the ship's course was therefore shaped for England.

I may observe, that the old Griper is now laid up as a hulk in Chichester Harbor, furnishing a residence and depot for the coast guard station.

Parry's Third Voyage.

In the spring of 1824 the Admiralty determined to give Capt. Parry another opportunity of carrying out the great problem which had so long been sought after, of a northwest passage to the Pacific, and so generally esteemed was this gallant commander that he had but to hoist his pennant, when fearless of all danger, and in a noble spirit of emulation, his former associates rallied around him.

The same two ships were employed as before, but Parry now selected the Hecla for his pennant. The staff of officers and men was as follows:—

Hecla.

Captain — W. E. Parry.
Lieutenants — J. L. Wynn, Joseph Sherer, and Henry Foster.
Surgeon — Samuel Neill, M. D.
Purser — W. H. Hooper.
Assistant Surgeon — W. Rowland.
Midshipmen — J. Brunton, F. R. M. Crozier, C. Richards, and H. N. Head.
Greenland Pilots — J. Allison, master; and G. Champion, mate.
49 Petty Officers, Seamen, and Marines.
Total complement, 62.

Fury.

Commander — H. P. Hoppner.
Lieutenants — H. T. Austin and J. C. Ross.
Surgeon — A. M'Laren.
Purser — J. Halse.
Assistant Surgeon — T. Bell.
Midshipmen — B. Westropp, C. C. Waller, and E. Bird.
Clerk — W. Mogg.
Greenland Pilots — G. Crawford, master; T. Donaldson, mate.
48 Petty Officers, Seamen, and Marines.
Total complement, 60.

The William Harris, transport, was commissioned to accompany the ships to the ice with provisions.

F

Among the promotions made, it will be seen, were Lieut. Hoppner to the rank of Commander, and second in command of the expedition. Messrs. J. Sherer, and J. C. Ross to be Lieutenants, and J. Halse to be Purser. The attempt on this occasion was to be made by Lancaster Sound through Barrow's Strait to Prince Regent Inlet. The ships sailed on the 19th of May, 1824, and a month afterward fell in with the body of the ice in lat. 60¾°. After transhipping the stores to the two vessels, and sending home the transport, about the middle of July they were close beset with the ice in Baffin's Bay, and "from this time (says Parry) the obstructions from the quantity, magnitude, and closeness of the ice, which were such as to keep our people almost constantly employed in heaving, warping, or sawing through it; and yet with so little success that, at the close of July, we had only penetrated seventy miles to the westward." After encountering a severe gale on the 1st of August, by which masses of overlaying ice were driven one upon the other, the Hecla was laid on her broadside by a strain, which Parry says must inevitably have crushed a vessel of ordinary strength; they got clear of the chief obstructions by the first week in September. During the whole of August they had not one day sufficiently free from rain, snow, or sleet, to be able to air the bedding of the ship's company.

They entered Lancaster Sound on the 10th of September, and with the exception of a solitary berg or two found it clear of ice. A few days after, however, they fell in with the young ice, which increasing daily in thickness, the ships became beset, and by the current which set to the east at the rate of three miles an hour, they were soon drifted back to the eastward of Admiralty Inlet, and on the 23d they found themselves again off Wollaston Island, at the entrance of Navy Board Inlet. By perseverance, however, and the aid of a strong easterly breeze, they once more managed to recover their lost ground, and on the 27th reached the entrance of Port Bowen on the eastern shore of Prince Regent Inlet, and here Parry resolved upon wintering; this making the fourth winter this enterprising commander had passed in these inhospitable seas.

The usual laborious process of cutting canals had to be resorted to, in order to get the ships near to the shore in secure and sheltered situations. Parry thus describes the dreary monotonous character of an arctic winter: —

"It is hard to conceive any one thing more like another than two winters passed in the higher latitudes of the polar regions, except when variety happens to be afforded by intercourse with some other branch of the whole family of man. Winter after winter, nature here assumes an aspect so much alike, that cursory observation can scarcely detect a single feature of variety. The winter of more temperate climates, and even in some of no slight severity, is occasionally diversified by a thaw, which at once gives variety and comparative cheerfulness to the prospect. But here, when once the earth is covered, all is dreary monotonous whiteness, not merely for days or weeks, but for more than half a year together. Whichever way the eye is turned, it meets a picture calculated to impress upon the mind an idea of inanimate stillness, of that motionless torpor with which our feelings have nothing congenial; of any thing, in short, but life. In the very silence there is a deadness with which a human spectator appears *out of keeping*. The presence of man seems an intrusion on the dreary solitude of this wintry desert, which even its native animals have for awhile forsaken."

During this year Parry tells us the thermometer remained below zero 131 days, and did not rise above that point till the 11th of April. The sun, which had been absent from their view 121 days, again blessed the crews with his rays on the 22d of February. During this long imprisonment, schools, scientific observations, walking parties, &c., were resorted to, but "our former amusements," says Parry, "being almost worn threadbare, it required some ingenuity to devise any plan that should possess the charm of novelty to recommend it." A happy idea was, however, hit upon by Commander Hoppner, at whose suggestion a monthly *bal masque* was held, to the great diversion of both officers and men, to the number of 120. The popular commander entered gayly into their recreations, and thus speaks of these polar masquerades :—

"It is impossible that any idea could have proved more happy, or more exactly suited to our situation Admirably dressed characters of various descriptions readily took their parts, and many of these were supported with a degree of spirit and genuine good humor which would not have disgraced a more refined assembly; while the latter might not have been disgraced by copying the good order, decorum, and inoffensive cheerfulness which our humble masquerades presented. It does especial credit to the dispositions and good sense of our men, that though all the officers entered fully into the spirit of these amusements, which took place once a month alternately on board of each ship, no instance occurred of any thing that could interfere with the regular discipline, or at all weaken the respect of the men toward their superiors. Ours were masquerades without licentiousness — carnivals without excess."

Exploring parties were sent out in several directions. Commander Hoppner and his party went inland, and after a fortnight's fatiguing journey over a mountainous, barren, and desolate country, where precipitous ravines 500 feet deep obstructed their passage, traveled a degree and three-quarters — to the latitude of 73° 19′, but saw no appearance of sea from thence.

Lieutenant Sherer, with four men, proceeded to the southward, and made a careful survey of the coast as far as 72¼°, but had not provisions sufficient to go round Cape Kater, the southernmost point observed in their former voyage.

Lieutenant J. C. Ross, with a similar party, traveled to the northward, along the coast of the Inlet, and from the hills about Cape York, observed that the sea was perfectly open and free from ice at the distance of twenty-two miles from the ships.

After an imprisonment of about ten months, by great exertions the ships were got clear from the ice, and on the 20th of July, 1825, upon the separation of the floe across the harbor, towed out to sea. Parry then made for the western shore of the Inlet, being desirous of examining the coast of North Somerset for any channel that might occur, a probability which later discoveries in that quarter have proved to be without foundation. On the 28th, when well in with the western shore, the Hecla, in spite of every exertion, was beset by floating ice, and after breaking two large ice anchors in endeavoring to heave in shore, was obliged to give up the effort and drift with the ice until the 30th. On the following day, a heavy gale came on, in which the Hecla carried away three hawsers, while the Fury was driven on shore, but was hove off at high water. Both ships were now drifted by the body of the ice down the Inlet, and took the ground, the Fury being so nipped and strained that she leaked a great deal, and four pumps kept constantly at work did not keep her clear of water. They were floated off at high water, but, late on the 2nd of August, the huge masses of ice once more forced the Fury on shore, and the Hecla narrowly escaped. On examining her and getting her off, it was found that she must be hove down and repaired; a basin was therefore formed for her reception and completed by the 16th, a mile further to the southward, within three icebergs grounded, where there were three or four fathoms of water. Into this basin she was taken on the 18th, and her stores and provisions being removed, she was hove down, but a gale of wind coming on and destroying the masses of ice which sheltered her, it became necessary to re-embark the stores, &c., and once more put to sea; but the unfortunate vessel had hardly got out of her harbor before, on the 21st, she was again driven on shore. After a careful survey and examination, it was found necessary to abandon her: Parry's opinion being thus expressed —

"Every endeavor of ours to get her off, or if got off, to float her to any known place of safety, would be at once utterly hopeless in itself, and productive of extreme risk to our remaining ship."

The loss of this ship, and the crowded state of the remaining vessel, made it impossible to think of continuing the voyage for the purposes of discovery.

"The incessant labor, the constant state of anxiety, and the frequent and imminent danger into which the surviving ship was thrown, in the attempts to save her comrade, which were continued for twenty-five days, destroyed every reasonable expectation hitherto cherished of the ultimate accomplishment of this object."

Taking advantage of a northerly wind, on the 27th the Hecla stretched across the Inlet for the eastern coast, meeting with little obstruction from the ice, and anchored in Neill's Harbor, a short distance to the southward of their winter quarters, Port Bowen, where the ship was got ready for crossing the Atlantic.

The Hecla put to sea on the 31st of August, and entering Barrow's Strait on the 1st of September, found it perfectly clear of ice. In Lancaster Sound, a very large number of bergs were seen; but they found an open sea in Baffin's Bay, till, on the 7th of September, when in latitude 75° 30′, they came to the margin of the ice, and soon entered a clear channel on its eastern side. From thirty to forty large icebergs, not less than 200 feet in height, were sighted.

On the 12th of October, Captain Parry landed at Peterhead, and the Hecla arrived at Sheerness on the 20th. But one man died during this voyage—John Page, a seaman of the Fury—who died of scurvy, in Neill's Harbor, on the 29th of August.

This voyage cannot but be considered the most unsuccessful of the three made by Parry, whether as regards the information gleaned on the subject of a northwest passage, or the extension of our store of geographical or scientific knowledge. The shores of this inlet were more naked, barren, and desolate than even Melville Island. With the exception of some hundreds of white whales, seen sporting about the southernmost part of the Inlet that was visited, few other species of animals were seen.

"We have scarcely," says Parry, "ever visited a coast on which so little of animal life occurs. For days together only one or two seals, a single sea-horse, and now and then a flock of ducks were seen."

He still clings to the accomplishment of the great object of a northwest passage. At page 184 of his official narrative, he says:—

"I feel confident that the undertaking, if it be deemed advisable at any future time to pursue it, will one day or other be accomplished; for — setting aside the accidents to which, from their very nature, such attempts must be liable, as well as other unfavorable circumstances which human foresight can never guard against, or human power control — I cannot but believe it to be an enterprise well within the reasonable limits of practicability. It may be tried often and fail, for several favorable and fortunate circumstances must be combined for its accomplishment; but I believe, nevertheless, that it will ultimately be accomplished."

"I am much mistaken, indeed," he adds, "if the northwest passage ever becomes the business of a single summer; nay, I believe that nothing but a concurrence of very favorable circumstances is likely ever to make a single *winter* in the ice sufficient for its accomplishment. But there is no argument against the possibility of final success; for we know that a winter in the ice may be passed not only in safety, but in health and comfort."

Not *one* winter alone, but two and three have been passed with health and safety in these seas, under a wise and careful commander.

Franklin's Second Expedition, 1825–26.

Undaunted by the hardships and sufferings he had encountered in his previous travels with a noble spirit of ardor and enthusiasm, Captain Franklin determined to prosecute the chain of his former discoveries from the Coppermine river to the most western point of the Arctic regions. A sea expedition, under the command of Captain Beechey was at the same time sent round Cape Horn to Behring's Straits, to co-operate with Parry and Franklin, so as to furnish provisions to the former, and a conveyance home to the latter.

Captain Franklin's offer was therefore accepted by the government, and leaving Liverpool in February, 1825, he arrived at New York about the middle of March. The officers under his orders were his old and tried companions and fellow sufferers in the former journey — Dr. Richardson and Lieutenant Back, with Mr. E. N. Kendal, a mate in the navy, who had been out in the Griper with Capt. Lyon, and Mr. T. Drummond, a naturalist. Four boats, specially prepared for the purposes of the expedition, were sent out by the Hudson's Bay Company's ship.

In July, 1825, the party arrived at Fort Chipewyan. It is unnecessary to go over the ground and follow them in their northern journey; suffice it to say, they reached Great Bear Lake in safety, and erected a winter dwelling on its western shore, to which the name of Fort Franklin was given. To Back and Mr. Dease, an officer in the Hudson's Bay Company's service, were intrusted the arrangements for their winter quarters.

From here a small party set out with Franklin down the Mackenzie to examine the state of the Polar Sea. On the 5th of September they got back to their companions, and prepared to pass the long winter of seven or eight months.

On the 28th of June, 1826, the season being sufficiently advanced, and all their preparations completed, the whole party got away in four boats to descend the Mackenzie to the Polar Sea. Where the river branches off into several channels, the party separated on the 3d of July, Captain Franklin and Lieutenant Back, with two boats and fourteen men, having with them the faithful Esquimaux interpreter, Augustus, who had been with them on the former expedition, proceeded to the westward, while Dr. Richardson and Mr. Kendal in the other two boats, having ten men under their command, set out in an easterly direction, to search the Coppermine River.

Franklin arrived at the mouth of the Mackenzie on the 7th of July, where he encountered a large tribe of fierce Esquimaux, who pillaged his boats, and it was only by great caution, prudence and forbearance, that the whole party were not massacred. After getting the boats afloat, and clear of these unpleasant visitors, Franklin pursued his survey, a most tedious and difficult one, for more than a month; he was only able to reach a point in latitude 70° 24′ N., longitude 149° 37′ W., to which Back's name was given; and here prudence obliged him to return, although, strangely enough, a boat from the Blossom was waiting not 160 miles west of his position to meet with him. The extent of coast surveyed was 374 miles. The return journey to Fort Franklin was safely accomplished, and they arrived at their house on the 31st of September, when they found Richardson and Kendal had returned on the first of the month, having accomplished a voyage of about 500 miles, or 902 by the coast line, between the 4th of July and the 8th of August. They had pushed forward beyond the strait named after their boats, the Dolphin and Union.

In aseending the Coppermine, they had to abandon their boats and carry their provisions and baggage.

Having passed another winter at Fort Franklin, as soon as the season broke up the Canadians were dismissed, and the party returned to England.

The cold experienced in the last winter was intense, the thermometer standing at one time at 58° below zero, but having now plenty of food, a weather-tight dwelling, and good health, they passed it cheerfully. Dr. Richardson gave a course of lectures on practical geology, and Mr. Drummond furnished information on natural history. During the winter, in a solitary hut on the Rocky mountains, he managed to collect 200 specimens of birds, animals, &c., and more than 1500 of plants.

When Captain Franklin left England to proceed on this expedition he had to undergo a severe struggle between his feelings of affection and a sense of duty. His wife (he has been married twice) was then lying at the point of death, and indeed died the day after he left England. But with heroic fortitude she urged his departure at the very day appointed, entreating him, as he valued her peace and his own glory, not to delay a moment on her account. His feelings, therefore, may be inferred, but not described, when he had to elevate on Garry Island a silk flag, which she had made and given him as a parting gift, with the instruction that he was only to hoist it on reaching the Polar Sea.

Beechey's Voyage.—1826–28.

H. M. sloop Blossom, 26, Captain F. W. Beechey, sailed from Spithead on the 19th of May, 1825, and her instructions directed her, after surveying some of the islands in the Pacific, to be in Behring's Straits by the summer or autumn of 1826, and contingently in that of 1827.

It is foreign to my purpose here to allude to those parts of her voyage anterior to her arrival in the Straits.

On the 28th of June the Blossom came to an anchor off the town of Petropolowski, where she fell in with the Russian ship of war Modeste, under the command of Baron Wrangel, so well known for his enterprise in the hazardous expedition by sledges over the ice to the northward of Cape Shelatskoi, or Errinos.

Captain Beechey here found dispatches informing him of the return of Parry's expedition. Being beset by currents and other difficulties, it was not till the 5th of July that the Blossom got clear of the harbor, and made the best of her way to Kotzebue Sound, reaching the appointed rendezvous at Chamiso Island on the 25th. After landing and burying a barrel of flour upon Puffin Rock, the most unfrequented spot about the island, the Blossom occupied the time in surveying and examining the neighboring coasts to the northeast. On the 30th she took her departure from the island, erecting posts or land-marks, and burying dispatches at Cape Krusenstern, near a cape which he named after Franklin, near Icy Cape.

The ship returned to the rendezvous on the evening of the 28th of August. The barrel of flour had been dug up and appropriated by the natives.

On the first visit of one of these parties, they constructed a chart of the coast upon the sand, of which, however, Captain Beechey at first took very little notice. "They, however, renewed their labor, and performed their work upon the sandy beach in a very ingenious and intelligible manner. The coast line was first marked out with a stick, and the distances regulated by the day's journey. The hills and ranges of mountains were next shown by elevations of sand or stone, and the islands represented by heaps of pebbles, their proportions being duly attended to. As the work proceeded, some of the bystanders occasionally suggested alterations, and Captain Beechey moved one of the Diomede Islands, which was misplaced. This was at first objected to by the hydrographer, but one of the party recollecting that the islands were seen *in one* from Cape Prince of Wales, confirmed its new position and made the mistake quite evident to the others, who were much surprised that Captain Beechey should have any knowledge of the subject. When the mountains and islands were erected, the villages and fishing-stations were marked by a number of sticks placed upright, in imitation of those which are put up on the coast wherever these people fix their abode. In time, a complete hydrographical plan was drawn from Cape Derby to Cape Krusenstern.

This ingenuity and accuracy of description on the part of the Esquimaux is worthy of particular remark, and has been verified by almost all the Arctic explorers.

The barge which had been dispatched to the eastward, under charge of Mr. Elson, reached to latitude 71° 23′ 31″ N., and longitude 156° 21′ 31″ W., where she was stopped by the ice which was attached to the shore. The farthest tongue of land they reached was named Point Barrow, and is about 126 miles northeast of Icy Cape, being only about 150 or 160 miles from Franklin's discoveries west of the Mackenzie river.

The wind suddenly changing to southwest, the compact body of ice began to drift with the current to the northeast at the rate of three and a half miles an hour, and Mr. Elson, finding it difficult to avoid large floating masses of ice, was obliged to come to an anchor to prevent being driven back. "It was not long before he was so closely beset in the ice, that no clear water could be seen in any direction from the hills, and the ice continuing to press against the shore, his vessel was driven upon the beach, and there left upon her broadside in a most helpless condition; and to add to his cheerless prospect the disposition of the natives, whom he found to increase in numbers as he advanced to the northward, was of a very doubtful character. At Point Barrow, where they were very numerous, their overbearing behavior, and the thefts they openly practiced, left no doubt of what would be the fate of his little crew, in the event of their falling into their power. They were in this dilemma several days, during which every endeavor was made to extricate the vessel but without effect, and Mr. Elson contemplated sinking her secretly in a lake that was near, to prevent her falling into the hands of the Esquimaux, and then making his way along the coast in a baidar, which he had no doubt he should be able to purchase from the natives. At length, however, a change of wind loosened the ice, and after considerable labor and trial, in which the personal strength of the officers was united to that of the seamen, Mr. Elson, with his shipmates, fortunately succeeded in effecting their escape.

Captain Beechey was very anxious to remain in Kotzebue Sound until the end of October, the period named in his instructions, but the rapid approach of winter, the danger of being locked up, having only five weeks' provisions left, and the nearest point at which he could replenish being some 2000 miles distant, induced his officers to concur with him in the necessity of leaving at once. A barrel of flour and other articles were buried on the sandy point of Chamiso, for Franklin, which it was hoped would escape the prying eyes of the natives.

After a cruise to California, the Sandwich Islands, Loochoo, the Bonin Islands, &c., the Blossom returned to Chamiso Island on the 5th of July, 1827. They found the flour and dispatches they had left the previous year unmolested. Lieut. Belcher was dispatched in the barge to explore the coast to the northward, and the ship followed her as soon as the wind permitted. On the 9th of September, when standing in for the northern shore of Kotzebue Sound, the ship drifting with the current took the ground on a sand-bank near Hotham Inlet, but the wind moderating, as the tide rose she went off the shoal apparently without injury.

After this narrow escape from shipwreck they beat up to Chamiso Island, which they reached on the 10th of September. Not finding the barge returned as expected, the coast was scanned, and a signal of distress found flying on the southwest point of Choris Peninsula, and two men waving a white cloth to attract notice. On landing, it was found that this party were the crew of the barge, which had been wrecked in Kotzebue Sound, and three of the men were also lost.

On the 29th a collision took place with the natives, which resulted in three of the seamen and four of the marines being wounded by arrows, and one of the natives killed by the return fire.

After leaving advices for Franklin, as before, the Blossom finally left Chamiso on the 6th of October. In a haze and strong wind she ran between the land and a shoal, and a passage had to be forced through breakers at the imminent danger of the ship's striking. The Blossom then made the best of her way home, reaching England in the first week of October, 1828.

Parry's Fourth, or Polar Voyage, 1827.

In 1826, Capt. Parry, who had only returned from his last voyage in the close of the preceding year, was much struck by the suggestions of Mr. Scoresby, in a paper read before the Wernerian Society, in which he sketched out a plan for reaching the highest latitudes of the Polar Sea, north of Spitzbergen, by means of sledge boats drawn over the smooth fields of ice which were known to prevail in those regions. Col. Beaufoy, F. R. S., had also suggested this idea some years previously. Comparing these with a similar plan originally proposed by Captain Franklin, and which was placed in his hands by Mr. Barrow, the Secretary of the Admiralty, Capt. Parry laid his modified views of the feasibility of the project, and his willingness to undertake it, before Lord Melville, the First Lord of the Admiralty, who, after consulting with the President and Council of the Royal Society, was pleased to sanction the attempt; accordingly, his old ship, the Hecla, was fitted out for the voyage to Spitzbergen, the following officers, (all of whom had been with Parry before,) and crew being appointed to her: —

Hecla.

Captain — W. E. Parry.
Lieutenants — J. C. Ross, Henry Foster, E. J. Bird, F. R. M. Crozier.
Purser — James Halse.
Surgeon — C. J. Beverley.

On the 4th of April, 1827, the outfit and preparations being completed, the Hecla left the Nore for the coast of Norway, touching at Hammerfest, to embark eight reindeer, and some moss (*Cenomyce rangiferiha*) sufficient for their support, the consumption being about 4 lbs. per day, but they can go without food for several days. A tremendous gale of wind, experienced off Hakluyt's Headland, and the quantity of ice with which the ship was in consequence beset, detained the voyagers for nearly a month, but on the 18th of June, a southerly wind dispersing the ice, they dropped anchor in a cove, on the northern coast of Spitzbergen, which appeared to offer a secure haven, and to which the name of the ship was given. On the 20th, the boats, which had been especially prepared in England for this kind of journey, were got out and made ready, and they left the ship on the 22d of June. A description of these boats may not here be out of place.

They were twenty feet long and seven broad, flat floored, like ferry boats, strengthened and made elastic by sheets of felt between the planking, covered with water-proof canvass. A runner attached to each side of the keel, adapted them for easy draught on the ice after the manner of a sledge. They were also fitted with wheels, to be used if deemed expedient and useful. Two officers and twelve men were attached to each boat, and they were named the Enterprise and Endeavor. The weight of each boat, including provisions and every requisite, was about 3780 lbs. Lieuts. Crozier and Foster were left on board, and Capt. Parry took with him in his boat Mr. Beverley, Surgeon, while Lieut. (now Capt. Sir James) Ross, and Lieut. (now Commander) Bird, had charge of the other.

The reindeer and the wheels were given up as useless, owing to the rough nature of the ice. Provisions for seventy-one days were taken — the daily allowance per man on the journey being 10 ozs. biscuit, 9 ozs. pemmican, 1 oz. sweetened cocoa powder (being enough to make a pint,) and one gill of rum; but scanty provision in such a climate, for men employed on severe labor; three ounces of tobacco were also served out to each per week.

As fuel was too bulky to transport, spirits of wine were consumed, which answered all the purposes required, a pint twice a day being found sufficient to warm each vessel, when applied to an iron boiler by a shallow lamp with seven wicks. After floating the boats for about eighty miles, they came to an unpleasant mixed surface of ice and water, where their toilsome journey commenced, the boats having to be laden and unladen several times according as they came to floes of ice or lanes of water, and they were drifted to the southward by the ice at the rate of four or five miles a day. Parry found it more advantageous to travel by night, the snow being then harder, and the inconvenience of snow blindness being avoided, while the party enjoyed greater warmth during the period of rest, and had better opportunities of drying their clothes by the sun.

I cannot do better than quote Parry's graphic description of this novel course of proceeding: "Traveling by night, and sleeping by day, so completely inverted the natural order of things that it was difficult to persuade ourselves of the reality. Even the officers and myself, who were all furnished with pocket chronometers, could not always bear in mind at what part of the twenty-hours we had arrived; and there were several of the men who declared, and I believe truly, that they never knew night from day during the whole excursion.

"When we rose in the evening, we commenced our day by prayers, after which we took off our fur sleeping-dresses and put on clothes for traveling; the former being made of camlet lined with raccoon skin, and the latter of strong blue cloth. We made a point of always putting on the same stockings and boots for traveling in, whether they had been dried during the day or not, and I believe it was only in five or six instances at the most that they were not either still wet or hard frozen. This indeed was of no consequence, beyond the discomfort of first putting them on in this state, as they were sure to be thoroughly wet in a quarter of an hour after commencing our journey; while, on the other hand, it was of vital importance to keep dry things for sleeping in. Being 'rigged' for traveling, we breakfasted upon warm cocoa and biscuit, and after stowing the things in the boats, and on the sledges, so as to secure them as much as possible from wet, we set off on our day's journey, and usually traveled four, five, or even six hours, according to circumstances."

In five days, notwithstanding their perseverance and continued journeys, they found, by observation at noon, on the 30th, that they had only made eight miles of direct northing.

At Walden Island, one of the Seven Islands, and Little Table Island, reserve supplies of provisions were deposited to fall back upon in case of necessity.

In halting early in the morning for the purposes of rest, the boats were hauled up on the largest piece of ice that offered the least chance of breaking through, or of coming in contact with other masses, the snow or wet was cleaned out and the sails rigged as awnings. "Every man then immediately put on dry stockings and fur boots, after which we set about the necessary repairs of boats, sledges, or clothes, and after serving the provisions for the succeeding day, we went to supper. Most of the officers and men then smoked their pipes, which served to dry the boats and awnings very much, and usually raised the temperature of our lodgings 10° or 15°. This part of the twenty-four hours was often a time, and the only one, of real enjoyment to us; the men told their stories, and fought all their battles o'er again, and the labors of the day, unsuccessful as they too often were, were forgotten. A regular watch was set during our resting time, to look out for bears, or for the ice breaking up round us, as well as to attend to the drying of the clothes, each man alternately taking this duty for one hour. We then concluded our day with prayers, and having put on our fur dresses, lay down to sleep with a degree of comfort which perhaps few persons would imagine possible under such circumstances, our chief inconvenience being, that we were somewhat pinched for room, and therefore obliged to stow rather closer than was quite agreeable."

This close stowage may be imagined when it is remembered that thirteen persons had to sleep in a boat seven feet broad. After sleeping about seven hours, they were roused from their slumbers by the sound of a bugle from the cook and watchman, which announced that their cocoa was smoking hot, and invited them to breakfast.

Their progress was of the most tedious and toilsome character, heavy showers of rain rendering the ice on many occasions a mass of "slush;" on others there was from six to eighteen inches of snow lying on the surface. Frequently the crew had to proceed on their hands and knees to secure a footing, and on one occasion they made such a snail-like progress that in two hours they only accomplished 150 yards. On the 12th of July, they had reached the latitude of 82° 14′ 28″. After five hours' unceasing labor on the 14th, the progress was but a mile and a half due north, though from three to four miles had been traversed, and ten at least walked, having made three journeys a great part of the way; launched and hauled up the boats four times, and dragged them over twenty-five separate pieces of ice. On the 18th, after eleven hours of actual labor, requiring for the most part the exertion of the whole strength of the party, they had traveled over a space not exceeding four miles, of which only two were made good.

But on halting on the morning of the 20th, having by his reckoning accomplished six and a half miles in a N. N. W. direction, the distance traversed being ten miles and a half, Parry found to his mortification from observation at noon, that they were not *five* miles to the northward of their place at noon on the 17th, although they had certainly traveled twelve miles in that direction since then.

On the 21st, a floe of ice on which they had lodged the boats and sledges, broke with their weight, and all went through with several of the crew, who, with the sledges were providentially saved.

On the 23d, the farthest northerly point was reached, which was about 82° 45′.

At noon on the 26th, the weather being clear, the meridian altitude of the sun was obtained, "by which," says Parry, "we found ourselves in latitude 82° 40′ 23″, so that since our last observation (at midnight on the

22d,) we had lost by drift no less than thirteen and a half miles, for we were now more than three miles to the southward of that observation, though we had certainly traveled between ten and eleven, due north in this interval! Again, we were but one mile to the north of our place at noon on the 21st, though we had estimated our distance made good at twenty-three miles." After encountering every species of fatigue and disheartening obstacles, in peril of their lives almost every hour, Parry now became convinced that it was hopeless to pursue the journey any further, and he could not even reach the eighty-third parallel; for after thirty-five days of continuous and most fatiguing drudgery, with half their resources expended, and the middle of the season arrived, he found that the distance gained in their laborious traveling was lost by the drift and sea of the ice with the southerly current during the period of rest. After planting their ensigns and pennants on the 26th, and making it a day of rest on the 27th, the return to the southward was commenced. Nothing particular occurred. Lieutenant Ross managed to bring down with his gun a fat she bear, which came to have a look at the boats, and after gormandizing on its flesh, an excess which may be excused considering it was the first fresh meat they had tasted for many a day, some symptoms of indigestion manifested themselves among the party.

On the outward journey very little of animal life was seen. A passing gull, a solitary rotge, two seals, and a couple of flies, were all that their eager eyes could detect. But on their return, these became more numerous. On the 8th of August, seven or eight narwhals were seen, and not less than 200 rotges, a flock of these little birds occuring in every hole of water. On the 11th, in latitude 81° 30′, the sea was found crowded with shrimps and other sea insects, on which numerous birds were feeding. On this day they took their last meal on the ice, being fifty miles distant from Table Island, having accomplished in fiteen days what had taken them thirty-three to effect on their outward journey. On the 12th, they arrived at this island. The bears had walked off with the relay of bread which had been deposited there. To an inlet lying off Table Island, and the most northern known land upon the globe, Parry gave the name of Ross, for "no individual," he observes, "could have exerted himself more strenuously to rob it of this distinction."

Putting to sea again, a storm obliged the boats to bear up for Walden Island. "Every thing belonging to us (says Captain Parry) was now completely drenched by the spray and snow; we had been fifty-six hours without rest, and forty-eight at work in the boats, so that by the time they were unloaded we had barely strength left to haul them up on the rocks. However, by dint of great exertion, we managed to get the boats above the surf; after which a hot supper, a blazing fire of drift wood, and a few hours quiet rest, restored us."

They finally reached the ship on the 21st of August, after sixty-one days' absence.

"The distance traversed during this excursion was 569 geographical miles; but allowing for the times we had to return for our baggage, during the greater part of the journey over the ice, we estimated our actual traveling at 978 geographical, or 1127 statute miles. Considering our constant exposure to wet, cold, and fatigue, our stockings having generally been drenched in snow-water for twelve hours out of every twenty-four, I had great reason to be thankful for the excellent health in which, upon the whole, we reached the ship. There is little doubt that we had all become in a certain degree gradually weaker for some time past; but only three men of our party now required medical care—two of them with badly swelled legs and general debility, and the other from a bruise, but even these three returned to their duty in a short time."

In a letter from Sir W. E. Parry to Sir John Barrow, dated November 25, 1845, he thus suggests some improvements on his old plan of proceedings:—

"It is evident (he says) that the causes of failure in

our former attempt, in the year 1827, were principally two: first, and chiefly, the broken, rugged, and soft state of the ice over which we traveled; and secondly, the drifting of the whole body of ice in a southerly direction.

"My amended plan is, to go out with a single ship to Spitzbergen, just as we did in the Hecla, but not so early in the season; the object for that year being merely to find secure winter quarters as far north as possible. For this purpose it would only be necessary to reach Hakluyt's Headland by the end of June, which would afford ample leisure for examining the more northern lands, especially about the Seven Islands, where, in all probability, a secure nook might be found for the ship, and a starting point for the proposed expedition, some forty or fifty miles in advance of the point where the Hecla was before laid up. The winter might be usefully employed in various preparations for the journey, as well as in magnetic, astronomical, and meteorological observations, of high interest in that latitude. I propose that the expedition should leave the ship in the course of the month of April, when the ice would present one hard and unbroken surface, over which, as I confidently believe, it would not be difficult to make good thirty miles per day, without any exposure to wet, and probably without snow blindness. At this season, too, the ice would probably be stationary, and thus the two great difficulties which we formerly had to encounter would be entirely obviated. It might form a part of the plan to push out supplies previously, to the distance of 100 miles, to be taken up on the way, so as to commence the journey comparatively light; and as the intention would be to complete the enterprise in the course of the month of May, before any disruption of the ice, or any material softening of the surface had taken place, similar supplies might be sent out to the same distance, to meet the party on their return."

The late Sir John Barrow, in his last work, commenting on this, says, "With all deference to so distinguished a sea officer, in possession of so much experience as Sir Edward Parry, there are others who express dislike of such a plan; and it is not improbable that many will be disposed to come to the conclusion, that so long as the Greenland Seas are hampered with ice, so long as floes, and hummocks, and heavy masses, continue to be formed, so long as a determined southerly current prevails, so long will any attempt to carry out the plan in question, in like manner fail. No laborious drudgery will ever be able to conquer the opposing progress of the current and the ice. Besides, it can hardly be doubted, this gallant officer will admit, on further consideration, that this unusual kind of disgusting and unseamanlike labor, is not precisely such as would be relished by the men; and, it may be said, is not exactly fitted for a British man-of-war's-man; moreover, that it required his own all-powerful example to make it even tolerable." Sir John therefore suggested a somewhat different plan. He recommended that two small ships should be sent in the early spring along the western coast of Spitzbergen, where usually no impediment exists, as far up as 80°. They should take every opportunity of proceeding directly to the north, where, in about 82°, Parry has told us the large floes had disappeared, and the sea was found to be loaded only with loose, disconnected, small masses of ice, through which ships would find no difficulty in sailing, though totally unfit for boats dragging; and as this loose ice was drifting to the southward, he further says, that before the middle of August a ship might have sailed up to the latitude of 82°, almost without touching a piece of ice. It is not then unreasonable to expect that beyond that parallel, even as far as the pole itself, the sea would be free of ice, during the six summer months of perpetual sun, through each of the twenty-four hours; which, with the aid of the current, would, in all probability, destroy and dissipate the polar ice.

The distance from Hakluyt's Headland to the pole is 600 geographical miles. Granting the ships to make only twenty miles in twenty-four hours, (on the supposition of much sailing ice to go through,) even in that case it would require but a month to enable the explorer to put his foot on the pivot or point of the axis on which the globe of the earth turns, remain there a month, if necessary, to obtain the sought-for information, and then, with a southerly current, a fortnight, probably less, would bring him back to Spitzbergen. *

In a notice in the Quarterly Review of this, one of the most singular and perilous journeys of its kind ever undertaken, except perhaps that of Baron Wrangell upon a similar enterprise to the northward of Behring's Straits, it is observed,—"Let any one conceive for a moment the situation of two open boats, laden with seventy days' provisions and clothing for twenty-eight men, in the midst of a sea covered nearly with detached masses and floes of ice, over which these boats were to be dragged, sometimes up one side of a rugged mass, and down the other, sometimes across the lanes of water that separate them, frequently over a surface covered with deep snow, or through pools of water. Let him bear in mind, that the men had little or no chance of any other supply of provisions than that which they carried with them, calculated as just sufficient to sustain life, and consider what their situation would have been in the event, by no means an improbable one, of losing any part of their scanty stock. Let any one try to imagine to himself a situation of this kind, and he will still have but a faint idea of the exertions which the men under Captain Parry had to make, and the sufferings and privations they had to undergo."

Captain Parry having thus completed his fifth voyage into the arctic regions, in four of which he commanded, and was second in the other, it may here be desirable to give a recapitulation of his services.

In 1818 he was appointed Lieutenant, commanding the Alexander, hired ship, as second officer with his uncle, Commander John Ross. In 1819, still as Lieu-

* Barrow's Voyages of Discovery, p. 316.

tenant, he was appointed to command the Hecla, and to take charge of the second arctic expedition, on which service he was employed two years. On the 14th of November, 1820, he was promoted to the rank of Commander.

On the 19th of December, 1820, the Bedfordean Gold Medal of the Bath and West of England Society for the Encouragement of Arts, Manufactures, and Commerce, was unanimously voted to him. On the 30th of December of that year, he was appointed to the Fury, with orders to take command of the expedition to the Arctic Sea. With the sum of 500 guineas, subscribed for the purpose, "the Explorer of the Polar Sea" was afterward presented with a silver vase, highly embellished with devices emblematic of the arctic voyages. And on the 24th of March, 1821, the city of Bath presented its freedom to Captain Parry, in a box of oak, highly and appropriately ornamented. On the 8th of November, 1821, he obtained his post-captain's rank. On the 22d of November, 1823, he was presented with the freedom of the city of Winchester; and, on the 1st of December, was appointed acting hydrographer to the Admiralty in the place of Captain Hind, deceased. In 1824 he was appointed to the Hecla, to proceed on another exploring voyage.

On the 22d of November, 1825, Captain Parry was formally appointed hydrographer to the Admiralty, which office he continued to hold until the 10th of November, 1826.

In December, 1825, he was voted the freedom of the borough of Lynn, in testimony of the high sense entertained by the corporation of his meritorious and enterprising conduct.

In April, 1827, he once more took the command of his old ship, the Hecla, for another voyage of discovery toward the North Pole. On his return in the close of the year, having paid off the Hecla at Deptford, he resumed, on the 2d of November, his duties as hydrographer to the Admiralty, which office he held until the 13th of May, 1829. Having received the honor of knighthood, he then resigned in favor of the present Admiral Beaufort, and, obtaining permission from the Admiralty, proceeded to New South Wales as resident Commissioner to the Australian Agricultural Com pany, taking charge of their recently acquired large territory in the neighborhood of Port Stephen. He returned from Australia in 1834. From the 7th of March, 1835, to the 3d of February, 1836, he acted as Poor Law Commissioner in Norfolk. Early in 1837, he was appointed to organize the Mail Packet Service, then transferred to the Admiralty, and afterward, in April, was appointed Controller of steam machinery to the Navy, which office he continued to hold up to December, 1846. From that period to the present time he has filled the post of Captain Superintendent of the Royal Navy Hospital at Haslar.

Captain John Ross's Second Voyage, 1829–33.

In the year 1829, Capt. Ross, the pioneer of arctic exploration in the 19th century, being anxious once more to display his zeal and enterprise as well as to retrieve his nautical reputation from those unfortunate blunders and mistakes which had attached to his first voyage, and thus remove the cloud which had for nearly ten years hung over his professional character, endeavored without effect to induce the government to send him out to the Polar Seas in charge of another expedition. The Board of Admiralty of that day, in the spirit of retrenchment which pervaded their councils, were, however, not disposed to recommend any further grant for research, even the Board of Longitude was abolished, and the boon of 20,000*l*. offered by act of parliament for the promotion of arctic discovery, also withdrawn by a repeal of the act.

Captain Ross, however, undaunted by the chilling indifference thus manifested toward his proposals by the Admiralty, still persevered, having devoted 3000*l*. out of his own funds toward the prosecution of the object he had in view. He was fortunate enough to meet with a public-spirited and affluent coadjutoı and supporter in the late Sir Felix Booth, the eminen distiller, and that gentleman nobly contributed 17,000*l*. toward the expenses. Captain Ross thereupon set to work, and purchased a small Liverpool steamer named the Victory, whose tonnage he increased to 150 tons. She was provisioned for three years. Captain Ross chose for his second in command his nephew, Commander James Ross, who had been with him on his first arctic expedition, and had subsequently accompanied Parry in all his voyages. The other officers of the vessel were — Mr. William Thom, purser; Mr. George M'Diarmid, surgeon; Thomas Blanky, Thos. Abernethy, and George Taylor, as 1st, 2d, and 3d, mates; Alexander Brunton and Allen Macinnes as 1st and 2d engineers; and nineteen petty officers and seamen; making a complement in all of 28 men.

The Admiralty furnished toward the purposes of the expedition a decked boat of sixteen tons, called the Krusenstern, and two boats which had been used by Franklin, with a stock of books and instruments.

The vessel being reported ready for sea was visited and examined by the late King of the French, the Lords of the Admiralty, and other parties taking an interest in the expedition, and set sail from Woolwich on the 23d of May, 1829. For all practical purposes the steam machinery, on which the commander had greatly relied, was found on trial utterly useless.

Having received much damage to her spars, in a severe gale, the ship put in to the Danish settlement of Holsteinberg, on the Greenland coast, to refit, and sailed again to the northward on the 26th of June. They found a clear sea, and even in the middle of Lancaster Sound and Barrow's Strait perceived no traces of ice or snow, except what appeared on the lofty summits of some of the mountains. The thermometer stood at 40°, and the weather was so mild that the officers dined in the cabin without a fire, with the skylight partially open. On the 10th of August they passed Cape York, and thence crossed over into Regent Inlet making the western coast between Sepping's and Elwin Bay on the 16th.

They here fell in with those formidable streams, packs, and floating bergs of ice which had offered such obstructions to Parry's ships. From their proximity to the magnetic pole, their compasses became useless as they proceeded southward. On the 13th they reached the spot where the Fury was abandoned, but no remnants of the vessel were to be seen. All her sails, stores, and provisions, on land, were, however, found; the hermetically-sealed tin canisters having kept the provisions from the attacks of bears; and the flour, bread, wine, spirits, sugar, &c., proved as good, after being here four years, as on the first day they were packed. This store formed a very seasonable addition, which was freely made available, and after increasing their stock to two years and ten months' supply, they still left a large quantity for the wants of any future explorers. On the 15th, crossing Cresswell Bay, they reached Cape Garry, the farthest point which had been seen by Parry. They were here much inconvenienced and delayed by fogs and floating ice. While mountains of ice were tossing around them on every side, they were often forced to seek safety by mooring themselves to these formidable masses, and drifting with them, sometimes forward, sometimes backward. In this manner on one occasion no less than nineteen miles were lost in a few hours; at other times they underwent frequent and severe shocks, yet escaped any serious damage.

Captain Ross draws a lively picture of what a vessel endures in sailing among these moving hills. He reminds the reader that ice is stone, as solid as if it were granite; and he bids him "imagine these mountains hurled through a narrow strait by a rapid tide, meeting with the noise of thunder, breaking from each other's precipices huge fragments, or rending each other asunder, till, losing their former equilibrium, they fell over headlong, lifting the sea around in breakers and whirling it in eddies There is not a moment in which it can be conjectured what will happen in the next; there is not one which may not be the last. The attention is troubled to fix on any thing amid such con fusion; still must it be alive, that it may seize on the single moment of help or escape which may occur Yet with all this, and it is the hardest task of all, there is nothing to be acted,— no effort to be made,— he must be patient, as if he were unconcerned or careless, waiting, as he best can, for the fate, be it what it may, which he cannot influence or avoid."

Proceeding southward, Ross found Brentford Bay, about thirty miles beyond Cape Garry, to be of considerable extent, with some fine harbors. Landing here, the British colors were unfurled, and the coast, named after the promoter of the expedition, was taken possession of in the name of the King. Extensive and commodious harbors, named Ports Logan, Elizabeth, and Eclipse, were discovered, and a large bay, which was called Mary Jones Bay. By the end of September the ship had examined 300 miles of undiscovered coast The winter now set in with severity, huge masses of ice began to close around them, the thermometer sank many degrees below freezing point, and snow fell very thick. By sawing through the ice, the vessel was got into a secure position to pass the winter, in a station which is now named on the maps Felix Harbor. The machinery of the steam engine was done away with, the vessel housed, and every measure that could add to the comfort of the crew adopted. They had abundance of fuel, and provisions that might easily be extended to three years.

On the 9th of January, 1831, they were visited by a large tribe of Esquimaux, who were better dressed and cleaner than those more to the northward. They displayed an intimate acquaintance with the situation and bearings of the country over which they had traveled, and two of them drew a very fair sketch of the neighboring coasts, with which they were familiar; this was revised and corrected by a learned lady named Teriksin,— the females seeming, from this and former instances, to have a clear knowledge of the hydrography and geography of the continent, bays, straits, and rivers which they had once traversed.

On the 5th of April, Commander Ross, with Mr. Blanky, the chief mate, and two Esquimaux guides, set out to explore a strait which was reported as lying to the westward, and which it was hoped might lead to the western sea. After a tedious and arduous journey, they arrived, on the third day, at a bay facing to the westward and discovered, further inland, an extensive lake, called by the natives Nie-tyle-le, whence a broad river flowed into the bay. Their guides informed them, however, there was no prospect of a water comunication south of their present position. Capt. Ross then traced the coast fifty or sixty miles further south.

Several journeys were also made by Commander Ross, both inland and along the bays and inlets. On the 1st of May, from the top of a high hill, he observed a large inlet, which seemed to lead to the western sea. In order to satisfy himself on this point, he set out again on the 17th of May, with provisions for three weeks, eight dogs, and three companions. Having crossed the great middle lake of the isthmus, he reached his former station, and thence traced an inlet which was found to be the mouth of a river named by them Garry. From the high hill, they observed a chain of lakes leading almost to Thom's Bay, the Victory's station in Felix Harbor. Proceeding northwest along the coast, they crossed the frozen surface of the strait which has since been named after Sir James Ross, and came to a large island which was called Matty; keeping along its northern shore, and passing over a narrow strait, which they named after Wellington, they found themselves on what was considered to be the mainland, but which the more recent discoveries of Simpson have shown to be an island, and which now bears the name of King William's Land. Still journeying onward, with difficulties continually increasing, from heavy toil and severe privation, the dogs became exhausted with fatigue, and a burden rather than an aid to the travelers.

One of their greatest embarrassments was, how to distinguish between land and sea. "When all is ice, and all one dazzling mass of white — when the surface of the sea itself is tossed up and fixed into rocks, while the land is, on the contrary, very often flat, it is not always so easy a problem as it might seem on a superficial view, to determine a fact which appears in words to be extremely simple." Although their provisions began to fall short, and the party were nearly worn out, Commander Ross was most desirous of making as much western discovery as possible; therefore, depositing every thing that could be dispensed with, he pushed on, on the 28th, with only four days' provisions, and reached Cape Felix, the most northern point of this island, on the following day. The coast here took a southwest direction, and there was an unbounded expanse of ocean in view. The next morning, after having traveled twenty miles farther, they reached a point, which Ross called Point Victory, situated in lat. 64° 46′ 19″, long. 98° 32′ 49″, while to the most distant one in view, estimated to be in long. 99° 17′ 58″, he gave the name of Cape Franklin. However loath to turn back, yet prudence compelled them to do so, for as they had only ten days' short allowance of food, and more than 200 miles to traverse, there could not be a moment's hesitation in adopting this step. A high cairn of stones was erected before leaving, in which was deposited a narrative of their proceedings.

The party endured much fatigue and suffering on their return journey; of the eight dogs only two survived, and the travelers in a most exhausted state arrived in the neighborhood of the large lakes on the 8th of June, where they fortunately fell in with a tribe of natives, who received them hospitably, and supplied them plentifully with fish, so that after a day's rest they resumed their journey, and reached the ship on the 13th. Captain Ross in the meanwhile had made a partial survey of the Isthmus, and discovered another large lake, which he named after Lady Melville.

After eleven months' imprisonment their little ship

once more floated buoyant on the waves, having been released from her icy barrier on the 17th of September, but for the next few days made but little progress, being beaten about among the icebergs, and driven hither and thither by the currents.

A change in the weather, however, took place, and on the 23d they were once more frozen in, the sea in a week after exhibiting one clear and unbroken surface. All October was passed in cutting through the ice into a more secure locality, and another dreary winter having set in, it became necessary to reduce the allowance of provisions. This winter was one of unparalleled severity, the thermometer falling 92° below freezing point. During the ensuing spring a variety of exploratory journeys were carried on, and in one of these Commander Ross succeeded in planting the British flag on the North Magnetic Pole. The position which had been usually assigned to this interesting spot by the learned of Europe, was lat. 70° N., and long. 98° 30′ W.; but Ross, by careful observations, determined it to lie in lat. 70° 5′ 17″ N., and long. 96° 46′ 45″ W., to the southward of Cape Nikolai, on the western shore of Boothia. But it has since been found that the center of magnetic intensity is a movable point revolving within the frigid zone.

"The place of the observatory," Ross remarks, "was as near to the magnetic pole as the limited means which I possessed enabled me to determine. The amount of the dip, as indicated by my dipping-needle, was 89° 59′, being thus within one minute of the vertical; while the proximity at least of this pole, if not its actual existence where we stood, was further confirmed by the action, or rather by the total inaction, of the several horizontal needles then in my possession."

Parry's observations placed it eleven minutes distant only from the site determined by Ross.

"As soon," continues Ross, "as I had satisfied my own mind on the subject, I made known to the party this gratifying result of all our joint labors; and it was then that, amidst mutual congratulations, we fixed the

British flag on the spot, and took possession of the North Magnetic Pole and its adjoining territory in the name of Great Britain and King William IV. We had abundance of materials for building in the fragments of limestone that covered the beach, and we therefore erected a cairn of some magnitude, under which we buried a canister containing a record of the interesting fact, only regretting that we had not the means of constructing a pyramid of more importance, and of strength sufficient to withstand the assaults of time and of the Esquimaux. Had it been a pyramid as large as that of Cheops, I am not quite sure that it would have done more than satisfy our ambition under the feelings of that exciting day."

On the 28th of August, 1831, they contrived to warp the Victory out into the open sea, and made sail on the following morning, but were soon beset with ice, as on the former occasion, being once more completely frozen in by the 27th of September.

On the previous occasion their navigation had been three miles; this year it extended to four. This protracted detention in the ice made their present position one of great danger and peril. As there seemed no prospect of extracting their vessel, the resolution was come to of abandoning her, and making the best of their way up the inlet to Fury Beach, there to avail themselves of the boats, provisions, and stores, which would assist them in reaching Davis' Straits, where they might expect to fall in with one of the whale ships.

On the 23d of April, 1832, having collected all that was useful and necessary, the expedition set out, dragging their provisions and boats over a vast expanse of rugged ice. "The loads being too heavy to be carried at once, made it necessary to go backward and forward twice, and even oftener, the same day. They had to encounter dreadful tempests of snow and drift, and to make several circuits in order to avoid impassable barriers. The general result was, that by the 12th of May they had traveled 329 miles to gain thirty in a direct line, having in this labor expended a month." After this preliminary movement, they bade a farewell to their little vessel, nailing her colors to the mast. Capt. Ross describes himself as deeply affected; this being the first vessel he had been obliged to abandon of thirty-six in which he had served during the course of forty-two years. On the 9th of June, Commander Ross and two others, with a fortnight's provisions, left the main body, who were more heavily loaded, to ascertain the state of the boats and supplies at Fury Beach. Returning they met their comrades on the 25th of June, reporting that they had found three of the boats washed away, but enough still left for their purpose, and all the provisions were in good condition. The remainder of the journey was accomplished by the whole party in a week, and on the 1st of July they reared a canvas mansion, to which they gave the name of Somerset House, and enjoyed a hearty meal.

By the 1st of August the boats were rendered serviceable, and a considerable extent of open sea being visible, they set out, and after much buffeting among the ice in their frail shallops, reached the mouth of the inlet by the end of August. After several fruitless attempts to run along Barrow's Strait, the obstructions of the ice obliged them to haul the boats on shore, and pitch their tents. Barrow's Strait was found, from repeated surveys, to be one impenetrable mass of ice. After lingering here till the third week in September, it was unanimously agreed that their only resource was to fall back on the stores at Fury Beach, and there spend their fourth winter. They were only able to get half the distance in the boats, which were hauled on shore in Batty Bay on the 24th of September, and the rest of their journey continued on foot, the provisions being dragged on sledges. On the 7th of October they once more reached their home at the scene of the wreck. They now managed to shelter their canvas tent by a wall of snow, and setting up an extra stove, made themselves tolerably comfortable until the increasing severity of the winter, and rigor of the cold, added to the tempestuous weather, made them perfect prisoners, and sorely tried their patience. Scurvy now began to attack several of the party, and on the 16th of February, 1833, Thomas, the carpenter, fell a victim to it, and two others died. "Their situation was becoming truly awful, since, if they were not liberated in the ensuing summer, little prospect appeared of their surviving another year. It was necessary to make a reduction in the allowance of preserved meats; bread was somewhat deficient, and the stock of wine and spirits was entirely exhausted. However, as they caught a few foxes, which were considered a delicacy, and there was plenty of flour, sugar, soups, and vegetables, a diet could be easily arranged sufficient to support the party."

While the ice remained firm, advantage was taken of the spring to carry forward a stock of provisions to Batty Bay, and this, though only thirty-two miles, occupied them a whole month, owing to their reduced numbers from sickness and heavy loads, with the journeyings to and fro, having to go over the ground eight times.

On the 8th of July they finally abandoned this depot, and encamped on the 12th at their boat station in Batty Bay, where the aspect of the sea was watched with intense anxiety for more than a month. On the 15th of August, taking advantage of a lane of water which led to the northward, the party embarked, and on the following morning had got as far as the turning point of their last year's expedition. Making their way slowly among the masses of ice with which the inlet was encumbered, on the 17th they found the wide expanse of Barrow's Strait open before them, and navigable, and reached to within twelve miles of Cape York. Pushing on with renewed spirits, alternately rowing and sailing, on the night of the 25th they rested in a good harbor on the eastern shore of Navy Board Inlet. At four on the following morning they were roused from their slumbers by the joyful intelligence of a ship being in sight, and never did men more hurriedly and energetically set out; but the elements conspiring against them, after being baffled by calms and currents, they had the misery to see the ship leave them with a fair breeze, and found it impossible to overtake her, or make themselves seen. A few hours later, however, their despair was relieved by the sight of another vessel which was lying to in a calm. By dint of hard rowing they were this time more for tunate, and soon came up with her; she proved to be the Isabella, of Hull, the very ship in which Ross had made his first voyage to these seas. Capt. Ross was told circumstantially of his own death, &c., two years previously, and he had some difficulty in convincing them that it was really he and his party who now stood before them. So great was the joy with which they were received, that the Isabella manned her yards, and her former commander and his gallant band of adventurers were saluted with three hearty cheers. The scene on board can scarcely be described; each of the crew vied with the other in assisting and comforting the party, and it cannot better be told than in Ross's own words:—

"The ludicrous soon took place of all other feelings; in such a crowd, and such confusion, all serious thought was impossible, while the new buoyancy of our spirits made us abundantly willing to be amused by the scene which now opened. Every man was hungry, and was to be fed; all were ragged, and were to be clothed; there was not one to whom washing was not indispensable, nor one whom his beard did not deprive of all human semblance. All, every thing too, was to be done at once: it was washing, shaving, dressing, eating, all intermingled; it was all the materials of each jumbled together, while in the midst of all there were interminable questions to be asked and answered on both sides; the adventures of the Victory, our own escapes, the politics of England, and the news which was now four years old.

"But all subsided into peace at last. The sick were

accommodated, the seamen disposed of, and all was done for us which care and kindness could perform.

"Night at length brought quiet and serious thoughts, and I trust there was not a man among us who did not then express, where it was due, his gratitude for that interposition which had raised us all from a despair which none could now forget, and had brought us from the very borders of a most distant grave, to life and friends and civilization. Long accustomed, however, to a cold bed on the hard snow or the bare rock, few could sleep amid the comfort of our new accommodations. I was myself compelled to leave the bed which had been kindly assigned me, and take my abode in a chair for the night, nor did it fare much better with the rest. It was for time to reconcile us to this sudden and violent change, to break through what had become habit, and inure us once more to the usages of our former days."

The Isabella remained some time longer to prosecute the fishery, and left Davis' Strait on her homeward passage on the 30th September. On the 12th of October they made the Orkney Islands, and arrived at Hull on the 18th. The bold explorers, who had long been given up as lost, were looked upon as men risen from the grave, and met and escorted by crowds of sympathizers. A public entertainment was given to them by the townspeople, at which the freedom of the town was presented to Captain Ross, and next day he left for London, to report to the Admiralty, and was honored by a presentation to the king at Windsor.

The Admiralty liberally rewarded all the parties, except indeed Captain Ross. Commander J. C. Ross was appointed to the guardship at Portsmouth to complete his period of service, and then received his post rank. Mr. Thom, the purser, Mr. M'Diarmid, the surgeon, and the petty officers, were appointed to good situations in the navy. The seamen received the usual double pay given to arctic explorers, up to the time of leaving their ship, and full pay from that date until their arrival in England.

A committee of the House of Commons took up the case of Captain Ross early in the session of 1834, and on their recommendation 5,000*l.* was granted him as a remuneration for his pecuniary outlay and privations.

A baronetcy, on the recommendation of the same committee, was also conferred by his Majesty William IV. on Mr. Felix Booth.

In looking back on the results of this voyage, no impartial inquirer can deny to Captain Ross the merit of having effected much good by tracing and surveying the whole of the long western coast of Regent Inlet, proving Boothia to be a peninsula, and setting at rest the probability of any navigable outlet being discovered from this inlet to the Polar Sea. The lakes, rivers and islands which were examined, proved with sufficient accuracy the correctness of the information furnished to Parry by the Esquimaux.

To Commander James Ross is due the credit of resolving many important scientific questions, such as the combination of light with magnetism, fixing the exact position of the magnetic pole. He was also the only person in the expedition competent to make observations in geology, natural history and botany. Out of about 700 miles of new land explored, Commander Ross, in the expeditions which he planned and conducted, discovered nearly 500. He had, up to this time, passed fourteen summers and eight winters in these seas.

The late Sir John Barrow, in his "Narrative of Voyages of Discovery and Research," p. 518, in opposition to Ross's opinion, asserted that Boothia was not joined to the continent, but that they were "completely divided by a navigable strait, ten miles wide and upward, leading past Back's Estuary, and into the Gulf (of Boothia,) of which the proper name is Akkolee, not Boothia; and moreover, that the two seas flow as freely into each other as Lancaster Sound does into the Polar Sea." This assumption has since been shown to be incorrect. Capt. Ross asserts there is a difference in the level of these two seas.

I may here fitly take a review of Captain Ross's services. He entered the navy in 1790, served fifteen years as a midshipman, seven as a lieutenant, and seven as a commander, and was posted on the 7th of December, 1818, and appointed to the command of the first arctic expedition of this century. On his return he received many marks of favor from continental sovereigns, was knighted and made a Companion of the Bath on the 24th of December, 1834; made a Commander of the Sword of Sweden, a Knight of the Second Class of St Anne of Prussia (in diamonds,) Second Class of the Legion of Honor, and of the Red Eagle of Prussia, and of Leopold of Belgium. Received the royal premium from the Geographical Society of London, in 1833, for his discoveries in the arctic regions; also gold medals from the Geographical Society of Paris, and the Royal Societies of Sweden, Austria, and Denmark. The freedom of the cities of London, Liverpool, and Bristol; six gold snuff-boxes from Russia, Holland, Denmark, Austria, London and Baden; a sword valued at 100 guineas from the Patriotic Fund, for his sufferings, having been wounded thirteen times in three different actions during the war; and one of the value of 200*l.* from the King of Sweden, for service in the Baltic and the White Sea. On the 8th of March, 1839, he was appointed to the lucrative post of British consul at Stockholm, which he held for six years.

Captain Back's Land Journey, 1833–35.

Four years having elapsed without any tidings being received of Capt. Ross and his crew, it began to be generally feared in England that they had been added to the number of former sufferers, in the prosecution of their arduous undertaking.

Dr. Richardson, who had himself undergone such frightful perils in the arctic regions with Franklin, was the first to call public attention to the subject, in a letter to the Geographical Society, in which he suggested a project for relieving them, if still alive and to be found;

and at the same time volunteered his services to the Colonial Secretary of the day, to conduct an exploring party.

Although the expedition of Capt. Ross was not undertaken under the auspices of government, it became a national concern to ascertain the ultimate fate of it, and to make some effort for the relief of the party, whose home at that time might be the boisterous sea, or whose shelter the snow hut or the floating iceberg. Dr. Richardson proposed to proceed from Hudson's Bay, in a northwest direction to Coronation Gulf, where he was to commence his search in an easterly direction. Passing to the north, along the eastern side of this gulf, he would arrive at Point Turnagain, the eastern point of his own former discovery. Having accomplished this, he would continue his search toward the eastward until he reached Melville Island, thus perfecting geographical discovery in that quarter, and a continued coast line might be laid down from the Fury and Hecla Strait to Beechey Point, leaving only the small space between Franklin's discovery and that of the Blossom unexplored. The proposal was favorably received; but owing to the political state of the country at the time, the offer was not accepted.

A meeting was held in November, 1832, at the rooms of the Horticultural Society, in Regent street, to obtain funds, and arrange for fitting out a private relief expedition, as the Admiralty and Government were unable to do this officially, in consequence of Captain Ross's expedition not being a public one. Sir George Cockburn took the chair, and justly observed that those officers who devoted their time to the service of science, and braved in its pursuit the dangers of unknown and ungenial climates, demanded the sympathy and assistance of all. Great Britain had taken the lead in geographical discovery, and there was not one in this country who did not feel pride and honor in the fame she had attained by the expeditions of Parry and Franklin; but if we wished to create future Parrys and Franklins, if we wished to encourage British enterprise and cou age, we must prove that the officer who is out of sight of his countrymen is not forgotten; that there is consideration for his sufferings, and appreciation of his spirit. This reflection will cheer him in the hour of trial, and will permit him, when surrounded by dangers and privations, to indulge in hope, the greatest blessing of man. Captain George Back, R. N., who was in Italy when the subject was first mooted, hastened to England, and offered to lead the party, and his services were accepted. A subscription was entered into, to defray the necessary expenses, and upward of 6000*l.* was raised; of this sum, at the recommendation of Lord Goderich, the then Secretary of State, the Treasury contributed 2000*l.*

After an interview with the king at Brighton, to which he was specially summoned, Captain Back made preparations for his journey, and laid down his plan of operations. In order to facilitate his views, and give him greater authority over his men, special instructions and authority were issued by the Colonial Office, and the Hudson's Bay Company granted him a commission in their service, and placed every assistance at his disposal throughout their territory in North America.

Every thing being definitely arranged, Capt. Back, accompanied by Dr. Richard King as surgeon and naturalist, with three men who had been on the expedition with Franklin, left Liverpool on the 17th of February, 1833, in one of the New York packet ships, and arrived in America after a stormy passage of thirty-five days. He proceeded on to Montreal, where he had great difficulty in preventing two of the men from leaving him, as their hearts began to fail them at the prospect of the severe journey with its attendant difficulties, which they had to encounter.

Four volunteers from the Royal Artillery corps here joined him, and some voyageurs having been engaged, the party left, in two canoes, on the 25th of April. Two of his party deserted from him in the Ottawa river.

On the 28th of June, having obtained his complement of men, he may be said to have commenced his journey. They suffered dreadfully from myriads of sand-flies and musquitoes, being so disfigured by their attacks that their features could scarcely be recognized. Horse-flies, appropriately styled "bull-dogs," were another dreadful pest, which pertinaciously gorged themselves, like the leech, until they seemed ready to burst.

"It is in vain to attempt to defend yourself against these puny bloodsuckers; though you crush thousands of them, tens of thousands arise to avenge the death of their companions, and you very soon discover that the conflict which you are waging is one in which you are sure to be defeated. So great at last are the pains and fatigue in buffeting away this attacking force, that in despair you throw yourself, half suffocated, in a blanket, with your face upon the ground, and snatch a few minutes of sleepless rest." Capt. Back adds that the vigorous and unintermitting assaults of these tormenting pests conveyed the moral lesson of man's helplessness, since, with all our boasted strength, we are unable to repel these feeble atoms of creation. "How," he says, "can I possibly give an idea of the torment we endured from the sand-flies? As we divided into the confined and suffocating chasms, or waded through the close swamps, they rose in clouds, actually darkening the air; to see or to speak was equally difficult, for they rushed at every undefended part, and fixed their poisonous fangs in an instant. Our faces streamed with blood, as if leeches had been applied, and there was a burning and irritating pain, followed by immediate inflammation, and producing giddiness, which almost drove us mad, and caused us to moan with pain and agony.

At the Pine portage, Captain Back engaged the services of A. R. McLeod, in the employ of the Hudson's Bay Company, and who had been fixed upon by Governor Simpson, to aid the expedition. He was accompanied by his wife, three children, and a servant; and had just returned from the Mackenzie River, with a large cargo of furs. The whole family were attached to the party, and after some detentions of a general and unimportant character they arrived at

Fort Chipewyan on the 20th of July. Fort Resolution, on Great Slave Lake, was reached on the 8th of August.

The odd assemblage of goods and voyageurs in their encampment are thus graphically described by the traveler, as he glanced around him.

"At my feet was a rolled bundle in oil-cloth, containing some three blankets, called a bed; near it a piece of dried buffalo, fancifully ornamented with long black hairs, which no art, alas, can prevent from insinuating themselves between the teeth, as you laboriously masticate the tough, hard flesh; then a tolerably clean napkin, spread by way of table-cloth, on a red piece of canvas, and supporting a tea-pot, some biscuits, and a salt-cellar; near this a tin plate, close by a square kind of box or safe of the same material, rich with a pale, greasy hair, the produce of the colony at Red River; and the last, the far-renowned *pemmican*, unquestionably the best food of the country for expeditions such as ours. Behind me were two boxes containing astronomical instruments, and a sextant lying on the ground, while the different corners of the tent were occupied by a washing apparatus, a gun, an Indian shot-pouch, bags, basins, and an unhappy-looking japanned pot, whose melancholy bumps and hollows seemed to reproach me for many a bruise endured upon the rocks and portages between Montreal and Lake Winnipeck. Nor were my crew less motley than the furniture of the tent. It consisted of an Englishman, a man from Stornaway, two Canadians, two Metifs or half-breeds, and three Iroquois Indians. Babel could not have produced a worse confusion of unharmonious sounds than was the conversation they kept up."

Having obtained at Fort Resolution all possible information, from the Indians and others, relative to the course of the northern rivers of which he was in search, he divided his crew into two parties, five of whom were left as an escort for Mr. McLeod, and four were to accompany himself in search of the Great Fish River, since appropriately named after Back himself.

On the 19th of August they began the ascent of the Hoar Frost River, whose course was a series of the most fearful cascades and rapids. The woods here were so thick as to render them almost impervious consisting chiefly of stunted firs, which occasioned infinite trouble to the party to force their way through added to which, they had to clamber over fallen trees through rivulets, and over bogs and swamps, until the difficulties appeared so appalling, as almost to dishearten the party from prosecuting their journey. The heart of Captain Back was, however, of too stern a cast to be dispirited by difficulties, at which less persevering explorers would have turned away discomfited, and cheering on his men, like a bold and gallant leader, the first in the advance of danger, they arrived at length in an open space, where they rested for awhile to recruit their exhausted strength. The place was, indeed, one of barrenness and desolation; crag was piled upon crag to the height of 2000 feet from the base, and the course of the river here, in a state of contraction, was marked by an uninterrupted line of foam.

However great the beauty of the scenery may be, and however resolute may be the will, severe toil will at length relax the spirits, and bring a kind of despondency upon a heart naturally bold and undaunted. This was found particularly the case now with the interpreter, who became a dead weight upon the party. Rapid now succeeded rapid; scarcely had they surmounted one fall than another presented itself, rising like an amphitheater before them to the height of fifty feet. They, however, gained at length the ascent of this turbulent and unfriendly river, the romantic beauty and wild scenery of which were strikingly grand, and after passing successively a series of portages, rapids, falls, lakes, and rivers, on the 27th Back observed from the summit of a high hill a very large lake full of deep bays and islands, and which has been named Aylmer Lake, after the Governor-General of Canada at that time. The boat was sent out with three men to search for the lake, or outlet of the river, which they discovered on the second day, and Captain Back himself, during their absence, also accidentally discovered its source in the Sand Hill Lake, not far from his encampment. Not prouder was Bruce when he stood on the green sod which covers the source of the Nile, than was Captain Back when he found that he was standing at the source of a river, the existence of which was known, but the course of which was a problem, no traveler had yet ventured to solve. Yielding to that pleasurable emotion which discoverers, in the first bound of their transport, may be pardoned for indulging, Back tells us he threw himself down on the bank and drank a hearty draught of the limpid water.

"For this occasion," he adds, "I had reserved a little grog, and need hardly say with what cheerfulness it was shared among the crew, whose welcome tidings had verified the notion of Dr. Richardson and myself, and thus placed beyond doubt the existence of the Thlew-ee-choh, or Great Fish River.

On the 30th of August, they began to move toward the river, but on reaching Musk-ox Lake, it was found impossible to stand the force of the rapids in their frail canoe, and as winter was approaching, their return to the rendezvous on Slave Lake was determined on.

At Clinton Colden Lake, some Indians visited them from the Chief Akaitcho, who, it will be remembered. was the guide of Sir John Franklin. Two of these Indians remembered Captain Back, one having accompanied him to the Coppermine River, on Franklin's first expedition.

At the Cat or Artillery Lake, they had to abandon their canoe, and perform the rest of the journey on foot over precipitous rocks, through frightful gorges and ravines, heaped with masses of granite, and along narrow ledges, where a false step would have been fatal.

At Fort Reliance, the party found Mr. McLeod had, during their absence, erected the frame-work of a comfortable residence for them, and all hands set to work to complete it. After many obstacles and difficulties, it was finished.

Dr. King joined them on the 16th of September, with two laden bateaux.

On the 5th of November, they exchanged their cold tents for the new house, which was fifty feet long by thirty broad, and contained four rooms, besides a spacious hall in the center, for the reception and accommodation of the Indians, to which a sort of rude kitchen was attached.

As the winter advanced, bands of starving Indians continued to arrive, in the hope of obtaining some relief, as little or nothing was to be procured by hunting. They would stand around while the men were taking their meals, watching every mouthful with the most longing, imploring look, but yet never uttered a complaint.

At other times they would, seated round the fire, occupy themselves in roasting and devouring small bits of their reindeer garments, which, even when entire, afforded them a very insufficient protection against a temperature of 102° below freezing point.

The sufferings of the poor Indians at this period are described as frightful. "Famine with her gaunt and bony arm," says Back, "pursued them at every turn, withered their energies, and strewed them lifeless on the cold bosom of the snow." It was impossible to afford relief out of their scanty store to all, but even small portions of the mouldy pemmican intended for the dogs, unpalatable as it was, was gladly received, and saved many from perishing. "Often," adds Back, "did I share my own plate with the children whose helpless state and piteous cries were peculiarly distressing; compassion for the full-grown may, or may not, be felt, but that heart must be cased in steel which is insensible to the cry of a child for food."

At this critical juncture, Akaitcho made his appearance with an opportune supply of a little meat, which in some measure enabled Captain Back to relieve the sufferers around him, many of whom, to his great delight, went away with Akaitcho. The stock of meat was soon exhausted, and they had to open their pemmican. The officers contented themselves with the short supply of half a pound a day, but the laboring men could not do with less than a pound and three-quarters. The cold now set in with an intensity which Captain Back had never before experienced,— the thermometer, on the 17th of January, being 70° below zero. "Such indeed, (he says,) was the abstraction of heat, that with eight large logs of dry wood on the fire, I could not get the thermometer higher than 12° below zero. Ink and paint froze. The sextant cases and boxes of seasoned wood, principally fir, all split. The skin of the hands became dry, cracked and opened into unsightly and smarting gashes, which we were obliged to anoint with grease. On one occasion, after washing my face within three feet of the fire, my hair was actually clotted with ice before I had time to dry it.".

The hunters suffered severely from the intensity of the cold, and compared the sensation of handling their guns to that of touching red-hot iron, and so excessive was the pain, that they were obliged to wrap thongs of leather round the triggers to keep their fingers from coming into contact with the steel.

The sufferings which the party now endured were great, and had it not been for the exemplary conduct of Akaitcho in procuring them game, it is to be doubted whether any would have survived to tell the misery they had endured. The sentiments of this worthy savage were nobly expressed —"The great chief trusts in us, and it is better that ten Indians perish, than that one white man should perish through our negligence and breach of faith."

On the 14th of February, Mr. McLeod and his family removed to a place half way between the fort and the Indians, in order to facilitate their own support, and assist in procuring food by hunting. His situation, however, became soon one of the greatest embarrassment, he and his family being surrounded by difficulties, privations, and deaths. Six of the natives near him sank under the horrors of starvation, and Akaitcho and his hunters were twelve days' march distant.

Toward the end of April, Capt. Back began to make arrangements for constructing boats for prosecuting the expedition once more, and while so employed, on the 25th a messenger arrived with the gratifying intelligence, that Capt. Ross had arrived safely in England, confirmation of which, was afforded in extracts from the *Times* and *Herald*, and letters from the long lost adventurers themselves. Their feelings at these glad tidings are thus described :—"In the fullness of our hearts we assembled together, and humbly offered up our thanks to that merciful Providence, who in the beautiful language of scripture hath said, 'Mine own will I bring again, as I did sometime from the deeps of the sea.' The thought of so wonderful a preservation overpowered for a time the common occurrences of life. We had just sat down to breakfast; but our appetite was gone, and the day was passed in a feverish state of excitement. Seldom, indeed, did my friend Mr. King or I indulge in a libation, but on this joyful occasion economy was forgotton; a treat was given to the men, and for ourselves the social sympathies were quickened by a generous bowl of punch." Capt. Back's former interpreter, Augustus, hearing that he was in the country, set out on foot from Hudson's Bay to join him, but getting separated from his two companions, the gallant little fellow was either exhausted by suffering and privations, or, caught in the midst of an open traverse, in one of those terrible snow storms which may be said to blow almost through the frame, he had sunk to rise no more, his bleached remains being discovered not far from the Riviere a Jean. "Such," says Capt. Back, "was the miserable end of poor Augustus, a faithful, disinterested, kind-hearted creature, who had won the regard, not of myself only, but I may add, of Sir J. Franklin and Dr. Richardson also, by qualities which, wherever found, in the lowest as in the highest forms of social life, are the ornament and charm of humanity."

On the 7th of June, all the preparations being completed, McLeod having been previously sent on to hunt, and deposit casks of meat at various stages, Back set out with Mr. King, accompanied by four voyagers and an Indian guide. The stores not required were buried, and the doors and windows of the house blocked up.

At Artillery Lake, Back picked up the remainder of his party, with the carpenters who had been employed preparing boats. The lightest and best was chosen and placed on runners plated with iron, and in this manner she was drawn over the ice by two men and six fine dogs. The eastern shore of the lake was followed, as it was found less rocky and precipitous than the opposite one. The march was prosecuted by night, the air being more fresh and pleasant, and the party took rest in the day. The glare of the ice, the difficulty encountered in getting the boat along, the ice being so bad that the spikes of the runners cut through instead of sliding over it, and the thick snow which fell in June, greatly increased the labor of getting along. The cold, raw wind pierced through them in spite of cloaks and blankets. After being caulked, the boat was launched on the 14th of June, the lake being sufficiently unobstructed to admit of her being towed along shore. The weather now became exceedingly unpleasant — hail, snow, and rain, pelted them one after the other for some time without respite, and then only yielded to squalls that overturned the boat. With alternate spells and haltings to rest, they however, gradually advanced on the traverse, and were really making considerable progress when pelting showers of sleet and drift so dimmed and confused the sight, darkening the atmosphere, and limiting their view to only a few paces before them, as to render it an extremely perplexing task to keep their course.

On the 23d of June, they fortunately fell in with a *cache* made for them by their *avant-courier*, Mr. McLeod, in which was a seasonable supply of deer and musk-ox flesh, the latter, however, so impregnated with the odor from which it takes its name, that the men declared they would rather starve three days than swallow a mouthful of it. To remove this unfavorable impression, Capt. Back ordered the daily rations to be served from it for his own mess as well as theirs, taking occasion at the same time, to impress on their minds the injurious consequences of voluntary abstinence, and the necessity of accommodating their tastes to such food as the country might supply. Soon after another *cache* was met with, thus making eleven animals in all, that had been thus obtained and secured for them by the kind care of Mr. McLeod.

On the 27th, they reached Sandy Hill Bay, where they found Mr. McLeod encamped. On the 28th, the boat being too frail to be dragged over the portage, about a quarter of a mile in length, was carried bodily by the crew, and launched safely in the Thlew-ee-choh or Fish River. After crossing the portage beyond Musk-ox Rapid, about four miles in length, and having all his party together, Captain Back took a survey of his provisions for the three months of operations, which he found to consist of two boxes of maccaroni, a case of cocoa, twenty-seven bags of pemmican of about 80 lbs. each, and a keg with two gallons of rum. This he considered an adequate supply if all turned out sound and good. The difficulty, however, of transporting a weight of 5000 lbs, over ice and rocks, by a circuitous route of full 200 miles, may be easily conceived, not to mention the pain endured in walking on some parts where the ice formed innumerable spikes that pierced like needles, and in other places where it was so black and decayed, that it threatened at every step to engulf the adventurous traveler. These and similar difficulties could only be overcome by the most steady perseverance, and the most determined resolution.

Among the group of dark figures huddled together in the Indian encampment around them, Capt. Back found his old acquaintance, the Indian beauty of whom mention is made in Sir John Franklin's narrative under the name of Green Stockings. Although surrounded with a family, with one urchin in her cloak clinging to her back, and several other maternal accompaniments, Capt. Back immediately recognized her, and called her by her name, at which she laughed, and said she was an old woman now, and begged that she might be relieved by the "medicine man" for she was very much out of health. However, notwithstanding all this, she was still the beauty of her tribe, and with that consciousness which belongs to all belles, savage or polite, she seemed by no means displeased when Back sketched her portrait.

Mr. McLeod was now sent back, taking with him ten persons and fourteen dogs. His instructions were to proceed to Fort Resolution for the stores expected to be sent there by the Hudson's Bay Company, to build a house in some good locality, for a permanent fishing station, and to be again on the banks of the Fish River by the middle of September, to afford Back and his party any assistance or relief they might require.

The old Indian chief Akaitcho, hearing from the interpreter that Capt. Back was in his immediate neighborhood, said, "I have known the chief a long time, and I am afraid I shall never see him again; I will go to him." On his arrival he cautioned Back against the dangers of a river which he distinctly told him the present race of Indians knew nothing of. He also warned him against the treachery of the Esquimaux, which he said was always masked under the guise of friendship, observing they would attack him when he least expected it. "I am afraid," continued the good old chief, "that I shall never see you again; but should you escape from the great water, take care you are not caught by the winter, and thrown into a situation like that in which you were on your return from the Coppermine, for you are alone, and the Indians cannot assist you."

The carpenters, with an Iroquois, not being further required, were dismissed to join Mr. McLeod, and on the 8th of July they proceeded down the river. The boat was now launched and laden with her cargo, which, together with ten persons, she stowed well enough for a smooth river, but not for a lake or sea way. The weight was calculated at 3360 lbs., exclusive of the awning, poles, sails, &c., and the crew.

Their progress to the sea was now one continued succession of dangerous and formidable falls, rapids, and cataracts, which frequently made Back hold his breath, expecting to see the boat dashed to shivers against some protruding rocks amidst the foam and fury at the foot of a rapid. The only wonder is how in their frail leaky boat they ever shot one of the rapids. Rapid after rapid, and fall after fall, were passed, each accompanied with more or less danger ; and in one instance the boat was only saved by all hands jumping into the breakers, and keeping her stern up the stream, until she was cleared from a rock that had brought her up.

They had hardly time to get into their places again, when they were carried with considerable velocity past a river which joined from the westward. After passing no less than five rapids within the distance of three miles, they came to one long and appalling one, full of rocks and large boulders ; the sides hemmed in by a wall of ice, and the current flying with the velocity and force of a torrent. The boat was lightened of her cargo, and Capt. Back placed himself on a high rock, with an anxious desire to see her run the rapid. He had every hope which confidence in the judgment and dexterity of his principal men could inspire, but it was impossible not to feel that one crash would be fatal to the expedition. Away they went with the speed of an arrow, and in a moment the foam and rocks hid them from view. Back at last heard what sounded in his ear like a wild shriek, and he saw Dr. King, who was a hundred yards before him, make a sign with his gun, and then run forward. Back followed with an agitation which may be easily conceived, when to his inexpressible joy he found that the shriek was the triumphant whoop of the crew, who had landed safely in a small bay below. For nearly one hundred miles of the distance they were impeded by these frightful whirlpools, and strong and heavy rapids.

On opening one of their bags of pemmican, the ingenuity of the Indians at pilfering was discovered, successive layers of mixed sand, stones, and green mea having been artfully and cleverly substituted for the dry meat. Fearful that they might be carrying heaps of stone instead of provision, Back had to examine carefully the remainder, which were all found sound and well-tasted. He began to fear, from the inclination of the river at one time toward the south, that it would be found to discharge itself in Chesterfield Inlet, in Hudson's Bay, but subsequently, to his great joy, it took a direct course toward the north, and his hopes of reaching the Polar Sea were revived. The river now led into several large lakes, some studded with islands, which were named successively after Sir H. Pelly, and Mr. Garry, of the Hudson's Bay Company; two others were named Lake Macdougall and Lake Franklin.

On the 28th of July, they fell in with a tribe of about thirty-five very friendly Esquimaux, who aided them in transporting their boat over the last long and steep portage, to which his men were utterly unequal, and Back justly remarks, to their kind assistance he is mainly indebted for getting to the sea at all.

It was late when they got away, and while threading their course between some sand-banks with a strong current, they first caught sight of a majestic headland in the extreme distance to the north, which had a coast-like appearance. This important promontory, Back subsequently named after our gracious Queen, then Princess Victoria.

"This, then," observes Back, "may be considered as the mouth of the Thlew-ee-choh, which after a violent and tortuous course of 530 geographical miles, running through an iron-ribbed country, without a single tree on the whole line of its banks, expanding into five large lakes, with clear horizon, most embarrassing to the navigator, and broken into falls, cascades, and rapids, to the number of eighty-three in the whole, pours its water into the Polar Sea, in lat. 67° 11′ N., and long. 94° 30′ W., that is to say, about thirty-seven miles more south than the Coppermine River, and nineteen miles more south than that of Back's River, (of Franklin,) at the lower extremity of Bathurst's Inlet."

For several days Back was able to make but slow progress along the eastern shore, in consequence of the solid body of drift-ice. A barren, rocky elevation of 800 feet high, was named Cape Beaufort, after the present hydrographer to the Admiralty. A bluff point on the eastern side of the estuary, which he considered to be the northern extreme, he named Cape Hay. Dean and Simpson, however, in 1839, traced the shore much beyond this. The difficulties met with here, began to dispirit the men. For a week or ten days they had a continuation of wet, chilly, foggy weather, and the only vegetation, fern and moss, was so wet that it would not burn; being thus without fuel, during this time they had but one hot meal. Almost without water, without any means of warmth, or any kind of warm or comforting food, sinking knee-deep, as they proceeded on land, in the soft slush and snow, no wonder that some of the best men, benumbed in their limbs and dispirited by the dreary and unpromising prospect before them, broke out for a moment, in low murmurings, that theirs was a hard and painful duty.

Captain Back found it utterly impossible to proceed, as he had intended, to the Point Turnagain of Franklin, and after vainly essaying a land expedition by three of the best walkers, and these having returned, after making but fifteen miles' way, in consequence of the heavy rains and the swampy nature of the ground, he came to the resolution of returning. Reflecting, he says, on the long and dangerous stream they had to ascend combining all the bad features of the worst rivers in the country, the hazard of the falls and the rapids, and the slender hope which remained of their attaining even a single mile further, he felt he had no choice. Assembling, therefore, the men around him, and unfurling the British flag, which was saluted with three cheers, he announced to them this determination. The latitude of this place was 68° 13′ 57″ N., and longitude 94° 58′ 1″ W. The extreme point seen to the northward on the western side of the estuary, in latitude 68° 46′ N., longitude 96° 20′ W., Back named Cape Richardson. The spirits of many of the men, whose health had suffered greatly for want of warm and nourishing food, now brightened, and they set to work with alacrity to prepare for their return journey. The boat being dragged across, was brought to the place of their former station, after which the crew went back four miles for their baggage. The whole was safely conveyed over before the evening, when the water-casks were broken up to make a fire to warm a kettle of cocoa, the second hot meal they had had for nine days.

On the 15th of August, they managed to make their way about twenty miles, on their return to the southward, through a breach in the ice, till they came to open water. The difficulties of the river were doubled in the ascent, from having to proceed against the stream. All the obstacles of rocks, rapids, sand-banks, and long portages had to be faced. In some days as many as sixteen or twenty rapids were ascended. They found, as they proceeded, that many of the deposits of provisions, on which they relied, had been discovered and destroyed by wolves. On the 16th of September, they met Mr. McLeod and his party, who had been several days at Sand Hill Bay, waiting for them. On the 24th, they reached the Ah-hel-dessy, where they met with some Indians. They were ultimately stopped by one most formidable perpendicular fall, and as it was found impossible to convey the boat further over so rugged and mountainous a country, most of the declivities of which were coated with thin ice, and the whole hidden by snow, it was here abandoned, and the party proceeded the rest of the journey on foot, each laden with a pack of about 75 lbs. weight.

Late on the 27th of September, they arrived at their old habitation, Fort Reliance, after being absent nearly four months, wearied indeed, but "truly grateful for the manifold mercies they had experienced in the course of their long and perilous journey." Arrangements were now made to pass the winter as comfortably as their means would permit, and as there was no probability that there would be sufficient food in the house for the consumption of the whole party, all except six were sent with Mr. McLeod to the fisheries. The Indians brought them provisions from time to time, and their friend Akaitcho, with his followers, though not very successful in hunting, was not wanting in his contributions. This old chieftain was, however, no longer the same active and important personage he had been in the days when he rendered such good service to Sir John Franklin. Old age and infirmities were creeping on him and rendering him peevish and fickle.

On the 21st of March following, having left directions with Dr. King to proceed, at the proper season, to the Company's factory at Hudson's Bay, to embark for England in their spring ships, Captain Back set out on his return through Canada, calling at the Fisheries to bid farewell to his esteemed friend, Mr. McLeod, and arriving at the Norway House on the 24th, where he settled and arranged the accounts due for stores, &c., to the Hudson's Bay Company. He proceeded thence to New York, embarked for England, and arrived at Liverpool on the 8th of September, after an absence of two years and a half. Back was honored with an audience of his Majesty, who expressed his approbation of his efforts — first in the cause of humanity, and next in that of geographical and scientific research. He has since been knighted ; and in 1835, the Royal Geographical Society awarded him their gold medal, (the Royal premium,) for his discovery of the Great Fish River, and navigating it to the sea on the arctic coast.

Dr. King, with the remainder of the party, (eight men,) reached England, in the Hudson's Bay Company's ship, in the following month, October.

Of Captain Back's travels it has been justly observed that it is impossible to rise from the perusal of them without being struck with astonishment at the extent of sufferings which the human frame can endure, and at the same time the wondrous display of fortitude which was exhibited under circumstances of so appalling a nature, as to invest the narrative with the character of a romantic fiction, rather than an unexaggerated tale of actual reality. He, however, suffered not despair nor despondency to overcome him, but gallantly and undauntedly pursued his course, until he returned to his native land to add to the number of those noble spirits whose names will be carried to posterity as the brightest ornaments to the country which gave them birth.

Captain Back's Voyage of the Terror.

In the year 1836, Captain Back, who had only returned the previous autumn, at the recommendation of the Geographical Society, undertook a voyage in the Terror up Hudson's Strait.

He was to reach Wager River, or Repulse Bay, and to make an overland journey, to examine the bottom of Prince Regent's Inlet, sending other parties to the north and west to examine the Strait of the Fury and Hecla, and to reach, if possible, Franklin's Point Turnagain.

Leaving England on the 14th of June, he arrived on the 14th of August at Salisbury Island, and proceeded up the Frozen Strait; off Cape Comfort the ship got frozen in, and on the breaking up of the ice by one of those frequent convulsions, the vessel was drifted right up the Frozen Channel, grinding large heaps that opposed her progress to powder.

From December to March she was driven about by the fury of the storms and ice, all attempts to release her being utterly powerless. She thus floated till the 10th of July, and for three days was on her beam-ends; but on the 14th she suddenly righted. The crazy vessel with her gaping wounds was scarcely able to transport the crew across the stormy waters of the Atlantic, but the return voyage which was rendered absolutely necessary, was fortunately accomplished safely.

I shall now give a concise summary of Captain Sir George Back's arctic services, so as to present it more readily to the reader:

In 1818 he was Admiralty Mate on board the Trent, under Franklin. In 1819 he again accompanied him on his first overland journey, and was with him in all those perilous sufferings which are elsewhere narrated. He was also as a Lieutenant with Franklin on his second journey in 1825. Having been in the interval promoted to the rank of Commander, he proceeded, in 1833, accompanied by Dr. King and a party, through Northern America to the Polar Sea, in search of Captain John Ross. He was posted on the 30th of September, 1835, and appointed in the following year to the command of the Terror, for a voyage of discovery in Hudson's Bay.

Messrs. Dease and Simpson's Discoveries.

In 1836 the Hudson's Bay Company resolved upon undertaking the completion of the survey of the northern coast of their territories, forming the shores of Arctic America, and small portions of which were left undetermined between the discoveries of Captains Back and Franklin.

They commissioned to this task two of their officers, Mr. Thomas Simpson and Mr. Peter Warren Dease, who were sent out with a party of twelve men from the company's chief fort, with proper aid and appliances. Descending the Mackenzie to the sea, they reached and surveyed in July, 1837, the remainder of the western part of the coast left unexamined by Franklin in 1825, from his Return Reef to Cape Barrow, where the Blossom's boats turned back.

Proceeding on from Return Reef two new rivers were discovered,—the Garry and the Colville; the latter more than a thousand miles in length. Although it was the height of summer, the ground was found frozen several inches below the surface, the spray froze on the oars and rigging of their boats, and the ice lay smooth and solid in the bays, as in the depth of winter.

On the 4th of August, having left the boats and proceeded on by land, Mr. Simpson arrived at Elson Bay which point Lieutenant Elson had reached in the Blossom's barge in 1826.

The party now returned to winter at Fort Confidence, on Great Bear Lake, whence they were instructed to prosecute their search to the eastward next season, and to communicate if possible with Sir George Back's expedition.

They left their winter quarters on the 6th of June, 1838, and descended Dease's River. They found the Coppermine River much swollen by floods, and encumbered with masses of floating ice. The rapids they had to pass were very perilous, as may be inferred from the following graphic description:—

"We had to pull for our lives to keep out of the suction of the precipices, along whose base the breakers raged and foamed with overwhelming fury. Shortly before noon, we came in sight of Escape Rapid of Franklin; and a glance at the overhanging cliff told us that there was no alternative but to run down with a full cargo. In an instant," continues Mr. Simpson, "we were in the vortex; and before we were aware, my boat was borne toward an isolated rock, which the boiling surge almost concealed. To clear it on the outside was no longer possible; our only chance of safety was to run between it and the lofty eastern cliff. The word was passed, and every breath was hushed. A stream which dashed down upon us over the brow of the precipice more than a hundred feet in height, mingled with the spray that whirled upward from the rapid, forming a terrific shower-bath. The pass was about eight feet wide, and the error of a single foot on either side would have been instant destruction. As, guided by Sinclair's consummate skill, the boat shot safely through those jaws of death, an involuntary cheer arose. Our next impulse was to turn round to view the fate of our comrades behind. They had profited by the peril we incurred, and kept without the treacherous rock in time."

On the 1st of July they reached the sea, and encamped at the mouth of the river, where they waited for the opening of the ice till the 17th. They doubled

Cape Barrow, one of the northern points of Bathurst's Inlet, on the 29th, but were prevented crossing the inlet by the continuity of the ice, and obliged to make a circuit of nearly 150 miles by Arctic Sound.

Some very pure specimens of copper ore were found on one of the Barry Islands. After doubling Cape Flinders on the 9th of August, the boats were arrested by the ice in a little bay to which the name of Boat Haven was given, situate about three miles from Franklin's farthest. Here the boats lingered for the best part of a month, in utter hopelessness. Mr. Simpson pushed on therefore on the 20th, with an exploring party of seven men, provisioned for ten days. On the first day they passed Point Turnagain, the limit of Franklin's survey in 1821. On the 23d they had reached an elevated cape, with land apparently closing all round to the northward, so that it was feared they had only been traversing the coast of a huge bay. But the perseverance of the adventurous explorer was fully rewarded.

"With bitter disappointment," writes Mr. Simpson, "I ascended the height, from whence a vast and splendid prospect burst suddenly upon me. The sea, as if transformed by enchantment, rolled its fierce waves at my feet, and beyond the reach of vision to the eastward, Islands of various shape and size overspread its surface; and the northern land terminated to the eye in a bold and lofty cape, bearing east northeast, thirty or forty-miles distant, while the continental coast trended away southeast. I stood, in fact, on a remarkable headland, at the eastern outlet of an ice-obstructed strait. On the extensive land to the northward I bestowed the name of our most gracious sovereign Queen Victoria. Its eastern visible extremity I called Cape Pelly, in compliment to the governor of Hudson's Bay Company."

Having reached the limits which prudence, dictated in the face of the long journey back to the boats, many of his men too being lame, Mr. Simpson retraced his steps, and the party reached Boat-haven on the 20th of August, having traced nearly 140 miles of new coast.

The boats were cut out of their icy prison, and commenced their re-ascent of the Coppermine on the 3d of September. At its junction with the Kendal River they left their boats, and shouldering their packs, traversed the barren grounds, and arrived at their residence on the lake by the 14th of September.

The following season these persevering explorers commenced their third voyage. They reached the Bloody Fall on the 22d of June, 1839, and occupied themselves for a week in carefully examining Richardson's River, which was discovered in the previous year, and discharges itself in the head of Back's Inlet. On the 3d of July they reached Cape Barrow, and from its rocky heights were surprised to observe Coronation Gulf almost clear of ice, while on their former visit it could have been crossed on foot.

They were at Cape Franklin a month earlier than Mr. Simpson reached it on foot the previous year, and doubled Cape Alexander, the northernmost cape in this quarter, on the 28th of July, after encountering a violent gale. They coasted the huge bay extending for about nine degrees eastward from this point, being favored with clear weather, and protected by the various islands they met from the crushing state of the ice drifted from seaward.

On the 10th of August they opened a strait about ten miles wide at each extremity, but narrowing to four or five miles in the center. This strait, which divides the main-land from Boothia, has been called Simpson's Strait.

On the 13th of August they had passed Richardson's Point and doubled Point Ogle, the furthest point of Back's journey in 1834.

By the 16th they had reached Montreal Island in Back's Estuary, where they found a deposit of provisions which Captain Back had left there that day five years. The pemmican was unfit for use, but out of several pounds of chocolate half decayed the men contrived to pick sufficient to make a kettleful acceptable drink in honor of the occasion. There were also a tin case and a few fish-hooks, of which, observes Mr. Simpson, "Mr. Deasé and I took possession, as memorials of our having breakfasted on the very spot where the tent of our gallant, though less successful precursor stood that very day five years before.

By the 20th of August they had reached as far as Aberdeen Island to the eastward, from which they had a view of an apparently large gulf, corresponding with that which had been so correctly described to Parry by the intelligent Esquimaux female as Akkolee.

From a mountainous ridge about three miles inland a view of land in the northeast was obtained supposed to be one of the southern promontories of Boothia. High and distant islands stretching from E. to E. N. E. (probably some in Committee Bay) were seen, and two considerable ones were noted far out in the offing. Remembering the length and difficulty of their return route, the explorers now retraced their steps. On their return voyage they traced sixty miles of the south coast of Boothia, where at one time they were not more than ninety miles from the site of the magnetic pole, as determined by Captain Sir James C. Ross. On the 25th of August they erected a high cairn at their farthest point, near Cape Herschel.

About 150 miles of the high, bold shores of Victoria Land, as far as Cape Parry, were also examined; Wellington, Cambridge, and Byron Bays being surveyed and accurately laid down. They then stretched across Coronation Gulf, and re-entered the Coppermine River on the 16th of September.

Abandoning here one of their boats, with the remains of their useless stores and other articles not required, they ascended the river and reached Fort Confidence on the 24th of September, after one of the longest and most successful boat voyages ever performed on the Polar Sea, having traversed more than 1600 miles of sea.

In 1838, before the intelligence of this last trip had been received, Mr. Simpson was presented by the Royal Geographical Society of London with the

Founder's Gold Medal, for discovering and tracing in 1837 and 1838 about 300 miles of the arctic shores; but the voyage which I have just recorded has added greatly to the laurels which he and his bold companions have achieved.

Dr. John Rae's Land Expedition, 1846–47.

Although a little out of its chronological order, I give Dr. Rae's exploring trip before I proceed to notice Franklin's last voyage, and the different relief expeditions that have been sent out during the past two years.

In 1846 the Hudson's Company dispatched an expedition of thirteen persons, under the command of Dr. John Rae, for the purpose of surveying the unexplored portion of the arctic coast at the northeastern angle of the American continent between Dease and Simpson's farthest, and the Strait of the Fury and Hecla.

The expedition left Fort Churchill, in Hudson's Bay, on the 5th of July, 1846, and returned in safety to York Factory on the 6th September in the following year, after having, by traveling over ice and snow in the spring, traced the coast all the way from the Lord Mayor's Bay of Sir John Ross to within eight or ten miles of the Fury and Hecla Strait, thus proving that eminent navigator to have been correct in stating Boothia to be a peninsula.

On the 15th of July the boats first fell in with the ice, about ten miles north of Cape Fullerton, and it was so heavy and closely packed that they were obliged to take shelter in a deep and narrow inlet that opportunely presented itself, where they were closed up two days.

On the 22d the party reached the most southerly opening of Wager River or Bay, but were detained the whole day by the immense quantities of heavy ice driving in and out with the flood and ebb of the tide, which ran at the rate of eight miles an hour, forcing up the ice and grinding it against the rocks with a noise like thunder. On the night of the 24th the boats anchored at the head of the Repulse Bay. The following day they anchored in Gibson's Cove, on the banks of which they met with a small party of Esquimaux; several of the women wore beads round their wrists, which they had obtained from Captain Parry's ship when at Igloolik and Winter Island. But they had neither heard nor seen anything of Sir John Franklin.

Learning from a chart drawn by one of the natives, that the isthmus of Melville peninsula was only about forty miles across, and that of this, owing to a number of large lakes, but five miles of land would have to be passed over, Dr. Rae determined to make his way over this neck in preference to proceeding by Fox's Channel through the Fury and Hecla Strait.

One boat was therefore laid up with her cargo in security, and with the other the party set out, assisted by three Esquimaux. After traversing several large lakes, and crossing over six "portages," on the 2d of August they got into the salt water, in Committee Bay, but being able to make but little progress to the northwest, in consequence of heavy gales and closely packed ice, he returned to his starting point, and made preparations for wintering, it being found impossible to proceed with the survey at that time. The other boat was brought across the isthmus, and all hands were set to work in making preparations for a long and cold winter.

As no wood was to be had, stones were collected to build a house, which was finished by the 2d of September. Its dimensions were twenty feet by fourteen, and about eight feet high. The roof was formed of oil-cloths and morse-skin coverings, the masts and oars of the boats serving as rafters, while the door was made of parchment skins stretched over a wooden frame.

The deer had already commenced migrating southward, but whenever he had leisure, Dr. Rae shouldered his rifle, and had frequently good success, shooting on one day seven deer within two miles of their encampment.

On the 16th of October, the thermometer fell to zero, and the greater part of the reindeer had passed; but the party had by this time shot 130, and during the remainder of October, and in November, thirty-two more were killed, so that with 200 partridges and a few salmon, their snow-built larder was pretty well stocked.

Sufficient fuel had been collected to last, with economy, for cooking, until the spring; and a couple of seals which had been shot produced oil enough for their lamps. By nets set in the lakes under the ice, a few salmon were also caught.

After passing a very stormy winter, with the temperature occasionally 47° below freezing point, and often an allowance of but one meal a day, toward the end of February preparations for resuming their surveys in the spring were made. Sleds, similar to those used by the natives, were constructed. In the beginning of March the reindeer began to migrate northward, but were very shy. One was shot on the 11th. Dr. Rae set out on the 5th of April, in company with three men and two Esquimaux as interpreters, their provisions and bedding being drawn on sleds by four dogs. Nothing worthy of notice occurs in this exploratory trip, till on the 18th Rae came in sight of Lord Mayor's Bay, and the group of islands with which it is studded. The isthmus which connects the land to the northward with Boothia, he found to be only about a mile broad. On their return the party fortunately fell in with four Esquimaux, from whom they obtained a quantity of seal's blubber for fuel and dog's food, and some of the flesh and blood for their own use, enough to maintain them for six days on half allowance.

All the party were more or less affected with snow blindness, but arrived at their winter quarters in Repulse Bay on the 5th of May, all safe and well, but as black as negroes, from the combined effects of frost-bites and oil smoke.

On the evening of the 13th May, Dr. Rae again started with a chosen party of four men, to trace the west shore of Melville peninsula. Each of the men carried about 70 lbs. weight.

Being unable to obtain a drop of water of nature's thawing, and fuel being rather a scarce article, they were obliged to take small kettles of snow under the blankets with them, to thaw by the heat of the body.

Having reached to about 69° 42′ N. lat., and 85° 8′ long., and their provisions being nearly exhausted, they were obliged, much to their disappointment, to turn back, when only within a few miles of the Hecla and Fury Strait. Early on the morning of the 30th of May, the party arrived at their snow hut on Cape Thomas Simpson. The men they had left there were well, but very thin, as they had neither caught nor shot any thing eatable, except two marmots, and they were preparing to cook a piece of parchment skin for their supper.

"Our journey," says Dr. Rae, "hitherto had been the most fatiguing I had ever experienced; the severe exercise, with a limited allowance of food, had reduced the whole party very much. However, we marched merrily on, tightening our belts — mine came in six inches — the men vowing that when they got on full allowance, they would make up for lost time."

On the morning of the 9th of June, they arrived at their encampment in Repulse Bay, after being absent twenty-seven days. The whole party then set actively to work procuring food, collecting fuel, and preparing the boats for sea; and the ice in the bay having broken up on the 11th of August, on the 12th they left their winter quarters, and after encountering head winds and stormy weather, reached Churchill River on the 31st of August.

A gratuity of 400*l.* was awarded o Mr. Rae, by the Hudson's Bay Company, for the important services he had thus rendered to the cause f science.

CAPTAIN SIR JOHN FRANKLIN'S LAST EXPEDITION. 1845–51.

THAT Sir John Franklin, now nearly six years absent, is alive, we dare not affirm; but that his ships should be so utterly annihilated that no trace of them can be discovered, or if they have been so entirely lost, that not a single life should have been saved to relate the disaster, and that no traces of the crew or vessels should have been met with by the Esquimaux, or the exploring parties who have visited and investigated those coasts, and bays, and inlets to so considerable an extent, is a most extraordinary circumstance. It is the general belief of those officers who have served in the former arctic expeditions, that whatever accident may have befallen the Erebus and Terror, they cannot wholly have disappeared from those seas, and that some traces of their fate, if not some living remnant of their crews, must eventually reward the search of the diligent investigator. It is possible that they may be found in quarters the least expected. There is still reason, then, for *hope*, and for the great and honorable exertions which that divine spark in the soul has prompted and still keeps alive.

"There is something," says the Athenæum, "intensely interesting in the picture of those dreary seas amid whose strange and unspeakable solitudes our lost countrymen are, or have been, somewhere imprisoned for so many years, swarming with the human life that is risked to set them free. No haunt was ever so exciting — so full of a wild grandeur and a profound pathos — as that which had just aroused the arctic echoes; that wherein their brothers and companions have been beating for the track by which they may rescue the lost mariners from the icy grasp of the Genius of the North. Fancy these men in their adamantine prison, wherever it may be, — chained up by the polar spirit whom they had dared, — lingering through years of cold and darkness on the stinted ration that scarcely feeds the blood, and the feeble hope that scarcely sustains the heart, — and then imagine the rush of emotions to greet the first cry from that wild hunting ground which should reach their ears! Through many summers has that cry been listened for, no doubt. Something like an expectation of the rescue which it should announce has revived with each returning season of comparative light, to die of its own baffled intensity as the long dark months once more settled down upon their dreary prison-house. — There is scarcely a doubt that the track being now struck, these long-pining hearts may be traced to their lair. But what to the anxious questioning which has year by year gone forth in search of their fate, will be the answer now revealed? The trail is found, — but what of the weary feet that made it? We are not willing needlessly to alarm the public sympathies, which have been so generously stirred on behalf of the missing men, — but we are bound to warn our readers against too sanguine an entertainment of the hope which the first tidings of the recent discovery is calculated to suggest. It is scarcely possible that the provisions which are sufficient for three years, and adaptable for four, can by any economy which implies less than starvation have been spread over five, — and scarcely probable that they can have been made to do so by the help of any accidents which the place of confinement supplied. We cannot hear of this sudden discovery of traces of the vanished crews as living men, without a wish which comes like a pang that it had been two years ago — or even last year. It makes the heart sore to think how close relief may have been to their hiding-place in former years — when it turned away. There is scarcely reason to doubt that had the present circumstances of the search occurred two years ago — last year perhaps — the wanderers would have been restored. Another year makes a frightful difference in the odds: — and we do not think the public will ever feel satisfied with what has been done in this matter if the oracle so long questioned, and silent so long, shall speak at last — and the answer shall be, 'It is too late.'"

In the prosecution of the noble enterprise on which all eyes are now turned, it is not merely scientific research and geographical discovery that are at present occupying the attention of the commanders of vessels sent out; the lives of human beings are at stake, and above all, the lives of men who have nobly periled every thing in the cause of national—nay, of universal progress and knowledge;—of men who have evinced on this and other expeditions the most dauntless bravery that any men can evince. Who can think of the probable fate of these gallant adventurers without a shudder?

Alas! how truthfully has Montgomery depicted the fatal imprisonment of vessels in these regions:—

There lies a vessel in that realm of frost,
Not wrecked, not stranded, yet forever lost;
Its keel embedded in the solid mass;
Its glistening sails appear expanded glass;
The transverse ropes with pearls enormous strung,
The yards with icicles grotesquely hung.
Wrapt in the topmast shrouds there rests a boy,
His old sea-faring father's only joy;
Sprung from a race of rovers, ocean born,
Nursed at the helm, he trod dry land with scorn,
Through fourscore years from port to port he veer'd;
Quicksand, nor rock, nor foe, nor tempest fear'd;
Now cast ashore, though like a hulk he lie,
His son at sea is ever in his eye.
He ne'er shall know in his *Northumbrian* cot,
How brief that son's career, how strange his lot;
Writhed round the mast, aud sepulchred in air,
Him shall no worm devour, no vulture tear;
Congeal'd to adamant his frame shall last,
Though empires change, till tide and time be past.
  Morn shall return, and noon, and eve, and night
Meet here with interchanging shade and light;
But from that barque no timber shall decay,
Of these cold forms no feature pass away;
Perennial ice around th' encrusted bow,
The peopled-deck, and full-rigg'd mast shall grow
Till from the sun himself the whole be hid,
Or spied beneath a crystal pyramid:
As in pure amber with divergent lines,
A rugged shell embossed with sea-weed, shines,
From age to age increased with annual snow,
This new *Mont Blanc* among the clouds may glow,
Whose conic peak that earliest greets the dawn,
And latest from the sun's shut eye withdrawn,

Shall from the Zenith, through incumbent gloom,
Burn like a lamp upon this naval tomb.
But when th' archangel's trumpet sounds on high,
The pile shall burst to atoms through the sky,
And leave its dead, upstarting at the call,
Naked and pale, before the Judge of all.

All who read these pages will, I am sure, feel the deepest sympathy and admiration of the zeal, perseverance, and conjugal affection displayed in the noble and untiring efforts of Lady Franklin to relieve or to discover the fate of her distinguished husband and the gallant party under his command, despite the difficulties, disappointments, and heart-sickening "hope deferred" with which these efforts have been attended. All men must feel a lively interest in the fate cf these bold men, and be most desirous to contribute toward their restoration to their country and their homes. The name of the present Lady Franklin is as "familiar as a household word" in every bosom in England; she is alike the object of our admiration, our sympathy, our hopes, and our prayers. Nay, her name and that of her husband is breathed in prayer in many lands — and, oh! how earnest, how zealous, how courageous, have been her efforts to find and relieve her husband, for, like Desdemona,

"She loved him for the dangers he had passed,
And he loved her that she did pity them."

How has she traversed from port to port, bidding "God speed their mission" to each public and private ship going forth on the noble errand of mercy — how freely and promptly has she contributed to their comforts. How has she watched each arrival from the north, scanned each stray paragraph of news, hurried to the Admiralty on each rumor, and kept up with unremitting labor a voluminous correspondence with all the quarters of the globe, fondly wishing that she had the wings of the dove, that she might flee away, and be with him from whom Heaven has seen fit to separate her so long.

An American poet well depicts her sentiments in the following lines: —

LADY FRANKLIN'S APPEAL TO THE NORTH.

Oh, where, my long lost-one! art thou,
  'Mid Arctic seas and wintry skies?
Deep, Polar night is on *me* now,
  And Hope, long wrecked, but mocks my cries
I am like thee! from frozen plains
  In the drear zone and sunless air,
My dying, lonely heart complains,
  And chills in sorrow and despair.

Tell me, ye Northern winds! that sweep
  Down from the rayless, dusky day —
Where ye have borne, and where ye keep,
  My well-beloved within your sway;
Tell me, when next ye wildly bear
  The icy message in your breath,
Of my beloved! Oh tell me where
  Ye keep him on the shores of death.

Tell me, ye Polar seas! that roll
  From ice-bound shore to sunny isle —
Tell me, when next ye leave the Pole,
  Where ye have chained my lord the while!
On the bleak Northern cliff I wait
  With tear-pained eyes to see ye come!
Will ye not tell me, ere too late?
  Or will ye mock while I am dumb?

Tell me, oh tell me, mountain waves!
  Whence have ye leaped and sprung to-day?
Have ye passed o'er their sleeping graves
  That ye rush wildly on your way?
Will ye sweep on and bear me too
  Down to the caves within the deep?
Oh, bring some token to my view
  That ye my loved one safe will keep!

Canst thou not tell me, Polar Star!
  Where in the frozen waste he kneels?
And on the icy plains afar
  His love to God and me reveals?
Wilt thou not send one brighter ray
  To my lone heart and aching eye?
Wilt thou not turn my night to day,
  And wake my spirit ere I die?

Tell me, oh dreary North! for now
  My soul is like thine Arctic zone;
Beneath the darkened skies I bow,
  Or ride the stormy sea alone!
Tell me of my beloved! for I
  Know not a ray my lord without!
Oh, tell me, that I may not die
  A sorrower on the sea of doubt!

In the early part of 1849, Sir E. Parry stated, that in offering his opinions, he did so under a deep sense of the anxious and even painful responsibility, both as regarded the risk of life, as well as the inferior consideration of expense involved in further attempts to rescue our gallant countrymen, or at least the surviving portion of them, from their perilous position.

But it was his deliberate conviction, that the time had not yet arrived when the attempt ought to be given up as hopeless : the further efforts making might also be the means of determining their fate, and whether it pleased God to give success to those efforts or not, the Lords of the Admiralty, and the country at large, would hereafter be better satisfied to have followed up the noble attempts already made, so long as the most distant hope remains of ultimate success.

In the absence of authentic information of the fate of the gallant band of adventurers, it has been well observed, the *terra incognita* of the northern coast of Arctic America, will not only be traced, but minutely surveyed, and the solution of the problem of centuries will engage the marked attention of the House of Commons, and the legislative assemblies of other parts of the world. The problem is very safe in their hands, so safe indeed that two years will not elapse before it is solved.

The intense anxiety and apprehension now so generally entertained for the safety of Sir John Franklin, and the crews of the Erebus and Terror, under his command, who, if still in existence, are now passing through the severe ordeal of a fifth winter, in those inclement regions, imperatively call for every available effort to be made for their rescue from a position so perilous ; and as long as one possible avenue to that position remains unsearched, the country will not feel satisfied that every thing has been done, which perseverance and experience can accomplish, to dispel the mystery which at present surrounds their fate.

Capt. Sir James Ross having returned successful from his antarctic expedition in the close of the preceding year, in the spring of 1845, the Lords Commissioners of the Admiralty, upon the recommendation of Sir John Barrow, determined on sending out another expedition to the North Pole.

Accordingly the command was given to Sir John Franklin, who re-commissioned the Erebus and Terror, the two vessels which had just returned from the South Polar Seas. The expedition sailed from Sheerness on the 20th of May, 1845. The following are the officers belonging to these vessels, and for whose safety so deep an interest is now felt:—

Erebus.

Captain — Sir John Franklin, K. C. H.
Commander — James Fitzjames, (Capt.)
Lieutenants — Graham Gore, (Commander,) Henry T. D. Le Vesconte, James William Fairholme.
Mates — Chas. F. des Vaux, (Lieut.,) Robert O'Sargent, (Lieut.)
Second Master — Henry F. Collins.
Surgeon — Stephen S. Stanley.
Assistant-Surgeon — Harry D. S. Goodsir, (acting.)
Paymaster and Purser — Chas. H. Osmer.
Ice-master — James Reid, acting.
58 Petty Officers, Seamen, &c.
Full Complement, 70.

Terror.

Captain — Fras R. M. Crozier.
Lieutenants — Edward Little, (Commander,) Geo. H. Hodgson, John Irving.
Mates — Frederick J. Hornby, (Lieutenant,) Robert Thomas, (Lieut.)
Ice-master — T. Blanky, (acting.)
Second Master — G. A. Maclean.
Surgeon — John S. Peddie.
Assistant-Surgeon — Alexander McDonald.
Clerk in Charge — Edwin J. H. Helpman.
57 Petty Officers, Seamen, &c.
Full Complement, 68.

Those officers whose rank is within parenthesis have been promoted during their absence.

The following is an outline of Capt. Franklin's services as recorded in O'Byrne's Naval Biography :—

Sir John Franklin, Kt., K. R. G., K. C. H., D. C. L., F. R. S., was born in 1786, at Spilsby, in Lincolnshire, and is brother of the late Sir W. Franklin, Kt., Chief Justice of Madras. He entered the navy in October, 1800, as a boy on board the Polyphemus, 64, Captain John Lawford, under whom he served as midshipman in the action off Copenhagen, 2d of April, 1801. He then sailed with Captain Flinders, in H. M. sloop Investigator, on a voyage of discovery to New Holland, joining there the armed store-ship Porpoise; he was wrecked on a coral reef near Cato Bank on the 17th of August, 1803. I shall not follow him through all his subsequent period of active naval service, in which he displayed conspicuous zeal and activity. But we find him taking part at the battle of Trafalgar, on the 21st of October, 1805, on board the Bellerophon, where he was signal midshipman. He was confirmed as Lieutenant, on board the Bedford, 74, 11th of February, 1808, and he then escorted the royal family of Portugal, from Lisbon to South America. He was engaged in very arduous services during the expedition against New Orleans, in the close of 1814, and was slightly wounded in boat service, and for his brilliant services on this occasion, was warmly and officially recommended for promotion. On the 14th of January, 1818, he assumed command of the hired brig Trent, in which he accompanied Captain D. Buchan, of the Dorothea, on the perilous voyage of discovery to the neighborhood of Spitzbergen, which I have fully recorded elsewhere. In April, 1819, having paid off the Trent in the preceding November, he was invested with the conduct of an expedition destined to proceed overland from the shores of Hudson's Bay, for the purpose more particularly of ascertaining the actual position of the mouth of the Coppermine River, and the exact trending of the shores of the Polar Sea, to the eastward of that river.

The details of this fearful undertaking, which endured until the summer of 1822, and in the course of which, he reached as far as Point Turnagain, in latitude 68° 19′ N., and longitude 109° 25′ W., and effected a journey altogether of 5550 miles, Captain Franklin has ably set forth in his "Narrative of a Journey to the Shores of the Polar Sea, in the year 1819-22," and which I have abridged in preceding pages. He was promoted to the rank of Commander, on the 1st of January, 1821, and reached his post rank on the 20th of November, 1822. On the 16th of February, 1825, this energetic officer again left England on another expedition to the Frozen Regions, having for its object a co-operation with Captains F. W. Beechey, and W. E. Parry, in ascertaining from opposite quarters the existence of a northwest passage. The results of this mission will be found in detail in Captain Franklin's "Narrative of a Second Expedition to the Shores of the Polar Sea, in 1825-7."

On his return to England, where he arrived on the 26th of Sept., 1827, Franklin was presented by the Geographical Society of Paris, with a gold medal valued at 1200 francs, for having made the most important acquisitions to geographical knowledge during the preceding year, and on the 29th of April, 1829, he received the honor of knighthood, besides being awarded in July following the Oxford degree of a D. C. L.

From 1830 to 1834, he was in active service in command of H. M. S. Rainbow, on the Mediterranean station, and for his exertions during that period as connected with the troubles in Greece, was presented with the order of the Redeemer of Greece. Sir John was created a K. C. H. on the 25th of January, 1836, and was for some time Governor of Van Diemen's Land. He married, on the 16th of August, 1823, Eleanor Anne, youngest daughter of W. Porden, Esq., architect, of Berners Street, London, and seconuly, on the 5th of November, 1828, Jane, second dauguter of John Griffin, Esq., of Bedford Place.

Captain Crozier was in all Parry's expeditions, having been midshipman in the Fury in 1821, in the Hecla in 1824, went out as Lieutenant in the Hecla, with Parry, on his boat expedition to the Pole in 1827, volunteered in 1836 to go out in search of the missing whalers and their crews to Davis' Straits, was made a Captain in 1841, and was second in command of the antarctic expedition under Sir James Ross, and on his return, appointed to the Terror, as second in command under Franklin.

Lieutenant Gore served as a mate in the last fearful voyage of the Terror, under Back, and was also with Ross in the antarctic expedition. He has attained his commander's rank during his absence.

Lieutenant Fairholme was in the Niger expedition.

Lieutenant Little has also been promoted during his absence, and so have all the mates.

Commander Fitzjames is a brave and gallant officer, who has seen much service in the East, and has attained to his post rank since his departure.

The Terror, it may be remembered, is the vessel in which Captain Sir G. Back made his perilous attempt to reach Repulse Bay, in 1836.

The Erebus and Terror were not expected home unless success had early rewarded their efforts, or some casualty hastened their return, before the close of 1847, nor were any tidings anticipated from them in the interval; but when the autumn of 1847 arrived, without any intelligence of the ships, the attention of H. M. Government was directed to the necessity of searching for, and conveying relief to them, in case of their being imprisoned in the ice, or wrecked, and in want of provisions and means of transport.

For this purpose a searching expedition in three divisions was fitted out by the government, in the early part of 1848. The investigation was directed to three different quarters simultaneously, viz: 1st, to that by which, in case of success, the ships would come out of the Polar Sea, to the westward, or Behring's Straits. This consisted of a single ship, the Plover, commanded by Captain Moore, which left England in the latter end of January, for the purpose of entering Behring's Strait. It was intended that she should arrive there in the month of July, and having looked out for a winter harbor, she might send out her boats northward and eastward, in which directions the discovery ships, if successful, would be met with. The Plover, however, in her first season, never even approached the place of her destination, owing to her setting off too late, and to her bad sailing properties.

Her subsequent proceedings, and those of her boats along the coast, will be found narrated in after pages.

The second division of the expedition was one of boats, to explore the coast of the Arctic Sea between the Mackenzie and Coppermine Rivers, or from the 135th to the 115th degree of W. longitude, together with the south coast of Wollaston Land, it being supposed, that if Sir John Franklin's party had been compelled to leave the ships and take to the boats, they would make for this coast, whence they could reach the Hudson's Bay Company's posts. This party was placed under the command of the faithful friend of Franklin, and the companion of his former travels, Dr. Sir John Richardson, who landed at New York in April, 1848, and hastened to join his men and boats, which were already in advance toward the arctic shore. He was, however, unsuccessful in his search.

The remaining and most important portion of this searching expedition consisted of two ships under the command of Sir James Ross, which sailed in May, 1848, for the locality in which Franklin's ships entered on this course of discovery, viz., the eastern side of Davis' Straits. These did not, however, succeed, owing to the state of the ice in getting into Lancaster Sound until the season for operations had nearly closed. These ships wintered in the neighborhood of Leopold Island, Regent Inlet, and missing the store-ship sent out with provisions and fuel, to enable them to stop out another year, were driven out through the Strait by the pack of ice, and returned home unsuccessful. The subsequent expeditions consequent upon the failure of the foregoing will be found fully detailed and narrated in their proper order.

Among the number of volunteers for the service of exploration, in the different searching expeditions, were the following:—Mr. Chas. Reid, lately commanding the whaling ship Pacific, and brother to the ice-master on board the Erebus, a man of great experience and respectability.

The Rev. Joseph Wolff, who went to Bokhara in search of Capt. Conolly and Col. Stoddart.

Mr. John McLean, who had passed twenty-five years as an officer and partner of the Hudson's Bay Company, and who has recently published an interesting narrative of his experience in the northwest regions.

Dr. Richard King, who accompanied Capt. Back in his land journey to the mouth of the Great Fish River.

Lieut. Sherard Osborn, R. N., who had recently gone out in the Pioneer, tender to the Resolute.

Commander Forsyth, R. N., who volunteered for all the expeditions, and was at last sent out by Lady Franklin in the Prince Albert.

Dr. McCormick, R. N., who served under Captain Sir E. Parry, in the attempt to reach the North Pole, in 1827, who twice previously volunteered his services in 1847.

Capt. Sir John Ross, who has gone out in the Felix, fitted out by the Hudson's Bay Company, and by private subscriptions; and many others.

Up to the present time no intelligence of any kind has been received respecting the expedition, and its fate is now exciting the most intense anxiety, not only on the part of the British government and public, but of the whole civilized world. The maratime powers of Europe and the United States are vying with each other as to who shall be the first to discover some trace of the missing navigators, and if they be still alive, to render them assistance. The Hudson's Bay Company have, with a noble liberality, placed all their available resources of men, provisions, and the services of their chief and most experienced traders, at the disposal of government. The Russian authorities have also given every facility for diffusing information and affording assistance in their territories.

In a letter from Sir John Franklin to Colonel Sabine, dated from the Whale Fish Islands, 9th of July, 1845, after noticing that, including what they had received from the transport which had accompanied them so far, the Erebus and Terror had on board provisions, fuel, clothing and stores for three years complete from that date, i. e. to July, 1848, he continues as follows:—"I hope my dear wife and daughter will not be over-anxious if we should not return by the time they have fixed upon; and I must beg of you to give them the benefit of your advice and experience when that arrives, for you know well, that even after the second winter, without success in our object, we should wish to try some other channel, if the state of our provisions, and the health of the crews justify it.

Capt. Dannett, of the whaler, Prince of Wales, while in Melville Bay, last saw the vessels of the expedition, moored to an iceberg, on the 26th of July, in lat. 74° 48′ N., long. 66° 13′ W., waiting for a favorable opening through the middle ice from Baffin's Bay to Lancaster Sound. Capt. Dannett states that during three weeks after parting company with the ships, he experienced very fine weather, and thinks they would have made good progress.

Lieut. Griffith, in command of the transport which accompanied them out with provisions to Baffin's Bay, reports that he left all hands well and in high spirits. They were then furnished, he adds, with every species of provisions for three entire years, independently of five bullocks, and stores of every description for the same period, with abundance of fuel.

The following is Sir John Franklin's official letter sent home by the transport:—

"*Her Majesty's Ship 'Erebus,'*
"*Whale-Fish Islands*, 12*th of July*, 1845.

"I have the honor to acquaint you, for the information of the Lords Commissioners of the Admiralty, that her Majesty's ships Erebus and Terror, with the transport, arrived at this anchorage on the 4th instant, having had a passage of one month from Stromness: the transport was immediately taken alongside this ship, that she might be the more readily cleared; and we have been constantly employed at that operation till last evening, the delay having been caused not so much in getting the stores transferred to either of the ships, as in making the best stowage of them below, as well as on the upper deck; the ships are now complete with supplies of every kind for three years; they are therefore very deep; but, happily, we have no reason to expect much sea as we proceed farther.

"The magnetic instruments were landed the same morning; so also were the other instruments requisite for ascertaining the position of the observatory; and it is satisfactory to find that the result of the observations for latitude and longitude accord very nearly with those assigned to the same place by Sir Edward Parry; those for the dip and variation are equally satisfactory, which were made by Captain Crozier with the instruments belonging to the Terror, and by Commander Fitzjames with those of the Erebus.

"The ships are now being swung, for the purpose of ascertaining the dip and deviation of the needle on board, as was done at Greenhithe, which, I trust, will be completed this afternoon, and I hope to be able to sail in the night.

"The governor and principal persons are at this time absent from Disco, so that I have not been able to receive any communication from head quarters as to the state of the ice to the north; I have, however, learnt from a Danish carpenter in charge of the Esquimaux at these islands, that though the winter was severe, the spring was not later than usual, nor was the ice later in breaking away hereabout; he supposes also that it is now loose as far as 74° latitude, and that our prospect is favorable of getting across the barrier, and as far as Lancaster Sound, without much obstruction.

"The transport will sail for England this day. I shall instruct the agent, Lieutenant Griffiths, to proceed to Deptford, and report his arrival to the Secretary of the Admiralty. I have much satisfaction in bearing my testimony to the careful and zealous manner in which Lieut. Griffiths has performed the service intrusted to him, and would beg to recommend him, as an officer who appears to have seen much service, to the favorable consideration of their lordships.

"It is unnecessary for me to assure their lordships of the energy and zeal of Captain Crozier, Commander Fitzjames, and of the officers and men with whom I have the happiness of being employed on this service.

"I have, &c.,

(Signed) JOHN FRANKLIN, Captain.

"The Right Hon. H. L. Corry, M. P."

It has often been a matter of surprise that but one of the copper cylinders which Sir John Franklin was instructed to throw overboard at stated intervals, to record his progress, has ever come to hand, but a recent sight of the solitary one which has been received proves to me that they are utterly useless for the purpose. A small tube, about the size of an ordinary rocket-case, is hardly ever likely to be observed among huge masses of ice, and the waves of the Atlantic and Pacific, unless drifted by accident on shore, or near some boat. The Admiralty have wisely ordered them to be rendered more conspicuous by being headed up in some cask or barrel, instructions being issued to Captain Collinson, and other officers of the different expeditions to that effect.

According to Sir John Richardson, who was on intimate terms with Sir John Franklin, his plans were to shape his course in the first instance for the neighborhood of Cape Walker, and to push to the westward in that parallel, or, if that could not be accomplished, to make his way southward, to the channel discovered on the north coast of the continent, and so on to Behring's Straits; failing success in that quarter, he meant to retrace his course to Wellington Sound, and attempt a passage northward of Parry's Islands, and if foiled there also, to descend Regent Inlet, and seek the passage along the coast discovered by Messrs. Dease and Simpson.

Captain Fitzjames, the second in command under Sir John Franklin, was much inclined to try the passage northward of Parry's Islands, and he would no doubt endeavor to persuade Sir John to pursue this course if they failed to the southward.

In a private letter of Captain Fitzjames to Sir John Barrow, dated January, 1845, he writes as follows: —

"It does not appear clear to me what led Parry down Prince Regent Inlet, after having got as far as Melville Island before. The northwest passage is certainly to be gone through by Barrow's Strait, but whether south or north of Parry's Group, remains to be proved. I am for going north, edging northwest till in longitude 140°, if possible."

I shall now proceed to trace, in chronological order and succession, the opinions and proceedings of the chief arctic explorers and public authorities, with the private suggestions offered and notice in detail the relief expeditions resulting therefrom.

In February, 1847, the Lords of the Admiralty state, that having unlimited confidence in the skill and resources of Sir John Franklin, they "have as yet felt no apprehensions about his safety; but on the other hand, it is obvious, that if no accounts of him should arrive by the end of this year, or, as Sir John Ross expects, at an earlier period, active steps must then be taken."

Captain Sir Edward Parry fully concurred in these views, observing, "Former experience has clearly shown that with the resources taken from this country, two winters may be passed in the polar regions, not only in safety, but with comfort; and if any inference can be drawn from the absence of all intelligence of the expedition up to this time, I am disposed to consider it rather in favor than otherwise of the success which has attended their efforts."

Captain Sir G. Back, in a letter to the Secretary of

the Admiralty, under date 27th of January, 1848, says, "I cannot bring myself to entertain more than ordinary anxiety for the safety and return of Sir John Franklin and his gallant companions."

Captain Sir John Ross records, in February, 1847, his opinion that the expedition was frozen up beyond Melville Island, from the known intentions of Sir John Franklin to put his ships into the drift ice at the western end of Melville Island, a risk which was deemed in the highest degree imprudent by Lieutenant Parry and the officers of the expedition of 1819–20, with ships of a less draught of water, and in every respect better calculated to sustain the pressure of the ice, and other dangers to which they must be exposed; and as it is now well known that the expedition has not succeeded in passing Behring's Strait, and if not totally lost, must have been carried by the ice that is known to drift to the southward on land seen at a great distance in that direction, and from which the accumulation of ice behind them will, as in Ross's own case, forever prevent the return of the ships; consequently they must be abandoned. When we remember with what extreme difficulty Ross's party traveled 300 miles over much smoother ice after they abandoned their vessel, it appears very doubtful whether Franklin and his men, 138 in number, could possibly travel 600 miles.

In the contingency of the ships having penetrated some considerable distance to the southwest of Cape Walker, and having been hampered and crushed in the narrow channels of the Archipelago, which there are reasons for believing occupies the space between Victoria, Wollaston, and Banks' Lands, it is well remarked by Sir John Richardson, that such accidents among ice are seldom so sudden but that the boats of one or of both ships, with provisions, can be saved; and in such an event the survivors would either return to Lancaster Strait, or make for the continent, according to their nearness.

Colonel Sabine remarks, in a letter dated Woolwich,

5th of May, 1847,—"It was Sir John Franklin's intention, if foiled at one point, to try in succession all the probable openings into a more navigable part of the Polar Sea: the range of coast is considerable in which memorials of the ships' progress would have to be sought for, extending from Melville Island, in the west, to the great Sound at the head of Baffin's Bay, in the east."

Sir John Richardson, when appealed to by the Admiralty in the spring of 1847, as regarded the very strong apprehensions expressed at that time for the safety of the expedition, considered they were premature, as the ships were specially equipped to pass two winters in the Arctic Sea, and until the close of that year, he saw no well-grounded cause for more anxiety than was naturally felt when the expedition sailed from this country on an enterprise of peril, though not greater than that which had repeatedly been encountered by others, and on one occasion by Sir John Ross for two winters also, but who returned in safety.

Captain Sir James C. Ross, in March, 1847, writes: "I do not think there is the smallest reason for apprehension or anxiety for the safety and success of the expedition; no one acqnainted with the nature of the navigation of the Polar Sea would have expected they would have been able to get through to Behring's Strait without spending at least two winters in those regions, except under unusually favorable circumstances, which all the accounts from the whalers concur in proving they have not experienced, and I am quite sure neither Sir John Franklin nor Captain Crozier expected to do so.

"Their last letters to me from Whale Fish Islands, the day previous to their departure from them inform me that they had taken on board provisions for three years on full allowance, which they could extend to four years without any serious inconvenience; so that we may feel assured they cannot want from that cause until after the middle of July, 1849; it therefore does not appear to me at all desirable to send after them until the spring of the next year." (1848.)

In the plan submitted by Captain F. W. Beechey, R. N., in April, 1847, after premising "that there does not at present appear to be any reasonable apprehension for the safety of the expedition," he suggested that it would perhaps be prudent that a relief expedition should be sent out that season to Cape Walker, where information of an important nature would most likely be found. From this vicinity one vessel could proceed to examine the various points and headlands in Regent Inlet, and also those to the northward, while the other watched the passage, so that Franklin and his party might not pass unseen, should he be on his return. At the end of the season the ships could winter at Port Bowen, or any other port in the vicinity of Leopold Island.

"In the spring of 1848," he adds, "a party should be directed to explore the coast, down to Hecla and Fury Strait, and to endeavor to communicate with the party dispatched by the Hudson's Bay Company in that direction; and in connection with this part of the arrangement, it would render the plan complete if a boat could be sent down Back's River to range the coast to the eastward of its mouth, to meet the above mentioned party; and thus, while it would complete the geography of that part of the American coast, it would at the same time complete the line of information as to the extensive measures of relief which their lordships have set on foot, and the precise spot where assistance and depots of provisions are to be found. This part of the plan has suggested itself to me from a conversation I had with Sir John Franklin as to his first effort being made to the westward and southwestward of Cape Walker. It is possible that, after passing the Cape, he may have been successful in getting down upon Victoria Land, and have passed his first winter (1845) thereabout, and that he may have spent his second winter at a still more advanced station, and even endured a third, without either a prospect of success, or of an extrication of his vessels within a given period of time.

"If, in this condition, which I trust may not be the

case, Sir John Franklin should resolve upon taking to his boats, he would prefer attempting a boat navigation through Sir James Ross's Strait, and up Regent Inlet, to a long land journey across the continent, to the Hudson's Bay Settlements, to which the greater part of his crew would be wholly unequal."

Sir John Richardson remarks upon the above suggestions, on the 5th of May, 1847,—"With respect to a party to be sent down Back's River to the bottom of Regent Inlet, its size and outfit would require to be equal with that of the one now preparing to descend the Mackenzie River, and it could scarcely with the utmost exertions be organized so as to start this summer. The present scarcity of provisions in the Hudson's Bay country precludes the hope of assistance from the Company's southern posts, and it is now too late to provide the means of transport through the interior of supplies from this country, which require to be embarked on board the Hudson's Bay ships by the 2d of June at the latest.

"Moreover there is no Company's post on the line of Back's River nearer than the junction of Slave River with Great Slave Lake, and I do not think that under any circumstances Sir John Franklin would attempt that route.

"In the summer of 1849, if the resources of the party I am to conduct remain unimpaired, as I have every reason to believe they will, much of what Capt. Beechey suggests in regard to exploring Victoria Land may be done by it, and indeed forms part of the original scheme. The extent of the examination of any part of the coast in 1848 depends, as I formerly stated, very much on the seasons of this autumn and next spring, which influence the advance of the boats through a long course of river navigation. As Governor Simpson will most likely succeed in procuring an Esquimaux to accompany my party, I hope by his means to obtain such information from parties of that nation as may greatly facilitate our finding the ships, should they be detained in that quarter.

"Were Sir John Franklin thrown upon the north coast of the continent with his boats, and all his crew, I do not think he would attempt the ascent of any river, except the Mackenzie. It is navigable for boats of large draught, without a portage, for 1300 miles from the sea, or within forty miles of Fort Chipewyan, one of the Company's principal depots, and there are five other posts in that distance. Though these posts could not furnish provisions to such a party, they could, by providing them with nets, and distributing the men to various fishing stations, do much toward procuring food for them.

"I concur generally in what Captain Beechey has said with regard to Behring's Straits, a locality with which he is so intimately acquainted, but beg leave to add one remark, viz: that in high northern latitudes the ordinary allowance of animal food is insufficient in the winter season to maintain a laboring man in health; and as Sir John Franklin would deem it prudent when detained a second winter to shorten the allowance, symptoms of scurvy may show themselves among the men, as was the case when Sir Edward Parry wintered two years in Fox's Channel.

"A vessel, therefore, meeting the Erebus and Terror this season in Behring's Straits, might render great service." *

The late Sir John Barrow, Bart., in a memorandum dated July, 1847, says:—

"The anxiety that prevails regarding Sir John Franklin, and the brave fellows who compose the crews of the two ships, is very natural, but somewhat premature; it arises chiefly from nothing having been received from them since fixed in the ice of Baffin's Bay, where the last whaling ship of the season of 1845 left them, opposite to the opening into Lancaster Sound. Hitherto no difficulty has been found to the entrance into that Sound. If disappointed, rather than return to the southward, with the view of wintering at or about Disco, I

* Parl. Paper, No. 264, Session 1848.

should be inclined to think that they would endeavor to enter Smith's Sound, so highly spoken of by Baffin, and which just now that gallant and adventurous Russian, Admiral Count Wrangel, has pointed out in a paper addressed to the Geographical Society as the starting place for an attempt to reach the North Pole; it would appear to be an inlet that runs up high to the northward, as an officer in one of Parry's ships states that he saw in the line of direction along that inlet, the sun at midnight skimming the horizon.

"From Lancaster Sound Franklin's instructions directed him to proceed through Barrow's Strait, as far as the islands on its southern side extended, which is short of Melville Island, which was to be avoided, not only on account of its dangerous coast, but also as being out of the direction of the course to the intended object. Having, therefore, reached the last known land on the southern side of Barrow's Strait, they were to shape a direct course to Behring's Strait, without any deviation, except what obstruction might be met with from ice, or from islands, in the midst of the Polar Sea, of which no knowledge had at that time been procured; but if any such existed, it would of course be left to their judgment, on the spot, how to get rid of such obstructions, by taking a northerly or a southerly course.

* * * * * * * *

"The only chance of bringing them upon this (the American) coast is the possibility of some obstruction having tempted them to explore an immense inlet on the northern shore of Barrow's Strait, (short of Melville Island,) called Wellington Channel, which Parry felt an inclination to explore, and more than one of the present party betrayed to me a similar inclination, which I discouraged, no one venturing to conjecture even to what extent it might go, or into what difficulties it might lead.

"Under all these circumstances, it would be an act of folly to pronounce any opinion of the state, condition, or position of those two ships; they are well suited for their purpose, and the only doubt I have is that of their being hampered by the screws among the ice."

Sir James C. Ross, in his outline of a plan for affording relief, submitted to the Admiralty in December, 1847, suggested that two ships should be sent out to examine Wellington Channel, alluded to in the foregoing memorandum of Sir John Barrow, and the coast between Capes Clarence and Walker. A convenient winter harbor might be found for one of the ships near Garnier Bay or Cape Rennell. From this position the coast line could be explored as far as it extended to the westward, by detached parties, early in the spring, as well as the western coast of Boothia, a considerable distance to the southward; and at a more advanced period of the season the whole distance to Cape Nicolai might be completed.

The other ship should then proceed alone to the westward, endeavoring to reach Winter Harbor, in Melville Island, or some convenient port in Banks' Land, in which to pass the winter.

From these points parties might be sent out early in the spring.

The first party should be directed to trace the western coast of Banks' Land, and proceed direct to Cape Bathurst or Cape Parry, on each of which Sir John Richardson proposes to leave depots of provisions for its use, and then to reach the Hudson's Bay Company's settlement at Fort Good Hope, on the Mackenzie, whence they might travel by the usual route of the traders to the principal settlement, and thence to England.

The second party should explore the eastern shore of Banks' Land, and make for Cape Krusenstern, where, or at Cape Hearne, they will find a *cache* of provision left by Sir John Richardson, with whom this party may communicate, and whom it may assist in completing the examination of Wollaston and Victoria Lands, or return to England by the route he shall deem most advisable.

Sir James Ross was intrusted with the carrying out

of this search, in the Enterprise and Investigator, and an account of the voyage and proceedings of these vessels will be found recorded in its chronological order.

The following letter from Dr. Richard King to the Lords of the Admiralty contains some useful suggestions, although it is mixed up with a good deal of egotistical remark:—

"17, *Saville Row*, *February*, 1848.

"'The old route of Parry, through Lancaster Sound and Barrow's Strait, as far as to the last land on its southern shore, and thence in a direct line to Behring's Straits, is the route ordered to be pursued by Franklin.'*

"The gallant officer has thus been dispatched to push his adventurous way between Melville Island and Banks' Land, which Sir E. Parry attempted for two years unsuccessfully. After much toil and hardship, and the best consideration that great man could give to the subject, he recorded, at the moment of retreat, in indelible characters, these impressive thoughts: 'We have been lying near our present station, with an easterly wind blowing fresh, for thirty-six hours together, and although this was considerably off the land, the ice had not during the whole of that time moved a single yard from the shore, affording a proof that there was no space in which the ice was at liberty to move to the westward. The navigation of this part of the Polar Sea is only to be performed by watching the occasional opening between the ice and the shore, and therefore, a continuity of land is essential for this purpose; such a continuity of land, which was here about to fail, as must necessarily be furnished by the northern coast of America, in whatsoever latitude it may be found.' Assuming, therefore, Sir John Franklin has been arrested between Melville Island and Banks' Land, where Sir E. Parry was arrested by difficulties which he considered insurmountable, and he has followed the advice of that gallant officer, and

* Barrow's Arctic Voyages, p. 11.

made for the continuity of America, he will have turned the prows of his vessel south and west, according as Banks' Land tends for Victoria or Wollaston Lands. It is here, therefore, that we may expect to find the expedition wrecked, whence they will make in their boats for the western land of North Somerset, if that land should not be too far distant.

"In order to save the party from the ordeal of a fourth winter, when starvation must be their lot, I propose to undertake the boldest journey that has ever been attempted in the northern regions of America, one which was justifiable only from the circumstances. I propose to attempt to reach the western land of North Somerset or the eastern portion of Victoria Land, as may be deemed advisable, by the close of the approaching summer; to accomplish, in fact, in one summer that which has not been done under two.

"I rest my hope of success in the performance of this Herculean task upon the fact, that I possess an intimate knowledge of the country and the people through which I shall have to pass, the health to stand the rigor of the climate, and the strength to undergo the fatigue of mind and body to which I must be subjected. A glance at the map of North America, directed to Behring's Strait in the Pacific, Barrow's Strait in the Atlantic, and the land of North Somerset between them, will make it apparent that, to render assistance to a party situated on that coast, there are two ways by sea and one by land. Of the two sea-ways, the route by the Pacific is altogether out of the question; it is an idea of by-gone days; while that by the Atlantic is so doubtful of success, that it is merely necessary, to put this assistance aside as far from certain, to mention that Sir John Ross found Barrow's Strait closed in the summer of 1832. To a land journey, then, alone we can look for success; for the failure of a land journey would be the exception to the rule, while the sea expedition would be the rule itself. To the western land of North Somerset, where Sir John Franklin is likely to be found, the Great Fish River is the direct and only route; and although the approach to it is through a country too poor and too difficult of access to admit of the transport of provisions, it may be made the medium of communication between the lost expedition and the civilized world, and guides be thus placed at their disposal to convey them to the hunting grounds of the Indians. Without such guides it is impossible that they can reach these hunting grounds. It was by the Great Fish River that I reached the Polar Sea while acting as second officer, in search of Sir John Ross. I feel it my duty, therefore, as one of two officers so peculiarly circumstanced, at the present moment to place my views on record, as an earnest of my sincerity. Even if it should be determined to try and force provision vessels through Barrow's Strait, and scour the vicinity in boats for the lost expedition, and should it succeed, it will be satisfactory to know that such a mission as I have proposed should be adopted; while, if these attempts should fail, and the service under consideration be put aside, it will be a source of regret that not only the nation at large will feel, but the whole civilized world. When this regret is felt, and every soul has perished, such a mission as I have proposed will be urged again and again for adoption; for it is impossible that the country will rest satisfied until a search be made for the remains of the lost expedition.

"The fact that all lands which have a western aspect are generally ice-free, which I dwelt largely upon when Sir John Franklin sailed, must have had weight with the gallant officer; he will therefore, on finding himself in a serious difficulty, while pushing along the eastern side of Victoria Land, at once fall upon the western land of North Somerset, as a refuge ground, if he have the opportunity. The effort by Behring's Strait and Banks' Land is praiseworthy in attempt, but forlorn in hope. In the former effort, it is assumed that Sir John Franklin has made the passage, and that his arrest is between the Mackenzie River and Icy Cape; in the latter, that Sir James Ross will reach Banks' Land, and trace its continuity to Victoria and Wollaston Land,

and thus make the 'passage.' First, We have no reason to believe that Sir John Franklin and Sir James Ross will be more fortunate than their predecessors, and we cannot trust to their success. Secondly, We are unable to assume that Sir James Ross will reach Bank's Land ; Sir E. Parry was unable to reach it, and only viewed it from a distance ; much less are we able to assume that the gallant officer will find a high road to Victoria Land, which is altogether a *terra incognita.*

"Mr. T. Simpson, who surveyed the arctic coast comprised between the Coppermine and Castor and Pollux Rivers, has set that question at rest, and is the only authority upon the subject. 'A further exploration,' remarks Mr. Simpson, from the most eastern limit of his journey, 'would necessarily demand the whole time and energies of another expedition, having some point of retreat much nearer to the scene of operations than Great Bear Lake, and Great Bear Lake is to be the retreat of Sir John Richardson.'

"What retreat could Mr. Simpson have meant but Great Slave Lake, the retreat of the land party in search of Sir John Ross? and what other road to the unexplored ground, the western land of North Somerset, could that traveler have meant than Great Fish River, that stream which I have pointed out as the ice free and high road to the land where the lost expedition is likely to be found,— to be the boundary of that passage which for three and a half centuries we have been in vain endeavoring to reach in ships?"

Captain Sir W. E. Parry, to whom Dr. King's proposal was submitted by the Admiralty, thus comments on it :—

"My former opinion, quoted by Dr. King, as to the difficulty of ships penetrating to the westward beyond Cape Dundas, (the southwestern extremity of Melville Island,) remains unaltered ; and I should expect that Sir John Franklin, being aware of this difficulty, would use his utmost efforts to get to the southward and westward before he approached that point, that is, between the 100th and 110th degree of longitude. The more I have considered this subject, (which has naturally occupied much of my attention lately,) the more difficult I find it to conjecture where the expedition may have stopped, either with or without any serious accident to the ships; but as no information has reached us up to this time, I conceive that there is some considerable probability of their being situated somewhere between the longitude I have just named; how far they may have penetrated to the southward, between those meridians, must be a matter of speculation, depending on the state of the ice, and the existence of land in a space hitherto blank on our maps.

"Be this as it may, I consider it not improbable, as suggested by Dr. King, that an attempt will be made by them to fall back on the western coast of North Somerset, wherever that may be found, as being the nearest point affording a hope of communication, either with whalers or with ships sent expressly in search of the expedition.

"Agreeing thus far with Dr. King, I am compelled to differ with him entirely as to the readiest mode of reaching that coast, because I feel satisfied that, with the resources of the expedition now equipping under Sir James Ross, the energy, skill, and intelligence of that officer will render it a matter of no very difficult enterprise to examine the coast in question, either with his ships, boats, or traveling parties; whereas an attempt to reach that coast by an expedition from the continent of America must, as it appears to me, be extremely hazardous and uncertain. And as I understand it to be their lordships' intention to direct Sir James Ross to station one of his ships somewhere about Cape Walker, while the other proceeds on the search, and likewise to equip his boats specially for the purpose of examining the various coasts and inlets, I am decidedly of opinion, that, as regards the western coast of North Somerset, this plan will be much more likely to answer the proposed object, than any overland expedition. This object will, of course, be the more easily accomplished in case of Sir James Ross finding the western coast of North Somerset navigable for his ships.

"In regard to Dr. King's suggestion respecting Vic toria Land and Wollaston Land, supposing Sir John Franklin's ships to have been arrested between the meridians to which I have already alluded, it does seem, by an inspection of the map, not improbable that parties may attempt to penetrate to the continent in that direction; but not being well acquainted with the facilities for reaching the coast of America opposite those lands in the manner proposed by Dr. King, I am not competent to judge of its practicability."

Nearly the whole of the west coast of North Somerset and Boothia was, (it will be found hereafter,) explored by parties in boats detached from Sir James Ross's ships in 1849.

I append, also, the most important portions of Sir James Ross's remarks on Dr. King's plan.

"Dr. King begins by assuming that Sir John Franklin has attempted to push the ships through to the westward, between Melville Island and Banks' Land, (although directly contrary to his instructions;) that having been arrested by insurmountable difficulties, he would have 'turned the prows of his vessels to the south and west, according as Banks' Land tends for Victoria or Wollaston Land;' and having been wrecked, or from any other cause obliged to abandon their ships, their crews would take to the boats, and make for the west coast of North Somerset.

"If the expedition had failed to penetrate to the westward between Banks' Land and Melville Island, it is very probable it would have next attempted to gain the continent by a more southerly course; and supposing that, after making only small progress, (say 100 miles,) to the southwest, it should have been then finally stopped or wrecked, the calamity will have occurred in about latitude 72½° N., and longitude 115° W. This point is only 280 miles from the Coppermine River and 420 miles from the Mackenzie, either of which would, therefore, be easily attainable, and at each of which, abundance of provision might be procured by them, and their return to England a measure of no great difficulty.

"At the point above mentioned, the distance from the west coast of North Somerset is probably about 360 miles, and the mouth of the Great Fish River full 500; at neither of these places could they hope to obtain a single day's provisions for so large a party; and Sir John Franklin's intimate knowledge of the impossibility of ascending that river, or obtaining any food for his party in passing through the Barren grounds, would concur in deterring him from attempting to gain either of these points.

"I think it most probable that, from the situation pointed out, he would, when compelled to abandon his ships, endeavor in the boats to retrace his steps, and passing through the channel by which he had advanced, and which we have always found of easy navigation, seek the whale ships which annually visit the west coast of Baffin's Bay.

"It is far more probable, however, that Sir John Franklin, in obedience to his instructions, would en deavor to push the ships to the south and west as soon as they passed Cape Walker, and the consequence of such a measure, owing to the known prevalence of westerly wind, and the drift of the main body of the ice, would be (in my opinion) their inevitable embarrassment, and if he persevered in that direction which he probably would do, I have no hesitation in stating my conviction he would never be able to extricate his ships, and would ultimately be obliged to abandon them. It is therefore in latitude 73° N. and longitude 105° W. that we may expect to find them involved in the ice, or shut up in some harbor. This is almost the only point in which it is likely they would be detained, or from which it would not be possible to convey information of their situation to the Hudson's Bay Settlements.

"If, then, we suppose the crews of the ships should be compelled, either this autumn or next spring, to abandon their vessels at or near this point, they would most assuredly endeavor, in their boats, to reach Lancaster Sound; but I cannot conceive any position in which they could be placed from which they would make for the Great Fish River, or at which any party descending that river would be likely to overtake them; and even if it did, of what advantage could it be to them?

"If Dr. King and his party, in their single canoe, did fall in with Sir John Franklin and his party on the west coast of North Somerset, how does he propose to assist them? he would barely have sufficient provision for his own party, and would more probably be in a condition to require rather than afford relief. He could only tell them what Sir John Franklin already knows, from former experience, far better than Dr. King, that it would be impossible for so large a party, or indeed any party not previously provided, to travel across the barren grounds to any of the Hudson's Bay Settlements."

"All that has been done by the way of search since February, 1848, tends," persists Dr. King, "to draw attention closer and closer to the western land of North Somerset, as the position of Sir John Franklin, and to the Great Fish (or Back) River, as the high road to reach it."

Dr. King has twice proposed to the Admiralty to proceed on the search by this route. "It would," he states, "be the happiest moment of my life (and my delight at being selected from a long list of volunteers, for the relief of Sir John Ross, was very great) if their lordships would allow me to go by my old route, the Great Fish River, to attempt to save human life a second time on the shores of the Polar Sea. What I did in search of Sir John Ross is the best earnest of what I could do in search of Sir John Franklin."

A meeting of those officers and gentlemen most conversant with arctic voyages was convened by the Lords Commissioners of the Admiralty on the 17th of January, 1849, at which the following were present:—Rear-Admiral Sir Francis Beaufort, K. C. B., Captain Sir W. E. Parry, R. N., Captain Sir George Back, R.

N., Captain Sir E. Belcher, R. N., Colonel Sabine, R. A., and the Rev. Dr. Scoresby.

A very pretty painting, containing portraits of all the principal arctic voyagers in consultation on these momentous matters, has been made by Mr. Pearse, artist, of 53, Berners Street, Oxford Street, which is well worthy of a visit. The beautiful Arctic Panorama of Mr. Burford, in Leicester Square, will also give a graphic idea of the scenery and appearance of the icy regions; the whole being designed from authentic sketches by Lieut. Browne, now of the Resolute, and who was out in the Enterprise in her trip in 1848, and also with Sir James Ross in his antarctic voyage.

The expedition under Sir James Ross having returned unsuccessful, other measures of relief were now determined on, and the opinions of the leading officers again taken.

Admiral Sir Francis Beaufort, in his report to the Lords Commissioners of the Admiralty, on November 24th, 1849, observes: —

"There are four ways only in which it is likely that the Erebus and Terror would have been lost — by fire, by sunken rocks, by storm, or by being crushed between two fields of ice. Both vessels would scarcely have taken fire together; if one of them had struck on a rock the other would have avoided the danger. Storms in those narrow seas, encumbered with ice, raise no swell, and could produce no such disaster; and therefore, by the fourth cause alone could the two vessels have been at once destroyed; and even in that case the crews would have escaped upon the ice (as happens every year to the whalers;) they would have saved their loose boats, and reached some part of the American shores. As no traces of any such event have been found on any part of those shores, it may therefore be safely affirmed that one ship at least, and both the crews, are still in existence; and therefore the point where they now are is the great matter for consideration.

"Their orders would have carried them toward Melville Island, and then out to the westward, where it is therefore probable that they are entangled among islands and ice. For should they have been arrested at some intermediate place, for instance, Cape Walker, or at one of the northern chain of islands, they would, undoubtedly, in the course of the three following years, have contrived some method of sending notices of their position to the shores of North Somerset or to Barrow's Strait.

"If they had reached much to the southward of Bank's Land, they would surely have communicated with the tribes on Mackenzie River; and if, failing to get to the westward or southward, they had returned with the intention of penetrating through Wellington Channel, they would have detached parties on the ice toward Barrow's Strait, in order to have deposited statements of their intentions.

"The general conclusion, therefore, remains, that they are still locked up in the Archipelago to the westward of Melville Island. Now, it is well known that the state of the weather alternates between the opposite sides of Northern America, being mild on the one when rigorous on the other; and accordingly, during the two last years, which have been unusually severe in Baffin's Bay, the United States whalers were successfully traversing the Polar Sea to the northward of Behring's Straits. The same severe weather may possibly prevail on the eastern side during the summer of 1850, and if so, it is obvious that an attempt should be now made by the western opening, and not merely to receive the two ships, if they should be met coming out (as formerly,) but to advance in the direction of Melville Island, resolutely entering the ice, and employing every possible expedient by sledging parties, by reconnoitering balloons, and by blasting the ice, to communicate with them.

"These vessels should be intrepidly commanded, effectively manned, and supplied with the best means for traveling across the ice to the English or to the Russian settlements, as it will be of the greatest importance to be informed of what progress the expedition has made; and for this purpose likewise the Plover will be of material service, lying at some advanced point near Icy Cape, and ready to receive intelligence, and to convey it to Petropaulski or to Panama.

"These vessels should enter Behring's Straits before the first of August, and therefore every effort should be now made to dispatch them from England before Christmas. They might water at the Falkland Islands, and again at the Sandwich Islands, where they would be ready to receive additional instructions via Panama, by one of the Pacific steamers, and by which vessel they might be pushed on some little distance to the northward.

"It seems to me likely that the ships have been pushing on, summer after summer, in the direction of Behring's Straits, and are detained somewhere in the space southwestward of Banks' Land. On the other hand, should they, after the first or second summer, have been unsuccessful in that direction, they may have attempted to proceed to the northward, either through Wellington Channel, or through some other of the openings among the same group of islands. I do not myself attach any superior importance to Wellington Channel as regards the northwest passage, but I understand that Sir John Franklin did, and that he strongly expressed to Lord Haddington his intention of attempting that route, if he should fail in effecting the more direct passage to the westward.

"The ships having been fully victualed for three years, the resources may, by due precautions, have been extended to four years for the whole crews; but it has occurred to me, since I had the honor of conferring with their lordships, that, if their numbers have been gradually diminished to any considerable extent by death, (a contingency which is but too probable, considering their unparalleled detention in the ice,) the resources would be proportionably extended for the survivors, whom it might, therefore, be found expedient to transfer to one of the ships, with all the remaining stores, and with that one ship to continue the endeavor to push westward, or to return to the eastward, as circumstances might render expedient; in that case, the necessity for quitting both the ships in the past summer might not improbably have been obviated.

"Under these circumstances, which, it must be admitted, amount to no more than mere conjecture, it seems to me expedient still to prosecute the search in both directions, namely, by way of Behring's Strait (to which I look with the strongest hope,) and also by that of Barrow's Strait. In the latter direction, it ought, I think, to be borne in mind, that the more than usual difficulties with which Sir James Ross had to contend, have, in reality, left us with very little more information than before he left England, and I cannot contemplate without serious apprehension, leaving that opening without still further search in the ensuing spring, in case the missing crews have fallen back to the eastern coast of North Somerset, where they would naturally look for supplies to be deposited for them, in addition to the chance of finding some of those left by the Fury. For the purpose of further pursuing the search by way of Barrow's Strait, perhaps two small vessels of 150 or 200 tons might suffice, but they must be square rigged for the navigation among the ice. Of course the object of such vessels would be nearly that which Sir James Ross's endeavors have failed to accomplish; and the provisions, &c., left by that officer at Whaler Point, as well as any which may be deposited in that neighborhood by the North Star, would greatly add to the resources, facilitate the operations, and lessen the risk of any attempt made in that direction.

"If, however, there be time to get ships to Behring's Straits by the first week in August, 1850, which would perhaps require the aid of steam vessels to accomplish with any degree of certainty, I recommend that the Enterprise and Investigator be forthwith equipped and dispatched there, with instructions to push through the ice to the E. N. E. as far as possible in the ensuing season, with the hope of meeting with at least one of the ships, or any of the parties which may have been detached from them. This attempt has never yet been made by any ships, and I cling very strongly to the belief that such an effort might be attended with success in rescuing at least a portion of our people.

"My reason for urging this upon their Lordships is, that the admirable instructions under which the Plover, assisted by the Herald, is acting, embraces only the search of the coast line eastward from Icy Cape; since the boats and baidars cannot effect any thing except by creeping along as opportunities offer, between the ice and the land, so that this plan of operations meets only the contingency of parties reaching, or nearly reaching, the land; whereas the chance of rescue would, as it appears to me, be immensely increased by ships pushing on, clear of the coast, toward Banks' Land and Melville Island, as far at least as might be practicable in the best five or six weeks of the season of 1850."

Captain Parry says—"Although this is the first attempt ever made to enter the ice in this direction, with ships properly equipped for the purpose, there is no reason to anticipate any greater difficulties in this navigation than those encountered in other parts of the North Polar Sea; and, even in the event of not succeeding in reaching Banks' Land in the summer of the present year, it may be possible to make such progress as to afford a reasonable hope of effecting that object in the following season (1851.) Indeed it is possible that, from the well known fact of the climate being more temperate in a given parallel of latitude, in going westward from the Mackenzie River, some comparative advantage may be derived in the navigation of this part of the Polar Sea.

"It is of importance to the security of the ships and of their crews that they should winter in some harbor or bay not at a distance from land, where the ice might be in motion during the winter; and it will be desirable, should no land be discovered fit for this purpose, in the space at present unexplored between Point Barrow and Banks' Land, that endeavors should be made to reach the continent about the mouth of the Mackenzie

River, or further eastward, toward Liverpool Bay, where there is reason to suppose that sufficient shelter may be found, and in which neighborhood, it appears, there is generally no ice to be seen from the shore for about six weeks in the months of August and September. Sir John Franklin's narrative of his second journey, that of Messrs. Dease and Simpson, and the Admiralty Charts, will furnish the requisite hydrographical information relative to this line of coast, so far as it has been attained.

"The utmost economy should be exercised in the use of provisions and fuel during the time the ships are in winter quarters; and if they should winter on or near the continent, there would probably be an opportunity of increasing their stock of provisions by means of game or fish, and likewise of fuel, by drift or other wood, to some considerable amount.

"If the progress of the ships in 1850 has been considerable — for instance, as far as the meridian of 120° W.— the probability is, that the most practicable way of returning to England will be, still to push on in the same direction during the whole season of 1851, with a view to reach Barrow's Strait, and take advantage, if necessary, of the resources left by Captain Sir James Ross at Whaler Point, near Leopold Harbor; if not the same season, at least after a second winter. If, on the other hand, small progress should have been made to the eastward at the close of the present summer, it might be prudent that when half the navigable season of 1851 shall have expired, no further attempts should be made in proceeding to the eastward, and that the remaining half of that season should be occupied in returning to the westward, with a view to escape from the ice by way of Behring's Straits after the winter of 1851–52, so as not to incur the risk of passing a third winter in the ice.

"During the summer season, the most vigilant lookout should be kept from the mast-heads of both ships night and day, not only for the missing ships, but for any detached parties belonging to them; and during the few hours of darkness which prevail toward the close of each season's navigation, and also when in winter quarters, signals, by fires, blue lights, rockets or guns, should be made as the means of pointing out the position of the ships to any detached parties belonging to the missing expedition. And in the spring before the ships can be released from the ice, searching parties might be sent out in various directions, either in boats or by land, to examine the neighboring coasts and inlets for any trace of the missing crews."

Captain Sir George Back also comments (1st of December, 1849,) on these intentions, in a letter to the Secretary of the Admiralty :—

"You will be pleased, Sir, to impress upon my Lords Commissioners, that I wholly reject all and every idea of any attempts on the part of Sir John Franklin to send boats or detachments over the ice to any part of the main-land eastward of the Mackenzie River, because I can say from experience, that no toil-worn and exhausted party could have the least chance of existence by going there.

"On the other hand, from my knowledge of Sir John Franklin, (having been three times on discovery together,) I much doubt if he would quit his ship at all, except in a boat; for any attempt to cross the ice a long distance on foot would be tempting death; and it is too laborious a task to sledge far over such an uneven surface as those regions generally present. That great mortality must have occurred, and that one ship, as Sir E. Beaufort hints at, may be lost, are greatly to be feared; and, as on all former expeditions, if the survivors are paralyzed by the depressing attacks of scurvy, it would then be impossible for them, however desirous they might be, to leave the ship, which must thus become their last most anxious abode.

"If, however, open water should have allowed Sir John Franklin to have resorted to his boats, then I am persuaded he would make for either the Mackenzie River, or, which is far more likely, from the almost *certainty he must have felt of finding provision*, Cape Clarence and Fury Point.

"I am aware that the whole cnances of life in this painful case depend on food; but when I reflect on Sir John Franklin's former extraordinary preservation under miseries and trials of the most severe description, living often on scraps of old leather and other refuse, I cannot despair of his finding the means to prolong existence till aid be happily sent him."

Dr. Sir John Richardson on the same day also sends in his opinion, as requested, on the proposed dispatch of the Enterprise and Investigator to Behring's Strait:

"It seems to me to be very desirable that the western shores of the Archipelago of Parry's Islands should be searched in a high latitude in the manner proposed by the hydrographer.

"If the proposed expedition succeeds in establishing its winter quarters among these islands, parties detached over the ice may travel to the eastward and southeastward, so as to cross the line of search which it is hoped Mr. Rae has been able to pursue in the present summer, and thus to determine whether any traces of the missing ships exist in localities the most remote from Behring's Strait and Lancaster Sound, and from whence shipwrecked crews would find the greatest difficulty in traveling to any place where they could hope to find relief.

"The climate of Arctic America improves in a sensible manner with an increase of western longitude. On the Mackenzie, on the 135th meridian, the summer is warmer than in any district of the continent in the same parallel, and it is still finer, and the vegetation more luxuriant on the banks of the Yucon, on the 150th meridian. This superiority of climate leads me to infer, that ships well fortified against drift-ice, will find the navigation of the Arctic Seas more practicable in its western portion than it has been found to the eastward. This inference is supported by my own personal experience, as far as it goes. I met with no ice in the month of August, on my late voyage, till I attained the 123d meridian, and which I was led, from that circumstance, to suppose coincided with the western limits of Parry's Archipelago.

'The greater facility of navigating from the west has been powerfully advocated by others on former occasions; and the chief, perhaps the only reason why the attempt to penetrate the Polar Sea from that quarter has not been resumed since the time of Cook is, that the length of the previous voyage to Behring's Strait would considerably diminish the store of provisions; but the facilities of obtaining supplies in the Pacific are now so augmented, that this objection has no longer the same force."

Captain F. W. Beechey, writing from Cheltenham, on the 1st of December, 1849, says:—

"I quite agree with Sir Francis Beaufort in what he has stated with regard to any casualties which Sir J. Franklin's ships may have sustained, and entirely agree with him and Sir Edward Parry, that the expedition is probably hampered among the ice somewhere to the southwestward of Melville Island; but there is yet a possibility which does not appear to have been contemplated, which is, that of the scurvy having spread among the crew, and incapacitated a large proportion of them from making any exertion toward their release, or that the whole, in a debilitated state, may yet be clinging by their vessels, existing sparingly upon the provision which a large mortality may have spun out, in the hope of relief.

"In the first case, that of the ships being hampered and the crews in good health, I think it certain that, as the resources of the ships would be expended in May last, Sir John Franklin and his crew have abandoned the ships, and pushed forward for the nearest point where they might reasonably expect assistance, and which they could reasonably reach.

"There are consequently three points to which it would be proper to direct attention, and as the case is urgent, every possible method of relief should be energetically pushed forward at as early a period as possible, and directed to those points, which, I need scarcely say, are Barrow's Strait, Behring's Strait, and the northern coast of America.

"Of the measures which can be resorted to on the northern coast of America, the officers who have had experience there, and the Hudson's Bay Company, will be able to judge; but I am of opinion that nothing should be neglected in that quarter; for it seems to me almost certain that Sir John Franklin and his crew, if able to travel, have abandoned their ships and made for the continent; and if they have not succeeded in gaining the Hudson's Bay outposts, they have been overtaken by winter before they could accomplish their purpose.

"Lastly as to the opinion which naturally forces itself upon us, as to the utility of the sending relief to persons whose means of subsistence will have failed them more than a year by the time the relief could reach them, I would observe, that a prudent reduction of the allowance may have been timely made to meet an emergency, or great mortality may have enabled the survivors to subsist up to the time required, or it may be that the crews have just missed reaching the points visited by our parties last year before they quitted them, and in the one case may now be subsisting on the supplies at Leopold Island, or be housed in eastward of Point Barrow, sustained by depots which have been fallen in with, or by the native supplies; so that under all the circumstances, I do not consider their condition so utterly hopeless that we should give up the expectation of yet being able to render them a timely assistance.

"The endeavors to push forward might be continued until the 30th of August, at latest, at which time, if the ships be not near some land where they can conveniently pass a winter, they must direct their course for the main-land, and seek a secure harbor in which they could remain. And on no account should they risk a winter in the pack, in consequence of the tides and shallow water lying off the coast.

"Should the expedition reach Herschel Island, or any other place of refuge on the coast near the mouth of the Mackenzie or Colville Rivers, endeavors should be made to communicate information of the ships' position and summer's proceedings through the Hudson's Bay Company or Russian settlements, and by means of interpreters; and no opportunity should be omitted of gaining from the natives information of the missing vessels, as well as of any boat expeditions that may have gone forward, as well as of the party under Dr. Rae.

"If nothing should be heard of Sir John Franklin in 1850, parties of observation should be sent forward in the spring to intercept the route the ship would have pursued, and in other useful directions between winter quarters and Melville Island; taking especial care that they return to the ship before the time of liberation of the ships arrives, which greatly depends upon their locality.

"Then, on the breaking up of the ice, should any favorable appearance of the ice present itself, the expedition might be left free to take advantage of such a prospect, or to return round Point Barrow; making it imperative, however, either to insure their return, so far as human foresight may be exercised, or the certainty of their reaching Melville Island at the close of that season, and so securing their return to England in 1852.

"If, after all, any unforeseen event should detain the ships beyond the period contemplated above, every exertion should be used, by means of boats and interpreters, to communicate with the Mackenzie; and should any casualty render it necessary to abandon the vessels, it should be borne in mind that the reserve-ship will remain at her quarters until the autumn of 1853, unless she hears of the safety of the ships and boats in other directions; while in the other quarter, Fort Macpherson, at the entrance of the Mackenzie, may be relied upon as an asylum.

"The Plover, or reserve-ship, should be provided with three years' provisions for her own crew, and for contingencies besides. She should be placed as near as possible to Point Barrow, and provided with interpreters, and the means of offering rewards for information; and she should remain at her quarters so long as there can be any occasion for her presence in the Arctic Seas; or, if she does not hear any thing of the expedition under Captain Collinson, as long as her provisions will last."

Sir John Richardson offers the following advice for this expedition:—"If," he says, "it should winter near the mouth of the Yucan or Colville, that river may be ascended in a boat in the month of June, before the sea ice begins to give way. The river varies in width from a mile and a half to two miles, and flows through a rich, well-wooded valley, abounding in moose deer, and having a comparatively mild climate. A Russian trading post has been built on it, at the dis tance of three or four days' voyage from the sea, with the current; but as the current is strong, from nine to twelve days must be allowed for its ascent, with the tracking line. It would be unsafe to rely upon receiving a supply of provisions at the Russian post, as it is not likely that any stock beyond what is necessary for their own use is laid up by the traders; and the moose deer being a very shy animal, is not easily shot by an unpracticed hunter; but the reindeer abound on the neighboring hills, and are much more approachable. The white-fronted goose also breeds in vast flocks in that district of the country, and may be killed in numbers, without difficulty, in the month of June.

"If the expedition should winter within a reasonable distance of the Mackenzie, Captain Collinson may have it in his power to send dispatches to England by that route.

"The river opens in June, and as soon as the ice ceases to drive, may be ascended in a boat, with a fair wind, under sail, or with a tracking line.

"The lowest post at present occupied by the Hudson's Bay Company on this river is Fort Good Hope. The site of this post has been changed several times, but it is at this time on the right bank of the river, in latitude 66° 16′ N., and is ten or eleven days' voyage from the sea. At Point Separation, opposite to the middle channel of the delta of the river, and on the promontory which separates the Peel and the Mackenzie, there is a case of pemmican (80 lbs.) buried, ten feet distant from a tree, which has its middle branches lopped off, and is marked on the trunk with a broad arrow in black paint. A fire was made over the pit in which the case is concealed, and the remains of the charcoal will point out the exact spot. This hoard was visited last year by a party from Fort Macpherson, Peel's River, when all was safe.

"Eight bags of pemmican, weighing 90 lbs. each, were deposited at Fort Good Hope in 1848, and would remain there last summer for the use of any boat parties that might ascend the river in 1849; but it is probable that part, or the whole, may have been used by the Company by next year.

"A boat party should be furnished with a small seine and a short herring net, by the use of which a good supply of fish may often be procured in the eddies or sandy bays of the Mackenzie. They should also be provided with a good supply of buck-shot, swan-shot, duck-shot, and gunpowder. The Loucheux and Hare Indians will readily give such provisions as they may happen to have, in exchange for ammunition. They will expect to receive tobacco gratuitously, as they are accustomed to do from the traders.

"The Mackenzie is the only water-way by which any of the Hudson's Bay Company's posts can be reached from the Arctic Sea. There is a post on the Peel River which enters the delta of the Mackenzie, but no supplies can be procured there. To the eastward of the Mackenzie no ship-party would have a chance of reaching a trading post, the nearest to the sea being Fort Resolution, on Great Slave Lake, situated on the 61st parallel of latitude, and the intervening hilly country, intersected by numerous lakes and rapid rivers, could not be crossed by such a party in less than an entire summer, even could they depend on their guns for a supply of food. Neither would be advisable for a party from the ships to attempt to reach the posts on the Mackenzie by way of the Coppermine River and Fort Confidence; as, in the absence of means of transport across Great Bear Lake, the journey round that irregular sheet of water, would be long and hazardous. Bear Lake River is more than fifty miles long, and Fort Norman, the nearest post on the Mackenzie, is thirty miles above its mouth. Mr. Rae was instructed to engage an Indian family or two to hunt on the tract of country between the Coppermine and Great Bear Lake in the summer of 1850; but no great reliance can be placed on these Indians remaining long there, as they desert their hunting quarters on very slight alarms, being in continual dread of enemies, real or imaginary.

"A case of pemmican was buried on the summit of the bank, about four or five miles from the summit of Cape Bathurst, the spot being marked by a pole planted in the earth, and the exact locality of the deposit by a fire of drift-wood, much of which would remain unconsumed.

"Another case was deposited in the cleft of a rock, on a small battlemented cliff, which forms the extreme part of Cape Parry. The case was covered with loose stones; and a pile of stones painted red and white, was erected immediately in front of it. This cliff resembles a cocked-hat in some points of view, and projects like a tongue from the base of a rounded hill, which is 500 or 600 feet high.

"Several cases of pemmican were left exposed on a ledge of rocks in latitude 68° 35′ N., opposite Lambert Island, in Dolphin and Union Strait, and in a bay to the westward of Cape Krusenstern, a small boat and ten pieces of pemmican were deposited under a high cliff, above high water mark, without concealment. The Esquimaux on this part of the coast are not numerous, and from the position of this hoard, it may escape discovery by them; but I have every reason to believe that the locality has been visited by Mr. Rae in the past summer. A deposit of larger size, near Cape Kendall, has been more certainly visited by Mr. Rae."

Captain Sir J. C. Ross writes from Haslar, 11th of February, 1850.

"With respect to the probable position of the Erebus and Terror, I consider that it is hardly possible they can be anywhere to the eastward of Melville Island, or within 300 miles of Leopold Island, for if that were the case, they would assuredly, during the last spring, have made their way to that point, with the hope of receiving assistance from the whale-ships which, for several years previous to the departure of that expedition from England, had been in the habit of visiting Prince Regent Inlet in pursuit of whales; and in that case they must have been met with, or marks of their encampments have been found by some of the numerous parties detached from the Enterprise and Investigator along the shores of that vicinity during the only period of the season in which traveling is practicable in those regions.

"It is probable, therefore, that during their first summer, which was remarkably favorable for the navigation of those seas, they have been enabled (in obedience to their orders) to push the ships to the westward of Banks' land, and have there become involved in the heavy pack of ice which was observed from Melville Island always to be setting past its westernmost point in a southeast direction, and from which pack they may not have been able to extricate their ships.

"From such a position, retreat to the eastward would be next to impossible, while the journey to the Mackenzie River, of comparatively easy accomplishment, together with Sir John Franklin's knowledge of the resources in the way and of its practicability, would strengthen the belief that this measure will have been adopted by them during the last spring.

"If this be assumed as the present position of the Erebus and Terror, it would manifestly be far more easy and safe to afford them relief by means of an expedition entering Behring's Straits, than from any other direction, as it would not be necessary for the ships to depart so far from the coast of North America as to preclude their keeping up a regular communication with the Russian settlements on the River Colville, or those of the Hudson's Bay Company near the mouth of the Mackenzie, while the whole space between any position in which the ships might winter, and Banks' Land could be thoroughly examined by traveling parties early in the spring, or by boats or steam launches at a more advanced period of the following season."

Mr. W. Snow, in a letter from New York, dated 7th of January, 1850, suggests a plan for a well organized expedition of as many men as could be fitted out from private funds. "For instance, let a party of 100 picked men, well disciplined and officered, as on board a ship, and accompanied with all the necessary food, scientific instruments, and every thing useful on such expeditions. proceed immediately, by the shortest and most available routes, to the lands in the neighborhood of the unexplored regions. If possible, I would suggest that they should proceed first to Moose Fort, on the southern part of Hudson's Bay, and thence by small craft to Chesterfield Inlet, or otherwise by land reach that quarter, so as to arrive there at the opening of summer. From this neighborhood let the party, minus ten men, be divided into three separate detachments, each with specific instructions to extend their researches in a northerly and northwesterly direction. The westernmost party to proceed as near as possible in a direct course to the easternmost limits of discovery yet made from Behring's Straits, and on no account to deviate from that course on the western side of it, but, if necessary, to the eastward. Let the central party shape a course as near as possible to the position of the Magnetic Pole; and the easternmost division direct to Prince Regent Inlet, or the westernmost point of discovery from the east, and not to deviate from that course easterly. Let each of these detachments be formed again into three divisions, each division thus consisting of ten men. Let the first division of each detachment pioneer the way, followed on the same track by the second and the third, at stated intervals of time. On the route, let the pioneers, at every spot necessary, leave distinguishing marks to denote the way, and also to give information to either of the other two principal detachments as may by chance fall into their track To second the efforts of the three detachments, let con stant succors and other assistance be forwarded by way of Moose Fort, and through the ten men left at Chesterfield Inlet; and should the object for which such an expedition was framed be happily accomplished by the return of the lost voyagers, let messengers be forwarded with the news, as was done with Captain Back, in the case of Captain Ross. Let each of the extreme detachments, upon arriving at their respective destinations, and upon being joined by the whole of their body, proceed to form plans for uniting with the central party, and ascertaining the results already obtained by each by sending parties in that direction. Also, let a chosen number be sent out from each detachment as exploring parties, wherever deemed requisite; and let no effort be wanted to make a search in every direction where there is a possibility of its proving successful.

"If a public and more extensive expedition be set on foot, I would most respectfully draw attention to the following suggestions:—Let a land expedition be formed upon a similar plan, and with the same number of men, say 300 or more, as those fitted out for sea. Let this expedition be formed into three great divisions; the one proceeding by the Athabasca to the Great Slave Lake, and following out Captain Back's discoveries; the second, through the Churchill district; or, with the third, according to the plan laid out for a private expedition alone; only keeping the whole of their forces as much as possible bearing upon the points where success may be most likely attainable.

"Each of these three great divisions to be subdivided and arranged also as in the former case. The expense of an expedition of this kind, with all the necessary outlay for provisions, &c., I do not think would be more than half what the same would cost if sent by sea; but of this I am not a competent judge, having no definite means to make a comparison. But there is yet another, and, I cannot help conceiving, a more easy way of obviating all difficulty on this point, and of reducing the expense considerably.

"It must be evident that the present position of the arctic voyagers is not very accessible, either by land or sea, else the distinguished leader at the head of the expedition would long ere this have tracked a route whereby the whole party, or at least some of them could return.

"In such a case, therefore, the only way to reach them is by, if I may use the expression, *forcing* an expedition on toward them; I mean, by keeping it constantly upheld and pushing onward. There may be, and indeed there are, very great difficulties, and difficulties of such a nature that, I believe, they would themselves cause another great difficulty in the procuring of men. But, if I might make another bold suggestion, I would respectfully ask our government at home, why not employ picked men from convicted criminals, as is done in exploring expeditions in Australia? Inducements might be held out to them; and by proper care they would be made most serviceable auxiliaries. Generally speaking, men convicted of offenses are men possessed of almost inexhaustible mental resources; and such men are the men who, with physical powers of endurance, are precisely those required. But this I speak of, merely, if sufficient free men could not be found, and if economy is studied."

Mr. John McLean, who has been twenty-five years a partner and officer of the Hudson's Bay Company, and has published an interesting narrative of his adventures and experience, writing to Lady Franklin from Canada West, in January, 1850, suggests the following very excellent plan as likely to produce some intelligence, if not to lead to a discovery of the party.

"Let a small schooner of some thirty or forty tons burden, built with a view to draw as little water as possible, and as strong as wood and iron could make her, be dispatched from England in company with the Hudson's Bay ships. This vessel would, immediately on arriving at York Factory, proceed to the Strait termed Sir Thomas Roe's Welcome, which divides Southampton Island from the main-land; then direct her course to Wager River, and proceed onward until interrupted by insurmountable obstacles. The party being safely landed, I would recommend their remaining stationary until winter traveling became practicable, when they should set out for the shores of the Arctic Sea, which, by a reference to Arrowsmith's map, appears to be only some sixty or seventy miles distant; then dividing in two parties or divisions, the one would proceed east, the other west; and I think means could be devised of exploring 250 or 300 miles in either direction; and here a very important question presents itself,— how and by what means is this enterprise to be accomplished?

"In the first place, the services of Esquimaux would be indispensable, for the twofold reason, that no reliable information can be obtained from the natives without their aid, and that they alone properly understand the art of preparing snow-houses, or 'igloes,' for winter encampment, the only lodging which the desolate wastes of the arctic regions afford. Esquimaux understanding the English language sufficiently well to answer our purpose, frequent the Hudson's Bay Company's post in Labrador, some of whom might be induced, (I should fain hope,) to engage for the expedition, or probably the 'half-breed' natives might do so more readily than the aborigines. They should, if possible, be strong, active men, and good marksmen, and not less than four in number. Failing in the attempt to procure the natives of Labrador, then I should think Esquimaux might be obtained at Churchill, in Hudson's Bay; the two who accompanied Sir John in his first land expedition were from this quarter."

An expedition of this kind is to be sent out by Lady Franklin this spring under the charge of Mr. Kennedy. There are various ways of accomplishing this object, the choice of which must mainly depend on the views and wishes of the officer who may undertake the com mand. Besides the northern route, or that by Regent Inlet, it is possible to reach Sir James Ross and Simpson's Straits from the south, entering Hudson's Bay, and passing up the Welcome to Rae Isthmus, or again by entering Chesterfield or Wager Inlet, and gaining the coast by Back's or the Great Fish River.

By either of these routes a great part of the exploration must be made in boats or on foot. In every case the main points to be searched are James Ross's Strait and Simpson's Strait, if indeed there be a passage in that direction, as laid down in Sir John Franklin's charts, though contradicted by Mr. Rae, and considered still doubtful by some arctic navigators.

The following extract from the Geographical Journal shows the opinion of Franklin upon the search of this quarter. Dr. Richardson says,*—"No better plan can be proposed than the one suggested by Sir John Franklin, of sending a vessel to Wager River, and carrying on the survey from thence in boats."

Sir John Franklin observes,†—"The Doctor alludes in his letter to some propositions which he knew I had made in the year 1828, at the command of his present Majesty, (William IV.,) on the same subject, and particularly to the suggestion as to proceeding from Repulse or Wager Bay. * * * A recent careful reading of all the narratives connected with the surveys of the Wager and Repulse Bays, and of Sir Edward Parry's Voyage, together with the information obtained from the Esquimaux by Sir Edward Parry, Sir John Ross, and Captain Back, confirm me in opinion that a successful delineation of the coast east of Point Turnagain to the Strait of the Fury and Hecla, would be best attained by an expedition proceeding from Wager Bay, the northern parts of which cannot, I think, be farther distant than forty miles from the sea, if the information received by the above-mentioned officers can be depended on."

Dr. McCormick particularly draws attention to Jones' and Smith's Sounds, recommending a careful examin

* Journal of Geographical Society, vol. vi. p. 40. † Ibid. p. 43.

ation of these to their probable termination in the Polar Sea :—

"Jones' Sound, with the Wellington Channel on the west, may be found to form an island of the land called 'North Devon.' All prominent positions on both sides of these Sounds should be searched for flag staves and piles of stones, under whcih copper cylinders or bottles may have been deposited, containing accounts of the proceedings of the missing expedition ; and if successful in getting upon its track, a clue would be obtained to the fate of our gallant countrymen."

The Wellington Channel he considers affords one of the best chances of crossing the track of the missing expedition.

To carry out this plan efficiently, he recommended that a boat should be dropped, by the ship conveying the searching party out, at the entrance to the Wellington Channel in Barrow's Strait ; from this point one or both sides of that channel and the northern shores of the Parry Islands might be explored as far west as the season would permit of. But should the ship be enabled to look into Jones' Sound, on her way to Lancaster Sound, and find that opening free from ice, an attempt might be made by the Boat Expedition to push through it into the Wellington Channel. In the event, however, of its proving to be merely an inlet, which a short delay would be sufficient to decide, the ship might perhaps be in readiness to pick up the boat on its return, for conveyance to its ultimate destination through Lancaster Sound ; or as a precaution against any unforeseen separation from the ship, a depot of provisions should be left at the entrance to Jones' Sound for the boat to complete its supplies from, after accomplishing the exploration of this inlet, and to afford the means, if compelled from an advanced period of the season or other adverse circumstances, of reaching some place of refuge, either on board a whaler or some one of the depots of provisions on the southern shores of Barrow's Strait.

Mr. Penny, in charge of the Lady Franklin, before sailing, observed :—

"If an early passage be obtained, I would examine Jones' Sound, as I have generally found in all my early voyages clear water at the mouth of that sound, and there is a probability that an earlier passage by this route might be found into Wellington Strait, which outlet ought by all means to be thoroughly examined at the earliest opportunity, since, if Sir J. Franklin had taken that route, with the hope of finding a passage westward, to the north of the Parry and Melville Islands, he may be beyond the power of helping himself. No trace of the expedition, or practical communication with Wellington Strait, being obtained in this quarter, I would proceed in time to take advantage of the first opening of the ice in Lancaster Sound, with the view of proceeding to the west and entering Wellington Strait, or, if this should not be practicable, of proceeding farther westward to Cape Walker, and beyond, on one or other of which places Sir John Franklin will probably have left some notices of his course."

The government has seen the urgent necessity of causing the Wellington Channel to be carefully examined; imperative orders were sent to Sir James Ross to search it, but he was drifted out of Barrow's Strait against his will, before he received those orders by the North Star.

I have already stated that Sir John Franklin's instructions directed him to try the first favorable opening to the southwest after passing Cape Walker; and failing in that, to try the Wellington Channel. Every officer in the British Service, as a matter of course, follows his instructions, as far as they are compatible with the exigencies of the case, be it what it may, nor ever deviates from them without good and justifiable cause. If, then, Sir John Franklin failed in finding an opening to the southwest of Cape Walker it is reasonable to suppose he obeyed his instructions, and tried the Wellington Channel. The second probability in favor of this locality is, that Sir John Franklin expressed o many of his friends a favorable opinion of the Wellington Channel, and, which is of far more consequence, intimated his opinion officially, and before the expedition was determined upon, that this strait seemed to offer the best chance of success.

Moreover, Capt. Fitzjames, his immediate second in command in the Erebus, was strongly in favor of the Wellington Channel, and always so expressed himself. See his letter, before quoted, to Sir John Barrow, p. 203.

Who can doubt that the opinion of Capt. Fitzjames, a man of superior mind, beloved by all who knew him, and in the service "the observed of all observers," would have great weight with Sir John Franklin, even if Sir John had not been himself predisposed to listen to him. What adds confirmation to these views is, that in 1840, a few years prior to the starting of the expedition, Col. Sabine published the deeply interesting "Narrative of Baron Wrangel's Expedition to the Polar Sea, undertaken between the years 1820 and 1823," and in his preface the translator points to the Wellington Channel as the most likely course for the successful accomplishment of the northwest passage. "Setting aside," he says, "the possibility of the existence of unknown land, the probability of an open sea existing to the north of the Parry islands, and communicating with Behring Strait, appears to rest on strict analogical reasoning." And again he adds, "all the attempts to effect the northwest passage, since Barrow's Strait was first passed in 1819, have consisted in an endeavor to force a vessel by one route or another through this land-locked and ice-encumbered portion of the Polar Ocean."

No examination has made kuown what may be the state of the sea to the north of the Parry Islands; whether similar impediments may there present themselves to navigation, or whether a sea may not there exist offering no difficulties whatever of the kind, as M. Von Wrangel has shown to be the case to the north of the Siberian Islands, and as by strict analogy we should be justified in expecting.

Colonel Sabine is an officer of great scientific experience, and from his having made several polar voyages, he has devoted great attention to all that relates to that quarter. He was in constant communication with Sir John Franklin when the expedition was fitting out, and it is but reasonable to suppose that he would be somewhat guided by his opinion.

We have, then, the opinions of Franklin himself, Colonel Sabine, and Captain Fitzjames, all bearing on this point, and we must remember that Parry, who discovered and named this channel, saw nothing when passing and re-passing it, but a clear open sea to the northward.

Lieut. S. Osborn, in a paper dated the 4th of January, 1850, makes the following suggestions :—

"General opinion places the lost expedition to the west of Cape Walker, and south of the latitude of Melville Island. The distance from Cape Bathurst to Banks' Land is only 301 miles, and on reference to a chart it will be seen that nowhere else does the American continent approach so near to the supposed position of Franklin's expedition.

"Banks' Land bears from Cape Bathurst N. 41° 49′, E. 302 miles, and there is reason to believe that in the summer season a portion of this distance may be traversed in boats.

"Dr. Richardson confirms previous reports of the ice being light on the coast east of the Mackenzie River to Cape Bathurst, and informs us that the Esquimaux had seen 'no ice to seaward for two moons.'

"Every mile traversed northward by a party from Cape Bathurst would be over that unknown space in which traces of Franklin may be expected. It is advisable that such a second party be dispatched from Cape Bathurst, in order that the prosecution of Dr. Rae's examination of the supposed channel between Wollaston and Victoria Lands may in no way be interfered with, by his attention being called to the westward."

In March, 1848, the Admiralty announced their intention of rewarding the crews of any whaling ships that brought accurate information of the missing expedition, with the sum of 100 guineas or more, according to circumstances. Lady Franklin also about the same time offered rewards of 2000*l.* and 3000*l.*, to be distributed among the owner, officers, and crew discovering and affording relief to her husband, or making extraordinary exertions for the above object, and, if required, bringing Sir John Franklin and his party to England.

In March, 1850, the following further rewards were offered by the British government to persons of any country:—

1st. To any party or person who in the judgment of the Board of Admiralty, shall discover and effectually relieve the crews of H. M. ships Erebus and Terror, the sum of 20,000*l.*, or,

2d. To any party or parties, &c., who shall discover and effectually relieve any portion of the crews, or shall convey such intelligence as shall lead to the relief of any of the crew, the sum of 10,000*l.*

3d. To any party or parties who shall by virtue of his or their efforts, first succeed in ascertaining their fate, 10,000*l.*

In a dispatch from Sir George Simpson to Mr. Rae, dated Lachine, the 21st of January, 1850, he says:—

"If they be still alive, I feel satisfied that every effort it may be in the power of man to make to succor them will be exerted by yourself and the Company's officers in Mackenzie River; but should your late search have unfortunately ended in disappointment, it is the desire of the Company that you renew your explorations next summer, if possible.

"By the annexed correspondence you will observe that the opinion in England appears to be that our explorations ought to be more particularly directed to that portion of the Northern Sea lying between Cape Walker on the east, Melville Island and Banks' Land to the north, and the continental shore or the Victoria Islands to the south.

"As these limits are believed to embrace the course that would have been pursued by Sir John Franklin, Cape Walker being one of the points he was particularly instructed to make for, you will therefore be pleased, immediately on the receipt of this letter, to fit out another exploring party, to proceed in the direction above indicated, but varying the route that may have been followed last summer, which party, besides their own examination of the coast and islands, should be instructed to offer liberal rewards to the Esquimaux to search for some vestiges of the missing expedition, and similar rewards should be offered to the Indians inhab iting near the coast and Peel's River, and the half-bred hunters of Mackenzie River, the latter being, perhaps, more energetic than the former; assuring them that whoever may procure authentic intelligence will be largely rewarded.

"Simultaneously with the expedition to proceed toward Cape Walker, one or two small parties should be dispatched to the westward of the Mackenzie, in the direction of Point Barrow, one of which might pass over to the Youcon River, and descending that stream to the sea, carry on their explorations in that quarter, while the other, going down the Mackenzie, might trace the coast thence toward the Youcon. And these parties must also be instructed to offer rewards to the natives to prosecute the search in all directions.

"By these means there is reason to believe that in the course of one year so minute a search may be made of the coast and the islands, that in the event of the expedition having passed in that direction, some trace of their progress would certainly be discovered.

"From your experience in arctic discovery, and peculiar qualifications for such an undertaking, I am in hopes you may be enabled yourself to assume the command of the party to proceed to the northward; and, as leaders of the two parties to explore the coast to the westward of the Mackenzie, you will have to select such officers of the Company's service within the district as may appear best qualified for the duty: Mr. Murray, I think, would be a very fit man for one of the leaders, and if one party be sent by way of the Youcon, he might take charge of it. In the event of your going on this expedition, you will be pleased to make over the charge of the district to Chief Trader Bell during your absence.

"In case you may be short-handed, I have by this conveyance instructed Chief Factor Ballenden to engage in Red River ten choice men, accustomed to boating, and well fitted for such a duty as will be required of them; and if there be a chance of their reaching Mackenzie River, or even Athabasca, before the breaking up of the ice, to forward them immediately.

"Should the season, however, be too far advanced to enable them to accomplish the journey by winter traveling, Mr. Ballenden is directed to increase the party to fourteen men, with a guide to be dispatched from Red River immediately after the opening of the navigation, in two boats, laden with provisions and flour, and a few bales of clothing, in order to meet, in some degree, the heavy drain that will be occasioned on our resources in provisions and necessary supplies in Mackenzie River. The leader of this party from Red River may, perhaps, be qualified to act as the conductor of one of the parties to examine the coast to the westward."

On the 5th of February, 1850, another consultation took place at the Admiralty among those officers most experienced in these matters, and their opinions in writing were solicited. It is important, therefore, to submit these as fully as possible to the consideration of the reader.

The first is the report of the hydrographer of the Admiralty, dated the 29th of January, 1850: —

"*Memorandum by Rear-Admiral Sir Francis Beaufort, K. C. B.*

"The Behring's Strait expedition being at length fairly off, it appears to me to be a duty to submit to their Lordships that no time should now be lost in equipping another set of vessels to renew the search on the opposite side, through Baffin's Bay; and this being the fifth year that the Erebus and Terror have been absent, and probably reduced to only casual supplies of food and fuel, it may be assumed that this search should be so complete and effectual as to leave unexamined no place in which, by any of the suppositions that have been put forward, it is at all likely they may be found.

"Sir John Franklin is not a man to treat his orders with levity, and therefore his first attempt was undoubtedly made in the direction of Melville Island, and not to the westward. If foiled in that attempt, he naturally hauled to the southward, and using Banks' Land as a barrier against the northern ice, he would try to make westing under its lee. Thirdly, if both of these roads were found closed against his advance, he perhaps availed himself of one of the four passages between the Parry Islands, including the Wellington Channel. Or, lastly, he may have returned to Baffin's Bay and taken the inviting opening of Jones' Sound.

"All those four tracks must therefore be diligently examined before the search can be called complete, and the only method of rendering that examination prompt and efficient will be through the medium of steam; while only useless expense and reiterated disappointment will attend the best efforts of sailing vessels, leaving the lingering survivors of the lost ships, as well as their relatives in England, in equal despair. Had Sir James Ross been in a steam vessel, he would not have been surrounded with ice and swept out of the Strait, but by shooting under the protection of Leopold Island, he would have waited there till that fatal field had passed to the eastward, and he then would have found a perfectly open sea up to Melville Island.

"The best application of steam to ice-going vessels would be Ericson's screw; but the screw or paddles of any of our moderate-sized vessels might be made to elevate with facility. Vessels so fitted would not require to be fortified in an extraordinary degree, not more than common whalers. From the log-like quiescence with which a sailing vessel must await the crush of two approaching floes, they must be as strong as wood and iron can make them; but the steamer slips out of the reach of the collision, waits till the shock is past, and then profiting by their mutual recoil, darts at once through the transient opening.

"Two such vessels, and each of them attended by two tenders laden with coals and provisions, would be sufficient for the main lines of search. Every prominent point of land where notices might have been left, would be visited, details of their own proceedings would be deposited, and each of the tenders would be left in proper positions, as points of rendezvous on which to fall back.

"Besides these two branches of the expedition, it would be well to allow the whaling captain (Penny,) to carry out his proposed undertaking. His local knowledge, his thorough acquaintance with all the mysteries of the ice navigation, and his well known skill and resources, seem to point him out as a most valuable auxiliary.

"But whatever vessels may be chosen for this service, I would beseech their lordships to expedite them; all our attempts have been deferred too long; and there is now reason to believe that very early in the season, in May or even in April, Baffin's Bay may be crossed before the accumulated ice of winter spreads over its surface. If they arrive rather too soon, they may very advantageously await the proper moment in some of the Greenland harbors, preparing themselves for the coming efforts and struggles, and procuring Esquimaux interpreters.

"In order to press every resource into the service of this noble enterprise, the vessels should be extensively furnished with means for blasting and splitting the ice, perhaps circular saws might be adapted to the steamers, a launch to each party, with a small rotary engine, sledges for the shore, and light boats with sledge bearings for broken ice-fields, balloons for the distribution of advertisements, and kites for the explosion of lofty fire-balls. And, lastly, they should have vigorous and numerous crews, so that when detachments are away, other operations should not be intermitted for want of physical strength.

"As the council of the Royal Society, some time ago, thought proper to remind their lordships of the propriety of instituting this search, it would be fair now to call on that learned body for all the advice and suggestions, that science and philosophy can contribute toward the accomplishment of the great object on which the eyes of all England and indeed of all the world, are now entirely fixed."

Captain Beechey, writing to the Secretary of the Admiralty, 7th of February, 1850, says:—

"The urgent nature of the case alone can justify the use of ordinary steamers in an icy sea, and great prudence and judgment will be required on the part of their commanders, to avoid being disabled by collision and pressure.

"I would also add, as an exception, that I think Leopold Island and Cape Walker, if possible, should both be examined, prior to any attempt being made to penetrate in other directions from Barrow's Strait, and that the bottom of Regent Inlet, about the Pelly Islands, should not be left unexamined. In the memorandum submitted to their lordships on the 17th of January, 1849, this quarter was considered of importance; and I am still of opinion, that, had Sir John Franklin abandoned his vessels near the coast of America, and much short of the Mackenzie River, he would have preferred the probability of retaining the use of his boats until he found relief in Barrow's Strait, to risking an overland journey *via* the before-mentioned river; it must be remembered, that at the time he sailed, Sir George Back's discovery had rendered it very probable that Boothia was an island.

"An objection to the necessity of this search seems to be, that had Sir John Franklin taken that route, he would have reached Fury Beach already. However, I cannot but think there will yet be found some good grounds for the Esquimaux sketch, and that their meaning has been misunderstood; and as Mr. M'Cormick is an enterprising person, whose name has already been before their lordships, I would submit, whether a boat expedition from Leopold Depot, under his direction, would not satisfactorily set at rest all inquiry upon this, now the only quarter unprovided for."

Captain Sir W. E. Parry states :—

"I am decidedly of opinion that the main search should be renewed in the direction of Melville Island and Banks' Land, including as a part of the plan the thorough examination of Wellington Strait and of the other similar openings between the islands of the group bearing my name. I entertain a growing conviction of the probability of the missing ships, or at least a considerable portion of the crews, being shut up at Mel ville Island, Banks' Land, or in that neighborhood, agreeing as I do with Rear Admiral Sir Francis Beaufort, in his report read yesterday to the Board that 'Sir John Franklin is not a man to treat his orders with levity,' which he would be justly chargeable with doing if he attached greater weight to any notions he might personally entertain than to the Admiralty instructions, which he well knew to be founded on the experience of former attempts, and on the best information which could then be obtained on the subject. For these reasons I can scarcely doubt that he would employ at least two seasons, those of 1845 and 1846, in an unremitting attempt to penetrate directly westward or southwestward to Behring's Strait.

"Supposing this conjecture to be correct, nothing can be more likely than that Sir John Franklin's ships, having penetrated in seasons of ordinary temperature a considerable distance in that direction, have been locked up by successive seasons of extraordinary rigor, thus baffling the efforts of their weakened crews to escape from the ice in either of the two directions by Behring's or Barrow's Straits.

"And here I cannot but add, that my own conviction of this probability—for it is only with probabilities that we have to deal—has been greatly strengthened by a letter I have lately received from Col. Sabine, of the Royal Artillery, of which I had the honor to submit a copy to Sir Francis Baring. Colonel Sabine having accompanied two successive expeditions to Baffin's Bay, including that under my command which reached Melville Island, I consider his views to be well worthy of their lordships' attention on this part of the subject.

"It must be admitted, however, that considerable weight is due to the conjecture which has been offered by persons capable of forming a sound judgment, that having failed, as I did, in the attempt to penetrate westward, Sir John Franklin might deem it prudent to retrace his steps, and was enabled to do so, in order to try a more northern route, either through Wellington Strait or some other of those openings between the Parry Islands to which I have already referred. And this idea receives no small importance from the fact, (said to be beyond a doubt,) of Sir John Franklin having, before his departure, expressed such an intention in case of failing to the westward.

"I cannot, therefore, consider the intended search to be complete without making the examination of Wellington Strait and its adjacent openings a distinct part of the plan, to be performed by one portion of the vessels which I shall presently propose for the main expedition.

"Much stress has likewise been laid, and I think not altogether without reason, on the propriety of searching Jones' and Smith's Sounds in the northwest parts of Baffin's Bay. Considerable interest has lately been attached to Jones' Sound, from the fact of its having been recently navigated by at least one enterprising whaler, and found to be of great width, free from ice, with a swell from the westward, and having no land visible from the mast-head in that direction. It seems more than probable, therefore, that it may be found to communicate with Wellington Strait; so that if Sir John Franklin's ships have been detained anywhere to the northward of the Parry Islands, it would be by Jones' Sound that he would probably endeavor to effect his escape, rather than by the less direct route of Barrow's Strait. I do not myself attach much importance to the idea of Sir John Franklin having so far retraced his steps as to come back through Lancaster Sound, and recommence his enterprise by entering Jones' Sound; but the possibility of his attempting his escape through this fine opening, and the report, (though somewhat vague,) of a cairn of stones seen by one of the whalers on a headland within it, seems to me to render it highly expedient to set this question at rest by a search in this direction, including the examination of Smith's Sound also."

I beg to cite next an extract from the letter of Dr. Sir John Richardson to the Secretary of the Admiralty:—

"*Haslar Hospital, Gosport, 7th of February*, 1850.

"With respect to the direction in which a successful search may be predicated with the most confidence, very various opinions have been put forth; some have supposed either that the ships were lost before reaching Lancaster Sound, or that Sir John Franklin, finding an impassable barrier of ice in the entrance of Lancaster Sound, may have sought for a passage through Jones' Sound. I do not feel inclined to give much weight to either conjecture. When we consider the strength of the Erebus and Terror, calculated to resist the strongest pressure to which ships navigating Baffin's Bay have been known to be subject, in conjunction with the fact that, of the many whalers which have been crushed or abandoned since the commencement of the fishery, the crews, or at least the greater part of them, have, in almost every case, succeeded in reaching other ships, or the Danish settlements, we cannot believe that the two discovery ships, which were seen on the edge of the middle ice so early as the 26th of July, can have been so suddenly and totally overwhelmed as to preclude some one of the intelligent officers, whose minds were prepared for every emergency, with their select crews of men, experienced in the ice, from placing a boat on the ice or water, and thus carrying intelligence of the disaster to one of the many whalers which remained for two months after that date in those seas, and this in the absence of any unusual catastrophe among the fishing vessels that season.

"With respect to Jones' Sound, it is admitted by all who are intimately acquainted with Sir John Franklin, that his first endeavor would be to act up to the letter of his instructions, and that therefore he would not lightly abandon the attempt to pass Lancaster Sound. From the logs of the whalers year after year, we learn that when once they have succeeded in rounding the middle ice, they enter Lancaster Sound with facility: had Sir John Franklin, then, gained that Sound, and from the premises we appear to be fully justified in concluding that he did so, and had he afterward encountered a compact field of ice, barring Barrow's Strait and Wellington Sound, he would then, after being convinced that he would lose the season in attempting to bore through it, have borne up for Jones' Sound, but not until he had erected a conspicuous landmark, and lodged a memorandum of his reason for deviating from his instructions.

"The absence of such a signal-post in Lancaster Sound is an argument against the expedition having turned back from thence, and is, on the other hand, a strong support to the suspicion that Barrow's Strait was as open in 1845 as when Sir W. E. Parry first passed it in 1819; that, such being the case, Sir John Franklin, without delay and without landing, pushed on to Cape Walker, and that, subsequently, in endeavoring to penetrate to the southwest, he became involved in the drift ice, which, there is reason to believe, urged by the prevailing winds and the set of the flood tides, is carried toward Coronation Gulf, through channels more or less intricate. Should he have found no opening at Cape Walker, he would, of course, have sought one further to the west; or, finding the southerly and westerly opening blocked by ice, he might have tried a northern passage.

"In either case, the plan of search propounded by

Sir Francis Beaufort seems to provide against every contingency, especially when taken in conjunction with Captain Collinson's expedition, *via* Behring's Strait, and the boat parties from the Mackenzie.

"I do not venture to offer an opinion on the strength or equipment of the vessels to be employed, or other merely nautical questions, further than by remarking, that the use of the small vessels, which forms part of Sir Francis Beaufort's scheme, is supported by the success of the early navigators with their very small craft, and the late gallant exploit of Mr. Shedden, in rounding Icy Cape and Point Barrow, in the Nancy Dawson yacht.

"And further, with respect to the comparative merits of the paddles and screw in the arctic seas, I beg leave merely to observe, that as long as the screw is immersed in water it will continue to act, irrespective of the tem perature of the air; but when, as occurs late in the autumn, the atmosphere is suddenly cooled below the freezing point of sea water, by a northerly gale, while the sea itself remains warmer, the paddles will be speedily clogged by ice accumulating on the floats as they rise through the air in every revolution. An incident recorded by Sir James C. Ross, furnishes a striking illustration of the powerful action of a cold wind; I allude to a fish having been thrown up by the spray against the bows of the Terror, and firmly frozen there, during a gale in a high southerly latitude. Moreover, even with the aid of a ready contrivance for topping the paddles, the flatness or hollowness of the sides of a paddle steamer renders her less fit for sustaining pressure; the machinery is more in the way of oblique beams for strengthening, and she is less efficient as a sailing vessel when the steam is let off."

Memorandum inclosed in Dr. M'Cormick's Letter of the 1st of January, 1850.

"In the month of April last, I laid before my Lords Commissioners of the Admiralty a plan of search for the missing expedition under the command of Captain

Sir John Franklin, by means of a boat expedition up Jones' and Smith's Sounds, volunteering myself to conduct it.

" In that plan I stated the reasons which had induced me to direct my attention more especially to the openings at the head of Baffin's Bay, which, at the time, were not included within the general scheme of search.

"Wellington Channel, however, of all the probable openings into the Polar Sea, possesses the highest degree of interest, and the exploration of it is of such paramount importance, that I should most unquestionably have comprised it within my plan of search, had not Her Majesty's ships Enterprise and Investigator been employed at the time in Barrow's Strait for the express purpose of examining this inlet and Cape Walker, two of the most essential points of search in the whole track of the Erebus and Terror to the westward ; being those points at the very threshold of his enterprise, from which Sir John Franklin would take his departure from the known to the unknown, whether he shaped a southwesterly course from the latter, or attempted the passage in a higher latitude from the former point.

" The return of the sea expedition from Port Leopold, and the overland one from the Mackenzie River, both alike unsuccessful in their search, leaves the fate of the gallant Franklin and his companions as problematical as ever; in fact, the case stands precisely as it did two years ago; the work is yet to be begun; every thing remains to be accomplished.

" In renewal of the search in the ensuing spring, more would be accomplished in boats than in any other way, not only by Behring's Strait, but from the eastward. For the difficulties attendant on icy navigation which form so insuperable a barrier to the progress of ships, would be readily surmounted by boats; by means of which the coast line may be closely examined for cairns of stones, under which Sir John Franklin would most indubitably deposit memorials of his progress in all prominent positions, as opportunities might offer.

"The discovery of one of these mementos would, in a. probability, afford a clue that might lead to the rescue of our enterprising countrymen, ere another and sixth winter close in upon them, should they be still in existence; and the time has not yet arrived for abandoning hope.

"In renewing once more the offer of my services, which I do most cheerfully, I see no reason for changing the opinions I entertained last spring; subsequent events have only tended to confirm them. I then believed, and I do so still, after a long and mature consideration of the subject, that Sir John Franklin's ships have been arrested in a high latitude, and beset in the heavy polar ice northward of the Parry Islands, and that their probable course thither has been through the Wellington Channel, or one of the sounds at the northern extremity of Baffin's Bay.

"This appears to me to be the only view of the case that can in any way account for the entire absence of all tidings of them throughout so protracted a period of time (unless all have perished by some sudden and overwhelming catastrophe.)

"Isolated as their position would be under such circumstances, any attempt to reach the continent of America at such a distance would be hopeless in the extreme: and the mere chance of any party from the ships reaching the top of Baffin's Bay at the very moment of a whaler's brief and uncertain visit would be attended with by far too great a risk to justify the attempt, for failure would insure inevitable destruction to the whole party; therefore their only alternative would be to keep together in their ships, should no disaster have happened to them, and by husbanding their remaining resources, eke them out with whatever wild animals may come within their reach.

"Had Sir John Franklin been able to shape a southwesterly course from Cape Walker, as directed by his instructions, the probability is, some intelligence of him would have reached this country ere this, (nearly five years having already elapsed since his departure from it.) Parties would have been sent out from his ships, either in the direction of the coast of America or Barrow's Strait, whichever happened to be the most accessible. Esquimaux would have been fallen in with, and tidings of the long-absent expedition have been obtained.

"Failing in penetrating beyond Cape Walker, Sir John Franklin would have left some notice of his future intentions on that spot, or the nearest accessible one to it; and should he then retrace his course for the Wellington Channel, the most probable conjecture, he would not pass up that inlet without depositing a further account of his proceedings, either on the western or eastern point of the entrance to it.

"Therefore, should my proposal meet with their Lordships' approbation, I would most respectfully submit, that the party I have volunteered to conduct should be landed at the entrance to the Wellington Channel, or the nearest point attainable by any ship that their Lordships may deem fit to employ in a future search, consistently with any other services that ship may have to perform; and should a landing be effected on the eastern side, I would propose commencing the search from Cape Riley or Beechey Island in a northerly direction, carefully examining every remarkable headland and indentation of the western coast of North Devon for memorials of the missing expedition; I would then cross over the Wellington Channel and continue the search along the northern shore of Cornwallis Island, extending the exploration to the westward as far as the remaining portion of the season would permit, so as to secure the retreat of the party before the winter set in, returning either by the eastern or western side of Cornwallis Island, as circumstances might indicate to be the most desirable at the time, after ascertaining the general extent and trending of the shores of that island.

"As, however, it would be highly desirable that Jones' Sound should not be omitted in the search, more especially as a whaler, last season, reached its entrance and reported it open, I would further propose, that the ship conveying the exploring party out should look into this opening on her way to Lancaster Sound, if circumstances permitted of her doing so early in the season; and, if found to be free from ice, the attempt might be made by the boat expedition to push through it to the westward in this latitude; and should it prove to be an opening into the Polar Sea, of which I think there can be little doubt, a great saving of time and distance would be accomplished. Failing in this, the ship should be secured in some central position in the vicinity of the Wellington Channel, as a *point d'appui* to fall back upon in the search from that quarter.

(Signed,) R. M'Cormick, R. N.

" *Twickenham*, 1*st of January*, 1850."

Outline of a Plan of an Overland Journey to the Polar Sea, by the Way of the Coppermine River, in Search of Sir John Franklin's Expedition, suggested in 1847.

" If Sir John Franklin, guided by his instructions, has passed through Barrow's Strait, and shaped a southwesterly course, from the meridian of Cape Walker, with the intention of gaining the northern coast of the continent of America, and so passing through the Dolphin and Union Strait, along the shore of that continent, to Behring's Strait;

" His greatest risk of detention by the ice throughout this course would be found between the parallels of 74° and 69° north latitude, and the meridians of 100° and 110° west longitude, or, in other words, that portion of the northwest passage which yet remains unexplored, occupying the space between the western coast of Boothia on the one side, and the island or islands forming Banks' and Victoria Lands on the other.

" Should the Erebus and Terror have been beset in the heavy drift-ice, or wrecked among it and the broken land, which in all probability exists there while contending with the prevalent westerly winds in this quarter;

"The Coppermine River would decidedly offer the most direct route and nearest approach to that portion of the Polar Sea, and, after crossing Coronation Gulf, the average breadth of the Strait between the Conti nent and Victoria Land is only about twenty-two miles.

"From this point a careful search should be commenced in the direction of Banks' Land ; the intervening space between it and Victoria Land, occupying about five degrees, or little more than 300 miles, could, I think, be accomplished in one season, and a retreat to winter quarters effected before the winter set in. As the ice in the Coppermine River breaks up in June, the searching party ought to reach the sea by the beginning of August, which would leave two of the best months of the year for exploring the Polar Sea, viz : August and September.

"As it would be highly desirable that every available day, to the latest period of the season, should be devoted to the search, I should propose wintering on the coast in the vicinity of the mouth of the Coppermine River, which would also afford a favorable position from which to recommence the search in the following spring, should the first season prove unsuccessful.

"Of course the object of such an expedition as I have proposed is not with the view of taking supplies to such a numerous party as Sir John Franklin has under his command ; but to find out his position, and acquaint him where a depot of provisions would be stored up for himself and crews at my proposed winter quarters, where a party should be left to build a house, establish a fishery, and hunt for game, during the absence of the searching party.

"To carry out this plan efficiently, the Hudson's Bay Company should be requested to lend their powerful cooperation in furnishing guides, supplies of pemmican, &c., for the party on their route and at winter quarters. Without entering into details here, I may observe, that I should consider one boat, combining the necessary requisites in her construction to fit her for either the river navigation, or that of the shores of the Polar Sea, would be quite sufficient, with a crew one half sailors, and the other half Canadian boatmen; the latter to be engaged at Montreal, for which place I would propose leaving England in the month of February.

"Should such an expedition even fail in its main object — the discovery of the position of the missing ships and their crews, the long-sought-for polar passage may be accomplished.

(Signed,) R. M'CORMICK, R. N.

"*Woolwich*, 1847."

Copy of a Letter from Lieutenant Sherard Osborn to the Lords Commissioners of the Admiralty.

"*Ealing, Middlesex, 4th January*, 1850.

"MY LORDS,— A second attempt to reach Sir John Franklin's expedition being about to be tried during the present year, I take the liberty of calling your attention to the inclosed proposition for an overland party to be dispatched to the shores of the Polar Sea, with a view to their traversing the short distance between Cape Bathurst and Banks' Land. My reasons for thus trespassing on your attention are as follows;

"1st. General opinion places the lost expedition to the west of Cape Walker, and south of the latitude of Melville Island.

"The distance from Cape Bathurst to Banks' Land is only 301 miles, and on reference to a chart it will be seen that nowhere else does the American continent approach so near to the supposed position of Franklin's expedition.

"2d. As a starting point, Cape Bathurst offers great advantages; the arrival of a party sent there from England may be calculated upon to a day; whereas the arrival of Captain Collinson in the longitude of Cape Barrow, or that of an eastern expedition in Lancaster Sound, will depend upon many uncontrollable contingencies. The distance to be performed is comparatively little, and the certainty of being able to fall back upon supplies offers great advantages. Captain

Collinson will have 680 miles of longitude to traverse between Cape Barrow and Banks' Land. An Eastern Expedition, if opposed by the ice, (as Sir James Ross has been,) and unable to proceed in their vessels farther than Leopold Harbor, will have to journey on foot 330 miles to reach the longitude of Banks' Land, and if any accident occur to their vessels, they will be in as critical a position as those they go to seek.

"3d. Banks' Land bears from Cape Bathurst N. 41° 49′ E. 302 miles, and there is reason to believe that in the summer season a portion of this distance may be traversed in boats.

"4th and 5th. Dr. Richardson confirms previous reports of the ice being light on the coast east of the Mackenzie River to Cape Bathurst, and informs us that the Esquimaux had seen no ice to seaward for two moons.

"6th. Every mile traversed northward by a party from Cape Bathurst would be over that unknown space in which traces of Franklin may be expected.

"7th. It is advisable that such a second party be dispatched from Cape Bathurst, in order that the prosecution of Dr. Rae's examination of the supposed channel between Wollaston and Victoria Lands may in no way be interfered with by his attention being called to the westward.

"8th. The *caches* of provisions made at different points of the Mackenzie and at Cape Bathurst, would enable a party to push down to their starting point with great celerity directly the River Mackenzie opens, which may be as early as May.

"I would also remind your Lordships that the proposed expedition would carry into execution a very important clause in the instructions given to Sir James Ross; viz: that of sending exploring parties from Banks' Land in a southwesterly direction toward Cape Bathurst or Cape Parry.

"In conclusion, I beg to offer my willing services toward the execution of the proposed plan; and seeking it from no selfish motives, but thoroughly impressed with its feasibility, you may rest assured, my lords, should I have the honor of being sent upon this service, that I shall not disappoint your expectations.

"I have, &c.,

(Signed,) "SHERARD OSBORN, Lieut., R. N."

Copy of a Letter from Colonel Sabine, R. A., to Captain Sir W. Edward Parry.

"*Castle-down Terrace, Hastings,*
"*15th of January*, 1850.

"There can be little doubt, I imagine, in the mind of any one who has read attentively Franklin's instructions, and, (in reference to them,) your description of the state of the ice and of the navigable water in 1819 and 1820, in the route which he was ordered to pursue; still less, I think, can there be a doubt in the mind of any one who had the advantage of being with you in those years, that Franklin, (always supposing no previous disaster,) must have made his way to the south-west part of Melville Island either in 1845 or 1846. It has been said that 1845 was an unfavorable season, and as the navigation of Davis' Strait and Baffin's Bay was new to Franklin, we may regard it as more probable that it may have taken him two seasons to accomplish what we accomplished in one. So far, I think, guided by his instructions and by the experience gained in 1819 and 1820, we may reckon pretty confidently on the first stage of his proceedings, and doubtless, in his progress he would have left memorials in the usual manner at places where he may have landed, some of which would be likely to fall in the way of a vessel following in his track. From the west end of Melville Island our inferences as to his further proceedings must become more conjectural, being contingent on the state of the ice and the existence of navigable water in the particular season. If he found the ocean, as we did, covered to the west and south, as far as the eye could reach from the summit of the highest hills, with ice of a thickness unparalleled in any other part of the Polar

Sea, he would, after probably waiting through one whole season in the hope of some favorable change, have retraced his steps, in obedience to the second part of his instructions, in order to seek an opening to the north which might conduct to a more open sea. In this case some memorial of the season passed by him at the southwest end of Melville Island, and also of his purpose of retracing his steps, would doubtless have been left by him; and should he subsequently have found an opening to the north, presenting a favorable appearance, there also, should circumstances have permitted, would a memorial have been left.

"He may, however, have found a more favorable state of things at the southwest end of Melville Island than we did, and may have been led thereby to attempt to force a passage for his ships in the direct line of Behring's Strait, or perhaps, in the first instance, to the south of that direction, namely, to Banks' Land. In such case two contingencies present themselves: first, that in the season of navigation of 1847 he may have made so much progress, that in 1848 he may have preferred the endeavor to push through to Behring's Strait, or to some western part of the continent, to an attempt to return by the way of Barrow's Strait; the mission of the Plover, the Enterprise, and the Investigator together with Dr. Rae's expedition, supply, I presume, (for I am but partially acquainted with their instructions,) the most judicious means of affording relief in this direction. There is, however, a second contingency; and it is the one which the impression left on my mind by the nature and general aspect of the ice in the twelve months which we ourselves passed at the southwest end of Melville Island, compels me, in spite of my wishes, to regard as the more probable, viz., that his advance from Melville Island in the season of 1847 may have been limited to a distance of fifty, or perhaps one hundred miles at farthest, and that in 1848 he may have endeavored to retrace his steps, but only with partial success. It is, I apprehend, quite a conceivable case, that under these circumstances, incapable of extricating the ships from the ice, the crews may have been, at length, obliged to quit them, and attempt a retreat, not toward the continent, because too distant, but to Melville Island, where certainly food, and probably fuel (seals,) might be obtained, and where they would naturally suppose that vessels dispatched from England for their relief would, in the first instance, seek them. It is quite conceivable also, I apprehend, that the circumstances might be such that their retreat may have been made without their boats, and probably in the April or May of 1849.

"Where the Esquimaux have lived, there Englishmen may live, and no valid argument against the attempt to relieve can, I think, be founded on the improbability of finding Englishmen alive in 1850, who may have made a retreat to Melville Island in the spring of 1849; nor would the view of the case be altered in any material degree, if we suppose their retreat to have been made in 1848 or 1849 to Banks' Land, which may afford facilities of food and fuel equal or superior to Melville Island, and a further retreat in the following year to the latter island as the point at which they would more probably look out for succor.

"Without disparagement, therefore, to the attempts made in other directions, I retain my original opinion, which seems also to have been the opinion of the Board of Admiralty, by which Ross's instructions were drawn up, that the most promising direction for research would be taken by a vessel which should follow them to the southwest point of Melville Island, be prepared to winter there, and, if necessary, to send a party across the ice in April or May to examine Banks' Land, a distance (there and back) less than recently accomplished by Ross in his land journey.

"I learn from Ross's dispatches, that almost immediately after he got out of Port Leopold (1849,) he was entangled in apparently interminable fields and floes of ice, with which, in the course of the summer, he was drifted down through Barrow's Strait and Baffin's Bay nearly to Davis' Strait. It is reasonable to presume, therefore, that the localities from whence this ice drifted are likely to be less encumbered than usual by accumulated ice in 1850. It is, of course, of the highest importance to reach Barrow's Strait at the earliest possible period of the season; and, connected with this point I learn from Captain Bird, whom I had the pleasure of seeing here a few days ago, a very remarkable fact, that the ice which prevented their crossing Baffin's Bay in 72° or 73° of latitude (as we did in 1819, arriving in Barrow's Strait a month earlier than we had done the preceding year, when we went round by Melville Bay, and nearly a month earlier than Ross did last year) was young ice, which had formed in the remarkably calm summer of last year, and which the absence of wind prevented their forcing a passage through, on the one hand, while on the other, the ice was not heavy enough for ice anchors. It was, he said, not more than two or two and a half feet thick, and obviously of very recent formation. There must, therefore, have been an earlier period of the season when this part of the sea must have been free from ice; and this comes in confirmation of a circumstance of which I was informed by Mr. Petersen (a Danish gentleman sent to England some months ago by the Northern Society of Antiquaries of Copenhagen, to make extracts from books and manuscripts in the British Museum,) that the Northmen, who had settlements some centuries ago on the west coast of Greenland, were in the habit of crossing Baffin's Bay in the latitude of Upernavic in the spring of the year, for the purpose of fishing in Barrow's Strait, from whence they returned in August; and that in the early months they generally found the passage across free from ice.

"In the preceding remarks, I have left one contingency unconsidered; it is that which would have followed in pursuance of his instructions, if Franklin should have found the aspect of the ice too unfavorable to the west and south of Melville Island to attempt to force a passage through it, and should have retraced his steps in hopes of finding a more open sea to the northward, either in Wellington Strait or elsewhere. It is quite conceivable that here also the expedition may have encountered, at no very great distance, insuperable difficulties to their advance, and may have failed in accomplishing a return with their ships. In this case, the retreat of the crews, supposing it to have been made across land or ice, would most probably be directed to some part of the coast on the route to Melville Island, on which route they would, without doubt, expect that succor would be attempted."

Mr. Robert A. Goodsir, a brother of Mr. H. D. Goodsir, the assistant-surgeon of Sir John Franklin's ship, the Erebus, left Stromness, as surgeon of the Advice, whaler, Capt. Penny, on the 17th of March, 1849, in the hopes of gaining some tidings of his brother; but returned unsuccessful after an eight months' voyage. He has, however, published a very interesting little narrative of the icy regions and of his arctic voyage.

In a letter to Lady Franklin, dated Edinburgh, 18th of January, 1850, he says:—"I trust you are not allowing yourself to become over-anxious. I know that, although there is much cause to be so, there is still not the slightest reason that we should despair. It may be presumptuous in me to say so, but I have never for a moment doubted as to their ultimate safe return, having always had a sort of presentiment that I would meet my brother and his companions somewhere in the regions in which their adventures are taking place. This hope I have not yet given up, and I trust that by next summer it may be fulfilled, when an end will be put to the suspense which has lasted so long, and which must have tried you so much."

The arctic regions, far from being so destitute of animal life as might be supposed from the bleak and inhospitable character of the climate, are proverbial for the boundless profusion of various species of the animal kingdom, which are to be met with in different localities during a great part of the year.

The air is often darkened by innumerable flocks of arctic and blue gulls, (*Lestris Parasiticus*, and *Larus glaucus*,) the ivory gull or snow-bird, (*Larus eburneus*,) the kittiwake, the fulmar or petrel, snow geese, terns, coons, dovekies, &c. The cetaceous animals comprise the great Greenland whale, (*Balæna mysticetus*,) the sea unicorn or narwhal, (*Monodon monoceros*,) the white whale or beluga, (*Delphinus leucos*,) the morse or walrus, (*Trichecus rosmarus*,) and the seal. There are also plenty of porpoises occasionally to be met with, and although these animals may not be the best of food, yet they can be eaten. Of the land animals I may instance the polar bear, the musk-ox, the reindeer, the arctic fox and wolves.

Parry obtained nearly 4000lbs. weight of animal food during his winter residence at Melville Island; Ross nearly the same quantity from birds alone when wintering at Port Leopold.

In 1719, the crews of two Hudson's Bay vessels, the Albany and Discovery, a ship and sloop, under the command of Mr. Barlow and Mr. Knight, were cast on shore on Marble Island, and it was subsequently ascertained that some of the party supported life for nearly three years. Mr. Hearne learned the particulars from some of the Esquimaux in 1729. The ship it appeared went on shore in the fall of 1719; the party being then in number about fifty, began to build their house for the winter. As soon as the ice permitted in the following summer the Esquimaux paid them another visit, and found the number of sailors much reduced, and very unhealthy.

Sickness and famine occasioned such havoc among them that by the setting in of the second winter, their number was reduced to twenty. Some of the Esquimaux took up their abode at this period on the opposite side of the harbor, and supplied them with what provisions they could spare in the shape of blubber, seal's flesh, and train oil.

The Esquimaux left for their wanderings in the spring, and on revisiting the island in the summer of 1721, only five of the crews were found alive, and these were so ravenous for food, that they devoured the blubber and seal's flesh raw, as they purchased it of the natives, which proved so injurious in their weak state, that three of them died in a few days. The two survivors, though very weak, managed to bury their comrades, and protracted their existence for some days longer.

"They frequently," in the words of the narrative, "went to the top of an adjacent rock, and earnestly looked to the south and east, as if in expectation of some vessels coming to their relief. After continuing there a considerable time, and nothing appearing in sight, they sat down close together, and wept bitterly. At length one of the two died, and the other's strength was so far exhausted, that he fell down and died also in attempting to dig a grave for his companion. The skulls and other large bones of these two men are now lying above ground close to the house."

Sir John Richardson, speaking of the amount of food to be obtained in the polar region, says, "Deer migrate over the ice in the spring from the main shore to Victoria and Wollaston Lands in large herds, and return in the autumn. These lands are also the breeding places of vast flocks of snow geese; so that with ordinary skill in hunting, a large supply of food might be procured on their shores, in the months of June, July, and August. Seals are also numerous in those seas, and are easily shot, their curiosity rendering them a ready prey to a boat party." In these ways and by fishing, the stock of provisions might be greatly augmented—and we have the recent example of Mr. Rae, who passed a severe winter on the very barren shores of Repulse Bay, with no other fuel than the withered tufts of a herbaceous andromada, and maintained a numerous party on the spoils of the chase alone for a whole year. Such instances, forbid us to lose hope. Should Sir John Franklin's provisions become so far inadequate to a winter's consumption, it is not likely that he would remain longer by his ships, but rather that in one body, or in several, the officers and crews, with boats cut down so as to be light enough to drag over the ice, or built expressly for that purpose, would endeavor to make their way eastward to Lancaster Sound, or southward to the main-land, according to the longitude in which the ships were arrested.

We ought not to judge of the supplies of food that can be procured in the arctic regions by diligent hunting, from the quantities that have been actually obtained on the several expeditions that have returned, and consequently of the means of preserving life there. When there was abundance in the ships, the address and energy of the hunting parties was not likely to be called forth, as they would inevitably be when the existence of the crews depended solely on their personal efforts, and formed their chief or only object in their march toward quarters where relief might be looked for. This remark has reference to the supposition that on the failure of the stock of provisions in the ships, the crews would, in separate parties under their officers, seek for succor in several directions.

With an empty stomach, the power of resisting external cold is greatly impaired; but when the process of digesting is going on vigorously, even with comparatively scanty clothing, the heat of the body is preserved. There is in the winter time, in high latitudes, a craving for fat or oleaginous food, and for such occasions the flesh of seals, walruses, or bears, forms a useful article of diet. Captain Cook says that the walrus is a sweet and wholesome article of food. Whales and seals would also furnish light and fuel. The necessity for increased food in very cold weather, is not so great when the people do not work.

Mr. Gilpin, in his narrative in the Nautical Magazine for March, 1850, writes thus: —

"About the 20th of June a small water bird, called the doveky, had become so numerous, and so many were daily shot by those who troubled themselves to go after them, that shooting parties from each ship, consisting of an officer and marine, were established at Whaler Point, where they remained the whole week, returning on board on Saturday night. In a week or so after this the coon, a much heavier bird, became more plentiful than the little doveky, and from this time to the middle of August, so successful and untiring were our sportsmen, that the crew received each a bird per man a day.

"The account kept on board the Investigator showed the number of birds killed to have amounted to about 4000, and yielding near 2500lbs. of meat. But more than this was obtained, as many were shot by individuals for amusement, and not always noted."

Mr. Goodsir, surgeon, when in the Advice whaler, on her voyage up Lancaster Sound, in the summer of 1849, speaking of landing on one of the Wollaston Islands, on the west side of Navy Board Inlet, says he disturbed about half a dozen pairs of the eider-duck (*Somateria mollissima.*) Their eggs he found to be within a few hours of maturity. There were, besides, numerous nests, the occupants of which had probably winged their way southward. Two brent geese, (*Anser bernicla,*) and a single pair of arctic terns, (*Sterna arctica,*) were most vociferous and courageous in defense of their downy offspring wherever he approached. These were the only birds he saw, with the exception of a solitary raven, (*Corvus corax,*) not very high overhead, whose sharp and yet musically bell-like croak came startling upon the ear.

Mr. Snow, in his account of the voyage of the Prince Albert, p. 162, says, (speaking of Melville Bay, at the northern head of Baffin's Bay,) "Innumerable quantities of birds, especially the little auk, (*Alca alle,*) and the doveky, (*Colymbus grylle,*) were now seen, (August 6th,) in every direction. They were to be observed in thousands, on the wing and in the water, and often on pieces of ice, where they were clustered together so thick that scores might have been shot at a time by two or three fowling pieces."

In passing up Lancaster Sound a fortnight later several shoal of eider-ducks and large quantities of other birds were also seen.

A BALLAD OF SIR JOHN FRANKLIN

"The ice was here, the ice was there,
The ice was all around." — COLERIDGE.

WHITHER sail you, Sir John Franklin?
Cried a whaler in Baffin's Bay;
To know if between the land and the Pole,
I may find a broad sea-way.

I charge you back, Sir John Franklin,
As you would live and thrive,
For between the land and the frozen Pole
No man may sail alive.

But lightly laughed the stout Sir John,
And spoke unto his men: —
Half England is wrong, if he is right;
Bear off to westward then.

O, whither sail you, brave Englishman?
Cried the little Esquimaux.
Between your land and the polar star
My goodly vessels go.

Come down, if you would journey there,
The little Indian said;
And change your cloth for fur clothing,
Your vessel for a sled.

But lightly laughed the stout Sir John,
And the crew laughed with him too;
A sailor to change from ship to sled,
I ween, were something new!

All through the long, long polar day,
The vessels westward sped;
And wherever the sail of Sir John was blown,
The ice gave way and fled.

Gave way with many a hollow groan,
And with many a surly roar;
But it murmured and threatened on every side,
And closed where he sailed before.

Ho! see ye not my merry man,
The broad and open sea?
Bethink ye what the whaler said,
Bethink ye of the little Indian's sled!
The crew laughed out in glee.

Sir John, Sir John, 't is bitter cold,
The scud drives on the breeze,
The ice comes looming from the north,
The very sunbeams freeze.

Bright summer goes, dark winter comes—
We cannot rule the year;
But long ere summer's sun goes down,
On yonder sea we'll steer.

The dripping icebergs dipped and rose,
  And floundered down the gale;
The ships were staid, the yards were manned,
  And furled the useless sail.

The summer 's gone, the winter 's come,
  We sail not on yonder sea;
Why sail we not, Sir John Franklin?
  — A silent man was he.

The winter goes, the summer comes,
  We cannot rule the year;
I ween, we cannot rule the ways,
  Sir John, wherein we 'd steer.

The cruel ice came floating on,
  And closed beneath the lee,
Till the thickening waters dashed no more,
'T was ice around, behind, before —
  My God! there is no sea!

What think you of the whaler now!
  What of the Esquimaux?
A sled were better than a ship,
  To cruise through ice and snow.

Down sank the baleful crimson sun;
  The northern-light came out,
And glared upon the ice-bound ships,
  And shook its spears about.

The snow came down, storm breeding storm,
  And on the decks was laid;
Till the weary sailor, sick at heart,
  Sank down beside his spade.

Sir John, the night is black and long,
  The hissing wind is bleak;
The hard, green ice is strong as death:—
  I prithee, captain, speak.

The night is neither bright nor short,
  The singing breeze is cold,
The ice is not so strong as hope,
  The heart of man is bold!

What hope can scale this icy wall,
  High o'er the main flag-staff?
Above the ridges the wolf and bear
Look down with a patient, settled stare —
  Look down on us and laugh.

The summer went, the winter came —
  We could not rule the year;
But summer will melt the ice again,
And open a path to the sunny main,
  Whereon our ships shall steer.

The winter went, the summer went,
  The winter came around;
But the hard, green ice was strong as death,
And the voice of hope sank to a breath,
  Yet caught at every sound.

Hark! heard you not the sound of guns?
  And there, and there again?
'T is some uneasy iceberg's roar,
  As he turns in the frozen main.

Hurra! hurra! the Esquimaux
  Across the ice-fields steal:
God give them grace for their charity!
  Ye pray for the silly seal.

Sir John, where are the English fields,
  And where the English trees,
And where are the little English flowers,
  That open in the breeze?

Be still, be still, my brave sailors!
  You shall see the fields again,
And smell the scent of the opening flowers,
  The grass, and the waving grain.

Oh! when shall I see my orphan child?
  My Mary waits for me;
Oh! when shall I see my old mother,
  And pray at her trembling knee?

Be still, be still, my brave sailors!
  Think not such thoughts again!
But a tear froze slowly on his cheek —
  He thought of Lady Jane.

Ah! bitter, bitter grows the cold,
  The ice grows more and more;
More settled stare the wolf and bear,
  More patient than before.

Oh! think you, good Sir John Franklin,
  We 'll ever see the land?
'T was cruel to send us here to starve,
  Without a helping hand.

'T was cruel, Sir John, to send us here,
  So far from help or home;
To starve and freeze on this lonely sea;
I ween, the Lords of the Admiralty
  Had rather send than come.

Oh! whether we starve to death alone,
  Or sail to our own country,
We have done what man has never done —
The open ocean danced in the sun —
  We passed the Northern Sea!

THE GOVERNMENT AND PRIVATE SEARCHING EXPEDITIONS AFTER SIR JOHN FRANKLIN.

THE following is a complete list of the several relief and exploring vessels which have been sent out during the last two years by the British government, by private individuals, and by the American nation:—

Ships.	Men.	Commanders.
1. H. M. S. Enterprise - -	68	Capt. Collinson.
2. H. M. S. Investigator - -	65	Com. M'Clure.
3. H. M. S. Plover - - -	52	Com. Moore.
4. H. M. S. Resolute - - -	68	Capt. H. Austin.
5. H. M. S. Assistance - -	60	Capt. E. Ommaney.
6. H. M. S. Intrepid, (screw steamer,) - - - - -	30	Lieut. S. Osborn.
7. H. M. S. Intrepid, (screw steamer,) - - - - -	38	Lieut. Cator.
8. The Lady Franklin - -	25	Mr. Penny.
9. The Sophia, (a tender to the above,) - - - - -	22	Mr. Stewart.
10. United States brig Advance - - - - -	20	Lieut. De Haven.
11. United States vessel Rescue - - - - -	18	Mr. S. P. Griffin.
12. Felix yacht - - - - -		Capt. Sir John Ross.
13. Mary, (tender to the Felix.)		
14. The North Star, Master and Commander Saunders.		
15. The Prince Albert - -	18	Com. Forsyth.

Of these vessels the Enterprise, Investigator, and Plover, are at present engaged on the western branch of search through Behring's Straits. The rest have all proceeded through Baffin's Bay to Lancaster Sound, and the channels branching out from thence, except the last two, which have returned home.

VOYAGE OF THE "ENTERPRISE" AND "INVESTIGATOR" UNDER CAPTAIN SIR JAMES C. ROSS, 1848–49.

In the spring of 1848, Captain Sir James C. Ross was placed in command of a well found and fitted expedition, with means and advantages of unusual extent, and with an object that could not fail to stimulate in the highest degree the energies and perseverance of all embarked in it. With the ever present feeling, too, that the lives of their countrymen and brother sailors depended, (under God's good providence,) upon their unflinching exertions, Captain Ross and his followers went forth in the confident hope that their efforts might be crowned with success.

The season was considerably advanced before the whole of the arrangements were completed, for it was not until the 12th of June, 1848, that Captain Ross left England, having under his charge the Enterprise and Investigator, with the following officers and crews:—

Enterprise, 540 *tons*.

Captain — Sir James C. Ross.
Lieutenants — R. J. L. M'Clure, F. L. McClintock, and W. H. J. Browne.
Master — W. S. Couldery, (acting.)
Surgeon — W. Robertson, (*b*) M. D.
Assistant-Surgeon — H. Matthias.
Clerk — Edward Whitehead.
Total complement, 68.

Investigator, 480 *tons*.

Captain — E. J. Bird.
Lieutenants — M. G. H. W. Ross, Frederick Robinson and J. J. Barnard.
Master — W. Tatham.
Surgeon — Robert Anderson.
Mates — L. J. Moore and S. G. Cresswell.
Second Master — John H. Allard.
Assistant-Surgeon — E. Adams.
Clerk in Charge — James D. Gilpin.
Total complement, 67.

The ships reached the Danish settlement of Uppernavick, situated on one of the group of Woman's Islands on the western shore of Baffin's Bay, on the 6th of July. Running through this intricate archipelago, they were made fast, on the 20th, to an iceberg aground off Cape Shackleton. The ships were towed, during the next few days, through loose streams of ice, and on the morning of the 26th were off the three islands of Baffin in latitude 74° N. Calms and light winds so greatly impeded any movement in the pack, that day after day passed away until the season had so far advanced as to preclude every hope of accomplishing much, if any thing, before the setting in of winter.

No exertions, however, were spared to take advantage of every opportunity of pushing forward, until, on the 20th of August, during a heavy breeze from the northeast, the ships under all sail bored through a pack of ice of but moderate thickness, but having among it heavy masses, through which it was necessary to drive them at all hazards. The shocks the ships sustained during this severe trial were great, but fortunately without serious damage to them. Getting into clear water in lat. 75½ N., and long. 68° W., on the 23d the ships stood in to Pond's Bay, but no traces of Esquimaux or other human beings were discovered, although signals were made and guns fired at repeated intervals. The ships were kept close to the land, and a rigid examination made of the coast to the northward, so that neither people nor boats could have passed without being seen. On the 26th the ships arrived off Possession Bay, and a party was sent on shore to search for any traces of the expedition having touched at this general point of rendezvous. Nothing was found but the paper left there recording the visit of Sir Edward Parry, on the very day (August 30th) in 1819. From this point the examination of the coast was continued with equal care. On the 1st of September they arrived off Cape York, and a boat's crew was sent on shore, to fix a conspicuous mark, and leave information for the guidance of any future party that might touch here.

I shall now take up the narrative in Sir James Ross's own words — "We stood over toward northeast cape until we came in with the edge of a pack, too dense for us to penetrate, lying between us and Leopold Island, about fourteen miles broad; we therefore coasted the north shore of Barrow's Strait, to seek a harbor further to the westward, and to examine the numerous inlets of that shore. Maxwell Bay, and several smaller indentations, were thoroughly explored, and, although we got near the entrance of Wellington Channel, the firm barrier of ice which stretched across it, and which had not broken away this season, convinced us all was impracticable in that direction. We now stood to the south-west to seek for a harbor near Cape Rennell, but found a heavy body of ice extending from the west of Cornwallis Island in a compact mass to Leopold Island. Coasting along the pack during stormy and foggy weather, we had difficulty in keeping the ships free during the nights, for I believe so great a quantity of ice was never before seen in Barrow's Strait at this period of the season."

Fortunately, after some days of anxious and arduous work, the ships were got through the pack, and secured in the harbor of Port Leopold on the 11th of September. No situation could be better adapted for the purpose than this locality; being at the junction of the four great channels of Barrow's Strait, Lancaster Sound, Prince Regent Inlet, and Wellington Channel, it was hardly possible for any party, after abandoning their ships, to pass along the shores of any of those inlets, without finding indications of the proximity of these ships.

The night following the very day of the ships' getting in, the main pack closed with the land, and completely sealed the mouth of the harbor. The long winter was passed in exploring and surveying journeys along the coasts in all directions. During the winter as many as fifty white foxes were taken alive, in traps made of empty casks set for the purpose. As it was well known how large a tract of country these animals traverse in search of food, copper collars, (upon which a notice of the position of the ships and depots of provisions was engraved,) were clinched round their necks, and they were then set free, in the hope that some of these four-footed messengers might be the means of conveying the intelligence to the Erebus and Terror, as the crews of those vessels would naturally be eager for their capture. The months of April and May were occupied by Capt. Ross, Lieut. McClintock, and a party of twelve men, in examining and thoroughly exploring all the inlets and smaller indentations of the northern and western coasts of Boothia peninsula, in which any ships might have found shelter.

From the high land in the neighborhood of Cape Bunny, Capt. Ross obtained a very extensive view, and observed that the whole space between it and Cape Walker to the west, and Wellington Strait to the north, was occupied by very heavy hummocky ice.

"The examination of the coast," Sir James Ross tells us, "was pursued until the 5th of June, when, having consumed more than half our provisions, and the strength of the party being much reduced, I was reluctantly compelled to abandon further operations, as it was, moreover, necessary to give the men a day of rest. But that the time might not wholly be lost, I proceeded with two hands to the extreme south point in sight from our encampment, distant about eight or nine miles."

This extreme point is situate in lat. 72° 38′ N., and long. 95° 40′ W., and is the west face of a small high peninsula. The state of the atmosphere being at the time peculiarly favorable for distinctness of vision, land of any great elevation might have been seen at the distance of 100 miles. The highest cape of the coast was not more than fifty miles distant, bearing nearly due south. A very narrow isthmus was found to separate Prince Regent Inlet from the western sea at Cresswell and Brentford Bays. The ice in this quarter proved to be eight feet thick. A large cairn of stones was erected, and on the 6th of June, the return journey was commenced. After encountering a variety of difficulties they reached the ships on the 23d, so completely worn out by fatigue, that every man was, from some cause or other, in the doctor's hands for two or three weeks. During their absence, Mr. Matthias, the assistant-surgeon of the Enterprise, had died of consumption. Several of the crews of both ships were in a declining state, and the general report of health was by no means cheering.

While Captain Ross was away, Commander Bird had dispatched other surveying parties in different directions. One, under the command of Lieutenant Barnard, to the northern shore of Barrow's Strait, crossing the ice to Cape Hind; a second, commanded by Lieutenant Browne, to the eastern shore of Regent Inlet; and a third party of six men, conducted by Lieutenant Robinson, along the western shore of the Inlet. The latter officer extended his examination of the coast as far as Cresswell Bay, several miles to the southward of Fury Beach. He found the house still standing in which Sir John Ross passed the winters of 1832–33, together with a quantity of the stores and provisions of the Fury, lost there in 1827. On opening some of the packages containing flour, sugar and peas, they were all found to be in excellent preservation, and the preserved soup as good as when manufactured. The labors of these searching parties were, however, of comparatively short duration, as they all suffered from snow-blindness, sprained ankles, and debility.

As it was now but too evident, from no traces of the absent expedition having been met with by any of these parties, that the ships could not have been detained anywhere in this part of the arctic regions, Captain Ross considered it most desirable to push forward to the westward as soon as his ships should be liberated. His chief hopes now centered in the efforts of Sir John Richardson's party; but he felt persuaded that Sir John Franklin's ships must have penetrated so far beyond Melville Island as to induce him to prefer making for the continent of America rather than seeking assistance from the whale ships in Baffin's Bay. The crews, weakened by incessant exertion, were now in a very unfit state to undertake the heavy labor which they had yet to accomplish, but all hands that were able were set to work with saws to cut a channel toward the point of the harbor, a distance of rather more than two miles, and on the 28th of August the ships got clear. Before quitting the port, a house was built of the spare spars of both ships, and covered with such of the housing cloths as could be dispensed with. Twelve months' provisions, fuel, and other necessaries were also left behind, together with the steam launch belonging to the Investigator, which, having been purposely lengthened seven feet, now formed a fine vessel, capable of conveying the whole of Sir John Franklin's party to the whale ships, if necessary.

The Investigator and Enterprise now proceeded toward the northern shore of Barrow's Strait, for the purpose of examining Wellington Channel, and, if possible, penetrating as far as Melville Island, but when about twelve miles from the shore, the ships came to the fixed land-ice, and found it impossible to proceed.

On the 1st of September a strong wind suddenly arising, brought the loose pack, through which they had been struggling, down upon the ships, which were closely beset. At times, during two or three days, they sustained severe pressure, and ridges of hummocks were thrown up all around; but after that time the temperature falling to near zero, it formed the whole body of ice into one solid mass.

The remainder of the narrative, as related by the Commander of the expedition in his official dispatch, will not bear abridgment.

"We were so circumstanced that for some days we could not unship the rudder, and when, by the laborious operation of sawing and removing the hummocks from under the stern, we were able to do so, we found it twisted and damaged; and the ship was so much strained, as to increase the leakage from three inches in a fortnight to fourteen inches daily. The ice was stationary for a few days; the pressure had so folded the lighter pieces over each other and they were so interlaced, as to form one entire sheet, extending from shore to shore of Barrow's Strait, and as far to the east and west as the eye could discern from the mast-head, while the extreme severity of the temperature had cemented the whole so firmly together that it appeared highly improbable that it could break up again this season. In the space which had been cleared away for unshipping the rudder, the newly-formed ice was fifteen inches thick, and in some places along the ship's side the thirteen-feet screws were too short to work. We had now fully made up our minds that the ships were fixed for the winter, and dismal as the prospect appeared, it was far preferable to being carried along the west coast of Baffin's Bay, where the grounded bergs are in such numbers upon the shallow banks off that shore, as to render it next to impossible for ships involved in a pack to escape destruction. It was, therefore, with a mixture of hope and anxiety that, on the wind shifting to the westward, we perceived the whole body of ice begin to drive to the eastward, at the rate of eight to ten miles daily. Every effort on our part was totally unavailing, for no human power could have moved either of the ships a single inch; they were thus completely taken out of our own hands, and in the center of a field of ice more than fifty miles in circumference, were carried along the southern shore of Lancaster Sound.

"After passing its entrance, the ice drifted in a more southerly direction, along the western shore of Baffin's Bay, until we were abreast of Pond's Bay, to the southward of which we observed a great number of icebergs stretching across our path, and presenting the fearful prospect of our worst anticipations. But when least expected by us, our release was almost miraculously brought about. The great field of ice was rent into innumerable fragments, as if by some unseen power."

By energetic exertion, warping, and sailing, the ships got clear of the pack, and reached an open space of water on the 25th of September.

"It is impossible," says Captain Ross, in his concluding observations, "to convey any idea of the sensation we experienced when we found ourselves once more at liberty, while many a grateful heart poured forth its praises and thanksgivings to Almighty God for this unlooked for deliverance."

"The advance of winter had now closed all the harbors against us; and as it was impossible to penetrate to the westward through the pack from which we had just been liberated, I made the signal to the Investigator of my intention to return to England."

After a favorable passage, the ships arrived home early in November, Captain Sir J. C. Ross reporting himself at the Admiralty on the 5th of November.

As this is the last arctic voyage of Sir James C. Ross, it is a fitting place for some record of his arduous services.

Captain Sir James Clarke Ross entered the navy in 1812, and served as volunteer of the first class, midshipman and mate until 1817, with his uncle Commander Ross. In 1818 he was appointed Admiralty midshipman in the Isabella, on Commander Ross's first voyage of discovery to the arctic seas. He was then midshipman in the two following years with Captain Parry, in the Hecla; followed him again in the Fury in his second voyage, and was promoted on the 26th of December, 1822. In 1824 and 1825, he was lieutenant in the Fury, under Captain Hoppner, on Parry's third voyage. In 1827, he was appointed first lieutenant of the Hecla, under Parry, and accompanied him in command of the second boat in his attempt to reach the North Pole. On his return he received his promotion to the rank of commander, the 8th of November, 1827. From 1829 to 1833, he was employed with his uncle as second in command in the Victory on the private expedition sent out by Mr. Felix Booth. During this period he planted, on the 1st of June, 1831, the British flag on the North Magnetic Pole. For this, on his return, he was presented by the Herald's College with an addition to his family arms of an especial crest, representing a flag-staff erect on a rock, with the union jack hoisted thereon, inscribed with the date, "1 June, 1831." On the 23d of October, 1834, he was promoted to the rank of Captain, and in the following year employed in making magnetic observations, preparatory to the general magnetic survey of England. In the close of 1836, it having been represented to the Ad miralty, from Hull, that eleven whale ships, having on board 600 men, were left in the ice in Davis' Strait, and in imminent danger of perishing, unless relief were forwarded to them, the Lords Commissioners resolved upon sending out a ship to search for them. Captain Ross, with that promptitude and humanity which has always characterized him, volunteered to go out in the depth of winter, and the Lieutenants, F. R. M. Crozier, Inman, and Ommaney, with the three mates, Jesse, Buchan, and John Smith, and Mr. Hallett, clerk in charge, joined him. They sailed from England on the 21st of December, and on arriving in Davis' Strait, after a stormy passage, found that nine of the missing ships were by that time in England, that the tenth was released on her passage, and that the other was in all probability lost, as some of her water-casks had been picked up at sea. From 1837 to 1838, Captain Ross was employed in determining the variation of the compass on all parts of the coast of Great Britain; and from 1839 to 1843, as Captain of the Erebus, in command of the antarctic expedition. In 1841, he was presented with the founder's medal of the Royal Geographical Society of London, for his discoveries toward the South Pole; and he has also received the gold medal of the Geographical Society of Paris. On the 13th of March, 1844, he received the honor of knighthood from the Queen, and in June of the same year the University of Oxford bestowed on him their honorary degree of D. C. L. In 1848, he went out, as we have just seen, in the Enterprise, in Command of one of the searching expeditions sent to seek for Franklin.

Voyage of H. M. S. "North Star."

The North Star, of 500 tons, was fitted out in the spring of 1849, under the command of Mr. J. Saunders, who had been acting master with Captain Back, in the Terror, in her perilous voyage to the Frozen Strait, in 1836.

The following are the officers of the ships :—

Master Commanding — J. Saunders.

Second Masters — John Way, M. Norman, H. B. Gawler.

Acting Ice-masters — J. Leach, and G. Sabestor.

Assistant Surgeon — James Rae, M. D.

Clerk in Charge — Jasper Rutter.

The North Star sailed from the river Thames, on the 26th of May, 1849, freighted with provisions for the missing expedition, and with orders and supplies for the Enterprise and Investigator.

The following is one of the early dispatches from the commander :—

"*To the Secretary of the Admiralty.*

"*H. M. S. North Star, July* 19, 1849,
lat. 74° 3′ *N., long.* 59° 40′ *W.*

"Sir,—I addressed a letter to their Lordships on the 18th ult., when in lat. 73° 30′ N., and long. 56° 53′ W., detailing the particulars of my proceedings up to that date, which letter was sent by a boat from the Lady Jane, whaler, which vessel was wrecked, and those boats were proceeding to the Danish settlements. Since then, I regret to state, our progress has been almost entirely stopped, owing to the ice being so placed across Melville Bay as to render it perfectly impassable.

"On the 6th inst., finding it impossible to make any progress, I deemed it advisable to run as far S. as 72°, examining the pack as we went along. At 72° 22′ the pack appeared slacker, and we entered it, and, after proceeding about twelve miles, found ourselves completely stopped by large floes of ice. We accordingly put back, and steered again for the northward.

"Having this day reached the latitude of 74° 3′ N., and long. 59° 40′ W., the ice appeared more open, and we stood in toward the land, when we observed two boats approaching, and which afterward, on coming alongside, were found to belong to the Prince of Wales, whaler, which vessel was nipped by the ice on the 12th inst., in Melville Bay.

"By the captain of the Prince of Wales I forward this letter to their Lordships, he intending to proceed in his boats to the Danish settlements.

"I have the honor to be, &c.

"J. SAUNDERS, Master and Commander.

"P. S.—Crew all well on board."

On the 29th of July, having reached the vicinity of the Devil's Thumb and Melville Bay, in the northerly part of Baffin's Bay, she was beset in an ice-field, with which she drifted helplessly about as the tide or wind impelled her, until the 16th of August, when, a slight opening in the ice appearing, an effort was made to heave through into clear water. This proved labor in vain, and no further move was made until the 21st of September, except as she drifted in the ice floe in which she was fixed. On the day last named she was driving before a hard gale from the S. S. W., directly down upon an enormous iceberg in Melville Sound, upon which if she had struck in the then prevailing weather, her total destruction would have been inevitable. Providentially a corner of the ice-field in which she was being carried furiously along came into violent collision with the berg, a large section was carried away, and she escaped. On the 29th of September, 1849, having been sixty-two days in the ice, she took up her winter quarters in North Star Bay, so called after herself, a small bay in Wolstenholme Sound, lying in 76° 33′ north latitude, and 68° 56′ west longitude; the farthest point to the north at which a British ship ever wintered. The ship was fixed about half a mile from the shore, and made snug for the winter, sails were unbent, the masts struck, and the ship housed over and made as warm and comfortable as circumstances would permit. The ice soon after took across the Sound, so that the crew could have walked on shore. The cold was intense; but two or three stoves warmed the ship, and the crews were cheered up and encouraged with all sorts of games and amusements, occasionally visiting the shore for the purpose of skylarking. There was, unfortunately, but little game to shoot. Former accounts gave this place a high character for deer and other animals; but the crew of the North Star never saw a single head of deer, and other animals were scarce; about fifty hares were killed. Foxes were numerous, and a number shot, but none taken alive. A few Esquimaux families occasionally visited the ship, and one poor man was brought on board with his feet so frozen that they dropped. He was placed under the care of the assistant-surgeon, Dr. Rae, who paid him much attention, and his legs were nearly cured; but he died from a pulmonary disorder after having been on board some six weeks. The North Star was not able to leave this retreat until the 1st of August, 1850, and got into clear water on the third of that month. On the 21st of August, she spoke the Lady Franklin, Captain Penny, and her consort the Sophia, and the following day the Felix, Sir John Ross, in Lancaster Sound. Captain Penny reported that he had left Captain Austin all well on the 17th of August. On the 23d of August, the North Star began landing the provisions she had carried out in Navy Board Inlet; 73° 44′ N. latitude, 80° 56′ W. longitude. She remained five days there, and was occupied four and a half in landing the stores, which were deposited in a ravine a short distance from the beach of Supply Bay, the bight in Navy Board Inlet, which the commander of the North Star so named. The position of the stores was indicated by a flag-staff, with a black ball, and a letter placed beneath a cairn of stones. They had previously tried to deposit the stores at Port Bowen, and Port Neale, but were prevented approaching them by the ice. On the 30th of August, the North Star saw and spoke the schooner Prince Albert, Commander Forsyth, in Possession Bay. On the 31st, a boat was sent to the Prince Albert, when Commander Forsyth came on board and reported that he had also been to Port Neale, but had not been able to enter for the ice, and had found one of the American ships sent out to search for Sir John Franklin ashore in Barrow's Strait, that he had tendered assistance, which had been declined by the American commander, as, his ship being uninjured, he believed his own crew competent to get her off. Commander Forsyth reported that Captain Austin had proceeded to Pond's Bay in the Intrepid, tender to the Assistance, to land letters. The North Star went on to Pond's Bay, but could not find any indication of Captain Austin's having been there. It is conjectured that he had passed the appointed spot in a fog. The North Star's people suffered much from the intense cold, but only lost five hands during her perilous trip and arctic winter quarters. She left there on September 9th, and reached Spithead on the 28th of September, 1850. Since his return Mr. Saunders has been appointed Master Attendant of the Dock-yard at Malta. The Admiralty have received dispatches from Captain Sir J. Ross, Captain Penny, and Captain Ommaney. Captain Ommaney, in the Assistance, dating from off Lancaster Sound, latitude 75° 46′ N., longitude 75° 49′ W., states that some Esquimaux had described to him a ship being hauled in during the last winter, and, on going to the spot, he found, from some papers left, that it was the North Star. He was proceeding to search in Lancaster Sound. Captain Penny, of the Lady Franklin, writing from Lancaster Sound, August 21, states, that having heard on the 18th from Captain Austin of a report from the Esquimaux, that Sir John Franklin's ships had been lost forty miles north, and the crews murdered, he went with an interpreter, but could find no evidence for the rumor, and came to the conclusion that the whole story had been founded on the North Star's wintering there. He considered that his interpreter, M. Petersen, had done much good by exposing the fallacy of the story of Sir J Ross's Esquimaux.

Her Majesty's Ships "Enterprise" and "Investigator" under Captain Collinson.

The Enterprise and Investigator were fitted out agair immediately on their return home, and placed undei the charge of Captain B. Collinson, C. B., with the fol lowing officers attached, to proceed to Behring's Strait, to resume the search in that direction :—

Enterprise, 340 *tons*.

Captain — R. Collinson.
Lieutenants — G. A. Phayre,* J. J. Barnard,* and C. T. Jago.
Master — R. T. G. Legg.
Second Master — Francis Skead.
Mate — M. T. Parks.
Surgeon — Robert Anderson.*
Assistant-Surgeon — Edward Adams.*
Clerk in Charge — Edward Whitehead.*
Total complement, 66.

Investigator.

Commander — R. J. M'Clure.*
Lieutenants — W. H. Haswell and S. G. Cresswell.*
Mates — H. H. Saintsbury and R. J. Wyniatt.
Second Master — Stephen Court.*
Surgeon — Alexander Armstrong, M. D.
Assistant-Surgeon — Hy. Piers.
Clerk in Charge — Joseph C. Paine.
Total complement, 66.

Those officers marked with a star had been with the ships in their last voyage.

These vessels sailed from Plymouth on the 20th of January, 1850. A Mr. Miertsching, a Moravian missionary, was appointed to the Enterprise, as interpreter. This gentleman is in the prime of life, of robust health, inured, by a service of five years in Labrador, to the hardships and privations of the arctic regions, and sufficiently acquainted with the language and manners of the Esquimaux to be able to hold friendly and unreserved intercourse with them.

The Investigator and the Enterprise were at the Sandwich Islands on June 29th. Captain Collinson purposed sailing in a few days, and expected to reach the ice about the 8th of July. Prior to his arrival, numerous whalers had started for the Strait, one in particular, under the command of a Captain Roys, with the expressed intention of endeavoring to earn the Franklin reward.

These vessels are intended to penetrate, if possible, to the western extremity of Melville Island, there to winter, and make further search, in the spring of 1851, for the crews of the lost ships.

In a letter from Captain Collinson to Commander Mc Clure, dated Oahu, June 29th, 1850, with a sight of which I have been favored at the Admiralty, he thus describes his intentions—"I intend making the pack close to the American shore, and availing myself of the first favorable opening west of the coast stream ; pressing forward toward Melville Island. In the event of meeting land, it is most probable that I would pursue the southern shore."

The latest letter received from Commander McClure is dated Kotzebue Sound, July 27th, 1850, and the following is an extract :—

"You will be glad to learn that to this we have been highly favored, carrying a fair wind from Whoa, which place we left on the 4th. We passed the Aleutian Islands on the 20th, in 172° 30′ W., and got fairly through the Straits to-day, and we consider we are upon our ground; the only detriment has been very dense fogs, which have rendered the navigation of the islands exceedingly nervous work; but as the object to be achieved is of so important a nature, all hazards must be run to carry out the intentions of those at home, which have very fortunately terminated without accident. We are now making the most of our wind, and we hope to meet an American whaler, of which I believe there are a great number fishing this season, and to whom we must intrust our last dispatches. Sincerely do I trust that, ere we return, some tidings of poor Sir John and his noble companions may reward our search; which will render the long-sought for passage, should it be our fortune to make it, one of the most memorable in the annals of our times, and relieve many an anxious breast"

Dispatches have been received at the Admiralty from Captain Kellet, C. B., of her Majesty's ship Herald, dated at sea, the 14th of October, 1850, on his return from Behring's Strait. The Herald had communicated with her Majesty's ship Plover, on the 10th of July, at Chamisso Island, where the Plover had passed the preceding winter. The two ships proceeded to the northward until they sighted the pack-ice, when the Herald returned to Cape Lisburne, in quest of Captain Collinson's expedition, and on the 31st fell in with her Majesty's ship Investigator, which had made a surprisingly short passage of twenty-six days from the Sandwich Islands. The Herald remained cruising off Cape Lisburne, and again fell in with the Plover on the 13th of August, on her return from Point Barrow, Commander Moore having coasted in his boats, and minutely examined the several inlets as far as that point from Icy Cape without gaining any intelligence of the missing expedition. Commander Moore and his boat's crew had suffered severely from exposure to cold. Captain Kellet, having fully victualed the Plover, ordered her to winter in Grantley Harbor (her former anchorage at Chamisso Island not being considered safe,) and then returned to the southward on his way to England.

Dispatches have also been received from Captain Collinson, C. B., of her Majesty's ship Enterprise, and Commander M'Clure, of her Majesty's ship Investigator of which the following are copies :—

"*Her Majesty's Ship 'Enterprise.'*
"*Port Clarence, Sept.* 13, 1850.

"Sir,—I have the honor to transmit an account of the proceedings of her Majesty's ship under my command since leaving Oahu on the 30th of June.

"Being delayed by light winds, we only reached the western end of the Aleutian Chain by the 29th of July, and made the Island of St. Lawrence on the 11th of August, from whence I shaped a course for Cape Lisburne, in anticipation of falling in with the Herald or the Plover. Not, however, seeing either of these vessels, and finding nothing deposited on shore, I went on to Wainwright Inlet, the last rendezvous appointed. Here we communicated on the 15th, and being alike unsuccessful in obtaining any information, I stood to the north, made the ice following morning, and reached the latitude 72° 40′ N. in the meridian of 159° 30′ W., without serious obstruction. Here, however, the pack became so close that it was impossible to make way in any direction except to the southward. Having extricated ourselves by noon on the 19th, we continued to coast along the edge of the main body, which took a southeasterly trend, running through the loose streams, so as not to lose sight of tight pack. At 4 A. M. on the 20th we were in the meridian of Point Barrow, and twenty-eight miles to the north of it, when we found open water to the N. E., in which we sailed, without losing sight of the ice to the north until the morning of the 21st, when we were obstructed by a heavy barrier trending to the southwest. A thick fog coming on, we made a board to the north, in order to feel the pack edge in the upper part of the bight, and not to leave any part unexplored. Having satisfied myself that no opening existed in this direction, we bore away to the south, running through heavy floes closely packed, and pushing to the eastward when an opportunity offered. In this, however, we were unsuccessful, being compelled to pursue a westerly course, the floes being very heavy and hummocky. By 8 P. M. we were within thirty miles of the land, and having clear weather, could see the ice closely packed to the south that left no doubt in my mind that a stop was put to our proceeding in this direction, by the ice butting so close on the shoal coast as to leave no chance that our progress along it would justify the attempt to reach Cape Bathurst, a distance of 570 miles, during the remaining portion of this season; and finding this opinion was coincided in by those officers on board qualified to form an opinion on the subject, I determined to lose no time in communicating with Point Barrow, but to attempt the passage further north, in hopes that the lane of water seen last year by the Herald and Plover would afford me an opening to the eastward. I therefore reluctantly proceeded again to the west, and turning the pack edge fifteen miles further to the south than it was on the day after we left Wainwright Inlet, we followed the edge of a loose pack greatly broken up, until we reached 163° W. long., when it took a sudden turn to the north, in which direction we followed it until the morning of the 27th, when we were in latitude 73° 20′, and found the pack to the westward trending southerly. I therefore plied to the eastward, endeavoring to make way, but such was its close condition that we could not work, although we might have warped through, had the condition of the ice in that direction afforded us any hope; but this, I am sorry to say, was not the case, and, on the contrary, the further we entered, the larger the floes became, leaving us, in thick weather, often in great difficulty where to find a lane. On the 29th the thermometer having fallen to 28°, and there being no prospect of our being able to accomplish any thing toward the fulfillment of their Lordships' instructions this season, I bore away for Point Hope, where I arrived on the 31st, and found a bottle deposited by the Herald, which informed me that it was intended to place the Plover in Grantley Harbor this season. I accordingly proceeded thither, with the view of taking her place for the winter, and enabling Commander Moore to recruit his ship's company by going to the southward. On my arrival I found her inside, preparing her winter quarters, and having examined and buoyed the bar, I attempted to take this vessel inside, but failed in doing so, owing to the change of wind from south to north having reduced the depth of water four feet, and had to relieve the ship of 100 tons, which was quickly done by the opportune arrival of the Herald, before she was released from a very critical position. The tides being irregular, the rise and fall depending principally on the wind, and that wind which occasions the highest water producing a swell on the bar, it became a question whether a considerable portion of the ensuing season might not be lost in getting the ship out of Grantley Harbor; and on consulting Captains Kellet and Moore, finding it to be their opinion, founded on the experience of two years, that the whalers coming from the south pass through the Strait early in June, whereas the harbors are blocked until the middle of July, I have come to the conclusion that I shall better perform the important duty confided in me by returning to the south, and replenishing my provisions, instead of wintering on the Asiatic Shore, where there is not a prospect of our being of the slightest use to the missing expedition. It is therefore my intention to proceed to Hong Kong, it being nearer than Valparaiso, and the cold season having set in, my stores and provisions will not be exposed to the heat of a double passage through the tropics; and as I shall not leave until the 1st of April, I may receive any further instructions their Lordships may please to communicate.

"The Plover has been stored and provisioned, and such of her crew as are not in a fit state to contend with the rigor of a further stay in these latitudes have been removed, and replaced by Captain Kellet, and the paragraphs referring to her in my instructions fulfilled

"I have directed Commander Moore to communicate annually with an Island in St. Lawrence Bay, in latitude 65° 38′ N., and longitude 170° 43′ W., which is much resorted to by the whalers, and where any communication their Lordships may be pleased to send may be deposited by them, as they are not in the habit of cruising on this side of the Strait; and I have requested Captain Kellet to forward to the Admiralty all the information on this head he may obtain at the Sandwich Islands.

"It is my intention to proceed again to the north, and remain in the most eligible position for affording assistance to the Investigator, which vessel, having been favored with a surprising passage from the Sandwich Islands, was fallen in with by the Herald on the

31st of July, off Point Hope, and again on the 5th of August, by the Plover, in latitude 70° 44′ N., and longitude 159° 52′W., when she was standing to the north under a press of sail, and in all probability reached the vicinity of Point Barrow, fifteen days previous to the Enterprise, when Captain M'Clure, having the whole season before him, and animated with the determination so vividly expressed in his letter to Captain Kellett, has most likely taken the inshore route, and I hope before this period reached Cape Bathurst; but as he will be exposed to the imminent risk of being forced on a shoal shore and compelled to take to his boats, I shall not forsake the coast to the northward of Point Hope until the season is so far advanced as to insure their having taken up their winter quarters for this season.

"I have received from my officers and ship's company that assistance and alacrity in the performance of their duty, which the noble cause in which we are engaged must excite, and I have the satisfaction to report that (under the blessing of God) owing to the means their Lordships have supplied in extra clothing and provisions, we are at present without a man on the sick list, notwithstanding the lengthened period of our voyage.

"I have, &c.,
RICHARD COLLINSON, Captain.
"The Secretary of the Admiralty."

"*Her Majesty's Discovery-ship 'Investigator,' at sea, latitude* 51° 26′ *N., longitude* 172° 35′ *W., July* 20.

SIR,—As I have received instructions from Captain Collinson, C. B., clear and unembarrassing, (a copy of which I inclose,) to proceed to Cape Lisburne in the hope of meeting him in that vicinity, as he anticipates being detained a day or two by the Plover in Kotzebue Sound, it is unnecessary to add that every exertion shall be made to reach that rendezvous, but can scarce venture to hope that even under very favorable circumstances I shall be so fortunate as to accomplish it ere the Enterprise will have rounded that cape, from her superior sailing, she hitherto having beaten us by eight days to Cape Virgins, and from Magellan Strait to Oahu six. It is, therefore, under the probable case that this vessel may form a detached part of the expedition that I feel it my duty to state, for the information of the Lords Commissioners of the Admiralty, the course which, under such a contingency, I shall endeavor to pursue, and have to request that you will lay the same before their Lordships.

"1. After passing Cape Lisburne, it is my intention to keep in the open water, which, from the different reports that I have read, appears about this season of the year to make between the American coast and the main pack as far to the northward as the 130th meridian, unless a favorable opening should earlier appear in the ice, which would lead me to infer that I might push more directly for Banks' Land, which I think is of the utmost importance to thoroughly examine. In the event of thus far succeeding, and the season continuing favorable for further operations, it would be my anxious desire to get to the northward of Melville Island, and resume our search along its shores and the islands adjacent as long as the navigation can be carried on, and then secure for the winter in the most eligible position which offers.

"2. In the ensuing spring, as soon as it is practicable for traveling parties to start, I should dispatch as many as the state of the crew will admit of in different directions, each being provided with forty days' provisions, with directions to examine minutely all bays, inlets and islands toward the northeast, ascending occasionally some of the highest points of land, so as to be enabled to obtain extended views, being particularly cautious in their advance to observe any indication of a break up in the ice, so that their return to the ship may be effected without hazard, even before the expenditure of their provisions would otherwise render it necessary.

"3. Supposing the parties to have returned without

obtaining any clue of the absent ships, and the vessel liberated about the 1st of August, my object would then be to push on toward Wellington Inlet, assuming that that channel communicates with the Polar Sea, and search both its shores, unless in doing so some indication should be met with to show that parties from any of Captain Austin's vessels had previously done so, when I should return, and endeavor to penetrate in the direction of Jones' Sound, carefully examining every place that was practicable. Should our efforts to reach this point be successful, and in the route no traces are discernible of the long missing expedition, I should not then be enabled longer to divest myself of the feelings, painful as it must be to arrive at such a conclusion, that all human aid would then be perfectly unavailing; and therefore, under such a conviction, I would think it my duty, if possible, to return to England, or at all events endeavor to reach some port that would insure that object upon the following year.

"4. In the event of this being our last communication, I would request you to assure their lordships that no apprehensions whatever need be entertained of our safety until the autumn of 1854, as we have on board three years of all species of provisions, commencing from the 1st of September proximo, which, without much deprivation, may be made to extend over a period of four years; moreover, whatever is killed by the hunting parties, I intend to issue in lieu of the usual rations, which will still further protract our resources.

"It gives me great pleasure to say that the good effects of the fruit and vegetables, (a large quantity of which we took on board at Oahu,) are very perceptible in the increased vigor of the men, who at this moment are in as excellent condition as it is possible to desire, and evince a spirit of confidence and a cheerfulness of disposition which are beyond all appreciation.

"5. Should difficulties apparently insurmountable encompass our progress, so as to render it a matter of doubt whether the vessel could be extricated, I should deem it expedient in that case not to hazard the lives of those intrusted to my charge after the winter of 1852, but in the ensuing spring quit the vessel with sledges and boats, and make the best of our way either to Pond's Bay, Leopold Harbor, the Mackenzie, or for whalers, according to circumstances.

"Finally. In this letter I have endeavored to give an outline of what I wish to accomplish, (and what, under moderately favorable seasons, appears to me attainable,) the carrying out of which, however, not resting upon human exertions, it is impossible even to surmise if any, or what, portion may be successful. But my object in addressing you is to place their Lordships in possession of my intentions up to the latest period, so far as possible, to relieve their minds from any unnecessary anxiety as to our fate; and having done this, a duty which is incumbent from the deep sympathy expressed by their Lordships, and participated in by all classes of our countrymen, in the interesting object of this expedition, I have only to add, that with the ample resources which a beneficent government and a generous country have placed at our disposal, (not any thing that can add to our comfort being wanting,) we enter upon this distinguished service with a firm determination to carry out, as far as in our feeble strength we are permitted, their benevolent intentions.

"I have, &c.,
"ROBERT M'CLURE, Commander."

"*Her Majesty's ship 'Enterprise,'*
"*Oahu, June* 29, 1850.

"MEMORANDUM.—As soon as Her Majesty's ship under your command is fully complete with provisions, fuel, and water, you will make the best of your way to Cape Lisburne, keeping a good look-out for the Herald, or casks, and firing guns in foggy weather, after passing Lawrence Bay. The whalers also may afford you information of our progress.

"Should you obtain no intelligence, you will understand that I intend to make the pack close to the American shore, and pursue the first favorable opening west of the Coast stream, pressing forward toward Melville Island. In the event of meeting land, it is most probable that I would pursue the southern shore, but conspicuous marks will be erected, if practicable, and information buried at a ten-foot radius.

"As it is necessary to be prepared for the contingency of your not being able to follow by the ice closing in, or the severity of the weather, you will in that case keep the Investigator as close to the edge of the pack as is consistent with her safety, and remain there until the season compels you to depart, when you will look into Kotzebue Sound for the Plover, or information regarding her position; and having deposited under her charge a twelve month's provisions, you will proceed to Valparaiso, replenish, and return to the Strait, bearing in mind that the months of June and July are the most favorable.

"A letter from the hydrographer relative to the variation of the compass is annexed; and you will bear in mind that the value of these observations will he greatly enhanced by obtaining the variation with the ship's head at every second or fourth point round the compass occasionally, and she should be swung for deviation in harbor as often as opportunity may offer.

"Should you not find the Plover, or that any casualty has happened to render her inefficient as a depot, you will take her place; and if, (as Captain Kellett supposes,) Kotzebue Sound has proved too exposed for a winter harbor, you will proceed to Grantley Harbor, leaving a notice to that effect on Chamisso Island. The attention of your officers is to be called, and you will read to your ship's company, the remarks of Sir J. Richardson concerning the communication with the Esquimaux, contained in the arctic report received at Plymouth.

"Your operations in the season 1851, cannot be guided by me, nor is there any occasion to urge you to proceed to the northeast; yet it will be highly desirable, previous to entering the pack, that you completed provisions from whalers, and obtained as much reindeer meat as possible. Captain Kellett's narrative will point out where the latter is to be had in most abundance, and where coal can be picked up on the beach; but husband the latter article during the winter, by using all the drift-wood in your power.

"In the event of leaving the Strait this season, you will take any weak or sickly men out of the Plover, and replace them from your crews, affording Commander Moore all the assistance in your power, and leaving with him Mr. Miertsching, the interpreter; instructions with regard to whose accommodations you have received, and will convey to the captain of the Plover. "RICHARD COLLINSON.

"*To Commander M'Clure, of her Majesty's ship 'Investigator.'*

"Should it be the opinion of Commander Moore that the services of the Investigator's ship's company in exploring parties during the spring would be attended with material benefit to the object of the expedition, he will, notwithstanding these orders, detain you for that purpose; but care must be taken that your efficiency as a sailing vessel is not crippled by the parties not returning in time for the opening of the sea.

"R. C."

"*Her Majesty's discovery ship 'Investigator,' July* 28, 1850. *Kotzebue Sound, latitude* 66° 54′ *N., longitude* 168° *W.*

"Sir,—I have the honor to acquaint you, for the information of the Lords Commissioners of the Admiralty, that to this date we have had a most excellent run. Upon getting clear of Oahu, on the morning of the 5th, we shaped a course direct for the Aleutian group, passing them in 172° 40′ W., upon the evening of the 20th; continued our course with a fine south-easterly breeze, but extremely thick and foggy weather, (which retarded the best of our way being made.) Got fairly out of Behring's Strait upon the evening of the

27th, and are now in a fair way of realizing their Lordships' expectations of reaching the ice by the beginning of August, our progress being advanced by the favorable circumstances of a fine southerly wind and tolerably clear weather. The latter we have known nothing of since the 19th, which, I can assure you, rendered the navigation among the islands a subject of much and deep anxiety, seldom having a horizon above 480 yards, that just enabled the dark outline of the land to be observed and avoided.

"It is with much satisfaction that I report the good qualities of this vessel, having well tried her in the heavy gales experienced during five weeks off Cape Horn, and in moderate weather among the intricate navigation of these islands, where so much depended upon her quick obedience to the helm, although laden with every species of stores and provisions for upward of three years. From these circumstances I am, therefore, fully satisfied she is as thoroughly adapted for this service as could be reasonably wished.

"I have not seen any thing of the Enterprise, nor is it my intention to lose a moment by waiting off Cape Lisburne, but shall use my best endeavors to carry out the intentions contained in my letter of the 20th, of which I earnestly trust their Lordships will approve.

"I am happy to be able to state that the whole crew are in excellent health and spirits, and every thing as satisfactory as it is possible to desire.

"I have, &c.,

"ROBERT M'CLURE, Commander.

"*The Secretary of the Admiralty.*"

VOYAGE OF H. M. S. "PLOVER," AND BOAT EXPEDITIONS UNDER COMMANDER PULLEN, 1848–51.

In the copy of the instructions issued from the Admiralty to Lieutenant, (now Commander,) Moore, of the Plover, dated 3d of January, 1848, he was directed to make the best of his way to Petropaulowski, touching at Panama, where she was to be joined by H. M.

M*

S. Herald, and afterward both vessels were to proceed to Behring's Strait, where they were expected to arrive about the 1st of July, and then push along the American coast, as far as possible, consistent with the certainty of preventing the ships being beset by the ice. The Plover was then to be secured for the winter in some safe and convenient port from whence boat parties might be dispatched, and the Herald was to return and transmit, *via* Panama, any intelligence necessary to England. Great caution was ordered to be observed in communicating with the natives in the neighborhood of Kotzebue Sound, should that quarter be visited, as the people in that part of the country differ in character from the ordinary Esquimaux, in being comparatively a fierce, agile, and suspicious race, well armed with knives, &c., for offense, and prone to attack. They were also ordered to take interpreters or guides from a small factory of the Russian-American Company in Norton Sound.

The Plover was safely ensconced for the winter of 1849–50 in Kotzebue Sound, after the termination of a hard season's work. She had, conjointly with the Herald, discovered to the north of Behring's Strait, two islands, and several apparently disconnected patches of very elevated ground. Lieut. Pullen had previously quitted her off Wainwright Inlet, with four boats, for the purpose of prosecuting his adventurous voyage along the coast to the mouth of the Mackenzie River, where he arrived safely on the 26th of August, after a perilous navigation of thirty-two days, but had obtained no clue or intelligence regarding the prime object of his expedition. At a later date he encountered at Fort Simpson, higher up the river, Dr. Rae, and gathered from that gentleman that the party led by him down the Coppermine, with the view of crossing over to Victoria or Wollaston Land, had, owing to the unusual difficulties created by the more than customary rigor of the season, met with entire failure; the farthest point attained being Cape Krusenstern.

Lieut. Pullen is occupied during the present year in

a journey from the mouth of the Mackenzie eastward, along the arctic coast, as far as Cape Bathurst, and this being successfully accomplished, he purposes attempting to cross the intervening space to Banks' Land. He is furnished with two boats, both open.

Lieut. W. H. Hooper, one of the party, in a recent letter to his father in London, writing from Great Slave Lake, under date June 27, 1850, gives some further details of their proceedings. Having had considerable trouble and a slight skirmish with some parties of Esquimaux, they were obliged to be continually on the watch. At the end of August, the party entered the Mackenzie River, and in a few days reached one of the Hudson's Bay Company's posts on the Peel River, a branch of the Mackenzie, where Commander Pullen left Lieut. Hooper and half the party to winter, while he proceeded farther up the river to a more important post at Fort Simpson. After remaining at Peel's River station about a fortnight, Mr. Hooper found that his party could not be maintained throughout the winter there, and in consequence determined on following Capt. Pullen, but was only able to reach Fort Norman, one of his party being frost-bitten on the journey. They thence made their way across to Great Bear Lake, where they passed the winter, subsisting on fish and water. Dr. Rae arrived there as soon as the ice broke up, and the party proceeded with him to Fort Simpson.

On the 20th of June, Commander Pullen and all his party left with the company's servants, and the stock of furs, on their way to the sea, to embark for England, when they were met, on the 25th, by a canoe with Admiralty dispatches, which caused them to retrace their steps ; and they are now on their route by the Great Slave Lake to Fort Simpson, and down the Mackenzie once more, to the Polar Sea, in search of Sir John Franklin.

"However grieving," Lieut. Hooper adds, "it is to be disappointed of returning home, yet I am nevertheless delighted to go again, and think that we do not hopelessly undertake another search, since our intended direction is considered the most probable channel for finding the missing ships or crews. We go down the Mackenzie, along the coast eastward to Point Bathurst, and thence strike across to Wollaston or Banks' Land. The season will, of course, much influence our proceedings; but we shall probably return up the hitherto unexplored river which runs into the Arctic Ocean from Liverpool Bay, between the Coppermine and Mackenzie."

The latest official dispatch from Commander Pullen is dated Great Slave Lake, June 28th. He had been stopped by the ice, and intended returning to Fort Simpson on the 29th. One of his boats was so battered about as to be perfectly useless; he intended patching up the other, and was also to receive a new boat belonging to the Hudson's Bay Company, from Fort Simpson. He had dismissed two of his party, as they were both suffering from bad health, but proposed engaging, at Fort Good Hope, two Hare Indians as hunters and guides, one of whom had accompanied Messrs. Dease and Simpson on their trips of discovery in 1838 and 1839. This would augment the party to seventeen persons in all.

"My present intentions," he says, "are to proceed down the Mackenzie, along the coast, to Cape Bathurst, and then strike across for Banks' Land; my operations must then, of course be guided by circumstances, but I shall strenuously endeavor to search along all coasts in that direction as far and as late as I can with safety venture; returning, if possible, by the Mackenzie, or by the Beghoola, which the Indians speak of as being navigable, as its head waters are, (according to Sir John Richardson,) only a nine-days' passage from Fort Good Hope; to meet which, or a similar contingency, I take snow shoes and sledges, &c.

"In conclusion, I beg to assure their Lordships of my earnest determination to carry out their views to the utmost of my ability, being confident, from the eagerness of the party, that no pains will be spared, no necessary labor avoided, and, by God's blessing, we hope to be successful in discovering some tidings of our gallant countrymen, or even in restoring them to their native land and anxious relatives."

Mr. Chief Factor Rae was about to follow Commander Pullen and his party from Portage La Loche.

Dr. Richardson observes that "Commander Pullen will require to be fully victualed for at least 120 days from the 20th of July, when he may be expected to commence his sea voyage; which, for sixteen men, will require forty-five bags of pemmican of 90 lbs. each. This is exclusive of a further supply which he ought to take for the relief of any of Franklin's people he may have the good fortune to find. After he leaves the main-land at Cape Bathurst, he would have no chance of killing deer till he makes Banks' Land, or some intervening island; and he must provide for the chance of being caught on the floe ice, and having to make his way across by the very tedious portages, as fully described by Sir W. E. Parry in the narative of his most adventurous boat voyage north of Spitzbergen.

"Mr. Rae can give Commander Pullen the fullest information respecting the depots of pemmican made on the coast.

"With respect to Commander Pullen's return from sea, his safest plan will be to make for the Mackenzie; but should circumstances place that out of his power, the only other course that seems to me to be practicable is for him to ascend a large river which falls into the bottom of Liverpool Bay, to the westward of Cape Bathurst. This river, which is named the Begloola Dessy by the Indians, runs parallel to the Mackenzie, and in the latitude of Fort Good Hope, (66° 30′ N.,) is not above five or six days' journey from that post. Hare Indians, belonging to Fort Good Hope, might be engaged to hunt on the banks of the river till the arrival of the party. The navigation of the river is unknown; but even should Commander Pullen be compelled to quit his boats, his Indian hunters, (of which he should at least engage two for his sea voyage,) will support and guide his party. Wood and animals are most certainly found on the banks of river-

"It is not likely that under any circumstances Commander Pullen should desire to reach the Mackenzie by way of the Coppermine River, and this could be effected only by a boat being placed at Dease River, for the transport of the party over Great Bear Lake. This would require to be arranged previously with Mr. Rae; and Commander Pullen should not be later in arriving at Fort Confidence than the end of September."

Voyage of the "Lady Franklin" and "Sophia," Government Vessels, under the command of Mr. Penny, 1850–51.

A vessel of 230 tons, named the Lady Franklin, fitted out at Aberdeen, with a new brig as a tender, built at Dundee, and named the Sophia, in honor of Miss S. Cracroft, the beloved and attached niece of Lady Franklin, and one of the most anxious watchers for tidings of the long missing adventurers, were purchased by the government last year.

The charge of this expedition was intrusted to Captain Penny, formerly commanding the Advice whaler, and who has had much experience in the icy seas, having been engaged twenty-eight years, since the age of twelve, in the whaling trade, and in command of vessels for fourteen years; Mr. Stewart was placed in charge of the Sophia.

The crew of the Lady Franklin number twenty-five, and that of the Sophia, twenty, all picked men.

These ships sailed on the 12th of April, 1850, provisioned and stored for three years. They were provided with a printing press, and every appliance to relieve the tedium of a long sojourn in the icy regions.

In the instructions issued by the Admiralty, it is stated that in accepting Captain Parry's offer of service, regard has been had to his long experience in arctic navigation, and to the great attention he has paid to the subject of the missing ships.

He was left in a great measure to the exercise of his

own judgment and discretion, in combining the most active and energetic search after the Erebus and Terror, with a strict and careful regard to the safety of the ships and their crews under his charge. He was directed to examine Jones' Sound at the head of Baffin's Bay, and if possible, penetrate through to the Parry Islands ; failing in this, he was to try Wellington Strait, and endeavor to reach Melville Island. He was to use his utmost endeavors, (consistent with the safety of the lives of those intrusted to his command,) to succor, in the summer of 1850, the party under Sir John Franklin, taking care to secure his winter-quarters in good time ; and 2dly, the same active measures were to be used in the summer of 1851, to secure the return of the ships under his charge to this country.

The Lady Franklin was off Cape York, in Baffin's Bay, on the 13th of August. From thence she proceeded, in company with H. M. S. Assistance, to Wolstenholme Sound. She afterward, in accordance with her instructions, crossed over to the west with the intention of examining Jones' Sound, but owing to the accumulation of ice, was unable to approach it within twenty-five miles. This was at midnight on the 18th. She, therefore, continued her voyage to Lancaster Sound, and onward to Wellington Channel, where she was seen by Commander Forsyth, of the Prince Albert, on the 25th of August, with her tender, and H. M. S. Assistance in company, standing toward Cape Hotham.

Voyage of H. M. Ships "Resolute" and "Assistance," with the Steamers "Pioneer" and "Intrepid" as Tenders, under command of Captain Austin, 1850–51.

Two fine teak-built ships of about 500 tons each, the Baboo and Ptarmigan, whose names were altered to the Assistance and Resolute, were purchased by the government in 1850, and sent to the naval yards to be properly fitted for the voyage to the polar regions.

Two screw-propeller steamers, intended to accompany

these vessels as steam tenders, were also purchased and similarly fitted; their names were changed from the Eider and Free Trade to the Pioneer and Intrepid.

The command of this expedition was intrusted to Captain Horatio T. Austin, C. B., who was first Lieutenant of the Fury, under Commander Hoppner, in Captain Sir E. Parry's third voyage, in 1824–25. The vessels were provisioned for three years, and their attention was also directed to the depots of stores lodged by Sir James Ross at Leopold Island, and at Navy Board Inlet by the North Star. The ships sailed in May, 1850. The officers employed in them were as follows:—

Resolute.

Captain — Horatio T. Austin, C. B.
Lieutenants — R. D. Aldrich, and W. H. J. Browne.
Mates — R. B. Pearse, and W. M. May.
Purser — J. E. Brooman.
Surgeon — A. R. Bradford.
Assistant, ditto — Richard King.
Midshipmen — C. Bullock, J. P. Cheyne.
Second Master — G. F. M'Dougall.
Total complement, 60 men.

Pioneer, screw steamer.

Lieut.-Commanding — Sherard Osborn.
Second Master — J. H. Allard.
Assistant-Surgeon — F. R. Picthorn.

Assistance.

Captain — E. Ommaney.
Lieutenants — J. E. Elliot, F. L. M'Clintock, and G. F. Mecham.
Surgeon — J. J. L. Donnett.
Assistant, ditto — J. Ward, (*a.*)
Mates — R. V. Hamilton, and J. R. Keane.
Clerk in Charge — E. N. Harrison.
Second Master — W. B. Shellabear.
Midshipman — C. R. Markham.
Total complement, 60 men.

Intrepid, screw steamer.

Lieut.-Commander —B. Cator.

Each of the tenders had a crew of 30 men.

Two of the officers appointed to this expedition, Lieutenants Browne and M'Clintock, were in the Enterprise under Captain Sir James C. Ross in 1848.

The Emma Eugenia transport was dispatched in advance with provisions to the Whale-Fish Islands, to await the arrival of the expedition.

It having been suggested by some parties that Sir John Franklin might have effected his passage to Melville Island, and been detained there with his ships, or that the ships might have been damaged by the ice in the neighboring sea, and that with his crews he had abandoned them and made his escape to that island, Captain Austin was specially instructed to use every exertion to reach this island, detaching a portion of his ships to search the shores of Wellington Channel and the coast about Cape Walker, to which point Sir John Franklin was ordered to proceed.

Advices were first received from the Assistance, after her departure, dated 5th of July; she was then making her way to the northward. The season was less favorable for exploring operations than on many previous years. But little ice had been met with in Davis' Strait, where it is generally found in large quantities, so that obstacles of a serious nature may be expected to the northward. Penny's ships had been in company with them.

Ice is an insurmountable barrier to rapid progress; fortifications may be breached, but huge masses of ice, 200 to 600 feet high, are not to be overcome.

On the 2d of July the Assistance was towed beneath a perpendicular cliff to the northward of Cape Shackleton, rising to the height of 1500 feet, which was observed to be crowded with the foolish guillemots, (*Uria troile.*) When the ship hooked on to an iceberg for the night, a party sent on shore for the purpose brought off 260 birds and about twenty dozen of their eggs. These birds only lay one egg each.

20

The following official dispatch has been since received from Captain Ommaney:—

"*Her Majesty's ship 'Assistance,' off Lancaster Sound, latitude* 75° 46′ *N., longitude* 75° 49′ *W., August* 17, 1850.

"Sir,—I have the honor to acquaint you, for the information of the Lords Commissioners of the Admiralty, that her Majesty's ship Assistance, and her tender, her Majesty's steam-vessel Intrepid, have this day succeeded in effecting a passage across to the west water, and are now proceeding to Lancaster Sound. Officers and crews all well, with fine clear weather, and open water as far as can be seen.

"Agreeably with instructions received from Captain H. Austin, we parted company on the 15th instant, at one A. M., off Cape Dudley Diggs, as the ice was then sufficiently open to anticipate no farther obstruction in effecting the north passage. He was anxious to proceed to Pond's Bay, and thence take up the examination along the south shores of Lancaster Sound, leaving me to ascertain the truth of a report obtained from the Esquimaux at Cape York respecting some ship or ships having been seen near Wolstenholme Island, after which to proceed to the north shores of Lancaster Sound and Wellington Channel.

"On passing Cape York, (the 14th inst.,) natives were seen. By the directions of Captain Austin I landed, and communicated with them, when we were informed that they had seen a ship in that neighborhood in the spring, and that she was housed in. Upon this intelligence I shipped one of the natives, who volunteered to join us as interpreter and guide.

"On parting with Captain Austin we proceeded toward Wolstenholme Island, where I left the ship and proceeded in her Majesty's steam-vessel Intrepid into Wolstenholme Sound, and by the guidance of the Esquimaux, succeeded in finding a bay about thirteen miles further in, and sheltered by a prominent headland. In the cairns erected here we found a document stating that the North Star had wintered in the bay, a copy of which I have the honor to transmit to their Lordships.

"Previous to searching the spot where the North Star wintered, I examined the deserted Esquimaux settlement. At this spot we found evident traces of some ship having been in the neighborhood, from empty preserved meat canisters and some clothes left near a pool of water, marked with the name of a corporal belonging to the North Star.

"Having ascertained this satisfactory information, I returned to Wolstenholme Island, where a document was deposited recording our proceedings. At 6 A. M., of the 16th inst., I rejoined the ship, and proceeded at two to the westward, and am happy to inform you that the passage across has been made without obstruction, towing through loose and straggling ice.

"The expedition was beset in Melville Bay, surrounded by heavy and extensive floes of ice, from the 11th of July to the 9th of August, 1850, when, after great exertion, a release was effected, and we succeeded in reaching Cape York by continuing along the edge of the land-ice, after which we have been favored with plenty of water.

"Captain Penny's expedition was in company during the most part of the time while in Melville Bay, and up to the 14th inst., when we left him off Cape Dudley Diggs — all well.

"In crossing Melville Bay we fell in with Sir John Ross and Captain Forsyth's expeditions. These Capt. Austin has assisted by towing them toward their destinations. The latter proceeded with him, and the former has remained with us.

"Having placed Sir John Ross in a fair way of reaching Lancaster Sound, with a fair wind and open water, his vessel has been cast off in this position. I shall, therefore, proceed with all dispatch to the examination of the north shores of Lancaster Sound and Wellington Channel, according to Captain Austin's directions.

"I have the honor to be, Sir, your most obedient humble servant.

"ERASMUS OMMANEY, Captain."

The Resolute got clear of the Orkneys on the 15th of May, and arrived with her consort and the two tenders at the Whale-Fish Islands on the 14th of June.

The Resolute was in Possession Bay on the 17th of August. From thence her proposed course was along the coast, northward and westward, to Whaler Point, situated at the southern extremity of Port Leopold, and afterward to Melville Island.

In order to amuse themselves and their comrades, the officers of the Assistance had started a MS. newspaper, under the name of the "Aurora Borealis." Many of my readers will have heard of the "Cockpit Herald," and such other productions of former days, in his Majesty's fleet. Parry, too, had his journal to beguile the long hours of the tedious arctic winter.

I have seen copies of this novel specimen of the 'fourth estate," dated Baffin's Bay, June, 1850, in which there is a happy mixture of grave and gay, prose and verse; numerous very fair acrostics are published. I append, by way of curiosity, a couple of extracts :—

"What insect that Noah had with him, were these regions named after?—The arc-tic."

" *To the editor of the Aurora Borealis.*

"SIR,— Having heard from an arctic voyager that he has seen 'crows'-nests' in those icy regions, I beg to inquire through your columns, if they are built by the crows, (*Corvus tintinnabulus*,) which Goodsir states to utter a metallic bell-like croak? My fast friend begs me to inquire when rook shooting commences in those diggings?

"A NATURALIST.

["We would recommend to 'A Naturalist' a visit to these 'crows'-nests,' which do exist in the arctic regions. We would also advise his fast friend to investigate these said nests more thoroughly; he would find them tenanted by very old birds (ice quarter-masters,) who would not only inform him as to the species of crows and the sporting season, but would give them a fair chance of showing him how a pigeon may be plucked. — EDITOR."]

VOYAGE OF CAPTAIN SIR JOHN ROSS IN THE "FELIX" PRIVATE SCHOONER, 1850–51.

IN April, 1850, Captain Sir John Ross having volunteered his services to proceed in the search, was enabled, by the liberality of the Hudson's Bay Company, who contributed 500*l*., and public subscription, to leave England in the Felix schooner, of 120 tons, with a picked crew, and accompanied by Commander C. Gervans Phillips, R. N. She also had the Mary, Sir John's own yacht of twelve tons, as a tender. Mr. Abernethy proceeded as ice-master, having accompanied Sir John in his former voyage to Boothia; and Mr. Sivewright was mate of the Felix. The vessels sailed from Scotland on the 23d of May, and reached Holsteinborg in June, where Captain Ross succeeded in obtaining a Danish interpreter who understood the Esquimaux language; he then proceeded on, calling at the Whale-Fish Islands, and passing northway through the Waygatt Strait, overtook, on the 10th of August, H. M. ships Assistance and Resolute, with their tenders the Intrepid and Pioneer, under the command of Captain Austin.

On the 13th of August, Captain Ommaney in the Assistance, and Sir John Ross in the Felix, being somewhere off Cape York, observed three male Esquimaux on the ice close by, and with these people it was prudently resolved to communicate. Accordingly, Lieutenant Cator in the Intrepid steamer, tender to the Assistance, and Commander Phillips in the whale-boat of the Felix, put off on this service. The Intrepid's people arrived first, but apparently without any means of expressing their desires, so that when the boat of the Felix, containing an Esquimaux interpreter, joined the party, the natives immediately gave signs of recognition and satisfaction, came into the boat without the least hesitation, and engaged themselves presently in a long and animated conversation with their countryman the interpreter. Half an hour was devoted to this interchange of intelligence, but with no immediate result, for the interpreter could only translate his native language into Danish, and as no person in the boat understood Danish, the information remained as inaccessible as before. In this predicament the boats returned with the intention of confronting the interpreter — whose christianized name is Adam Beek — with Sir John Ross himself. As Sir John, however, was pushing ahead in the Felix toward Cape Dudley Diggs, and as Adam appeared anxious to disburden himself of his newly acquired information, the boats dropped on board the Prince Albert, another of the exploring vessels in the neighborhood, and there put Adam in communication with the captain's steward, John Smith, who "understood a little of the language," as Sir John Ross says, or "a good deal," as Commander Phillips says, and who presently gave such an account of the intelligence as startled every body on board. Its purport was as follows;—That in the winter of 1846, when the snow was falling, two ships were crushed by the ice a good way off in the direction of Cape Dudley Diggs, and afterward burned by a fierce and numerous tribe of natives; that the ships in question were not whalers, and that epaulettes were worn by some of the white men; that a part of the crews were drowned, that the remainder were some time in huts or tents apart from the natives, that they had guns, but no balls, and that being in a weak and exhausted condition, they were subsequently killed by the natives with darts or arrows. This was the form given to the Esquimaux story by John Smith, captain's steward of the Prince Albert. Impressed with the importance of these tidings, Captain Ommaney and Commander Phillips immediately made their report to Captain

Austin in the Resolute, which was then in company with the Felix near Cape Dudley Diggs. Captain Austin at once decided upon investigating the credibility of the story, and with this view dispatched a message to the Lady Franklin, another of the exploring ships, which lay a few miles off, and which had on board a regular Danish interpreter. This interpreter duly arrived, but proceeded forthwith to translate the story by a statement "totally at variance" with the interpretation of "the other," whom, as we are told, he called a liar and intimidated into silence; though no sooner was the latter left to himself than he again repeated his version of the tale, and stoutly maintained its accuracy. Meantime an additional piece of information became known, namely, that a certain ship had passed the winter safely housed in Wolstenholme Sound — a statement soon ascertained by actual investigation to be perfectly true. The following is an extract of a letter from —

Captain Sir John Ross, R. N., to Captain W. A. B. Hamilton, R. N., Secretary of the Admiralty.

"'*Felix' discovery yacht, off Admiralty Inlet,*
"*Lancaster Sound, August* 22.

"SIR,— I have to acquaint you, for the information of the Lords Commissioners of the Admiralty, that the Felix discovery yacht, with her tender, the Mary, after obtaining an Esquimaux interpreter at Holsteinborg, and calling at Whale-Fish Islands, proceeded northway through the Waygatt Straits, and overtook her Majesty's discovery ships, under the command of Captain Austin on the 11th of August; and on the 12th the senior officer and the second in command having cordially communicated with me on the best mode of performing the service on which we are mutually embarked, arrangements were made and concluded for a simultaneous examination of every part of the eastern side of a northwest passage in which it was probable that the missing ships could be bound: documents to that effect were exchanged, and subsequently assented to by Captains Forsyth and Penny.

"On the 13th of August natives were discovered on the ice near to Cape York, with whom it was deemed advisable to communicate. On this service, Lieutenant Cator, in the Intrepid, was detached on the part of Captain Austin, and on my part Commander Phillips, with our Esquimaux interpreter, in the whale-boat of the Felix. It was found by Lieutenant Cator that Captain Penny had left with the natives a note for Captain Austin, but only relative to the state of the navigation; however, when Commander Phillips arrived, the Esquimaux, seeing one apparently of their own nation in the whale-boat, came immediately to him, when a long conversation took place, the purport of which could not be made known, as the interpreter could not explain himself to any one, either in the Intrepid or the whale-boat, (as he understands only the Danish besides his own language,) until he was brought on board the Prince Albert, where John Smith, the captain's steward of that vessel, who had been some years at the Hudson's Bay settlement of Churchill, and understands a little of the language, was able to give some explanation of Adam Beek's information, which was deemed of such importance that Captains Ommaney, Phillips, and Forsyth, proceeded in the Intrepid to the Resolute, when it was decided by Captain Austin to send for the Danish Interpreter of the Lady Franklin, which, having been unsuccessful in an attempt at getting through the ice to the westward, was only a few miles distant. In the mean time it was known that, in addition to the first information, a ship, which could only be the North Star, had wintered in Wolstenholme Sound, called by the natives Ourinak, and had only left it a month ago. This proved to be true, but the interpretation of the Dane was totally at variance with the information given by the other, who, although for obvious reasons he did not dare to contradict the Dane, subsequently maintained the truth of his statement, which induced Captain Austin to dispatch the Intrepid with Captains

Ommaney and Phillips, taking with them both our interpreters, Adam Beek and a young native who had been persuaded to come as one of the crew of the Assistance, to examine Wolstenholme Sound. In the mean time it had been unanimously decided that no alteration should be made in our previous arrangement, it being obvious that while there remained a chance of saving the lives of those of the missing ships who may be yet alive, a further search for those who had perished should be postponed, and accordingly the Resolute, Pioneer, and Prince Albert parted company on the 15th. It is here unnecessary to give the official reports made to me by Commander Phillips, which are of course transmitted by me to the Secretary of the Hudson's Bay Company, which, with the information written in the Esquimaux language by Adam Beek, will no doubt be sent to you for their Lordships' information; and it will be manifest by these reports that Commander Phillips has performed his duty with sagacity, circumspection, and address, which do him infinite credit, although it is only such as I must have expected from so intelligent an officer; and I have much satisfaction in adding that it has been mainly owing to his zeal and activity that I was able, under disadvantageous circumstances, to overtake her Majesty's ships, while by his scientific acquirements and accuracy in surveying, he has been able to make many important corrections and valuable additions to the charts of the much-frequented eastern side of Baffin's Bay, which has been more closely observed and navigated by us than by any former expedition, and, much to my satisfaction, confirming the latitude aud longitude of every headland I had an opportunity of laying down in the year 1818.

"I have only to add that I have much satisfaction in co-operating with her Majesty's expedition. With such support and with such vessels so particularly adapted for the service, no exertion shall be wanting on my part. But I cannot conclude this letter without acknowledging my obligations to Commodore Austin and Captain Ommaney for the assistance they have afforded me, and for the cordiality and courtesy with which I have been treated by these distinguished officers and others of the ships under their orders. Animated as we are with an ardent and sincere desire to rescue our imperiled countrymen, I confidently trust that our united exertions and humble endeavors may, under a merciful Providence, be completely successful.

"I am, with truth and regard, Sir, your faithful and obedient servant,

"JOHN ROSS, Captain, R. N."

By the accounts brought home by Commander Forsyth from Lancaster Sound, to the 25th of August, it is stated that Sir John Ross, in the Felix, intended to return to England.

The ice was at that period very heavy, extending all around from Leopold Island, at the entrance of Regent Inlet, to Cape Farewell, to the westward, so as to prevent the possibility of any of the vessels pushing on to Cape Walker. When the Prince Albert was between Cape Spencer and Cape Innes, in Wellington Channel, Mr. Snow went at noon to the mast-head, and saw H. M. Ship Assistance as near as possible within Cape Hotham, under a press of sail. Her tender, the Intrepid, was not seen, but was believed to be with her. Captain Penny, with his two ships, the Lady Franklin and Sophia, was endeavoring to make his way up the same Channel, but it was feared the ice would ultimately be too strong for him, and that he would have to return home, leaving Captain Austin's squadron only to winter in the ice.

The American man-of-war brig Rescue was close beset with the ice near Cape Bowen.

The Pioneer was with the Resolute on the 17th August.

AMERICAN SEARCHING EXPEDITION.— UNITED STATES' SHIPS, "ADVANCE" AND "RESCUE," UNDER THE COMMAND OF LIEUTENANT DE HAVEN, 1850–51.

IN the spring of 1849, Lady Franklin made a touching and pathetic appeal to the feelings of the American nation, in the following letter to the President of the Republic:—

The Lady of Sir John Franklin to the President.

"*Bedford-place*, *London*, *4th April*, 1849.

"SIR,—I address myself to you as the head of a great nation, whose power to help me I cannot doubt, and in whose disposition to do so I have a confidence which I trust you will not deem presumptuous.

"The name of my husband, Sir John Franklin, is probably not unknown to you. It is intimately connected with the northern part of that continent of which the American republic forms so vast and conspicuous a portion. When I visited the United States three years ago, among the many proofs I received of respect and courtesy, there was none which touched and even surprised me more than the appreciation everywhere expressed to me of his former services in geographical discovery, and the interest felt in the enterprise in which he was then known to be engaged."

* * * * *

[Her ladyship here gives the details of the departure of the expedition, and the measures already taken for its relief.]

* * * * *

"I have entered into these details with the view of proving that, though the British government has not forgotten the duty it owes to the brave men whom it has sent on a perilous service, and has spent a very large sum in providing the means for their rescue, yet that, owing to various causes, the means actually in operation for this purpose are quite inadequate to meet the extreme exigence of the case; for, it must be remembered, that the missing ships were victualed for three years only, and that nearly four years have now elapsed, so that the survivors of so many winters in the ice must be at the last extremity. And also, it must be borne in mind, that the channels by which the ships may have attempted to force a passage to the westward, or which they may have been compelled, by adverse circumstances, to take, are very numerous and complicated, and that one or two ships cannot possibly, in the course of the next short summer, explore them all.

"The Board of Admiralty, under a conviction of this fact, has been induced to offer a reward of 20,000*l.* sterling to any ship or ships, of any country, or to any exploring party whatever, which shall render efficient assistance to the missing ships, or their crews, or to any portion of them. This announcement, which, even if the sum had been doubled or trebled, would have met with public approbation, comes, however, too late for our whalers, which had unfortunately sailed before it was issued, and which, even if the news should overtake them at their fishing-grounds, are totally unfitted for any prolonged adventure, having only a few months' provision on board, and no additional clothing. To the American whalers, both in the Atlantic and Pacific, I look with more hope, as competitors for the prize, being well aware of their numbers and strength, their thorough equipment, and the bold spirit of enterprise which animates their crews. But I venture to look even beyond these. I am not without hope that you will deem it not unworthy of a great and kindred nation to take up the cause of humanity which I plead, in a national spirit, and thus generously make it your own.

"I must here, in gratitude, adduce the example of the imperial Russian government, which, as I am led to hope by his Excellency, the Russian embassador in London, who forwarded a memorial on the subject, will send out exploring parties this summer, from the Asiatic side of Behring's Strait, northward, in search of the lost vessels. It would be a noble spectacle to the world, if three great nations, possessed of the widest empires on the face of the globe, were thus to unite their efforts in the truly christian work of saving their perishing fellow-men from destruction.

"It is not for me to suggest the mode in which such benevolent efforts might best be made. I will only say, however, that if the conceptions of my own mind, to which I do not venture to give utterance, were realized, and that in the noble competition which followed, American seamen had the good fortune to wrest from us the glory, as might be the case, of solving the problem of the unfound passage, or the still greater glory of saving our adventurous navigators from a lingering fate which the mind sickens to dwell on, though I should in either case regret that it was not my own brave countrymen in those seas whose devotion was thus rewarded, yet should I rejoice that it was to America we owed our restored happiness, and should be forever bound to her by ties of affectionate gratitude.

"I am not without some misgivings while I thus address you. The intense anxieties of a wife and of a daughter may have led me to press too earnestly on your notice the trials under which we are suffering, (yet not we only, but hundreds of others,) and to presume too much on the sympathy which we are assured is felt beyond the limits of our own land. Yet, if you deem this to be the case, you will still find, I am sure, even in that personal intensity of feeling, an excuse for the fearlessness with which I have thrown myself on your generosity, and will pardon the homage I thus pay to your own high character, and to that of the people over whom you have the distinction to preside. "I have, &c.,

(Signed) "JANE FRANKLIN."

To which the following reply was received :—

Mr. Clayton to Lady Jane Franklin.

"*Department of State, Washington,*
"*25th April*, 1849.

"MADAM,—Your letter to the President of the United States, dated April 4th, 1849, has been received by him, and he has instructed me to make to you the following reply:—

"The appeal made in the letter with which you have honored him, is such as would strongly enlist the sympathy of the rulers and the people of any portion of the civilized world.

"To the citizens of the United States, who share so largely in the emotions which agitate the public mind in your own country, the name of Sir John Franklin has been endeared by his heroic virtues, and the sufferings and sacrifices which he has encountered for the benefit of mankind. The appeal of his wife and daughter, in their distress, has been borne across the waters, asking the assistance of a kindred people to save the brave men who embarked in this unfortunate expedition; and the people of the United States, who have watched with the deepest interest that hazardous enterprise, will now respond to that appeal, by the expression of their united wishes that every proper effort may be made by this government for the rescue of your husband and his companions.

"To accomplish the objects you have in view, the attention of American navigators, and especially of our whalers, will be immediately invoked. All the information in the possession of this government, to enable them to aid in discovering the missing ships, relieving their crews and restoring them to their families, shall be spread far and wide among our people; and all that the executive government of the United States, in the exercise of its constitutional powers, can effect, to meet this requisition on American enterprise, skill and bravery, will be promptly undertaken.

"The hearts of the American people will be deeply touched by your eloquent address to their Chief Magistrate, and they will join with you in an earnest prayer to Him whose spirit is on the waters, that your husband and his companions may yet be restored to their country and their friends.

"I have, &c.,

(Signed) "JOHN M. CLAYTON."

A second letter was also addressed by Lady Franklin to the President in the close of that year, after the forced return of Captain Sir James Ross, from whose active exertions so much had been expected —

The Lady of Sir John Franklin to the President.

"*Spring Gardens, London,* 11*th Dec.,* 1849.

"SIR,—I had the honor of addressing myself to you, in the month of April last, in behalf of my husband, Sir John Franklin, his officers and crews, who were sent by Her Majesty's government, in the spring of 1845, on a maritime expedition for a discovery of the northwest passage, and who have never since been heard of.

"Their mysterious fate has excited, I believe, the deepest interest throughout the civilized world, but nowhere more so, not even in England itself, than in the United States of America. It was under a deep conviction of this fact, and with the humble hope that an appeal to those general sentiments would never be made altogether in vain, that I ventured to lay before you the necessities of that critical period, and to ask you to take up the cause of humanity which I pleaded, and generously make it your own.

"How nobly you, sir, and the American people, responded to that appeal, — how kindly and courteously that response was conveyed to me, — is known wherever our common language is spoken or understood; and though difficulties, which were mainly owing to the advanced state of the season, presented themselves after your official announcement had been made known to our government, and prevented the immediate execution of your intentions, yet the generous pledge you had given was not altogether withdrawn, and hope still remained to me that, should the necessity for renewed measures continue to exist, I might look again across the waters for the needed succor.

"A period has now, alas, arrived, when our dearest hopes as to the safe return of the discovery ships this autumn are finally crushed by the unexpected, though forced return of Sir James Ross, without any tidings of them, and also by the close of the arctic season. And not only have no tidings been brought of their safety or of their fate, but even the very traces of their course have yet to be discovered; for such was the concurrence of unfortunate and unusual circumstances attending the efforts of the brave and able officer alluded to, that he was not able to reach those points where indications of the course of discovery ships would most probably be found. And thus, at the close of a second season since the departure of the recent expedition of search, we remain in nearly the same state of ignorance respecting the missing expedition as at the moment of its starting from our shores. And in the mean time our brave countrymen, whether clinging still to their ships, or dispersed in various directions, have entered upon a fifth winter in those dark and dreary solitudes, with exhausted means of sustenance, while yet their expected succor comes not!

"It is in the time, then, of their greatest peril, in the day of their extremest need, that I venture, encouraged by your former kindness, to look to you again for some active efforts which may come in aid of those of my own country, and add to the means of search. Her Majesty's Ministers have already resolved on sending an expedition to Behring's Strait, and doubtless have other necessary measures in contemplation, supported as they are, in every means that can be devised for this humane purpose, by the sympathies of the nation, and by the generous solicitude which our Queen is known to feel in the fate of her brave people imperiled in their country's service. But, whatever be the measures contemplated by the Admiralty, they cannot be such as will leave no room or necessity for more, since it is only by the multiplication of means, and those vigorous and instant ones, that we can hope, at this last stage, and in this last hour, perhaps, of the lost navigators' existence, to snatch them from a dreary grave. And surely, till the shores and seas of those frozen regions have been swept in all directions, or until some memorial be found to attest their fate, neither England, who sent them out, nor even America, on whose shores they have been launched in a cause which has interested the world for centuries, will deem the question at rest.

"May it please God so to move the hearts and wills of a great and kindred people, and of their chosen Chief Magistrate, that they may join heart and hand in the generous enterprise! The respect and admiration of the world, which watches with growing interest every movement of your great republic, will follow the chivalric and humane endeavor, and the blessing of them who were ready to perish shall come to you!

"I have, &c.,

(Signed) JANE FRANKLIN.

"*His Excellency the President of the United States.*"

In a very admirable letter addressed to Lady Franklin in February, 1850, by Lieut. Sherard Osborn, R. N., occur the following remarks and suggestions, which appear to me so explicit and valuable that I publish them entire: —

"*Great Ealing, Middlesex, 6th February*, 1850.

"MY DEAR LADY FRANKLIN. — It is of course of vital importance that the generous co-operation of the Americans in the rescue of Sir John Franklin and his crews be directed to points which call for search, and at the same time give them a clear field for the exercise of their energy and emulation. It would be a pity, for instance, if they should be merely working on the same ground with ourselves, while extensive portions of the Arctic Sea, in which it is equally probable the lost expedition may be found, should be left unexamined; and none, in my opinion, offers a better prospect of successful search than the coasts of Repulse Bay, Hecla and Fury Strait, Committee Bay, Felix Harbor, the estuary of the Great Fish River, and Simpson's Strait, with the sea to the northwest of it. My reasons for saying so are as follows; —

"Suppose Sir John Franklin to have so far carried out the tenor of his orders as to have penetrated south-west from Cape Walker, and to have been either 'cast away,' or hopelessly impeded by ice, and that either in the past or present year he found it necessary to quit his ships, they being anywhere between 100° and 108° west longitude, and 70° and 73° north latitude. Now, to retrace his steps to Cape Walker, and thence to Regent Inlet, would be no doubt the first suggestion that would arise. Yet there are objections to it: firstly, he would have to contend against the prevailing set of the ice, and currents, and northerly wind; secondly, if no whalers were found in Lancaster Sound, how was he to support his large party in regions where the musk ox or reindeer is never seen? thirdly, leaving his ships in the summer, he knew he could only reach the whaling ground in the fall of the year; and, in such case, would it not be advisable to make rather for the southern than the northern limit of the seas visited by the whalers? fourthly, by edging to the south rather than the north, Sir John Franklin would be falling back to, rather than going from, relief, and increase the probabilities of providing food for his large party.

"I do not believe he would have decided on going due south, because the lofty land of Victoria Island was in his road, and when he did reach the American shore, he would only attain a desert, of whose horrors he no doubt retained a vivid recollection; and a lengthy land journey of more than 1000 miles to the Hudson's Bay settlements was more than his men were capable of.

"There remains, therefore, but one route for Sir John under such circumstances to follow; and it decidedly has the following merits, that of being in a direct line for the southern limit of the whale fishery; that of leading through a series of narrow seas adapted for the navigation of small open boats; that of being the most expeditious route by which to reach Fort Churchill, in Hudson's Bay; that of leading through a region visited by Esquimaux and migratory animals; and this route is through the 'Strait of Sir James Ross,' across the narrow isthmus of Boothia Felix, (which, as you reminded me to-day, was not supposed to exist when Sir John Franklin left England, and has been since discovered,) into the Gulf of Boothia, where he could either pass by Hecla and Fury Strait into the fishing-ground of Hudson's Strait, or else go southward down Committee Bay, across the Rae Isthmus into Repulse Bay, and endeavor from there to reach some vessels in Hudson's Bay, or otherwise Fort Churchill.

"It is not unlikely either, that when Franklin had got to the eastern extremity of James Ross's Strait, and found the land to be across his path where he had expected to find a strait, that his party might have divided, and the more active portion of them attempted to ascend the Great Fish River, where we have Sir George Back's authority for supposing they would find, close to the arctic shores, abundance of food in fish, and herds of reindeer, &c., while the others traveled on the road I have already mentioned.

"To search for them, therefore, on this line of retreat, I should think highly essential, and if neglected this year, it must be done next; and if not done by the Americans, it ought to be done by us.

"I therefore suggest the following plan:—Suppose a well-equipped expedition to leave America in May, and to enter Hudson's Strait, and then divide into two divisions. The first division might go northward, through Fox's Channel to Hecla and Fury Strait, examine the shores of the latter carefully, deposit provisions at the western extreme, erect conspicuous beacons, and proceed to Melville or Felix Harbor, in Boothia, secure their vessel or vessels, and dispatch, as soon as circumstances would allow, boat parties across the neck of the isthmus into the western waters. Here let them divide, and one party proceed through James Ross's Strait, carefully examining the coast, and push over sea, ice, or land, to the northwest as far as possible. The other boat party to examine the estuary of the Great

Fish River, and thence proceed westward along the coast of Simpson's Strait, and, if possible, examine the broad bay formed between it and Dease's Strait.

"The second division, on parting company, might pass south of Southampton Island, and coast along from Chesterfield Inlet northward to Repulse Bay, a boat party with two boats might cross Rae Isthmus into the bottom of Committee Bay, with instructions to visit both shores of the said bay, and to rendezvous at the western entrance of Hecla and Fury Strait. The second division (be it one or more vessels) should then pass into Fox's Channel, and turning through Hecla and Fury Strait, pick up the boats at the rendezvous; and thence, if the first division have passed on all right, and do not require reinforcement, the second division should steer northward along the unknown coast, extending as far as Cape Kater; from Cape Kater proceed to Leopold Island, and having secured their ships there, dispatch boat or traveling parties in a direction southwest from Cape Rennell, in North Somerset, being in a parallel line to the line of search we shall adopt from Cape Walker, and at the same time it will traverse the unknown sea beyond the Islands lately observed by Captain Sir James Ross.

"Some such plan as this would, I think, insure your gallant husband being met or assisted, should he be to the south or the west of Cape Walker, and attempt to return by a southeast course, a direction which, I think, others as well as myself would agree in thinking a very rational and probable one.

"I will next speak of an argument which has been brought forward in consequence of no traces of the missing expedition having been discovered in Lancaster Sound; that it is quite possible, if Franklin failed in getting through the middle ice from Melville Bay to Lancaster Sound, that, sooner than disappoint public anxiety and expectation of a profitable result arising from his expedition, he may have turned northward, and gone up Smith's Sound; every mile beyond its entrance was new ground, and therefore a reward to the discoverer. It likewise brought them nearer the pole, and may be they found that open sea of which Baron Wrangel speaks so constantly in his journeys over the ice northward from Siberia.

"It is therefore desirable that some vessels should carefully examine the entrance of this sound, and visit all the conspicuous headlands for some considerable distance within it; for it ought to be borne in mind, that localities perfectly accessible for the purpose of erecting beacons, &c., one season, may be quite impracticable the next, and Franklin, late in the season and pressed for time, would not have wasted time, scaling bergs to reach the shore and pile up cairns, of which, in all the sanguine hope of success, he could not have foreseen the necessity.

"Should any clue be found to the lost expedition in this direction, to follow it up would, of course, be the duty of the relieving party, and every thing would depend necessarily upon the judgment of the commanders.

"In connection with this line of search, I think a small division of vessels, starting from Spitzbergen, and pushing from it in a northwest direction, might be of great service; for on reference to the chart, it will be seen that Spitzbergen is as near the probable position of Franklin (if he went north about,) on the east, as Behring's Strait is upon the west; and the probability of reaching the meridian of 80° west from Spitzbergen is equally as good as, if not better than, Behring's Strait, and, moreover, a country capable of supporting life always in the rear to fall back upon.

"Sherard Osrorn,
"Lieutenant Royal Navy.

"To Lady Franklin."

Debate in the American Congress.

The following remarks of honorable members and senators, in defense of the bill for carrying out Mr. Grinnell's expedition, will explain the grounds on which the government countenance was invoked for the noble undertaking:—

"Mr. MILLER: I prefer that the government should have the entire control of this enterprise; but, Sir, I do not think that can be accomplished; at all events, it cannot within the time required to produce the good results which are to be hoped from this expedition. It is well known to all that the uncertain fate of Sir John Franklin and his companions has attracted the attention and called forth the sympathies of the civilized world. This government, Sir, has been indifferent to the call. An application, an appeal was made to this government of no ordinary character; one which was cheerfully entertained by the President, and which he was anxious should be complied with. But it is known to the country and to the Senate that, although the President had every disposition to send out an expedition in search of Sir John Franklin, it was found upon inquiry that we had no ships fitted for the occasion, and that the Executive had no authority to procure them for an expedition of this kind, and suitable for this sort of navigation. The Executive was therefore obliged, for want of authority to build the ships, to forego further action on this noble enterprise, until Congress should meet, and authorize the expedition.

"In the mean time, Mr. Grinnell, one of the most respectable and worthy merchants of the city of New York, understanding the difficulty that the government had in fitting out the expedition, has gone to work, and with his own means has built two small vessels especially prepared for the expedition; and he now most generously tenders them to the government, not to be under his own control, but the control of the government, and to be made part of the navy of the United States. The honorable senator from Alabama (Mr. King) is mistaken with regard to the terms and effect of this resolution. This resolution places these two ships under the control of the government, as much so as if they were built expressly for the navy of the United States. Their direction, their fitting out, their officers and men, are all to be under the control of the Executive. Their officers are to be officers of our navy — their seamen the seamen of our navy — so that the expedition will be as thoroughly under the control of this government as if the ships belonged to us. Now, Sir, I should have no objections myself to amend this resolution so as to authorize the purchase of these two small vessels at once, and make them a part of our naval establishment; but, when I recollect the magnanimous feeling which urged this noble-hearted merchant to prepare these ships, I know that that same feeling would forbid him to make merchandise of that which he has devoted to humanity. He offers them for this great cause; they are his property, prepared for this enterprise, and he offers them to us to be used by the government in this great undertaking. We must either accept them for the purpose to which he has dedicated them, or reject them altogether. If we refuse these ships, we will defeat the whole enterprise, and lose all opportunity of participation in a work of humanity which now commands the attention of the world.

"If we refer this resolution back to the committee, and they report a bill authorizing government to build ships to carry on the expedition on its own account, it would be attended with very great delay, and, in my opinion defeat the object we have in view. In a case of this kind time is every thing. It must be done speedily, if done at all. Every hour's delay may be worth the life of a man. Sir John Franklin and his companions may ere this have perished, but our hope is that they are still living in some narrow sea, imprisoned by walls of ice, where our succor may yet reach them. But, Sir, whether our hopes are fallacious or not, the public feeling — the feeling of humanity — is, that the fate of Sir John Franklin should, if possible, be ascertained, and as soon as possible. The public mind will never be satisfied till an expedition from this country, or from some other country, shall have ascertained their fate. I therefore trust that this resolution, as it is, will be acted upon at once, and that it will receive the unanimous vote of the Senate. * * * *

"I am so impressed Mr. President, with the importance of time as regards the disposal of this question, that I hesitate even to occupy the attention of the Senate for a few moments; and I only do so for the purpose of correcting some views which have been expressed by the senator from Mississippi. * * * The question is, whether we shall adopt this resolution, and immediately send forth this expedition for the purpose of accomplishing this great object, or whether we shall throw back this resolution to drag its slow course through Congress, in the form of another bill, to make an appropriation for the purpose of building vessels. For what object? To secure, as the senator says, to the United States, the sole honor and glory of this expedition. Sir, if this expedition is got up merely for honor and glory either to the United States or to an individual, I will have nothing whatever to do with it. Sir, there is a deeper and a higher sentiment that has induced the action of Congress on this subject. It is to engage in a great work of humanity, to do that which is not only being done by the government of England, but by private individuals, who are fitting out expeditions at their own expense, and sending them to the northern seas, for the purpose of discovering the fate of this great man, who had periled his life in the cause of science and of commerce.

"Mr President, I have been informed that a private expedition is now being fitted out in England under the direction of that great commander, or I may call him the king of the Polar Seas, Sir John Ross, who is going again to devote himself and his life to this perilous expedition. Sir, altogether I have not had heretofore much confidence in the success of this expedition, yet when I consider the reputation of Sir John Ross, and the fact that he is better acquainted with those seas than any other man living, and understanding that he entertains the belief that Sir John Franklin and his companions are yet alive, and may be rescued, — I say, finding such a man as Sir John Ross engaged in an expedition of this kind, I am not without hope that our efforts may, under Providence, be crowned with success.

But the honorable senator says that nothing is likely to be derived from this expedition but honor and glory, and that that is to be divided between the government of the United States and a private individual. Sir, is there nothing to be derived from the performance of an act of humanity but honor and glory? Sir, it is said that in this instance both the government and the individual alluded to are engaged in the same work. Well, Sir, what objection can there be to that connection? Does the honorable senator from Mississippi envy the individual his share of the honor and glory? Does he desire to monopolize it all to the United States? I hope he has no such feeling as that.

"But, Mr. President, the honorable senator made use of an expression which I think he will withdraw. He intimated, if I understood him rightly, some suspicion that this was a matter of speculation on the part of Mr. Grinnell.

"Mr. Foote: I said I had heard such a thing suggested; but I do not make any such charge myself.

"Mr. Miller: I have heard this urged as an objection heretofore, but I am satisfied that if the senator from Mississippi knew the character and the history of this gentleman, he would not even repeat that he had heard such an insinuation. Sir, although this is a liberal donation from an individual, the sum need not alarm gentlemen about after claims. These ships are but small ships; and it is necessary that they should be small in order that they may be effective. One of them is, I understand, 150 tons, and the other 90 tons. They have cost, I believe, 30,000 dollars. Now, when we find this merchant devoting his property, not for the purpose of building ships to convey merchandise to the markets of the world; when we find him retiring from the ordinary course of commercial pursuit in which all the world is engaged, and devoting a portion of his fortune to the building of ships that can be used for no other purpose but in this voyage of humanity, can it be imagined that any thought of speculation on his part could have influenced his conduct? No, Sir. On the contrary, it is a high and worthy motive ; and I think it ought to receive the approbation of this and all other intelligent Christian nations, to see a merchant, who, while the commercial world are encompassing the globe by sea and land in quest of profit and of gold, is dedicating himself to his great object, and devoting a part of his fortune to the cause of humanity, and offering to government, not as a bounty, but because the government, with all its means, has not the power and the time to prepare vessels to do this work. That, Sir, is the object.

"Now, if we do not accept these ships, there will be an end of this expedition. Sir, shall it be said, that this government has lost such an opportunity as this of exhibiting the deep interest which our people feel both in the cause of science and humanity, and that, too, at the very time when we are entering into treaties and compacts with all the commercial nations of the world, for the purpose of extending commerce and civilization, and opening communications of trade from sea to sea? When the government is not only doing all by its own power, but also acting in concert with our private citizens in constructing rail-roads and canals, and by various other modes extending commercial civilization throughout the world, shall it be said that we, at this moment, refused, through the fear of losing a little honor and glory and national dignity, to accept two ships — the only two ships in America that can do the work — in the accomplishment of this great enterprise? I hope not. Let us not, then, cavil and waste time about these little matters. If the work is to be done at all it must be done now, and done, as I conceive, by the adoption of this resolution.

Governor Seward spoke as follows in the Senate on the same subject: — "I am happy to perceive, Mr. President, indications all around the chamber that there is no disagreement in regard to the importance, or in relation to the propriety, of a search on the part of this nation, by the government itself, or by individual citizens, for the lost and heroic navigator. Since so much is conceded, and since I come from the State whence this proposition emanates, I desire to notice, in a very few words, the objections raised against the mode of carrying the proposed design into effect. It is always the case, I think, when great objects and great enterprises which are feasible are hindered or defeated, that they are hindered or defeated, not so much by want of agreement concerning the measures themselves, as by diversity of opinion concerning the mode of carrying them into execution. Since this is so generally the case, the rule which I always adopt, and which seems to be a safe one, is, that where I cannot have my own way of obtaining a great public object, I will accept the best other way which opens before me. Now, I cordially agree with those honorable Senators who would have preferred that at some appropriate time, and in some proper and unobjectionable manner, the government should have moved for the attainment of this object, as a government, and have made it exclusively the act of the nation. And I would have preferred this, not so much on account of the glory that it is supposed would have followed it, as because of the beneficence of the enterprise. Enterprises which spring from a desire of glory are very apt to end in disappointment. True national glory is always safely attained by prosecuting beneficent designs, whatever may be their success. I say, Sir, then, that I would have preferred the alternative suggested; but the fact is, without stopping to inquire where the fault lies, or whether there be fault at all, the government has not moved, and the reason which has been assigned is, I have no doubt, the true one. I do not know that it has ever been contradicted or called in question; that reason is, that the Navy of the United States contains no vessels adapted to the enterprise, but consists of ships constructed and fitted for very different objects and purposes than an exploring expedition amid the ice-bound seas of the arctic pole. Our naval marine consists of vessels adapted to the purposes of convoys, military armament, and the suppression of the slave-trade on the coast of Africa. The executive portions of the government failed for want of vessels suitable to be employed in this particular service. It therefore devolved upon the Legislature of the United States. But, although we have been here now nearly five months, no Committee of either House, no member of either House of Congress has proposed to equip a national fleet for this purpose. While this fact exists on one side, it is to be remarked on the other, that the time has arrived in which the movement must be made if it is to be made at all, and also that a careful investigation, made by scientific and practical men, has revived the hope in Europe and America that the humane object can be attained. There can, then, be no delay allowed for considering whether the manner for carrying the design into effect could not be changed. Let us, then, practically survey the case as it comes before us. The government of the United States has really no vessels adapted to the purpose. To say nothing of the expense, the government has not time to provide, prepare, or equip vessels for the expedition. Under such circumstances, a citizen of the United States tenders to the government vessels of his own, precisely adequate in number, and exactly fitted in construction and equipment, for the performance of the duty to be assumed. Since he offers them to the government, what reason can we assign for refusing them? No reason can be assigned, except that he is too generous, and offers to *give* us the use of the vessels instead of demanding compensation for it. Well, Sir, if we do accept them it can be immediately carried into execution, with a cheering prospect of attaining the great object which the United States and the civilized world have such deep interest in securing. Then the question resolves itself into this — the question raised by the honorable Senator from Alabama (Mr. King) — whether, in seeking so beneficent an object, it is consistent with the dignity of the nation to combine individual action with a national enterprise. I do not think, Mr. President, that that honorable Senator will find himself obliged to insist upon this objection after he shall have carefully examined the bill before us. He will find that it converts the undertaking into a national enterprise. The vessels are to be accepted not as individual property, but as national vessels. They will absolutely cease to be under the direction, management, or control of the owners, and will become at once national ships, and for the time, at least, and for all the purposes of the expedition, a part of the national marine.

"Now, Sir, have we not postal arrangements with various foreign countries carried into effect in the same way, and is the dignity of the nation compromised by them? During the war with Mexico, the government continually hired ships and steamboats from citizens for military operations. Is the glory of that war tarnished by the use of those means? The government in this case, as in those cases, is in no sense a partner. It assumes the whole control of the vessels, and the enterprise becomes a national one. The only circumstance remaining to be considered is, whether the government can accept the loan of the service of the vessels without making compensation. Now, Sir, I should not have had the least objection, and, indeed, it would have been more agreeable to me if the government could have made an arrangement to have paid a compensation. But I hold it to be quite unnecessary in the present case because the character of the person who tenders these vessels, and the circumstances and manner of the whole transaction, show that it is not a speculation. No compensation is wanted. It would only be a ceremony on the part of the government to offer it, and a ceremony on the part of the merchant to decline it. I am, therefore, willing to march directly to the object, and to assume that these ceremonies have been duly performed, that the government has offered to pay, and the noble-spirited merchant declined to receive.

"Now, then, is there any thing derogatory from the dignity and independence of this nation in employing the vessels? Certainly not, since that employment is indispensable. If it were not indispensable I do not think that the dignity of the Republic would be impaired ; I think, on the contrary, that it would be enhanced and elevated. It is a transaction worthy of the nation, a spectacle deserving the contemplation and respect of mankind, to see that not only does the nation prosecute, but that it has citizens able and willing to contribute, voluntarily and without compulsion, to an enterprise so interesting to the cause of science and of humanity. It is indeed a new and distinct cause for national pride, that an individual citizen, not a merchant prince, as he would be called in some other countries, but a republican merchant, comes forward in this way and moves the government and co-operates with it. It illustrates the magnanimity of the nation and of the citizen. Sir, there is nothing objectionable in this feature of the transaction. It results from the character of the government, which is essentially popular, that there are perpetual debates on the question how far measures and enterprises, for the purposes of humanity and science, are consistent with the constitutional organization of the government, although they are admitted to be eminently compatible with the dignity, character, and intelligence of the nation. All our enterprises, more or less, are carried into execution, if they are carried into execution at all, not by the direct action of the government, but by the lending of its favor, countenance, and aid to individuals, to corporations, and to States. Thus it is that we construct railroads and canals, and found colleges and universities.

"Nor is this mode of prosecuting enterprises of great pith and moment peculiar to this government. There was a navigator who went forth from a port in Spain, some three or four hundred years ago, on an enterprise quite as doubtful and quite as perilous as this. After trying unsuccessfully several States, he was forced to be content with the sanction, and little more than the sanction and patronage of the Court of Madrid. The scanty treasures devoted to that undertaking were the private contributions of a Queen and her subjects, and the vessels were fitted out and manned at the expense of merchants and citizens, which gave a new world to the kingdom of Castile and Leon.

"Entertaining these views now, whatever my opinion might have been under other circumstances, I shall vote against a recommittal, and in favor of the bill, as the surest way of preventing its defeat, and of attaining the sublime and beneficent object which it contemplates."

The committee of both Houses of Congress, to whom Mr. Grinnell's petition for men and supplies was referred, made a unanimous report in favor; and the vessels left on their daring and generous errand.

The following are the joint resolutions which passed both Houses of Congress and were approved by General Taylor, authorizing the President of the United States to accept and attach to the U. S. Navy the two vessels, offered by Mr. Grinnell, to be sent to the arctic seas in search of Sir John Franklin and his companions:

"Resolved by the Senate and House of Representatives of the United States of America in Congress assembled, That the President be, and he is hereby authorized and directed, to receive from Henry Grinnell, of the city of New York, the two vessels prepared by him for an expedition in search of Sir John Franklin and his companions, and to detail from the Navy such commissioned and warrant officers, and so many seamen as may be necessary for said expedition, and who may be willing to engage therein. The said officers and men shall be furnished with suitable rations, at the discretion of the President, for a period not exceeding three years, and shall have the use of such necessary instruments as are now on hand and can be spared from the Navy, to be accounted for or returned by the officers who shall receive the same.

"Sec. 2. Be it further resolved, That the said vessels, officers, and men shall be in all respects under the laws and regulations of the Navy of the United States until their return, when the said vessels shall be delivered to the said Henry Grinnell: Provided, That the United States shall not be liable to any claim for compensation in case of the loss, damage or deterioration of the said vessels, or either of them, from any cause or in any manner whatever, nor be liable to any demand for the use or risk of the said vessels or either of them."

Directly the fact became known that the American government had nobly come forward to aid in the search which was being so strenuously made, the different learned societies of the metropolis vied with each other in testifying the estimation in which this noble conduct was held.

At the annual meeting of the Royal Society, on the 7th of June, upon the motion of Sir Charles Lennox, seconded by the late Marquis of Northampton, a vote of thanks was carried with the utmost enthusiasm, expressive of the gratitude of the Society to the American government, and of their deep sense of the kind and brotherly feeling which had prompted so liberal an act of humanity. A similar vote was carried, on the 11th of June, at a general meeting of the Royal Geographical Society, (of which Sir John Franklin was long one of the vice-presidents.)

The American expedition consists of two brigantines — now enrolled in the United States Navy — the Advance, of 144 tons, and the Rescue, 91 tons. These vessels have been provided and fitted out by the generous munificence of Mr. Henry Grinnell, a merchant of New York, at an expense to him of between 5000*l.* and 6000*l.* The American government also did much toward fitting and equipping them. The Advance was two years old, and the Rescue quite new. Both vessels were strengthened in every part, and put in the most complete order for the service in which they were to be engaged. They are under the command of Lieutenant Edward S. De Haven, who was employed in Commander Wilkes' expedition in 1843 ; Mr. S. P. Griffin, acting master, has charge of the Rescue. The other officers of the expedition are Messrs. W. H. Murdaugh, acting-master ; T. W. Broadhead, and R. R. Carter, passed midshipmen ; Dr. E. K. Kane, passed assistant-surgeon ; Mr. Benjamin Finland, assistant-surgeon ; W

S. Lovell, midshipman; H. Brooks, boatswain; and a complement of thirty-six seamen in the two vessels — the crew of the Advance consisting of fifteen men, and the Rescue thirteen men. The vessels left New York on the 25th of May, 1850. Their proposed destination is through Barrow's Strait, westward to Cape Walker, and round Melville Island. They were provisioned for three years.

Whatever may be the result of this expedition, as connected with the fate of the gallant Sir John Franklin, it is one which reflects the highest honor upon the philanthropic individual who projected it, and upon the officers and men engaged therein.

A dispatch has been received from Lieutenant De Haven, dated off Leopold Island, August 22d, which reports the progress of the expedition thus far. The Advance, in company with her consort, the Rescue, sailed from the Whale Fish Islands on the 29th of June; after many delays and obstructions from calms, stream ice, and the main pack, they forced a passage through it for a considerable distance, but at last got wedged up in the pack immovably until the 29th of July, when by a sudden movement of the floes, an opening presented itself, and under a press of sail the vessels forced their way into clear water. They encountered a heavy gale, which, with a thick fog, made their situation very dangerous, the huge masses of ice being driven along by the strength of the wind and current with great fury. By the aid of warping in calm weather, they reached Cape Yorke on the 15th of August, and a little to the eastward met with two Esquimaux, but could not understand much from them. Between Cape Yorke and Cape Dudley Diggs, while delayed by calms, being in open water, they hauled the ships into the shore at the Crimson Cliffs of Beverley, (so named from the red snow on them,) and filled their water casks from a mountain stream.

On the 18th, with a fair wind, they shaped their course for the western side of Baffin's Bay, and met the pack in streams and very loose, which they cleared entirely by the following day — getting into the north waters, where they fell in with Captain Penny's two vessels, which having been unsuccessful in their efforts to enter Jones' Sound, were now taking the same course up Lancaster Sound. On the 19th, in a violent gale, the Advance parted company with the Rescue. On the morning of the 21st of August, the fog cleared, and Lieutenant De Haven found he was off Cape Crawford, on the south ern shore of the Sound. Here he fell in with the Felix schooner, under Captain Sir John Ross, from whom he learned that Commodore Austin was at Pond's Bay with two of his vessels, seeking for information, while the other two had been dispatched to examine the north shore of the Sound. Lieutenant De Haven proposed proceeding on from Port Leopold to Wellington Channel, the appointed place of rendezvous with his consort.

Captain Forsyth's Remarkable Voyage in the "Prince Albert."

In April, 1850, a branch expedition to aid those vessels sent out by the government was determined on by Lady Franklin, who contributed largely toward its outfit; a considerable sum being also raised by public subscription. The expenses of this expedition were nearly 4000*l.*, of which 2500*l.* were contributed by Lady Franklin herself. The object of this expedition was the providing for the search of a portion of the Arctic Sea, which it was distinctly understood could not be executed by the vessels under Captain Austin; but the importance of which had been set forth, by arctic and other authorities, in documents printed in the Parliamentary Papers.

The unprovided portion alluded to, includes Regent Inlet, and the passages connecting it with the western sea, James Ross's Strait, and other localities, S. W. of Cape Walker, to which quarter Sir John Franklin was required by his instructions to proceed in the first instance. This search is assumed to be necessary on the following grounds: —

1. The probability of Sir John Franklin having abandoned his vessels to the S. W. of Cape Walker.

2. The fact that, in his charts, an open passage is laid down from the west into the south part of Regent Inlet.

3. Sir John Franklin would be more likely to take this course through a country known to possess the resources of animal life, with the wreck of the Victory in Felix Harbor for fuel, and the stores of Fury Beach farther north in view, than to fall upon an utterly barren region of the north coast of America.

4. He would be more likely to expect succor to be sent to him by way of Lancaster Sound and Barrow's Strait, into which Regent Inlet opens, than in any other direction.

In corroboration of the necessity of this part of the search, I would refer generally to the Parliamentary papers of 1848–9 and 50. As an individual opinion, I may quote the words of Captain Beechey, p. 31 of the first series. "If, in this condition," (that of being hopelessly blocked up to the S. W. of Cape Walker,) "which I trust may not be the case, Sir John Franklin should resolve upon taking to his boats, he would prefer attempting a boat navigation through Sir James Ross's Strait, and up Regent Inlet, to a long land journey across the continent to the Hudson Bay Settlements, to which the greater part of his crew would be wholly unequal." And again, in his letter to the Secretary of the Admiralty, 7th of February, 1850, Captain Beechey writes, " * * * * the bottom of Regent Inlet, about the Pelly Islands, should not be left unexamined. In the memorandum submitted to their Lordships, 17th of January, 1849, this quarter was considered of importance, and I am still of opinion that had Sir John Franklin abandoned his vessels near the coast of America, and much short of the Mackenzie River, he would have preferred the probability of retaining the use of his boats until he found relief in Barrow's Strait, to risking an overland journey *via* the before-mentioned river; and it must be remembered that at the time he sailed, Sir George Back's discovery had rendered it very probable that Boothia was an island.

The memorandum alluded to by Captain Beechey as having been submitted to the Lords of the Admiralty on the 17th of January, 1849, was, the expression of the unanimous opinion of the arctic officers assembled by command of the Admiralty to deliberate upon the best means to be taken for the relief of the missing expedition; and in this report, clause 14 is expressly devoted to the recommendation of the search of Regent Inlet.

The necessity for the proposed search may be thus further developed. Sir John Franklin may have abandoned his ships, when his provisions were nearly exhausted somewhere about the latitude of 73° N., long. 105° W.; in short, at any point S. W. of Cape Walker, not further W. than long. 110°. And in such case, rather than return north, (which might be indeed impracticable) or moving south upon the American Continent, of which (upon the coast,) the utter barrenness was already well known to him, he might prefer a southeastern course, with a view of passing in his boats, either through James Ross's, or through Simpson's Straits, into the Gulf of Boothia, and so up into Regent Inlet to the house and stores left at Fury Beach, the only depot of provisions known to him. The advantages of such a course might appear to him very great.

1. Two open passages being laid down in his charts into Regent Inlet, by James Ross's Strait, and by Simpson's Strait, a means of boat transport for his party would be afforded, of which alone perhaps their exhausted strength and resources might admit; such a course would obviously recommend itself to a commander who had experienced the frightful difficulties of a land journey in those regions.

2. The proposed course would lead through a part, the Isthmus of Boothia, in which animal life is known at some seasons to abound.

3. The Esquimaux who have been found on the Isthmus of Boothia are extremely well disposed and friendly.

4. It is the direct route toward the habitual yearly resort of the whalers on the west coast of Baffin's Bay and Davis' Strait; indeed those ships occasionally descend Regent Inlet to a considerable distance south.

5. There are two persons attached to the expedition who are well acquainted with this region and its resources — viz., Mr. Blanky, ice master, and Mr. MacDonald, assistant surgeon, of the Terror. The former was with Sir John Ross in the Victory. The latter has made several voyages in whaling vessels and is acquainted with the parts lying between Regent Inlet and Davis' Strait. Where so few among the crews of the missing ships have had any local experience, the concurrent knowledge of two persons would have considerable weight.

6. Opinions are very greatly divided as to the part in which Sir John Franklin's party may have been arrested, and as to the course they may have taken in consequence. It would be therefore manifestly unfair, and most dangerous, to reason out and magnify any one hypothesis at the expense of the others. The plan here alluded to sought to provide for the probability of the Expedition having been stopped shortly after passing to the southwest of Cape Walker. The very open season of 1845 was followed by years of unusual severity until 1849. It is therefore very possible that retreat as well as onward progress has been impossible — that safety alone has become their last object. The hope of rescuing them in their last extremity depends, then, (as far as human means can insure it,) on the multiplying of simultaneous efforts in every direction. Captain Austin's vessels will, if moving in pairs, take two most important sections only, of the general search, and will find they have enough to do to reach their several points of operation this season.

The necessity for this search was greatly enhanced by the intelligence received about this time in England of the arrival of Mr. Rae and Commander Pullen at the Mackenzie River, thus establishing the fact, that Sir John Franklin's party had not reached any part of the coast between Behring's Strait and the Coppermine River, while the check which Mr. Rae received in his course to the north of the Coppermine, tended to give increased importance to the quarter eastward of that position.

Commander Charles Codrington Forsyth, R. N., an enterprising young officer, who had not long previously been promoted in consequence of his arduous services in surveying on the Australian, African, and American shores, and who had rendered good service to the government by landing supplies on the east coast of Africa, under circumstances of great difficulty during the Kafir war, had volunteered unsuccessfully for all the government expeditions, but was permitted by the Admiralty to command this private branch expedition, in which he embarked without fee or reward — on the noble and honorable mission of endeavoring to relieve his long-imprisoned brother officers.

The Prince Albert, a small clipper vessel of about ninety tons, originally built by Messrs. White, of Cowes, in October, 1848, for the fruit trade, was accordingly hastily fitted out and dispatched from Aberdeen, and Captain Forsyth was instructed to winter, if possible, in Brentford Bay, in Regent Inlet, and thence send parties to explore the opposite side of the isthmus and the various shores and bays of the Inlet She had a crew of twenty, W. Kay and W. Wilson acting as first and second mates, and Mr. W. P. Snow as clerk. She sailed on the 5th of June, and was consequently the last vessel that left, and yet is the first that has reached home, having also brought some account of the track of Franklin's expedition.

The Prince Albert arrived off Cape Farewell, July 2d, entered the ice on the 19th, and on the 21st, came up with Sir John Ross in a labyrinth of ice. She proceeded up Lancaster Sound and Barrow's Strait, fell in with most of the English ships in those seas, and also with the American brig Advance, sailing some time in company, and attempted to enter Regent Inlet and Wellington Channel. She left the Advance aground near

THE ADVANCE LEADING THE PRINCE ALBERT, NEAR LEOPOLD ISLAND.

Cape Riley, at the entrance of Wellington Channel, though not in a situation supposed to be dangerous. Commander Forsyth, in his official letter to the Lords of the Admiralty, says that "traces of the missing expedition under Sir John Franklin had been found at Cape Riley and Beechey Island, at the entrance to the Wellington Channel. We observed five places where tents had been pitched, or stones placed as if they had been used for keeping the lower part of the tents down, also great quantities of beef, pork, and birds' bones, a piece of rope, with the Woolwich naval mark on it, (yellow,) part of which I have inclosed." Having entered Wellington Channel, and examined the coast as far as Point Innis, and finding no further traces of the missing vessels, and it being impracticable to penetrate further to the west, Commander Forsyth returned to Regent Inlet, but meeting no opening there, the season being near at hand when the ice begins to form, and his vessel not of a strength which would enable it to resist a heavy pressure of ice, he determined on returning without further delay to England, after examining a number of points along the coast.

On the 25th of August, a signal staff being observed on shore at Cape Riley, Mr. Snow was sent by Captain Forsyth to examine it. He found that the Assistance, Captain Ommaney, had been there two days before, and had left the following notice:—

"This is to certify that Captain Ommaney, with the officers of her Majesty's ships Assistance and Intrepid, landed upon Cape Riley on the 23d August, 1850, where he found traces of encampments, and collected the remains of materials, which evidently proved that some party belonging to her Majesty's ships had been detained on that spot. Beechey Island was also examined, where traces were found of the same party. This is also to give notice that a supply of provisions and fuel is at Cape Riley. Since 15th August, they have examined the north shore of Lancaster Sound and Barrow's Strait, without meeting with any other traces. Captain Ommaney proceeds to Cape Hotham and Cape

Walker in search of further traces of Sir John Franklin's expedition. Dated on board her Majesty's ship Assistance, off Cape Riley, the 23d August, 1850."

The seamen who were dispatched from the Assistance to examine these remains, found a rope with the naval mark, evidently belonging to a vessel which had been fitted out at Woolwich, and which, in all probability, was either the Erebus or the Terror. Other indications were also noticed, which showed that some vessel had visited the place besides the Assistance. Captain Forsyth left a notice that the Prince Albert had called off Cape Riley on the 25th of August, and then bore up to the eastward. Captain Forsyth landed at Possession Bay on the 29th August, but nothing was found there to repay the search instituted.

The Prince Albert arrived at Aberdeen, on the 22d of October, after a quick passage, having been absent something less than four months.

Captain Forsyth proceeded to London by the mail train, taking with him, for the information of the Admiralty, the several bones, (beef, pork, &c.,) which were found on Cape Riley, together with a piece of rope of about a foot and a half in length, and a small piece of canvas with the Queen's mark upon it, both in an excellent state of preservation ; placing it almost beyond a doubt that they were left on that spot by the expedition under Sir John Franklin.

Captain Forsyth, during his short trip, explored regions which Sir James Ross was unable to reach the previous year. He was at Wellington Channel, and penetrated to Fury Beach, where Sir E. Parry abandoned his vessel, (the Fury,) in 1825, after she had taken the ground. It is situated in about 72° 40′ N. latitude, and 91° 50′ W. longitude. This is a point which has not been reached by any vessel for twenty years past. It was found, however, utterly impossible to land there on account of the packed ice. The whole of the coasts of Baffin's Bay have also now been visited without result.

The intelligence which Capt. Forsyth brought home

has, as a matter of course, excited the most intense interest in naval circles, and among the friends and relatives of the parties absent in the Erebus and Terror, the more so inasmuch as it has been ascertained at Chatham Dockyard that the rope which Captain Forsyth found on the spot when he visited it, and copied Capt. Ommaney's notice, is proved by its yellow mark to have been manufactured there, and certainly since 1824; and moreover, from inquiries instituted, very strong evidence has been elicited in favor of the belief that the rope was made between the years 1841 and 1849. That the trail of the Franklin expedition, or some detachment of it, has been struck, there cannot be the slightest doubt in the mind of any one who has read the dispatches and reports. That Captain Ommaney felt satisfied on this score is evident from the terms of the paper he left behind him. The squadron, it appears, were in full cry upon the scent on the 25th of August, and we must wait patiently, but anxiously, for the next accounts of the results of their indefatigable researches, which can hardly reach us from Barrow's Strait before the autumn of 1851.

There can be no doubt now in the mind of any one, that the Arctic Searching Expeditions have at length come upon *traces*, if not the track of Sir John Franklin. The accounts brought by Captain Forsyth must have at least satisfied the most desponding that there is still hope left—that the ships have not foundered in Baffin's Bay, at the outset of the voyage, nor been crushed in the ice, and burned by a savage tribe of Esquimaux, who had murdered the crew. That the former *might* have happened, all must admit; but to the latter, few, we imagine, will give their assent, notwithstanding the numerous cruel rumors promulgated from time to time. It would be idle to dwell upon so impossible an event. Where could this savage tribe spring from? Mr. Saunders describes the natives of Wolstenholme Sound as the most miserable and helpless of mortals. *They* had no articles obtained from Europeans; and he was of opinion that there were no settlements further north; and if there were, doubtless they would be even more impotent than these wretched beings. That the ship might have foundered *all* must admit. The President did so with many a gallant soul on board. The Avenger ran on the Sorelli, and 300 brave fellows, in an instant, met with a watery grave; and till the sea shall give up her dead, who can count the thousands that lie beneath the billows of the mighty ocean? We have now certain evidence that Franklin's ships did not founder — not, at least, in Baffin's Bay; and our own belief, (says a well-informed and competent writer in the Morning Herald,) is that the pennant still floats in the northern breeze, amid eternal regions of snow and ice.

The voyage performed by the Prince Albert has thus been the means of keeping alive our hopes, and of informing us, up to a certain point, of the progress of the expeditions, and the situation of the different ships, of which we might have been left in a state of utter ignorance till the close of this year. Every thing connected with the navigation of the arctic seas is a chance, coupled, of course, with skill; and in looking at this voyage performed by Lady Franklin's little vessel, it must be obvious to every one that Captain Forsyth has had the chance of an open season, and the skill to make use of it.

"Live a thousand years," and we may never see such another voyage performed. We have only to look at all that have preceded. Parry, it is true, in one year ran to Melville Island, and passing a winter, got back to England the following season — and this is at present the *ne plus ultra* of arctic navigation. Sir John Ross, we know, went out in the Victory to Regent Inlet, and was frozen in for four years, and all the world gave him up for lost — but "there's life in the old dog yet," as the song has it.

Sir James Ross was frozen in at Leopold Harbor, and only got out, after passing a winter, to be carried away in a floe of ice into Baffin's Bay, which no human skill could prevent.

Sir George Back was to make a summer's cruise to Wager Inlet, and return to England. The result every one knows or may make themselves acquainted with, by reading the fearful voyage of the Terror, an abstract of which I have already given. It would be superfluous to enumerate many other of our series of polar voyages, but it is pretty evident that Captain Forsyth's voyage, performed in the summer months of 1850, will be handed down to posterity as one of the most remarkable, if not the most remarkable, that has ever been accomplished in the arctic seas — the expedition consisting of one solitary small vessel.

The main object of the voyage, it is true, has not been accomplished, but as all the harbors in Regent Inlet were frozen up, and it was utterly impossible to cut through a vast tract of ice, extending for perhaps four or five miles, to get the ship to a secure anchorage, under these circumstances, Captain Forsyth had no alternative but to return, and in doing so, he has, in the opinion of all the best-informed officers, displayed great good sense and judgment rather than remain frozen in at the Wellington Channel, where he only went to reconnoiter, and where he had no business whatever, his instructions being confined to Regent Inlet.

ADVANCE AND RESCUE BEATING TO WINDWARD OF AN ICEBERG.

THE AMERICAN ARCTIC EXPEDITION.

THE FIRST GRINNELL EXPEDITION IN THE ADVANCE AND RESCUE, SENT OUT BY HENRY GRINNELL, ESQ., UNDER COMMAND OF LIEUTENANT DE HAVEN, IN THE YEARS 1850 AND 1851.

THE safe return of the expedition sent out by Mr. Henry Grinnell, an opulent merchant of New York city in search of Sir John Franklin and his companions, is an event of much interest; and the voyage, though not resulting in the discovery of the long-absent mariners, presents many considerations satisfactory to the parties immediately concerned, and the American public in general.

Mr. Grinnell's expedition consisted of only two small brigs, the Advance of 140 tons; the Rescue of only 90 tons. The former had been engaged in the Havana trade; the latter was a new vessel built for the merchant service. Both were strengthened for the arctic voyage at a heavy cost. They were then placed under the directions of our Navy Board, and subject to naval regulations, as if in permanent service. The command was given to Lieut. E. De Haven, a young naval officer who accompanied the United States exploring expedition. The result has proved that a better choice could not have been made. His officers consisted of Mr. Murdoch, sailing-master; Dr. E. K. Kane, surgeon and naturalist; and Mr. Lovell, midshipman. The Advance had a crew of twelve men when she sailed; two of them complaining of sickness, and expressing a desire to return home, were left at the Danish settlement at Disco Island, on the coast of Greenland.

The Expedition left New York on the 23d of May, 1850, and was absent a little more than sixteen months. They passed the eastern extremity of Newfoundland ten days after leaving Sandy Hóok, and then sailed east-northeast, directly for Cape Comfort, on the coast of Greenland. The weather was generally fine, and only a single accident occurred on the voyage to that country of frost and snow. Off the coast of Labrador they met an iceberg making its way toward the tropics. The night was very dark, and as the huge voyager had no "light out," the Advance could not be censured for running foul. She was punished, however, by the loss of her jib-boom, as she ran against the iceberg at the rate of seven or eight knots an hour.

The voyagers did not land at Cape Comfort, but turning northward, sailed along the southwest coast of Greenland, sometimes in the midst of broad acres of broken ice, (particularly in Davis' Straits,) as far as Whale Island. On the way the anniversary of our national independence occurred; it was observed by the seamen by "splicing the main-brace"—in other words, they were allowed an extra glass of grog on that day.

From Whale Island, a boat, with two officers and four seamen, was sent to Disco Island, a distance of about 26 miles, to a Danish settlement there, to procure skin clothing and other articles necessary for use during the rigors of a polar winter. The officers were entertained at the government house; the seamen were comfortably lodged with the Esquimaux, sleeping in fur bags at night. They returned to the ship the following day, and the expedition proceeded on its voyage. When passing the little Danish settlement of Upernavick, they were boarded by natives for the first time. They were out in government whale-boats, hunting for ducks and seals. These hardy children of the Arctic Circle were not shy, for through the Danes, the English whalers, and government expeditions, they had become acqnainted with men of other latitudes.

When the expedition reached Melville Bay, which, on account of its fearful character, is also called the *Devil's Nip*, the voyagers began to witness more of the grandeur and perils of arctic scenes. Icebergs of

PERILOUS SITUATION OF THE ADVANCE AND RESCUE IN MELVILLE BAY.

all dimensions came bearing down from the Polar seas, like vast squadrons, and the roar of their rending came over the waters like the booming of heavy broadsides of contending navies. They also encountered immense floes, with only narrow channels between, and at times their situation was exceedingly perilous. On one occasion, after heaving through fields of ice for five consecutive weeks, two immense floes, between which they were making their way, gradually approached each other, and for several hours they expected their tiny vessels — tiny when compared with the mighty objects around them — would be crushed. An immense calf of ice, six or eight feet thick, slid under the Rescue, lifting her almost "high and dry," and careening her partially upon her beam ends. By means of ice-anchors, (large iron hooks,) they kept her from capsizing. In this position they remained about sixty hours, when, with saws and axes, they succeeded in relieving her. The ice now opened a little, and they finally warped through into clear water. While they were thus confined, polar bears came around them in abundance, greedy for prey, and the seamen indulged a little in the perilous sports of the chase.

The open sea continued but a short time, when they again became entangled among bergs, floes, and hummocks, and encountered the most fearful perils. Sometimes they anchored their vessels to icebergs, and sometimes to floes or masses of hummock. On one of these occasions, while the cook, an active Frenchman, was upon a berg, making a place for an anchor, the mass of ice split beneath him, and he was dropped through the yawning fissure into the water, a distance of almost thirty feet. Fortunately the masses, as is often the case, did not close up again, but floated apart, and the poor cook was hauled on board more dead than alive, from excessive fright. It was in this fearful region that they first encountered pack-ice, and there they were locked in from the 7th to the 23d of July. During that time they were joined by the yacht Prince Albert, commanded by Captain Forsyth, of the Royal Navy, and together the three vessels were anchored, for a while, to an immense field of ice, in sight of the Devil's Thumb. That high, rocky peak, situated in latitude 74° 22′, was about thirty miles distant, and with the dark hills adjacent, presented a strange aspect where all was white and glittering. The pack and the hills are masses of rock, with occasionally a lichen or a moss growing upon their otherwise naked surfaces. In the midst of the vast ice-field loomed up many lofty bergs, all of them in motion — slow and majestic motion.

From the Devil's Thumb the American vessels passed onward through the pack toward Sabine's Islands, while the Prince Albert essayed to make a more westerly course. They reached Cape York at the beginning of August. Far across the ice, landward, they discovered, through their glasses, several men, apparently making signals; and for a while they rejoiced in the belief that they saw a portion of Sir John Franklin's companions. Four men, (among whom was our sailor-artist,) were dispatched with a whale-boat to reconnoiter. They soon discovered the men to be Esquimaux, who, by signs, professed great friendship, and endeavored to get the voyagers to accompany them to their homes beyond the hills. They declined; and as soon as they returned to the vessel, the expedition again pushed forward, and made its way to Cape Dudley Digges, which they reached on the 7th of August.

At Cape Dudley Digges they were charmed by the sight of the Crimson Cliffs, spoken of by Captain Parry and other arctic navigators. These are lofty cliffs of dark brown stone, covered with snow of a rich crimson color. It was a magnificent sight in that cold region, to see such an apparently warm object standing out in bold relief against the dark blue back-ground of a polar sky. This was the most northern point to which the expedition penetrated. The whole coast which they had passed from Disco to this cape is high, rugged, and barren, only some of the low points, stretching into the sea, bearing a species of dwarf fir. Northeast from the cape rise the Arctic Highlands, to an unknown alti-

THE ADVANCE, RESCUE, AND PRINCE ALBERT NEAR THE DEVIL'S THUMB.

tude ; and stretching away northward is the unexplored Smith's Sound, filled with impenetrable ice.

From Cape Dudley Digges, the Advance and Rescue, beating against wind and tide in the midst of the ice-fields, made Wolstenholme Sound, and then changing their course to the southwest, emerged from the fields into the open waters of Lancaster Sound. Here, on the 18th of August, they encountered a tremendous gale, which lasted about twenty-four hours. The two vessels parted company during the storm, and remained separate several days. Across Lancaster Sound, the Advance made her way to Barrow's Straits, and on the 22d discovered the Prince Albert on the southern shore of the straits, near Leopold Island, a mass of lofty, precipitous rocks, dark and barren, and hooded and draped with snow. The weather was fine, and soon the officers and crews of the two vessels met in friendly greeting. Those of the Prince Albert were much astonished, for they (being towed by a steamer,) left the Americans in Melville Bay on the 6th, pressing northward through the pack, and could not conceive how they so soon and safely penetrated it. Captain Forsyth had attempted to reach a particular point, where he intended to remain through the winter, but finding the passage thereto completely blocked up with ice, he had resolved, on the very day when the Americans appeared, to " 'bout ship," and return home. This fact, and the disappointment felt by Mr. Snow, are mentioned in our former article.

The two vessels remained together a day or two, when they parted company, the Prince Albert to return home, and the Advance to make further explorations. It was off Leopold Island, on the 22d of August, that the "mad Yankee" took the lead through the vast masses of floating ice, so vividly described by Mr. Snow, and so graphically portrayed by the sailor-artist. "The way was before them," says Mr. Snow, who stood upon the deck of the Advance ; "the stream of ice had to be either gone through boldly, or a long *detour* made; and, despite the heaviness of the stream, *they pushed the vessel through in her proper course.* Two or three shocks, as she came in contact with some large pieces, were unheeded ; and the moment the last block was past the bow, the officer sung out, 'So : steady as she goes on her course ;' and came aft as if nothing more than ordinary sailing had been going on. I observed our own little bark nobly following in the American's wake ; and as I afterward learned, she got through it pretty well, though not without much doubt of the propriety of keeping on in such procedure after the 'mad Yankee,' as he was called by our mate."

From Leopold Island the Advance proceeded to the northwest, and on the 25th reached Cape Riley, another amorphous mass, not so regular and precipitate as Leopold Island, but more lofty. Here a strong tide, setting in to the shore, drifted the Advance toward the beach, where she stranded. Around her were small bergs and large masses of floating ice, all under the influence of the strong current. It was about two o'clock in the afternoon when she struck. By diligent labor in removing every thing from her deck to a small floe, she was so lightened, that at four o'clock the next morning she floated, and soon every thing was properly replaced.

Near Cape Riley the Americans fell in with a portion of an English Expedition, and there also the Rescue, left behind in the gale in Lancaster Sound, overtook the Advance. There was Captain Penny with the Sophia and Lady Franklin; the veteran Sir John Ross, with the Felix, and Commodore Austin, with the Resolute steamer. Together the navigators of both nations explored the coast at and near Cape Riley, and on the 27th they saw in a cove on the shore of Beechey Island, or Beechey Cape, on the east side of the entrance to Wellington Channel, unmistakable evidence that Sir John Franklin and his companions were there in April, 1846. There they found many articles known to belong to the British Navy, and some that were the property of the Erebus and Terror, the ships under the command of Sir John. There lay, bleached

THE ADVANCE STRANDED AT CAPE RILEY.

to the whiteness of the surrounding snow, a piece of canvas, with the name of the Terror, marked upon it with indestructible charcoal. It was very faint, yet perfectly legible. Near it was a guide board, lying flat upon its face, having been prostrated by the wind. It had evidently been used to direct exploring parties to the vessels, or rather, to the encampment on shore. The board was pine, thirteen inches in length and six and a half in breadth, and nailed to a boarding pike eight feet in length. It is supposed that the sudden opening of the ice, caused Sir John to depart hastily, and in so doing, this pike and its board were left behind. They also found a large number of tin canisters, such as are used for packing meats for a sea voyage; an anvil block: remnants of clothing, which evinced, by numerous patches and their thread-bare character, that they had been worn as long as the owners could keep them on; the remains of an India Rubber glove, lined with wool; some old sacks; a cask, or tub, partly filled with charcoal, and an unfinished rope-mat, which, like other fibrous fabrics, was bleached white.

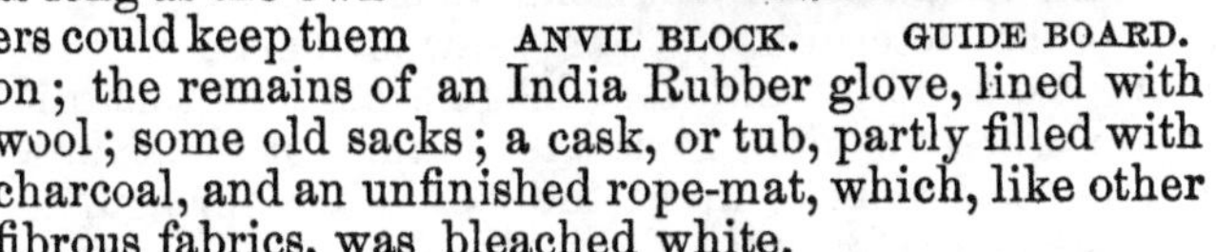

ANVIL BLOCK. GUIDE BOARD.

But the most interesting, and at the same time most melancholy traces of the navigators, were three graves, in a little sheltered cove, each with a board at the head, bearing the name of the sleeper below. These inscriptions testify positively when Sir John and his companions were there. The board at the head of the grave on the left has the following inscription:

"Sacred to the memory of JOHN TORRINGTON, who departed this life, January 1st, A D., 1846, on board her Majesty's ship Terror, aged 20 years."

On the center one—"Sacred to the memory of JOHN HARTNELL, A. B., of her Majesty's ship Erebus; died, January 4th, 1846, aged 25 years. 'Thus saith the Lord of Hosts, Consider your ways;' Haggai, chap. i. 5, 7."

On the right—"Sacred to the memory of W. BRAINE, R. M., of her Majesty's ship Erebus, who died April 3d, 1846, aged 32 years. 'Choose you this day whom you will serve:' Joshua, chap. xxiv., part of the 15th verse."

THREE GRAVES AT BEECHEY.

How much later than April 3d (the date upon the last-named head-board,) Sir John remained at Beechey, can not be determined. They saw evidences of his having gone northward, for sledge tracks in that direction were visible. It is the opinion of Dr. Kane that, on the breaking up of the ice, in the spring, Sir John passed northward with his ships through Wellington Channel, into the great Polar basin, and that he did not return. This, too, is the opinion of Captain Penny, and he zealously urges the British government to send a powerful screw steamer to pass through that

THE ADVANCE AND RESCUE AT BARLOW'S INLET.

channel, and explore the theoretically more hospitable coasts beyond. This will doubtless be undertaken another season, it being the opinions of Captains Parry, Beechey, Sir John Ross, and others, expressed at a conference with the board of Admiralty, in September, that the season was too far advanced to attempt it the present year. Dr. Kane, in a letter to Mr. Grinnell, since the return of the expedition, thus expresses his opinion concerning the safety of Sir John and his companions. After saying, "I should think that he is now to be sought for north and west of Cornwallis Island," he adds, "as to the chance of the destruction of his party by the casualties of ice, the return of our own party after something more than the usual share of them, is the only fact that I can add to what we knew when we set out. The hazards from cold and privation of food may be almost looked upon as subordinate. The snow-hut, the fire and light from the moss-lamp fed with blubber, the seal, the narwhal, the white whale, and occasionally abundant stores of migratory birds, would sustain vigorous life. The scurvy, the worst visitation of explorers deprived of permanent quarters, is more rare in the depths of a polar winter, than in the milder weather of the moist sum mer; and our two little vessels encountered both seasons without losing a man."

Leaving Beechey Cape, our expedition forced its way through the ice to Barrow's Inlet, where they narrowly escaped being frozen in for the winter. They endeavored to enter the Inlet, for the purpose of making it their winter quarters, but were prevented by the mass of pack-ice at its entrance. It was on the 4th of September, 1850, when they arrived there, and after remaining seven or eight days, they abandoned the attempt to enter. On the right and left of the above picture, are seen the dark rocks at the entrance of the Inlet, and in the center of the frozen waters and the range of hills beyond. There was much smooth ice within the Inlet, and while the vessels lay anchored to the "field," officers and crew exercised and amused themselves by skating. On the left of the Inlet, (in dicated by the dark conical object,) they discovered a Cairn, (a heap of stones with a cavity,) eight or ten feet in height, which was erected by Captain Ommaney of the English Expedition then in the polar waters. Within it he had placed two letters, for "Whom it might concern." Commander De Haven also deposited a letter there. It is believed to be the only post-office in the world, free for the use of all nations. The rocks, here, presented vast fissures made by the frost; and at the foot of the cliff on the right that powerful agent had cast down vast heaps of debris.

From Barlow's Inlet, our expedition moved slowly westward, battling with the ice every rood of the way, until they reached Griffin's Island, at about 96° west longitude from Greenwich. This was attained on the 11th, and was the extreme westing made by the expedition. All beyond seemed impenetrable ice; and, despairing of making any further discoveries before the winter should set in, they resolved to return home. Turning eastward, they hoped to reach Davis' Strait by the southern route, before the cold and darkness came on; but they were doomed to disappointment. Near the entrance to Wellington Channel they became completely locked in by hummock-ice, and soon found themselves drifting with an irresistible tide up that channel toward the pole.

Now began the most perilous adventures of the navigators. The summer day was drawing to a close; the diurnal visits of the pale sun were rapidly shortening, and soon the long polar night, with all its darkness and horrors, would fall upon them. Slowly they drifted in those vast fields of ice, whither, or to what result, they knew not. Locked in the moving yet compact mass; liable at every moment to be crushed; far away from land; the mercury sinking daily lower and lower from the zero figure, toward the point where that metal freezes, they felt small hope of ever reaching home again. Yet they prepared for winter comforts and winter sports, as cheerfully as if lying safe in Barlow's Inlet. As the

ADVANCE AND RESCUE DRIFTING IN WELLINGTON SOUND.

winter advanced, the crews of both the vessels went on board the larger one. They unshipped the rudders of each, to prevent their being injured by the ice, covered the deck of the Advance with felt, prepared their stores, and made arrangements for enduring the long winter, now upon them. Physical and mental activity being necessary for the preservation of health, they daily exercised in the open air for several hours. They built ice huts, hunted the huge white bears and the little polar foxes, and when the darkness of the winter night had spread over them they arranged in-door amusements and employments.

Before the end of October, the sun made its appearance for the last time, and the awful polar night closed in. Early in November they wholly abandoned the Rescue, and both crews made the Advance their permanent winter home. The cold soon became intense; the mercury congealed, and the spirit thermometer indicated 46° below zero! Its average range was 30° to 35°. They had drifted helplessly up Wellington Channel, almost to the latitude from whence Captain Penny saw an open sea, and which all believe to be the great polar basin, where there is a more genial clime than that which intervenes between the Arctic Circle and the 75th degree. Here, when almost in sight of the open ocean, that mighty polar tide, with its vast masses of ice, suddenly ebbed, and our little vessels were carried back as resistlessly as before, through Barrow's Straits into Lancaster Sound! All this while the immense fields of hummock-ice were moving, and the vessels were in hourly danger of being crushed and destroyed. At length, while drifting through Barrow's Straits, the congealed mass, as if crushed together by the opposite shores, became more compact, and the Advance was elevated almost seven feet by the stern, and keeled two feet eight inches, starboard. In this position she remained, with very little alteration for five consecutive months; for, soon after entering Baffin's Bay in the midst of the winter, the ice became frozen in one immense tract, covering millions of acres. Thus frozen in, sometimes more than a hundred miles from land, they drifted slowly along the southwest coast of Baffin's Bay, a distance of more than a thousand miles from Wellington Channel. For eleven weeks that dreary night continued, and during that time the disc of the sun was never seen above the horizon. Yet nature was not wholly forbidding in aspect. Sometimes the Aurora Borealis would flash up still further northward; and sometimes Aurora Parhelia — mock suns and mock moons — would appear in varied beauty in the starry sky. Brilliant, too, were the northern constellations; and when the real moon was at its full, it made its stately circuit in the heavens, without descending below the horizon, and lighted up the vast piles of ice with a pale luster, almost as great as the morning twilights of more genial skies.

Around the vessels the crews built a wall of ice; and in ice huts they stowed away their cordage and stores to make room for exercise on the decks. They organized a theatrical company, and amused themselves and the officers with comedy well performed. Behind the pieces of hummock each actor learned his part, and by means of calico they transformed themselves into female characters, as occasion required. These dramas were acted on the deck of the Advance, sometimes while the thermometer indicated 30° below zero, and actors and audiences highly enjoyed the fun. They also went in parties during that long night, fully armed, to hunt the polar bear, the grim monarch of the frozen North, on which occasions they often encountered perilous adventures. They played at foot-ball, and exercised themselves in drawing sledges, heavily laden with provisions. Five hours of each twenty-four, they thus exercised in the open air, and once a week each man washed his whole body in cold snow water. Serious sickness was consequently avoided, and the scurvy which attacked them soon yielded to remedies.

Often during that fearful night, they expected the disaster of having their vessels crushed. All through November and December, before the ice became fast they slept in their clothes, with knapsacks on their backs, and sledges upon the ice, laden with stores, not knowing at what moment the vessels might be demolished, and themselves forced to leave them, and make their way toward land. On the 8th of December, and the 23d of January, they actually lowered their boats and stood upon the ice, for the crushing masses were making the timbers of the gallant vessel creak and its decks to rise in the center. They were then ninety miles from land, and hope hardly whispered an encouraging idea of life being sustained. On the latter occasion, when officers and crew stood upon the ice, with the ropes of their provision sledges in their hands, a terrible snow-drift came from the northeast, and intense darkness shrouded them. Had the vessel then been crushed, all must have perished. But God, who ruled the storm, also put forth His protecting arm and saved them.

Early in February the northern horizon began to be streaked with gorgeous twilight, the herald of the approaching king of day; and on the 18th the disc of the sun first appeared above the horizon. As its golden rim rose above the glittering snow-drifts and piles of ice, three hearty cheers went up from those hardy mariners, and they welcomed their deliverer from the chains of frost as cordially as those of old who chanted,

> "See! the conquering hero comes,
> Sound the trumpet, beat the drums."

Day after day it rose higher and higher, and while the pallid faces of the voyagers, bleached during that long night, darkened by its beams, the vast masses of ice began to yield to its fervid influences. The scurvy disappeared, and from that time, until their arrival home, not a man suffered from sickness. As they slowly drifted through Davis' Straits, and the ice gave indications of breaking up, the voyagers made preparations for sailing. The Rescue was re-occupied, (May 13th, 1851,) and her stone-post, which had been broken by the ice in Barrow's Straits, was repaired. To accomplish this, they were obliged to dig away the ice which was from 12 to 14 feet thick around her, as represented in the engraving. They reshipped their rudders ; removed the felt covering ; placed their stores on deck, and then patiently awaited the disruption of the ice This event was very sudden and appalling. It began to give way on the 5th of June, and in the space of twenty minutes the whole mass, as far as the eye could reach, became one vast field of moving floes. On the 10th of June, they emerged into open water, a little south of the Arctic Circle, in latitude 65° 30′. They immediately repaired to Godhaven, on the coast of Greenland, where they refitted, and, unappalled by the perils through which they had just passed, they once more turned their prows northward to encounter anew the ice squadrons of Baffin's Bay. Again they traversed the coast of Greenland to about the 73d degree, when they bore to the westward, and on the 7th and 8th of July, passed the English whaling fleet near the Dutch Islands. Onward they pressed through the accumulating ice to Baffin's Island, where, on the 11th, they were joined by the Prince Albert, then out upon another cruise. They continued in company until the 3d of August, when the Albert departed for the westward, determined to try the more southern passage. Here again our expedition encountered vast fields of hummock-ice, and were subjected to the most imminent perils. The floating ice, as if moved by adverse currents, tumbled in huge masses, and reared upon the sides of the sturdy little vessels like monsters of the deep intent upon destruction. These masses broke in the bulwarks, and sometimes fell over upon the decks with terrible force, like rocks rolled over a plain by mountain torrents. The noise was fearful ; so deafening that the mariners could scarcely hear each other's voices. The sounds of these rolling masses, together with the rending of the icebergs floating near, and the vast floes, produced a din like the discharge of a thousand pieces of ordnance upon a field of battle.

Finding the north and west closed against further progress, by impenetrable ice, the brave De Haven was

THE ADVANCE IN DAVIS' STRAITS, JUNE 5, 1851.

balked, and turning his vessels homeward, they came out into an open sea, somewhat crippled, but not a plank seriously started. During a storm off the banks of Newfoundland, a thousand miles from New York, the vessels parted company. The Advance arrived safely at the Navy Yard at Brooklyn on the 30th of September, and the Rescue joined her there a few days afterward. Toward the close of October, the government resigned the vessels into the hands of Mr. Grinnell, to be used in other service, but with the stipulation that they are to be subject to the order of the Secretary of the Navy in the spring, if required for another expedition in search of Sir John Franklin.

We have thus given a very brief account of the principal events of interest connected with the American Arctic Expedition; a full report of which, and detailed narratives have been published. Aside from the success which attended our little vessels in encountering the perils of the polar seas, there are associations which must forever hallow the effort as one of the noblest exhibitions of the true glory of nations. The navies of America and England have before met upon the ocean, but they met for deadly strife. Now, too, they met for strife, equally determined, but not with each other. They met in the holy cause of benevolence and human sympathy, to battle with the elements beneath the Arctic Circle; and the chivalric heroism which the few stout hearts of the two nations displayed in that terrible conflict, redounds a thousand-fold more to the glory of the actors, their governments, and the race, than if four-score ships, with ten thousand armed men had fought for the mastery of each other upon the broad ocean, and battered hulks and marred corpses had gone down to the coral caves of the sea, a dreadful offering to the demon of Discord. In the latter event, troops of widows and orphan children would have sent up a cry of wail; now, the heroes advanced manfully to rescue husbands and fathers to restore them to their wives and children. How glorious the thought! and how suggestive of the beauty of that fast approaching day, when the nations shall sit down in peace as united children of one household.

Winter in the Arctic Ocean.

The following narrative, showing the way the winter of 1851–52 was passed by those engaged in the recent arctic expedition, is from the official report made by Lieut. De Haven, the Commander of the expedition:

"On the morning of the 13th Sept., 1850, the wind having moderated sufficiently, we got under way, and working our way through some streams of ice, arrived in a few hours at 'Griffith's' Island, under the lee of which we found our consort made fast to the shore, where she had taken shelter in the gale, her crew having suffered a good deal from the inclemency of the weather. In bringing to under the lee of the island, she had the misfortune to spring her rudder, so that on joining us, it was with much difficulty she could steer. To insure her safety and more rapid progress, she was taken in tow by the Advance, when she bore up with a fine breeze from the westward. Off Cape Martyr, we left the English squadron under Capt. Austin. About ten miles further to the east, the two vessels under Capt. Penny, and that under Sir John Ross, were seen secured near the land. At 8 P. M., we had advanced as far as Cape Hotham. Thence as far as the increasing darkness of the night enabled us to see, there was nothing to obstruct our progress, except the bay ice. This, with a good breeze, would not have impeded us much; but unfortunately the wind, when it was most required, failed us. The snow, with which the surface of the water was covered, rapidly cemented, and formed a tenacious coat, through which it was impossible with all our appliances to force the vessels. At 8 P. M., they came to a dead stand, some ten miles to the east of Barlow's Inlet.

"The following day the wind hauled to the southward, from which quarter it lasted till the 19th. During this period the young ice was broken, its edges squeezed up

ADVANCE AND RESCUE DURING THE WINTER OF 1850–51.

like hammocks, and one floe overrun by another until it all assumed the appearance of heavy ice. The vessels received some heavy nips from it, but they withstood them without injury. Whenever a pool of water made its appearance, every effort was made to reach it, in hopes that it would lead us into Beechey Island, or some other place where the vessel might be placed in security; for the winter set in unusually early, and the severity with which it commenced, forbade all hopes of our being able to return this season. I now became anxious to attain a point in the neighborhood, from whence by means of land parties, in the spring, a goodly extent of Wellington Channel might be examined.

"In the mean time, under the influence of the south wind, we were being set up the channel. On the 18th we were above Cape Bowden, the most northern point seen on this shore by Parry. The land on both shores was seen much further, and trended considerably to the west of north. To accouut for this drift, the fixed ice of Wellington Channel, which we had observed in passing to the westward, must have been broken up and driven to the southward by the heavy gale of the 12th. On the 19th the wind veered to the north, which gave us a southerly set, forcing us at the same time with the western shore. This did not last long; for the next day the wind hauled again to the south, and blew fresh, bringing the ice in upon us with much pressure. At midnight it broke up all around us, so that we had work to maintain the Advance in a safe position, and keep her from being separated from her consort, which was immovably fixed in the center of a large floe.

"We continued to drift slowly to the N. N. W., until the 22d, when our progress appeared to be arrested by a small low island, which was discovered in that direction, about seven miles distant. A channel of three or four miles in width separated it from Cornwallis Island. This latter island, trending N. W. from our position, terminated abruptly in an elevated cape, to which I have given the name of Manning, after a warm personal friend and ardent supporter of the expedition.

Between Cornwallis Island and some distant high land visible in the north, appeared a wide channel leading to the westward. A dark, misty-looking cloud which hung over it, (technically termed frost-smoke,) was indicative of much open water in that direction. This was the direction in which my instructions, referring to the investigations of the National Observatory, concerning the winds and currents of the ocean, directed me to look for open water. Nor was the open water the only indication that presented itself in confirmation of this theoretical conjecture as to a milder climate in that direction. As we entered Wellington Channel, the signs of animal life became more abundant, and Captain Penny, commander of one of the English expeditions, who afterward penetrated on sledges much toward the region of the 'frost-smoke,' much further than it was possible for us to do in our vessels reported that he actually arrived on the borders of this open sea.

"Thus, these admirably drawn instructions, deriving arguments from the enlarged and comprehensive system of physical research, not only pointed with emphasis to an unknown sea into which Franklin had probably found his way, but directed me to search for traces of his expedition in the very channel at the entrance of which it is now ascertained he had passed his first winter. The direction in which search with most chances of success is now to be made for the missing expedition, or for traces of it, is no doubt in the direction which is so clearly pointed out in my instructions. To the channel which appeared to lead into the open sea over which the cloud of 'frost-smoke' hung as a sign, I have given the name of Maury, after the distinguished gentleman at the head of our National Observatory, whose theory with regard to an open sea to the north is likely to be realized through this channel. To the large mass of land visible between N. W. to N. N. E., I gave the name of Grinnell, in honor of the head and heart of the man in whose philanthropic mind originated the idea of this expedition, and to whose munificence it owes its existence.

"To a remarkable peak bearing N. N. E. from us, distant about forty miles, was given the name of Mount Franklin. An inlet or harbor immediately to the north of Cape Bowden was discovered by Mr. Griffin in his land excursion from Point Innes, on the 27th of August, and has received the name of Griffin Inlet. The small island mentioned before was called Murdaugh's Island, after the acting master of the Advance. The eastern shore of Wellington Channel appeared to run parallel with the western, but it became quite low, and being covered with snow, could not be distinguished with certainty, so that its continuity with the high land to the north was not ascertained. Some small pools of open water appearing near us, an attempt was made about fifty yards, but all our combined efforts were of no avail in extricating the Rescue from her icy cradle. A change of wind not only closed the ice up again, but threatened to give a severe nip. We unshipped her rudder and placed it out of harm's way.

"September 22d, was an uncomfortable day. The wind was from N. E. with snow. From an early hour in the morning, the floes began to be pressed together with so much force that their edge was thrown up in immense ridges of rugged hummocks. The Advance was heavily nipped between two floes, and the ice was piled up so high above the rail on the starboard side as to threaten to come on board and sink us with its weight. All hands were occupied in keeping it out. The pressure and commotion did not cease till near midnight, when we were very glad to have a respite from our labors and fears. The next day we were threatened with a similar scene, but it fortunately ceased in a short time. For the remainder of September, and until the 4th of October, the vessels drifted but little. The winds were very light, the thermometer fell to minus 12, and ice formed over the pools in sight, sufficiently strong to travel upon. We were now strongly impressed with the belief that the ice had become fixed for the winter, and that we should be able to send out traveling parties from the advanced position for the examination of the lands to the northward Stimulated by this fair prospect, another attempt was made to reach the shore in order to establish a depot of provisions at or near Cape Manning, which would materially facilitate the progress of our parties in the spring; but the ice was still found to be detached from the shore, and a narrow lane of water cut us from it.

"During the interval of comparative quiet, preliminary measures were taken for heating the Advance and increasing her quarters, so as to accomodate the officers and crew of both vessels. No stoves had as yet been used in either vessel; indeed they could not well be put up without placing a large quantity of stores and fuel upon the ice. The attempt was made to do this, but a sudden crack in the floe where it appeared strongest, causing the loss of several tons of coal, convinced us that it was not yet safe to do so. It was not until the 20th of October, we got fires below. Ten days later the housing cloth was put over, and the officers and crew of the Rescue ordered on board the Advance for the winter. Room was found on the deck of the Rescue for many of the provisions removed from the hold of this vessel. Still a large quantity had to be placed on the ice. The absence of fire below had caused much discomfort to all hands ever since the beginning of September, not so much from the low temperature, as from the accumulation of moisture by condensation, which congealed as the temperature decreased, and covered the wood work of our apartments with ice. This state of things soon began to work its effect upon the health of the crews. Several cases of scurvy appeared among them, and notwithstanding the indefatigable attention and active treatment resorted to by the medical officers, it could not be eradicated — its progress, however, was checked.

"All through October and November, we were drifted to and fro by the changing wind, but never passing out of Wellington Channel. On the 1st of November, the new ice had attained the thickness of 37 inches. Still, frequent breaks would occur in it, often in fearful proxnnity to the vessels. Hummocks consisting of massive granite-like blocks, would be thrown up to the height of twenty, and even thirty feet. This action in the ice was accompanied with a variety of sounds impossible to be described, but when heard never failed to carry a feeling of awe into the stoutest hearts. In the stillness of an arctic night, they could be heard several miles, and often was the rest of all hands disturbed by them. To guard against the worst that could happen to us — the destruction of the vessels — the boats were prepared and sledges built. Thirty days' provisions were placed in for all hands, together with tents and blanket bags for sleeping in. Besides this, each man and officer had his knapsack containing an extra suit of clothes. These were all kept in readiness for use at a moment's notice.

"For the sake of wholesome exercise, as well as to inure the people to ice traveling, frequent excursions were made with our laden sledges. The officers usually took the lead at the drag ropes, and they, as well as the men underwent the labor of surmounting the rugged hummocks, with great cheerfulness and zeal. Notwithstanding the low temperature, all hands usually returned in a profuse perspiration. We had also other sources of exercise and amusements, such as foot-ball, skating, sliding, racing, with theatrical representations on holidays and national anniversaries. These amusements were continued throughout the winter, and contributed very materially to the cheerfulness and general good health of all hands. The drift had set us gradually to the S. E., until we were about five miles to the S. W. of Beechey Island. In this position we remained comparatively stationary about a week. We once more began to entertain a hope that we had become fixed for the winter, but it proved a vain one, for on the last day of November a strong wind from the westward set in, with thick snowy weather. The wind created an immediate movement in the ice. Several fractures took place near us, and many heavy hummocks were thrown up. The floe in which our vessels were imbedded, was being rapidly encroached upon, so that we were in momentary fear of the ice breaking from around them, and that they would be once more broken out and left to the tender mercies of the crashing floes.

"On the following day (the 1st of December) the weather cleared off, and the few hours of twilight which we had about noon, enabled us to get a glimpse of the land. As well as we could make it out, we appeared to be off Gascoigne Inlet. We were now clear of Wellington Channel, and in the fair way of Lancaster Sound, to be set either up or down, at the mercy of the prevailing winds and currents. We were not long left in doubt as to the direction we had to pursue. The winds prevailed from the westward, and our drift was steady and rapid toward the mouth of the Sound. The prospect before us was now any thing but cheering. We were deprived of our last fond hope, that of becoming fixed in some position whence operations could be carried on by means of traveling parties in the spring. The vessels were fast being set out of the region of search. Nor was this our only source of uneasiness. The line of our drift was from two to five miles from the north shore, and whenever the moving ice met with any of the capes or projecting points of land, the obstruction would cause fractures in it, extending off to and far beyond us. Cape Hurd was the first and most prominent point — we were but two miles from it on the 3d of December. Nearly all day the ice was both seen and heard to be in constant motion at no great distance from us. In the evening a crack on our floe took place not more than twenty-five yards ahead of the Advance. It opened in the course of the evening to the width of 190 yards.

"No further disturbance took place until noon of the 5th, when we were somewhat startled by the familiar and unmistakable sound of the ice grinding against the side of the ship. Going on deck, I perceived that another crack had taken place, passing along the length of the vessel. It did not open more than a foot; this, however, was sufficient to liberate the vessel, and she rose several inches bodily, having become more buoyant since she froze in. The following day, in the evening the crack opened several yards, leaving the sides of the Advance entirely free, and she was once more supported by and rode in her own element. We were not, though, by any means, in a pleasant situation. The floes were considerably broken in all directions around us, and one crack had taken place between the two vessels. The Rescue was not disturbed in her bed of ice.

"December 7th, at 8 A. M., the crack in which we were, had opened and formed a lane of water fifty-six feet wide, communicating ahead at the distance of sixty feet with ice of about one foot in thickness, which had formed since the 3d. The vessel was secured to the largest floe near us (that on which our spare stores were deposited.) At noon, the ice was again in motion, and began to close, affording us the pleasant prospect of an inevitable nip between two floes of the heaviest kind. In a short time the prominent points took our side, on the starboard, just about the main-rigging, and on the port under the counter, and at the fore-rigging; thus bringing three points of pressure in such a position that it must have proved fatal to a larger or less strengthened vessel. The Advance, however, stood it bravely. After trembling and groaning in every joint, the ice passed under and raised her about two and a half feet. She was let down again for a moment, and then her stern was raised about five feet. Her bows being unsupported, were depressed almost as much. In this *uncomfortable position* we remained. The wind blew a gale from the eastward, and the ice all around was in dreadful commotion, excepting, fortunately, that in immediate contact with us. The commotion in the ice continued all through the night; and we were in momentary expectation of the destruction of both vessels. The easterly gale had set us some two or three miles to the west. As soon as it was light enough to see on the 9th, it was discovered that the heavy ice on which the Rescue had been imbedded for so long a time, was entirely broken up, and piled up around her in massive hummocks. On her pumps being sounded, I was gratified to learn that she remained tight, notwithstanding the immense straining and pressure she must have endured.

"During this period of trial, as well as in all former and subsequent ones, I could not avoid being struck with the calmness and decision of the officers, as well as the subordination and good conduct of the men, without an exception. Each one knew the imminence of the peril that surrounded us, and was prepared to abide it with a stout heart. There was no noise, no confusion. I did not detect, even in the moment when the destruction of the vessel seemed inevitable, a single desponding look among the whole crew; on the contrary, each one seemed resolved to do his whole duty, and every thing went on cheerily and bravely. For my own part, I had become quite an invalid, so much so as to prevent my taking an active part in the duties of the vessel as I had always done, or even from incurring the exposure necessary to proper exercise. However, I felt no apprehensions that the vessel would not be properly taken care of, for I had perfect confidence in one and all by whom I was surrounded. I knew them to be equal to any emergency, but I felt under special obligations to the gallant commander of the Rescue, for the efficient aid he rendered me. With the kindest consideration, and the most cheerful alacrity, he volunteered to perform the executive duties during the winter, and relieve me from every thing that might tend in the least to retard my recovery.

"During the remainder of December, the ice remained quiet immediately around us, and breaks were all strongly cemented by new ice. In our neighborhood, however, cracks were daily visible. Our drift to the eastward averaged nearly six miles per day; so that on the last of the month we were at the entrance of the Sound, Cape Osborn bearing north from us.

"January, 1851.— On passing out of the Sound, and opening Baffin's Bay, to the north was seen a dark horizon, indicating much open water in that direction. On the 11th, a crack took place between us and the Rescue, passing close under our stern, and forming a lane of water eighty feet wide. In the afternoon the floes began to move, the lane was closed up, and the edges of the ice coming in contact with so much pressure, threatened the demolition of the narrow space which separated us from the line of fracture. Fortunately, the floes again separated, and assumed a motion by which the Rescue passed from our stern to the port bow, and increased her distance from us 709 yards, where she came to a stand. Our stores that were on the ice were on the same side of the cracks as the Rescue, and of course were carried with her. The following day the ice remained quiet, but soon after midnight, on the 13th, a gale having sprung up from the westward, it once more got into violent motion. The young ice in the crack near our stern was soon broken up, the edges of the thick ice came in contact, and fearful pressures took place, forcing up a line of hummocks which approached within ten feet of our stern. The vessel trembled and complained a great deal.

"At last the floe broke up around us into many pieces, and became detached from the sides of the vessel. The scene of frightful commotion lasted until 4 A. M. Every moment I expected the vessel would be crushed or overwhelmed by the massive ice forced up far above our bulwarks. The Rescue being further removed on the other side of the crack from the line of crushing, and being firmly imbedded in heavy ice, I was in hopes would remain undisturbed. This was not the case; for, on sending to her as soon as it was light enough to see, the floe was found to be broken away entirely up to her bows, and there formed into such high hummocks that her bowsprit was broken off, together with her head, and all the light wood work about it. Had the action of the ice continued much longer, she must have been destroyed. We had the misfortune to find sad havoc had been made among the stores and provisions left on the ice; and few barrels were recovered; but a large portion were crushed and had disappeared.

"On the morning of the 14th there was again some motion in the floes. That on the port side moved off from the vessel two or three feet and there became stationary. This left the vessel entirely detached from the ice round the water line, and it was expected she would once more resume an upright position. In this, however, we were disappointed, for she remained with her stern elevated, and a considerable lift to starboard, being held in this uncomfortable position by the heavy masses which had been forced under her bottom She retained this position until she finally broke out in the spring. We were now fully launched into Baffin's Bay, and our line of drift began to be more southerly, assuming a direction nearly parallel with the western shore of the Bay at a distance of from 40 to 70 miles from it.

"After an absence of 87 days, the sun, on the 29th of January, rose his whole diameter above the southern horizon, and remained visible more than an hour. All hands gave vent to delight on seeing an old friend again, in three hearty cheers. The length of the days now went on increasing rapidly, but no warmth was yet experienced from the sun's rays; on the contrary the cold became more intense. Mercury became congealed in February, also in March, which did not occur at any other period during the winter. A very low temperature was invariably accompanied with clear and calm weather, so that our coldest days were perhaps the most pleasant. In the absence of wind, we could take exercise in the open air without any inconvenience from the cold. But with a strong wind blow ing, it was dangerous to be exposed to its chilling blasts for any length of time, even when the thermometer indicated a comparatively moderate degree of temperature.

"The ice around the vessels soon became cemented again and fixed, and no other rupture was experienced until it finally broke up in the spring, and allowed us to escape. Still we kept driving to the southward along with the whole mass. Open lanes of water were

visible at all times from aloft; sometimes they would be formed within a mile or two of us. Narwhals, seals, and dovekys were seen in them. Our sportsmen were not expert enough to procure any, except a few of the latter; although they were indefatigable in their exertions to do so. Bears would frequently be seen prowling about; only two were killed during the winter; others were wounded, but made their escape. A few of us thought their flesh very palatable and wholesome; but the majority utterly rejected it. The flesh of the seal, when it could be obtained, was received with more favor.

"As the season advanced, the cases of scurvy became more numerous, yet they were all kept under control by the unwearied attention and skillful treatment of the medical officers. My thanks are due to them, especially to Passed Assistant Surgeon Kane, the senior medical officer of the expedition. I often had occasion to consult him concerning the hygiene of the crew, and it is in a great measure owing to the advice which he gave and the expedients which he recommended, that the expedition was enabled to return without the loss of one man. By the latter end of February the ice had become sufficiently thick to enable us to build a trench around the stern of the Rescue, sufficiently deep to ascertain the extent of the injury she had received in the gale at Griffith's Island. It was not found to be material; the upper gudgeon alone had been wrenched from the stern post. It was adjusted, and the rudder repaired in readiness for shipping, when it should be required. A new bowsprit was also made for her out of the few spare spars we had left, and every thing made seaworthy in both vessels before the breaking up of the ice.

"In May, the noon-day began to take effect upon the snow which covered the ice; the surface of the floes became watery, and difficult to walk over. Still the dissolution was so slow in comparison with the mass to be dissolved, that it must have taken it a long period to become liberated from this cause alone. More was expected from our southerly drift, which still continued, and must soon carry us into a milder climate and open sea. On the 19th of May, the land about Cape Searle was made out, the first that we had seen since passing Cape Walter Bathurst, about the 20th of January. A few days later we were off Cape Walsingham, and on the 27th, passed out of the Arctic Zone.

"On the 1st of April, a hole was cut in some ice that had been forming since our first besetment in September; it was found to have attained the thickness of 7 feet 2 inches. In this month, (April,) the amelioration of the temperature became quite sensible. All hands were kept at work, cutting and sawing the ice around the vessels, in order to allow them to float once more. With the Rescue, they succeeded, after much labor, in attaining this object; but around the stern of the Advance, the ice was so thick that our 13 feet saw was too short to pass through it; her bows and sides, as far aft as the gangway, were liberated. After making some alteration in the Rescue for the better accommodation of her crew, and fires being lighted on board of her several days previous, to remove the ice and dampness, which had accumulated during the winter, both officers and crew were transferred to her on the 24th of April. The stores of this vessel, which had been taken out, were restored, the housing cloth taken off, and the vessel made in every respect ready for sea. There was little prospect, however, of our being able to reach the desired element very soon. The nearest water was a narrow lane more than two miles distant. To cut through the ice which intervened, would have been next to impossible. Beyond this lane, from the mast-head, nothing but intermediate floes could be seen. It was thought best to wait with patience, and allow nature to work for us.

"June 6th, a moderate breeze from S. E. with pleasant weather — thermometer up to 40 at noon, and altogether quite warm and melting day. During the morning a peculiar cracking sound was heard on the floe. I was inclined to impute it to the settling of the snow drifts as they were acted upon by the sun, but in the afternoon, about 5 o'clock, the puzzle was solved very lucidly, and to the exceeding satisfaction of all hands. A crack in the floe took place between us and the Rescue, and in a few minutes thereafter, the whole immense field in which we had been imbedded for so many months, was rent in all directions, leaving not a piece of 100 yards in diameter. The rupture was not accompanied with any noise. The Rescue was entirely liberated, the Advance only partially. The ice in which her after part was imbedded, still adhered to her from the main chains aft, keeping her stern elevated in its unsightly position. The pack, (as it may now be called,) became quite loose, and but for our pertinacious friend acting as an immense drag upon us, we might have made some headway in any desired direction. All our efforts were now turned to getting rid of it. With saws, axes, and crowbars, the people went to work with a right good will, and after hard labor for 48 hours succeeded. The vessel was again afloat, and she righted. The joy of all hands vented itself spontaneously in three hearty cheers. The after part of the false keel was gone, being carried away by the ice. The loss of it, however, I was glad to perceive, did not materially affect the sailing or working qualities of the vessel. The rudders were shipped, and we were once more ready to move, as efficient as on the day we left New York.

"Steering to the S. E. and working slowly through the loose but heavy pack, on the 9th we parted from the Rescue in a dense fog, she taking a different lead from the one the Advance was pursuing."

Ground for Hope.

Mr. Wm. Penny, of Aberdeen, states in a letter to the Times, that Capt. Martin, who, when commanding the whaler Enterprise, in 1845, was the last person to communicate with Sir. J. Franklin, has just informed him that the Enterprise was alongside the Erebus, in Melville Bay, and Sir John Franklin invited him, (Capt. Martin,) to dine with him, which the latter de clined doing, as the wind was fair to go south. Sir John, while conversing with Capt. Martin, told him that he had five years' provisions, which he could make last seven, and his people were busily engaged in salting down birds, of which they had several casks full already, and twelve men were out shooting more. "To see such determination and foresight," observes Mr. Penny, "at that early period, is really wonderful, and must give us the greatest hopes." Mr. Penny says that Capt. Martin is a man of fortune, and of the strictest integrity.

The following is the deposition of Capt. Martin, just received in the London Times, of Jan. 1, 1852, containing the facts above alluded to:

Robert Martin, now master and commander of the whaleship Intrepid, of Peterhead, solemnly and sincerely declares that on the 22d day of July, 1845, when in command of the whale ship Enterprise, of Peterhead, in lat. 75° 10′, long. 66° W., calm weather, and towing, the Erebus and Terror were in company. These ships were alongside the Enterprise for about fifteen minutes. The declarant conversed with Sir John Franklin, and Mr. Reid, his ice-master. The conversation lasted all the time the ships were close. That Sir John, in answer to a question by the declarant if he had a good supply of provisions, and how long he expected them to last, stated that he had provisions for five years, and if it were necessary he could "make them spin out seven years;" and he said further, that he would lose no opportunity of killing birds, and whatever else was useful that came in the way, to keep up their stock, and that he had plenty of powder and shot for the purpose. That Sir John also stated that he had already several casks of birds salted, and had then two shooting parties out — one from each ship. The birds were very numerous; many would fall at a single shot, and the declarant has himself killed forty at a shot with white pease. That the birds are very agreeable food, are in taste and size somewhat like young pigeons, and are called by the sailors "rotges."

That on the 26th or 28th of said month of July, two parties of Sir John's officers, who had been out shooting, dined with the declarant on board the Enterprise. There was a boat with six from each ship. Their conversation was to the same effect as Sir John's. They spoke of expecting to be absent four or five, or perhaps six years. These officers also said that the ships would winter where they could find a convenient place, and in spring push on as far as possible, and so on year after year, as the determination was to push on as far as practicable.

That on the following day, an invitation was brought to the declarant, verbally, to dine with Sir John, but the wind shifted, and the Enterprise having cut through the ice about a mile and a half, the declarant was obliged to decline the invitation. That he saw the Erebus and Terror for two days longer; they were still lying at an iceberg, and the Enterprise was moving slowly down the country. That so numerous were the birds mentioned, and so favorable was the weather for shooting them, that a very large number must have been secured during the time the declarant was in sight of the two ships. The Prince of Wales whaler was also within sight during the most of the time. That from the state of the wind and weather for a period of 10 days, during part of which the declarant was not in sight of the two ships, the best opportunity was afforded for securing the birds. That the birds described are not to be found at all places on the fishing ground during the whaling season, but are met with in vast numbers every season on certain feeding banks and places for brooding, and it appeared at the time by the declarant to be a most fortunate circumstance that the Erebus and Terror had fallen in with so many birds, and that the state of the weather was so favorable for securing large numbers of them. The declarant has himself had a supply of the same description of birds, which kept fresh and good during three months, at Davis' Strait, and the last were as good as the first of them.

Which declaration, above written, is now made conscientiously, believing the same to be true.

ROBERT MARTIN.

Declared, December, 29th, 1851, before

R. GRATH, Provost of Peterhead.

A Summer's Search for Sir John Franklin, with a Pass into the Polar Basin, by Commander E. A. Inglefield, in the Screw Steamer Isabel, in 1852.

The profound interest which the heroism and mysterious fate of Sir John Franklin, have excited in the public mind, occasioned other expeditions to start in pursuit of him, both from England and the United States, the details of whose adventures are in the highest degree entertaining. On the 12th of July, 1852, Commander Inglefield took his departure in the English steamer Isabel, from Fair Island; and sailed forth toward the frozen realms of the north, to which so many other bold adventurers had already been attracted. His crew consisted of seventeen persons, including two ice-masters, a mate, surgeon, engineer, stoker, two carpenters, cook, and eight able seamen, who had been whalers. The two ice-masters, Messrs. Abernethy and Manson, were already well known in "Arctic Cirles," as having been connected with former expeditions, and as having great experience in the perils incident to adventurous travel in that perilous zone. The vessel was provided with fuel and provisions for several years.

On the 30th of July the expedition gained their first distant glimpse of the snowy mountains of Greenland. On the same day the first icebergs sailed majestically past them. Ere midnight the Isabel was completely surrounded by those massive monuments of the northern seas. Already the utmost caution was necessary to prevent a fatal collision between them and the little steamer which slowly and adroitly elbowed her way through their rolling masses. In spite of the utmost prudence, the Isabel occasionally struck; instantly she trembled from stem to stern, recoiled for a moment, but then again recovered and advanced upon her way. The advantages of a screw-steamer for the purposes of navigating polar seas filled with floating ice, were already apparent at this early stage of the expedition. The propelling power being placed at the stern of the vessel, and not at the sides, enabled her to worm her way unresisted through very many narrow defiles, which a steamship of ordinary structure, or even a sailing vessel could not have done.

On the 7th of August the expedition reached the neighborhood of Fiskernoes, a Danish settlement; and they were there visited by some Esquimaux in their canoes. Guided by these pilots they entered the harbor on which their village is built. They visited the Danish governor, M. Lazzen, and were kindly entertained by him. A few goats supplied his family with milk, and a very small garden protected from the storms of that climate by artificicial means, afforded them a few vegetables during the summer months. M. Lazzen furnished the vessel with some salmon, codfish, and milk. The residence of the governor in this inhospitable region, consisted of a small house two stories high, built in an antique but substantial manner. A Danish clergyman visits this obscure and remote spot once every two weeks, and preaches to the governor and to the colony of rude Esquimaux over whom he rules.

On the 10th of August the Isabel resumed her journey. She then sailed for the harbor of Lievely, in which the expedition obtained a few supplies of sugar, soap, and plank, which they needed; but they failed to obtain here either dogs or interpreters. On the 15th, they found themselves off Upernavick, a settlement in which they obtained these necessaries. This Greenland village consists of two or three wooden houses for the Danish settlers, and a few mud huts for the Esquimaux. In sailing out from this harbor the steam-engine suddenly stopped, and neither the commander nor the engineer was able to discover the difficulty. They were completely puzzled, until at length it was ascertained that the screw at the stern had caught in a loose cable which floated in the water, which had become wound around the screw so tightly, and in such a manner, as to eventually impede its revolutions and stop the engine.

After the adjustment of this singular and unusual difficulty, the vessel continued her voyage. On the 17th of August she reached Buchan Islands, passing in her way innumerable icebergs of gigantic size, which reeled and tumbled in the deep, and occasionally split up into many fragments, with a roar more grand and deafening than that of thunder. On this day the vessel lost her main-boom; which in falling on the deck, struck the standard compass and damaged it. In a short time the injuries to both were repaired, and the Isabel held on her hyperborean way.

Having arrived at Wolstenholme Sound, the navigators examined the site of the former winter quarters of the "North Star," and had the melancholy pleasure of inspecting the lonely graves where the remains of several of her crew were laid to repose. Captain Inglefield and his officers and men went on shore with pickaxes and shovels. The place is called North Ornenak; and one Adam Beek, a seamen in one of the former Arctic expeditions, had asserted that here Sir John Franklin had been assailed by the savage and starving natives; that here he and his crew had been massacred; and that here in large *cairns* they had been buried. The story was an improbable one; but Captain Inglefield determined to examine the spot thoroughly, and test the truth of the report. Several large *cairns* were indeed here found, composed of heavy rough stones. They were immediately pulled down and their interiors inspected. But nothing was discovered save a large quantity of fish bones and the bones of other animals, which seem to have been deposited there for some future use. In the village itself, composed of a few underground hovels, occupied by half starved Esquimaux, were found a quantity of seal and walrus flesh, intended to supply the wants of nature during the nine long months of winter, which these wretched beings are compelled each year to endure.

Captain Inglefield determined to continue the thorough examination of the shores of Wolstenholme Sound. He did so, and discovered several islands which were not to be found on any chart. These islands he respectively termed the Three Sister Bees, Manson Isle, and Abernethy Isle. During this portion of the cruise, the voyageurs had not encountered as yet much of the severe extremes of northern cold. It was still mid-summer, and the trim steamer was able in the absence of compact ice, to sail rapidly through known and unknown seas, in opposition both to tide and wind. On the 25th, the Isabel reached the Cary Islands; and from this point began the voyage of Captain Inglefield into untraveled waters, and into regions which had not been explored, at least in a northward direction, by any of his predecessors. At this point, in the summer months, a few wretched Esquimaux manage to support existence; and Captain Inglefield carefully examined their huts to ascertain whether any memento of the expedition of Sir John Franklin might exist among them. No article of European manufacture was found, except a knife-blade stamped B. Wilson, set in an ivory handle, a broken tin canister, and several small pieces of steel, curiously fixed in a piece of bone. A piece of rope was also obtained, having an eye in it; but this was supposed to have drifted ashore from some whaling vessel. No trace of the lost navigators had as yet been seen since the commencement of this expedition.

Captain Inglefield resumed his voyage, and as he rapidly invaded those new seas, through the tireless power of steam, he discovered many new islands, at that period of the year free from their monstrous burdens of ice, to which he gave appropriate names. One he called Northumberland Island, another Herbert Island, and a third, Milne Island. At this point a strait, to which he applied the name of Murchison, opened out in an eastern direction, and invited them to enter on its exploration, with tempting prospects of discovery. But as Sir John Franklin's instructions had been to travel northward and westward from this point, if he ever reached it, it was evidently necessary to follow that designated route, if the intention to seek him was still retained. Accordingly Captain Inglefield was compelled to relinquish the exploration of this summer sea. On the 26th of August the Isabel reached Cape Alexander, and still boldly steering northward, the gallant craft passed the confines of the Polar Sea, and was about to make her adventurous dip into the Polar Basin. The soundings at this point were 145 fathoms. It was at this time the hope of Captain I. that from this point he might find his way to Behring's Strait, and might discover the missing navigator somewhere upon this remote line of travel.

Even in this distant northern latitude, the weather still remained fair and temperate. The splendors of that clime in mid-summer, transcend the power of language to depict. The sun, shooting his unobstructed rays far into the northern hemisphere, tinges the boundless fields of half-melted snow with crimson hues; and a brightness and brilliancy fill the heavens, which almost remind the observer of the boasted beauties and charms of an Italian sky. Those Polar solitudes now resounded with the unaccustomed echoes of the steamship, which glided rapidly over half frozen wastes, which sailing vessels could only have traversed at a very slow and tedious rate.

Captain Inglefield was now exploring what is known as Smith's Sound, the upper or northern continuation of Baffin's Bay. The western shore of this body of water, which forms a part of the Polar Ocean, was composed of a high range of frozen mountains. These were called after the Prince of Wales. The extreme northern point of these mountains received the name of Victoria Head, in honor of the British queen. Thus also on the eastern shore of this sea, the most northern point discovered by Captain I. he named after the Danish monarch, Frederick VII. After steaming several days longer in a north-western direction, an observation was made of the position of the vessel, when it was found that she had reached 78° 28′ 21″ north latitude. From this it appears that Captain Inglefield has the credit, according to his own computation, of reaching the distance of 140 miles further north than had been attained by any previous navigator. The vessel was now surrounded by immense floating icebergs. The frozen shores of the ocean receded far away to the east and to the west. A furious storm of wind and hail drove directly in the face of the bold navigators, as they continued their course toward the pole. No traces of Sir John Franklin had yet been discovered. To further persist in the course in which they were then sailing, was only calculated to hem them in with the oceans of ice which the rapidly approaching winter would congeal around them; and the moment had arrived, in the progress of the expedition, when it became necessary to determine what final course should be pursued. While the commander and his officers were deliberating on the most suitable decision to be selected, the vessel was suddenly surrounded with perils such as she had not encountered since the commencement of the voyage. A vast land-pack of ice had floated from the west, unperceived through the heavy fog; and immediately the Isabel became involved in its angry, turbulent, and dangerous embrace. The swell lifted the ship far into the pack; and the violence and fury of the troubled masses were indicated by the loud roar of the waters surging on the vast floe-pieces by which the vessel was surrounded. The frightful chaos of rolling masses, tossing the vessel to and fro like a feather in their midst, seemed to render escape from the impending peril of being either crushed or submerged, almost impossible. The only possibillity of rescue consisted in threading their way amid the rolling and tossing fragments, by the aid of the steam engine, after first getting the head of the vessel free from its contact with the ice. As the vessel carefully and slowly went forward amid the floating ice, immense masses dropped astern one after another into her wake. She escaped at length through every danger; though the edges of the fan of the screw were brightened from frequent abrasion against the ice.

Captain Inglefield now continued to sail eastward. He passed by and observed new islands which were then unknown and nameless, to which he applied appropriate epithets. On the 1st of September the sea had become so completely encumbered with the floating ice as to make the further progress of the vessel both difficult and dangerous, Captain Inglefield then determined to steer for the purpose of meeting the squadron of Sir Edward Belcher, which had also been sent out for the purpose of searching those seas for Sir John Franklin by the British government; and which would winter there in accordance with their instructions. Captain Inglefield was induced to pursue this course in order that he might carry his surplus provisions, stores, and coals to that squadron; and that he might convey to them the latest news and information from England. It was his intention then, unless some special service required his exertions, to return to England with intelligence from the squadron of Sir E. Belcher, and the prospects of success which still attended their labors of discovery. That squadron Captain Inglefield knew was then stationed at Beechey Island, and thither he immediately steered.

So severe had the weather already become, that the heavy seas which broke over the Isabel continually froze, and her bows became one mass of ice, binding the anchor fast to her side. After several days of rapid sailing, Beechey Island was reached; but the

North Star alone was found there. The rest of Sir E. Belcher's squadron had sailed, about three weeks before, up Wellington channel, and it was supposed that he had steered thence through the open waters beyond Parry Strait.

It was on this Island that Captain Inlegfield was shown the three graves of some of Sir John Franklin's crew, to which reference has already been made on page 376 of this volume. Plunging through the snow which was knee-deep, he reached, under the guidance of one of the officers of the North Star, those sad and lonely resting places of mortality. He found them unchanged from what they had been when visited by Lieutenant De Haven; and he was informed by his guide that a polar bear of monstrous size was frequently seen keeping his grim and cheerless vigils over the dead, and sitting on the graves. Captain Inglefield picked up some of the meat canisters which lay scattered on the island, and some relics of canvas and wood which were supposed to have belonged to the missing ships. He obtained from the commander of the North Star all the information necessary in reference to the condition and prospects of Sir John Belcher and Captain Kellett, both of whom held commands in that squadron. They had as yet discovered no trace of Sir John Franklin; but it was their purpose to pass the winter in the Polar Seas, for the purpose of renewing their researches in the ensuing spring.

As this voyage of the Isabel was only a summer cruise, and as the vessel was neither adapted nor intended to confront the overwhelming rigors of the winter season in the Arctic regions, it was but proper that, as the season was now rapidly advancing, Captain Inglefield should resume his voyage homeward, to escape the greater perils which delay would entail. Accordingly, on the 10th of September the Isabel commenced to sail in a southern direction. On the 12th she reached Mount Possession. On the 14th she was opposite Cape Bowen. Captain Inglefield landed here to examine the traces of a cairn, which was said to exist. But he saw nothing save the large and deep footprints of a great Polar bear, and those of the small Arctic fox.

Here the further progress of the Isabel along the coast was stopped by the presence of vast fields of ice. It became necessary to press along the edge of the pack, and seek for an opening to permit her to advance. This pack seemed to have been collected here by the immense icebergs which had run aground on the Hecla and Griper banks, and thence drifted south by the continual current which existed on those western shores. The pack stretched away, as far as the eye could reach, both southward and northward. A storm of snow came on, such as one sees only in Arctic latitudes. The sea also became exceedingly rough and boisterous; and wave after wave broke over the whole length of the vessel. Each plunge filled the rigging and hung the spars with monstrous icicles; and the waves froze as they flooded the deck, the ropes, and the sails; so that the hands of the sailors were frozen fast the instant they touched either of them.

On the 21st of September the weather moderated, and the Isabel boldly dashed through the crevices and channels of the pack. Pancake ice was rapidly forming around them, giving the mariners warning that they must soon vacate that locality, or else be frozen in, beyond the power of deliverance, for the winter. Rapidly the Isabel dashed forward, impelled by the unwearied power of her engine. By noon on the 23d, she had cleared the pack, had traveled a hundred and seventeen miles in twenty-four hours, and found herself in 69° north latitude. Here Captain Inglefield encountered a gale of the utmost fury, which continued during five days incessantly. The ocean waves now attained the size of mountains, and exceeded in violence and fury even those which lash the bold promontory of Cape Horn, where the waters of two great oceans roll together in hostile rivalry. Vast waves continually flooded the decks fore and aft. Torrents of water drenched almost every portion of the vessel, carrying the seamen with it into the lee scuppers. The drifting sleet and snow drove so fiercely into the eyes of the sailors, that it was almost impossible for them to see, or to execute orders. Nevertheless, the gallant ship sailed manfully through it all, and safely outrode the gale, though with the loss of her spare spars, and the total ribboning of her sails.

In order to repair this damage Captain Inglefield was compelled, after the storm lulled, to steer for the nearest port of Holsteinburg, in order to make repairs. This port he reached on the 2d of October. During the week which the captain spent here, the anniversary of the birth-day of the king of Denmark occurred; which gave an occasion for the observation of the peculiarities of the Esquimaux tribes, who here live as the remotest subjects of that monarch, under the superintendence of a governor sent from Copenhagen. An entertainment was given at the house of the governor. Esquimaux of both sexes attended, danced their native dances, drank their brandy-punch furnished both by the governor and by Captain Inglefield, and became elated and uproarious in the extreme. The governor's wife was an Esquimaux woman; and Captain Inglefield had the honor of executing with her the intricate mazes of an Esquimaux quadrille, to the monotonous scraping of a crippled fiddle, bound around and held together with divers strings and splinters.

On the 7th of October the Isabel again put to sea, and again she encountered a storm of unusual violence. The helmsman was very nearly washed overboard. On the 13th the gale moderated, and the vessel then continued her way across the Atlantic. No incident worthy of special notice occurred during the rest of the homeward voyage. On the 4th of November the Isabel anchored at Stromness, having been absent precisely four months from the day of starting. And although this expedition, taking place as it did in the summer months, was devoid of the usual extreme horrors and vicissitudes which attend Arctic researches, it accomplished results which were by no means of secondary importance. Captain Inglefield carefully examined the unknown eastern shore of the Polar Basin, as far north as 78° 35′, throwing considerable light upon the disputed question, whether Baffin's Bay opens into the Polar Basin. He also explored the waters of the shores of Smith Sound, in search of Sir John Franklin, but in vain. Jones Sound was then examined, with the same result, and he ascertained the probable fact that this sound is a gulf having no outlet, except perhaps by some small frozen strait into the Polar Sea. Lancaster Sound was also visited, and the western coast of Baffin's Bay as far south as the river Clyde. Throughout a coast of six hundred continuous miles, many alterations and additions were made in the geography of those countries. And altogether, for a private expedition of no very great expense, executed in a small vessel, though amply provisioned and stored, the results attained were as important as could reasonably have been expected.

Eighteen months in the Polar Regions in search of Sir John Franklin's Expedition, in the years 1850–51, by Lieutenant Sherard Osborn, with the Steam Vessels Pioneer and Intrepid.

In May, 1850, this expedition was fitted out at Woolwich, for the purpose of continuing the search after the missing mariners. The instructions of the British Admirality to the commander were, that he should examine Barrow's Straits south-westerly to Cape Walker, westerly toward Melville Island, and north-westerly up Wellington Channel.

On the 26th of May the expedition approached the shores of Greenland, and came within view of Cape Farewell. They proceeded rapidly on until they reached their first place of stoppage, the Whale Fish Isles. A day was spent here in taking in provisions and fowls. From this point the view of the shores of Greenland at a distance was picturesque in the extreme. Its glaciers, its lofty peaks, and its frozen headlands presented every variety of shape; while between them and the vessels, the sea was covered with an infinite variety of tossing icebergs of every possible size and proportion, exhibiting the richest emerald hues, and glowing with the deepest azure tints. The awful silence of the scene was impressive in the highest degree, a silence which would often be suddenly broken by a distant roar reverberating along the surface of the deep, and among the frozen masses. It was the breaking up of some vast icebergs, whose fragments would roll over into the sea, plunge beneath its surface, and cover the spot of its descent with foam and spray. This process was repeated at short intervals, in every direction of the compass around them, and as far as their eyes could reach.

The 29th of June still found Captain Osborn cruising opposite the northern extremity of Greenland. He here began to experience the dangers that accompanied the necessity which he sometimes felt of anchoring to icebergs. This operation is frequently indispensable in Arctic regions, when progress in the required direction is for a time impossible. The icebergs in consequence of their immense size are often aground, and thus seamen may anchor fast to them in two hundred fathoms of water, without any more trouble than digging a hole in the iceberg, and inserting a hook into it, called an ice-anchor. This is attached to a whale line, which enables the ship to ride out under the lee of this natural breakwater, and often thus to escape both the violence of the winds, and the rude shocks of a lee pack.

But the dangers which sometimes accompany this process are considerable. Sometimes the very first stroke of the man setting the ice-anchor, causes a portion of the iceberg to break off, and the persons employed in the work run great risk of being crushed by the falling masses. Sometimes pieces of ice become detached from the upper portions of the berg, and falling on the ships below, have injured spars, and crushed sailors to death. Occasionally these masses have been so immense as even to sink the vessel.

On the 6th of July Captain Osborn had his first experience of the real perils of the Arctic world. All hands were at dinner when the news suddenly came down from the deck, that a vast body of ice was approaching under the pressure of a strong southerly gale. A heavy brown vapor preceded it, under which the ice gleamed fiercely, and the floes were rapidly pressing together. The best security against danger in cases of this kind, is the preparation of docks in the body of the ice, which are cut in the portion which is firm and solid. Into these the ships are then inserted, and they are thus protected from the collisions of the loose fragments. In this case one hundred persons were instantly on the solid ice, their triangles were rigged, and their long ice-saws were at work. A hundred manly voices accompanied their labor with the jolly sailor songs of merry old England. The ice was about three feet in thickness, and the saws employed were ten feet in length. Very soon the vast cavity intended to receive the ships began to take form and shape, and they then were removed into them. The relief was much needed; for the pressure of the pack extended itself some ten miles to the north of the position of the vessels; the collisions between the floes and the iceberg became prodigious; and had the ships been between them, they would inevitably have suffered severely. But safely ensconced in their docks, the expert seamen could gaze with pleasure at the sublime spectacle presented for many miles on either side of them.

In spite of the vigilance of Capt Osborn, his ships became entangled on the 20th of July, in the midst of a heavy pack, six feet in thickness. So great was the pressure that every plank and timber was cracking and groaning. The vessels were thrown over on their sides, and lifted up bodily, the bulkheads cracking, the decks arching from the strain, and even the scupper-pieces turning out from their mortices. The ice was rapidly piling up as high as the bulwarks, around the vessels. There seemed to be no possible remedy against the destruction of the ships. The sailors quickly brought their bundles of clothes on deck, for the purpose of taking refuge on the ice. At this moment a deep dent in the side of the Pioneer, and the breaking of twenty-one of her timbers, indicated her great danger. But fortunately, at the very moment when it was thought that she must be crushed to pieces, the strain of the floe-edge suddenly eased, and the ship was saved from destruction.

From the 20th to the 31st of July the squadron continued to pursue their route; yet so impenetrable was the ice, that but *seven* miles was made during the whole of that interval, in the right direction! By the 13th of August the squadron had passed through Mellville Bay, and had reached Cape York. They were still a considerable distance from the chief point of research. Yet here they were detained for two days in chasing up the groundless fabrication of Adam Beek, alluded to in the previous article, in reference to the destruction of Sir John Franklin and his crews at this point, by the native Esquimaux.

On the 15th of August Captain Osborn struck westward, and entered a wide sea of water which seemed unobstructed by the ice. The shores of this portion of Baffin's Bay, which is termed the West Land, appeared to be free from snow, and to be even comparatively verdant and genial. At Button's Point the commander landed, and was able, at this season of the summer, to kill both deer and salmon. The natives of this region had here erected numerous unroofed winter houses, of the rudest structure; and the navigators discovered many cairns, standing generally in pairs. These were instantly pulled down, for the purpose of discovering their hidden contents. Nothing however was found of a suspicious or suggestive nature. These cairns seemed to be nothing but marks erected by the Esquimaux, to enable them to discover, on the return of winter, the places where they had stored their sea-blubber *caché*. A ring of stones several feet high were all the indications of these Esquimaux huts which appeared above the surface of the ground.

It was on the 22d of August that this expedition entered Lancaster Sound. This is the great gate-way to those Arctic waters, around which so many thrilling associations cluster of maritime adventure, suffering, and discovery. It was first explored by the bold Baffin, two hundred years ago, and was named by him after the duke of Lancaster. Baffin termed it a sound. Sir John Ross, forty years since, discovered that it was a bay; and Parry, who has not unfitly been termed the prince of Arctic navigators, until the vastly superior abilities and services of the immortal Kane justly deprived him of that honorable eminence, explored this bay throughout the extent of 600 miles toward Behring's Straits.

It was to complete the exploration of the remaining 600 miles of this unknown region, that the expedition of Sir John Franklin and his 140 gallant associates had been devoted. Hence in pursuing this line of travel and adventure, Lieutenant Osborn justly supposed that he was following the most probable and most certain course to ascertain the fate of that lost and unfortunate expedition. He had already discovered one important fact in reference to the phenomena of the Arctic regions; or if he had not absolutely discovered it, he ascertained its certainty. This was that the iceberg, the most wonderful peculiarity of those climes, is the creation of the glacier. It had formally been supposed, even by the most learned, that the iceberg was the accumulation of the ice and snow which the lapse of ages had produced; that a vast circle of ice many miles in height and depth, surrounded the pole like an eternal belt; that these huge cupolas of ice towered far up into the cheerless heavens of the north; transcending in size and altitude the utmost creations of human architecture; and that these stupendous icebergs were merely fragments which had become detached, probably by their own weight, from the parent mass, and had then floated away into more southern seas. This fanciful conception has now been exploded; and it is proved that the iceberg is only known to exist where there is land of a nature adapted to form the glacier. Accordingly, Captain Osborn reasoned that where icebergs burdened the ocean, glacier lands could not be far distant; and he directed the movements of his exploring squadron accordingly. It was by following this principle that Sir James Ross discovered the circumpolar continent of Queen Victoria's Land, in the Southern or Antarctic hemisphere.

On the 26th of August the ships entered Regent's Inlet. The nights were only two hours in duration. Next day a pack of ice was discovered some 10 miles to the eastward. They instantly sailed westward, giving the intruders very wide sea-room. They soon reached Beechey's Island, on which the three graves of Sir John Franklin's seamen were to be found, and other evidences which showed that he had sojourned there during 1845–46, the first winter of their absence. This circumstance confuted the opinions of those who held that Sir John Franklin had perished in the depths of Baffin's Bay on his outward voyage; and proved that he had advanced safely to a very remote point in Arctic travel and discovery. On Beechey's Island Captain Osborn saw another mournful trace of Sir John Franklin. It was the remnant of a garden, with a neatly shaped oval outline, the borders carefully covered with moss, lichen, and anemones, which he had transplanted from a more genial clime; and these even yet continued to show some traces of vitality. At some distance from this garden the foundations of a store-house were discovered. These consisted of an interior and exterior embankment, into which oak and elm scantling had been stuck, as supports to the roofing. Within the enclosure some empty coal-sacks were found, and some wood shavings. It is probable that this store-house had been constructed by Sir John Franklin to preserve a portion of the abundant provisions with which his decks had been encumbered when he left Whale Fish Islands. Captain Osborn also discovered a pair of Cashmere gloves which had been laid out to dry by one of the lost crews; on each of which a small stone had been placed to prevent them from being swept away by the wind. They had rested there, having been probably forgotten by their owner, ever since 1846!

Again on this occasion were the three lonely graves of Sir John Franklin's seamen scanned by a sailor's eye, and wept over by those gallant adventurers. These graves are simple and neat in their appearance, such as British sailors erect over the bodies of their departed messmates, in every quarter of the globe, whether in the frozen zones of the north, the coral-girded isles of the south, the verdant and spicy vales of the east, or the gold-gifted climes of the west. They are graves which remind the observer of some quiet church-yard in England or in our own land, where the departed sleep beneath the very eaves of the humble sanctuary, surrounded by the green turf, the waving grass, and the blooming rose, with which the hand of affection, or the undisturbed fruitfulness of nature has surrounded them. One grave of the three is especially suggestive of mournful thoughts. It is that of "J. Hartnell, B. A., of the ship Erebus; died January 4th, 1846. Aged 25 years." Here was a youth who had been reared amid the classic shades and the ennobling associations of one of England's great universities—either a Cantab or an Oxonian—and strange to say, he was destined to lay his form to take its long last sleep in the lonely and cheerless solitude of that frozen zone; and that, too, in the prime of his years, and far distant from all that was connected with the brilliant hopes of his youthful days!

When about to leave Beechey Island, Captain Osborn found it difficult to determine what course should be taken. It was evident that Sir John Franklin had selected one of three routes, in 1846. The first was south-west by Cape Walker; the second, north-west by Wellington Channel; the third, west by Melville Island. Vague reports were current among the crews, that some of Captain Penny's people had seen sledge-marks on the eastern shores of Erebus and Terror Bay. Captain Osborn determined in person, first to explore Beechey Island, in that direction. He landed on the north shore of Union Bay, at the base of the cliffs of Cape Spencer, and soon discovered a deep sledge-mark which had been cut through the edge of one of the ancient natural terraces on the beach. It was in a line between the cairn of meat cans which Franklin had erected on the northern spur of Beechey Island, to a valley between the Capes Ennes and Bowden. From its appearance, it had been evidently an outward-bound sledge, and its depth denoted that it was heavily laden. It was an additional evidence of the former presence of Franklin on that island. Upon further examination, various other sledge-marks were discovered on the island. At one spot they were very numerous, and proved that there a rendezvous had been appointed for the purpose of landing some of the contents of the ships. From this point some of the sledge-marks ran northward into a gorge through the hills; others were directed toward Caswell's Tower, a singular mass of limestone rock, on the shore of Radstock Bay, which served as a useful landmark to all vessels approaching either from the east or the west.

Captain Osborn here divided his party, and each followed the sledge-marks in an opposite direction. He discovered the site of a circular tent, which had evidently been constructed and used by a shooting party from the Erebus or Terror. The stones which had been used to confine the canvas to its place, lay around. Several large stones well blackened with smoke, indicated where the fire-place had been; and porter-bottles, meat-cans, pieces of paper, and feathers, were strewed about. Yet no written line or mark was detected, to throw any light on the great mystery which occupied their minds. After seven hours of hard walking, Captain Osborn and his men returned to the ships. Such were all the traces which the utmost industry and scrutiny could discover of Sir John Franklin, in this last known spot of his habitation. From the 1st to the 4th of September the ships lay waiting for an opening in the fixed ice, to enable them to resume their voyage. At length on the 5th, the appearance of the ice and the direction of the wind being favorable, Captain Osborn immediately gave orders to proceed across Wellington Channel toward Barlow Inlet.

Before this course had been pursued for any distance, the channel became blocked up with a vast field of floating ice. A northerly gale began to blow furiously over its surface; and the ships of the squadron were swept along with the ice, in whose embrace they were, out of the channel toward Leopold Island. The squadron drifted at the rate of a mile per hour, toward the south-east. Suddenly an opening in the pack occurred, and the steam-engine was instantly brought into requisition, to enable the seamen to extricate themselves. Soon they reached again the open water; and found themselves near the squadron of Captain Penny, and the American vessels, commanded by De Haven. These were then making sail under a full press of canvas for Cape Hotham.

When in this position on the 11th of September, 1850, the Arctic winter descended on the adventurers. The heavens became overclouded with blackness, and the atmosphere filled with hail, snow, and sleet. A heavy sea began to roll, and the loose fragments of the rapidly congealing ice again to close around them. A snug harbor was happily discovered for the winter, between Capes Hotham and Martyr, on the south side of Cornwallis Island. Here the Pioneer and Intrepid were taken and secured. Several parties were sent out to carry provisions and establish depots on the intended routes of the different expeditions which would explore this region in the spring of 1851. Lieutenant McClintock carried out a depot toward Melville Island, and Lieutenant Aldrich, taking another toward Lowther Island. Lieutenant Mecham was also sent to examine Cornwallis Island, between Assistance Harbor and Cape Martyr, for traces of the progress of Sir John Franklin.

Captain Osborn determined to embrace this opportunity to connect the search from the spot where Lieutenant Mecham left the coast, to the point at which Lieutenant McClintock again took it up, thus completing the survey of this whole region, through which it was very naturally inferred that Sir John Franklin had passed. He started on the 10th of October, provided with five day's provisions. The party consisted of six persons. The thermometer was six degrees above zero, and accordingly they did not suffer from the severity of the weather. After a march of three hours they came to Cape Martyr. Striking inward on Cornwallis Island, Captain Osborn came suddenly in view of a structure which at once excited the utmost interest, with the hope that it might be some unknown monument of the lost navigators. It was a round, conical-shaped building, twenty feet in circumference at the base. The apex had fallen in, but the height of what remained was five feet six inches. It was well built, and those who had reared it seemed to have well understood the strength of the arched roof, to resist the weight of the immense amount of snow which falls in those regions. Much skill was exhibited in the arrangement of the slates of limestone with which the building was constructed. The stones of the apex which had fallen within the walls were quickly removed, but they discovered nothing which could enlighten them as to the origin of the structure. Yet it was evident from the thick moss which adhered to the walls, that it was not of recent origin, and that in fact it must have been built many years before the date of Sir John Franklin's voyage. The position of this mysterious monument was lonely in the extreme. It seemed to be a solitary landmark in that polar world, of the former and transient abode of some unknown visitant; and it bore clear evidence that it was not the product of the labor of the rude Esquimaux, who sometimes in their summer wanderings reached even these remote latitudes. Nothing more of interest was discovered on Cornwallis Island; and Captain Osborn returned to his ships.

On the 17th of October the commander of the ships which composed this squadron, determined that as soon as they could commence operations in the ensuing spring, Captain Penny was to continue the exploration of Wellington Channel, while Captain Osborn was to continue his researches toward Melville Island, and from Cape Walker toward the south-west. With the settlement of this arrangement, all the labors of the squadron for the year 1850 closed, as the utmost rigors of a polar winter were now upon them. The upper decks were then covered in. The stoves and warming apparatus were set to work. The boats were secured on the ice. All the lumber was removed from the upper decks. The masts and yards were made as snug as possible; and rows of posts were placed between the ships, to designate the way amid the darkness and storms of winter. Holes were cut through the ice in order to obtain a ready supply of water in case of fire; and arrangements were made to ensure the cleanliness of the ships and the crews. On the 8th of November several officers ascended the heights of Griffith's Island, and at noon caught the last glimpse of the sun, which they were destined to see, for some months; though it was then 17 miles below the horizon, and the rays which they beheld were those only of refraction. The precise position of the vessels was 74½° of north latitude.

Though the sun had ceased to visit those Arctic heavens, it must not be supposed that the bold navigators were in darkness. The southern horizon was illumed each day during several hours at noon, by a deep and rosy red light, mixed with pink and blue. Toward the north the prevalent appearance of the heavens was a cold, bluish-black. During the rest of the twenty-four hours, a gray twilight prevailed around them, except when the moon was full. At that period a subdued splendor was cast over the frozen face of nature, which finds no parallel in the natural phenomena of other and more favored climes. The loveliness of an Arctic moonlight none can know, save those who themselves have seen it.

Thus shut out from all the world, the adventurers endeavored to wear away the monotonous months of winter. The festivals of Christmas and New Year were observed with unusual glee and festivity, with such means as were within their reach. Sometimes the weather was too severe to permit any communication between the vessels. During a portion of the time, the snow was drifted to such immense heights around the ships, that it excluded all view of the surrounding wastes. The vessels only three hundred yards distant from each other, were often invisible. Frequently as the furious storms of the north swept over the surrounding ice for many miles, the floor vibrated and trembled with the violence of the shock, and communicated this singular motion to the vessels. The aurora borealis alone disappointed those who were connected with this expedition. It was deficient in brilliancy of color. It was also inferior in extent to what they anticipated. The series of concentric semi-circles of light were subdued by dark spaces between them, which diminished its luster and general splendor. The snow fell almost incessantly. When heavy gales blew the vessels were nearly smothered; and vast drifts 15 feet thick above the decks, had to be removed by the continual labors of the seamen.

Amid such scenes as these, the long winter slowly passed away. Early in March the crews began to stir. On the 11th of that month the thermometer was 41° below zero; and yet this temperature was not considered as too severe for active operations. On the 4th of April, 1851, preparations were made to travel on sledges, for the purpose of pursuing the inland searches. Captain Ommaney was directed to cross Barrow's Strait and Cape Walker. Lieutenant Aldrich was sent with two sledges and 14 men toward the unknown channel of Byam-Martin Island. Lieutenant McCormick was dispatched to Melville Island, to prosecute his researches as far as Winter Harbor, with two sledges and 13 men. Other officers were sent in other directions; making in all fifteen sledges, manned by 105 men, who were thus distributed in various directions, in order to obtain information and indications of the career and fate of the squadron of Sir John Franklin.

It was the 12th of April when these expeditions started forth from the ships. Our space forbids us to follow all their adventures, which were exciting and perilous in the extreme, over vast tracts of snow and ice, of the most monstrous and irregular shapes. The whole coast of Cape Walker's Land was surveyed. Many of the seamen became snow-blind, and many had frozen feet. They beheld vast tracts of snow-covered land hugged by the icy seas, over which a silence and solitude sullenly brooded, not unlike that of a primitive chaos. Most of the sledge parties accomplished journeys of 500 miles, in various directions, during the fifty days the expedition lasted. After the lapse of this period, or nearly so, all the parties returned to the ships. Some had searched the whole western coast of Bathurst Island. Some had been to Winter Harbor, Bushman Cove, and Cape Dundas. Others had explored the whole eastern coast of Mellville Island. In eighty days the company under Lieutenant McClintock had traveled 800 miles, dragging their sledges containing their provisions after them. He and his men had performed the greatest labor of any of their associates. Yet nowhere, amid all these various researches, in every possible and available direction, had the least trace been detected of Sir John Franklin, no tradition of his presence, no monument or evidence of his fate!

On the 14th of August, 1851, the vessels steered for Jones' Sound, which they entered on the evening of the 15th. This sound was discovered to be the narrowest about the entrance. The scenery of the shores is magnificent. Ten miles inland a huge dome of pure white snow ascended to the height of 4,000 feet, presenting one of the most singular spectacles which could well be imagined. Reaching Cape Hardwicke, which was discovered to be in fact a group of islands, they struck eastward toward Cape Clarence, which seemed to be the utmost limit of the land in that direction. Proceeding onward in their southern route, the squadron soon came in sight of Cary Isles, and then of the flat-topped region between Cape York and Dudley Digges. The steamers then rapidly advanced on their homeward way. On the 28th of August they reached Wolstenholme Island. Here they were stopped by the floating ice; and anchoring fast to an iceberg, they awaited the first opening which might occur. Here began traces again of the nomade Esquimaux; and thus they seemed to have returned to communion with the rest of mankind. By the 1st of September the vessels still remained closely packed in the ice; and nothing appeared to the view from the mast-head, except the boundless horizon of the frozen ocean. It was nevertheless necessary for Captain Osborn to make a bold push of some description, to be released from his confinement, for starvation itself might soon surprise his associates in their imprisonment. In a day or two a fortunate slackening of the ice encouraged them to attempt on entering. So difficult and slow was their progress, that they did not advance more than the ship's length during the period, and after the labors, of an hour. By dint of constant screwing and heaving, however, some advance was made. Gradually the sea became more open; and then the powers of the steam-engine were brought into play. A moment's further delay might have secured their detention for the whole winter, in those inhospitable and frozen climes. After a day of excessive exertions, the ships had wormed their way through the floating ice to the open sea which lay to the south of it, and thus again were free.

On the 5th of September the squadron commenced its unobstructed voyage of return to England. In eight days they reached the latitude of Cape Farewell, and at length safely anchored at Grimby, in the River Humber, precisely three weeks after the commencement of their homeward-bound voyage. The expedition had indeed failed either to rescue Sir John

Franklin, or even to solve the great mystery of his fate; nevertheless it had made "assurance doubly sure" that he had not been lost in the regions which they had visited, but that he must have proceeded on his adventurous way to a very remote and unequaled extreme of northern latitude. It ascertained that, if he had perished at all, he had perished in the execution of one of the boldest and most desperate resolutions ever entertained by man, to explore if possible, the utmost limits of the accessible earth; and to arrive as near to the North Pole as it was possible for human heroism, endurance, and determination to approach.

But other interesting and valuable researches were made by this expedition, which deserve notice. These established the fact that the Esquimaux tribes which now inhabit portions of the Arctic Zone, were once very numerous along the whole northern shore of Barrow's Straits and Lancaster Sound, and that formerly the Esquimaux were among the most widely diffused races on the earth, so far as superficial extent is concerned. From Melville Island on the west, to the isolated inhabitants of Northern Greenland, called Arctic Highlands, many strange and ancient remains were discovered in various sheltered nooks and corners on the shore, such as rude houses, *cachés*, hunting posts, and graves, which clearly proved that inhabitants once dwelt in this sad and solitary clime, who have now either become exterminated, or have emigrated to some more genial region.

The origin of this people seems to have been in the north-eastern extremity of Asia; for on the banks of the Lena and the Indigirka, and along the whole extent of the frozen *Tundra*, which faces the Polar Seas, as well as in New Siberia, the same species of circular stone huts, the same whalebone rafters, the same rude axes made of stones, and the same primitive implements of the chase, are still found to exist, and are used alike by the Esquimaux of Hudson Straits and

Greenland, the Innuit of North America, and the Tchuktches of Behring's Straits. It is probable, therefore, that these people first reached the American continent from the east of Asia. The Tchuktches are the only tribe of Siberia who have maintained their independence; and have defied, assisted by the horrid rigors of nature, the overwhelming power of Russia. The other tribes of Siberia narrate how one of the races called by them the Omoki, whose homes were as numerous on the banks of the Lena as the stars of an Arctic night, did formally remove to unknown regions; supposed by them to be in a north-eastern direction. They also tell of another tribe, termed the Onkillon, who, having been attacked by the Tchuktches, took shelter in a distant land to the northward from Cape Jakan. This land has now been found actually to exist in that direction.

These people eventually reached the shores of Davis' Straits and the Atlantic Ocean; and some of them even advanced as far as Lancaster Sound, along the Parry Group. Compelled by the necessities of food, and attracted by the products of fishing and hunting, they eventually reached Behring's Straits; and thus this unfortunate race extended over a vast proportion of those inhospitable but habitable realms which lie nearest to the Pole. Among the proofs of this fact furnished by the researches of Captain Osborn's expedition, may be mentioned the following: Ruins of the description already mentioned, were found between Bathurst and Cornwallis Land, on the whole southern shore of Cornwallis Island, on Capes Spencer and Riley, on Radstock Bay, Ommaney Harbor, Cape Warrender, and on the shores of Jones' Sound. Formerly, also, many Esquimaux lived even at the head of Baffin's Bay. On the coast northward of Cape York, many deserted villages and dead bodies have been found; clearly indicating the existence of a people who have now either become extinct, or have congregated in a less rigorous locality. All these tribes and races, whatever they may have been, undoubtedly belonged to the general Esquimaux family, who first originated in the north-eastern extremity of Asia.

Arctic Searching Expedition; a Journal of a Boat-voyage through Rupert's Land and the Arctic Sea, in Search of Sir John Franklin, by Sir John Richardson, in 1851.

The commander of this expedition was directed by the British admiralty to leave England in a mail-steamer for Halifax and New York; and from the latter place to proceed to Montreal, in order to confer with Sir George Simpson, governor of the Hudson Bay company's settlements. He was ordered thence to travel by Lake Huron to Saut Ste. Marie and Lake Superior, and there embark with a small crew, and sail along the chain of lakes until he overtook Mr. Bell, whom it was supposed he would find at Isle a la Crosse.

With four boats well adapted to this service, Sir John Richardson was ordered to proceed and examine the extensive North American coast between the Mackenzie and Coppermine Rivers. Passing the winter at Fort Good Hope, or Confidence, near Great Bear Lake, he was directed in the following spring to resume his journey, and explore the passages between Wollaston, Banks', and Victoria Lands, so as to cross the routes of Sir J. C. Ross' detached parties; and thence to return again to Great Bear Lake. It was hoped that this comparatively novel and untried direction of search, might probably reveal some satisfactory indications or memorials of the fate and situation of Sir John Franklin.

The length of this interior navigation to the Arctic Sea from Montreal, is about 4,400 miles. Sixteen hundred of these are performed on the Mackenzie

River and its tributaries. The boats employed in this expedition measured 30 feet in length, six in breadth, three in depth; and were provided with masts, sails, oars, anchors, and tools; and each weighed half a ton. A crew of five men was deemed sufficient for each. Among the seamen selected to man the boats, were sappers, miners, carpenters, blacksmiths, armorers, and engineers. These four boats properly provisioned, were embarked, together with the men of the expedition, on board the "Prince of Wales" and "Westminster," bound to York Factory, one of the posts of the Hudson Bay company; and there both ships eventually arrived, after a stormy passage, with the boats and their respective crews. In May, 1851, Sir John Richardson and his chief associate, Mr. Rae, left the house of Mr. Ballenden, at Saut Ste. Marie, near Lake Superior, and entered on the active duties of their expedition.

We will omit some details of their travels, as long as these continue through those intermediate regions which are not directly connected with the Arctic Zone; and which throw but little light upon the peculiarities of that remote portion of the earth. The expedition pursued its designated route, until at length they entered the estuary of the Mackenzie River. At four o'clock in the morning they embarked, and crossing a shallow bar at the end of a sand-bank, they steered between Richards' Island and the main land. They soon perceived about 200 Esquimaux coming toward them in their canoes, and three umiaks filled with women and children. It was necessary to beat off these intruders, who by hanging on to the sides of the boats impeded their progress; nor were the voyagers certain that no hostile attack was intended by these half-starved and importunate semi-savages.

As soon as these two parties in the several boats came in contact, a buisy scene of barter began to be enacted. The Esquimaux had arrows, bows, knives of copper, or of bone, and articles of that description to sell; and for these they received in return knives, files, hatchets, awls, and needles. The articles obtained by the explorers were indeed of little service to them; but they wished to conciliate the Esquimaux; and inasmuch as the latter considered a gift without an equivalent accepted in return as an insult, it was necessary to barter with them in order to furnish them the articles which they desired. The English boats were much incommoded by the crowds of Esquimaux who were disposed to hold on to their sides, and it became necessary to use violence sometimes to compel them to release their grasp. At length the boat commanded by Lieutenant Clark was attacked by the Esquimaux around it. An attempt was made to plunder it. A struggle ensued between the crew of six men and the assailants, and a musket was fired by Lieutenant Clark, as a signal to his associates for assistance. The other boats then immediately wore around, and came to the protection of the assailed. Muskets were presented, and an attack threatened by the English sailors; the effect of which demonstration was, to induce the Esquimaux at once to desist from all further aggressive operations, and resume friendly relations.

Thus, as the boats pursued their way, they were accompanied by the Esquimaux canoes. At length as they began to lose sight of the land entirely, the Esquimaux gradually fell behind them, and returned to their encampment on the shore of the estuary. During this intercourse between the voyagers and the natives, the inquiries of the former were directed to obtaining information in reference to the discovery ships. But the natives uniformly persisted in declaring, that they knew nothing about any white people, or any ships on their coast. They all denied having been present in any interviews which took place between their countrymen and the navigators of those seas in previous years. One person alone, in answer to the inquiries of Captain Richardson, declared that a party of white men were living on a neighboring island, called Richards' Island. But as the expedition had visited and examined that locality but a day two previously, his assertion was known to be false. Captain Richardson requested his interpreter to inform the Esquimaux that he had recently been there, and knew that he was lying; which declaration only called forth a hearty laugh from the Esquimaux, whose only desire was, by a fabricated story, to induce the expedition to sojourn longer in the neighborhood, and waste its time in fruitless researches.

These Esquimaux are a singular race, and one of their distinctive peculiarities is, that they are strictly a littoral people. They live only on the shore, and they inhabit an area of nearly 5,000 miles of seaboard. Their habitations extend from the Straits of Belle-isle to the Peninsula of Alaska. Throughout this vast extent of region there is no material variation in their dialect, except what may be justly termed provincialisms. An interpreter born on the east main or western shore of James' Bay, experienced no difficulty in understanding the language of the Esquimaux of the estuary of the Mackenzie; although the distance between the two localities was at least 2,500 miles. Traces of the encampments of this same race have been discovered as far north on the American continent as the foot of the boldest adventurer has trodden. Their capacity to endure the privations of these frozen and rugged regions, results evidently from their disposition to subsist on blubber, and their long practiced ability to inhabit houses and huts constructed of ice and snow. They employ drift-timber whenever it is accessible; but they can do without it, and can find a good substitute in the fabrication of their weapons, sledges, and boat-frames, in the teeth and bones of whales, morses, and other sea-monsters. They associate together in large numbers, to engage in the pursuit of the whale; and this fact indicates the possession of no small degree of natural hardihood and intelligence. Those of the Esquimaux who have been received into the service of the Hudson Bay company, at the distant fur-posts, have very soon acquired the habits of their white associates, and proved eventually to be more industrious, intelligent, and trustworthy than domesticated Indians. Among themselves a great deal of honesty prevails; and the private hunting-grounds of the different families are secure from all depredations from other members of the nation. But their dexterity and pertinacity in thieving the property of strangers are very remarkable. They are brave in their conflicts, and are devoid of the pusillanimity of the Indians of the southern zones. All their peculiarities, both personal and national, serve to establish the position advanced in the preceding article of this work, that the various Esquimaux tribes possess one and the same origin, and that they emanated originally from the north-eastern extremity of the continent of Asia.

As soon as the Esquimaux canoes had disappeared from view, the boats were steered toward the opposite shore, at a spot where there were several winter habitations of the natives. This place is situated about eight miles to the eastward of Point Warren. The buildings are placed on a spot where the water is sufficiently deep for a boat to come close to the beach; so that the natives may be able to tow a whale or seal to the place where they intend to cut it up. The houses themselves were constructed of drift-timber, strongly built together, and covered with a layer of earth from one to two feet in thickness. Light and air are admitted through a small low door at one extremity; and even this aperture in winter is closed by a slab of ice. In that case their greasy lamps supply them to some extent with heat, as well as with light. These huts are large enough to permit ten or twelve people to seat themselves around the fire, built in the center on the ground. In winter the imperfect admission of fresh air, and the effluvia arising from their greasy and filthy bodies, render their abodes not only disagreeable in the extreme, but also exceedingly unwholesome. Yet these peculiarities characterize the whole Esquimaux tribes throughout the whole extent and variety of their diffusion.

Having resumed their route on the 4th of August, Captain Richardson pulled for three hours across Copland Hutchinson Inlet, and landed at length on its eastern shore. This inlet is about 10 miles in width, and its mouth is obstructed by sand banks. Having computed their position, they found it to be 69° 44′ north latitude; and the variation of the needle was 58° east. This whole coast is low, though in the inland, some sandy cliffs were discovered. The soil was soft, boggy, and treacherous, and the whole country was covered over with ponds and small lakes.

On the 8th of August the expedition reached Cape Brown. Here they came in contact again with the Esquimaux. After the usual exchange of articles had been completed, inquiries were made in reference to the missing ships. The Esquimaux declared that no large ships had ever visited that coast; and that these were the only white men whom they had ever seen. It seems that Captain Richardson had visited this coast twenty-three years before on a commercial expedition; and had then met some of these same people. But they denied having the least knowledge or recollection of him or of his associates.

Captain Richardson crossed Russel Inlet, and passed Cape Brown. They then reached Cape Dalhousie and pitched their tent upon the beach. This island and the cape are flat; but toward the sea there are steep cliffs 40 and 50 feet in height. There are also deep ravines in the interior, produced by the melting of the snows in the beginning of summer. From this point the boats steered across Liverpool Bay, and approached Nicholson Island. They then landed and encamped off Cape Maitland. The surface of this cape is level, but its shores are girt with rugged cliffs 80 feet in height. A frozen surface is constantly exposed to view, and permanent ground-ice is everywhere to be found, twenty inches beneath the surface of the soil. Vegetation is very meager and scanty.

From this point the expedition proceeded to Harrowby Bay, and Baillie's Islands. They landed at the latter place at evening, and pitched their tent to pass the night in repose. They soon discovered a large fleet of Esquimaux canoes approaching in the form of a crescent, in the dim twilight. The object of the natives was to trade; but as Captain Richardson wished his men to have an opportunity to repose during the night, he ordered a ball to be fired across the path of the canoes. This immediately stopped their further progress; and an interpreter then informed the Esquimaux that there would be no bartering that night, but that if they would return in the morning their wishes should be gratified. After a short consultation the Esquimaux seemed to be satisfied with this arrangement and retired. At two o'clock the next morning the expedition resumed their journey, and soon met the approaching Esquimaux. From them they ascertained that their summer season here continues only during two months, of which this (August) was one; that during this period they have no ice whatever; and that they carried on their black-whale fishing. The extent of their operations usually consists in the capture of two whales during the whole summer—sometimes, though rarely, they obtain three. Sometimes they are altogether unsuccessful and secure none. In that case the succeeding winter generally proves to be one of great want and hardship. Their ignorance of the rest of the world may be inferred from the following incident: One of them asserted to Captain Richardson that Cape Bathurst was an island. When the latter denied this assertion, the Esquimaux responded with great sincerity, "Are not all lands islands?" At this point Captain Richardson buried some pemmican and erected a signal-post. A hole was dug on the top of the cliff, in which a case of pemmican was deposited, with a memorandum explaining the purposes of the expedition. The utmost care was used in replacing the turf so as to avoid detection; some drift timber was then placed on the spot and burned; and a pole painted red and white was planted at a distance of 10 feet. To induce the Esquimaux not to disturb the post, some articles of value were suspended upon it. Soon several Esquimaux were seen running toward the pole; they quickly stripped it of its hangings; but did not disturb the signal itself.

From this point the expedition proceeded to the south-east of Cape Bathurst, along the shore, which sometimes rose to the height of 250 feet. At Point Trail, in north latitude 70° 19′, the bituminous shale had been ignited and burned; and the bank had crumbled down from the destruction of the beds, presenting a most singular appearance.

August the 11th the expedition continued their route along the coast, and at length reached Point Stivens, and on the 13th landed on the shores of Sellwood Bay. Their next sojourn was on one of the western points which terminate Cape Parry. This portion of the cape presents a singular aspect when approaching it from the sea. It is an eminence 500 feet in height, which far surmounts all the surrounding region. In the neighborhood of this spot, at Cocked-Hat Point, a letter was deposited with a case of pemmican; over which were placed fragments of limestones, covered with red paint. It was here that the members of this expedition first saw the drift-ice. They sailed on past Clapperton Island, Point Pearce, and Point Keats. The first indications of the approach of winter now began to force themselves upon their notice; for the sea became covered with thin ice, which sometimes very essentially impeded their progress. At Cape Parry they still saw traces of the Esquimaux; they had the first severe frost during the night; and the ice already exceeded an inch in thickness.

On the 12th of September the expedition nearly reached Cape Kendall. It had progressed thus far along the north-western coast of the North American continent, without meeting any traces of Sir John Franklin. At this point the sea became so obstructed with ice that it was impossible to pursue the journey along the sea-shore, although they were still at some considerable distance from the Coppermine River, the appointed boundary of their travels. Captain Richardson, determined to continue the journey by land. The company provided themselves with thirteen day's provisions of pemmican, with cooking utensils, bedding, snow-shoes, astronomical instruments, fowling-pieces, ammunition, and portable boat, nets, and lines. Each man was compelled to carry a load of sixty-five pounds. The boats of the expedition were left behind on the shore, and the tent with a few cooking articles and hatchets, were abandoned to the Esquimaux.

On the 3d of September at six o'clock in the morning, the journey commenced. They pursued a direct course toward the bottom of Back's Inlet. The snow was deep, and advance was laborious and difficult. So heavy was the way that most of the men were willing to leave behind them their carbines. At night they halted under a basalt cliff 200 feet in height. The sea was here full of ice. They still occasionally met Esquimaux, whose services they employed in ferrying them over the numerous inlets which interrupted their way along the coast. Among the Esquimaux whom Captain Richardson met, were two who are mentioned by Mr. Simpson. One of these was recognized by a large wen which marked his forehead; and the other by his being crippled, and using crutches.

They had been very kindly treated by Messrs. Dease and Simpson; and they were therefore disposed to be friendly, together with their whole tribe, toward the white people. The travelers bought skin-boots from them, which proved of very great service. Captain Richardson permitted none of his men to enter their huts, or to offer any indignity to these harmless and forlorn beings. He himself visited one of their cabins, both for the purpose of obtaining a glimpse of their household appearance, and to present some needles and other articles to their women. He found in one hut six or seven females sewing, seated in a circle. They were nearly naked, and very dirty. On his entrance they seemed both ashamed and afraid. Captain Richardson shrewdly conjectured that, as these people had heard of the approach of the strangers, they had purposely rendered themselves as repulsive as possible, by rubbing mud and ashes on their faces and persons. They received his presents in a friendly manner; but seemed quite relieved when the hardy old mariner took his leave. This is a singular circumstance, as illustrating how, in every clime and country under heaven, men's passions, their fears, and their artifices are uniformly and invariably the same!

At length the travelers arrived on the shores of Richardson's River. This river was discovered in 1822, by some hunters of Sir John Franklin's party, and its outlet was then erroneously supposed to be only five miles west of the Coppermine. In 1839 Mr. Simpson explored this river, and ascertained that it falls into Back's Inlet in north latitude 67° 53′ 57″. Having crossed this river in a small boat of Lieutenant Halkett, which could carry but two persons at once, they resumed their march. In a short time they gained the summit of the ridge which divided the valley of the Richardson from that of the Coppermine River. This ridge was now covered with snow. From its summit they saw in the distance the Coppermine; and at three o'clock in the afternoon they reached its banks, several miles above Bloody Fall.

On the 10th of September the company struck the Kendal River, at some distance from its junction with the Coppermine. They walked nearly three miles along its banks, seeking for a crossing place. No such spot being found, they were compelled to construct a raft, and thus transport themselves over. This raft could bear but three persons at a time; nevertheless all of them passed over in safety. From this point they traveled directly across the country toward Dease River. Some snow fell both during the day, and also during the succeeding night. On the 12th they reached a tributary stream of the Kendal River, and forded it; the ice-cold water rising up to their waists. On the 14th the march took a south-western direction. They found the soil cracked, hummocky, and swampy; and it became exceedingly wearisome and difficult for pedestrians. On the 15th they crossed a branch of the River Dease by fording it; and at four o'clock in the afternoon the whole party reached Fort Confidence, the present appointed termination of their journey, and their quarters for the ensuing winter.

It is proper that we should here interrupt the narrative of Captain Richardson's expedition in search of Sir John Franklin, by detailing some of the information which he obtained in reference to the Esquimaux race—one of the most interesting and important items of Arctic observation and scrutiny. We have already given a few details on this subject on a previous page; and the additional light thrown upon it by the researches of Captain Richardson, are both valuable and entertaining. The views presented by Captain R. of this widely diffused people, are, as will be seen, those which describe them as they exist on the northern coast of the American continent—being quite a different locality from that depicted by Captain Osborn.

The term Esquimaux is probably derived from the words, *Ceux qui miaux;* or it may have originated from the shouts of *Teymô* which the natives uttered, when they surrounded the first exploring ships in their canoes. The sailors of the Hudson Bay company's vessels still call them *Seymôs.* The word Esquimaux does not belong to the language of the nation. These invariably call themselves *Inu-it, the people,* from *I-nuk, a man.*

One peculiarity of this race is that they alone, of all the aboriginal races, are known to inhabit portions of both the old and the new continents. Their language and their customs, in consequence of the peculiarity of their position, have also remained strangely unaltered by any contact or collision with the rest of the world. They confine themselves to the shores; and neither wander inland, nor cross extensive seas. They extend along the whole northern boundary of America, from Behring's Straits to the Straits of Bellisle, and along both shores of Greenland and Labrador. Their appearance is singular. Their faces are egg-shaped, with considerable prominence in the cheek bones. Their foreheads are narrow and taper upwards. Their chins are conical but not acute. Generally their noses are broad and depressed. Their profiles, in consequence of the receding both of the forehead and the chin, present a more curved outline than is found in any other variety of the Caucasian race. Their complexions are not red, but of an intermediate hue between red and white. They have little or no beards; but the hair of the head is long, straight, thick, and coarse. The men are of medium size, broad-shouldered, and muscular. In both sexes the hands and feet are small and well formed. The teeth, especially of the young girls, are generally of superior regularity and beauty.

The chief subsistence of this extensive race depends upon hunting and fishing. In the spring the opening rivers give them the opportunity to spear and capture the fish which at that period ascend the streams to spawn. Then also they hunt the reindeer, which bring forth their young on the coasts and islands before the snow is entirely melted on the ground. They also take a large quantity of swans, geese, and ducks. The months of July and August are employed in the capture of whales; and when they are successful in this, their own sustenance for the ensuing year is secured. During the two summer months they live in tents made of skins, and then they provide their stores of food for winter use. At mid-winter they are usually in total darkness. At that period they live in houses framed of drift timber, which are thickly covered with earth. They have no windows in their dwellings, and they enter by a low trap door inserted either on the side, or in the roofs. The floor is covered with rude timber, and they have no fireplace. A large flat stone is placed in the center which supports a lamp, by the flame of which they often cook. The Esquimaux hunter can trap the seal, notwithstanding the great acuteness and vigilance of that animal; and his plunder also serves to assist in sustaining Esquimaux life in the spring months.

The summer architecture of this race is peculiar. By that period of the year, the snow has acquired a sufficient degree of coherence to form a light building material; and of this material the Esquimaux erect comfortable huts which are dome-shaped, and are often used in preference to their tents. They first trace a circle on the smooth surface of the snow. The sides are built of slabs of ice instead of brick or granite. The summit is composed of similar slabs; and the floor is laid with the same material. Each slab in the building is carefully fitted to its place, where it becomes congealed and frozen into the solid mass. All the crevices are plugged up, and the seams carefully closed, by throwing loose snow over the fabric. The walls are only three or four inches in thickness, and therefore nearly translucent; so that they admit an agreeable light to the interior from without. All the furniture, consisting of seats, tables, and sleeping places, are formed of snow, and are covered with rein-deer or seal skins, which render them quite comfortable. Often these houses are built contiguous to each other, with low galleries running between them. These houses are durable, and the sun rarely acquires sufficient strength in that clime either to thaw or to destroy them.

The Esquimaux who live on the estuary of the Mackenzie river, carry on a traffic with the western Esquimaux from the region of Point Barrow and Behring's Straits, whom they meet half-way between their respective homes on the coast. The central Esquimaux have but little traffic with the Europeans, and articles of Russian manufacture are never or rarely seen further east than Point Atkinson. Those who live between Behring's Straits and the Mackenzie pierce the lower lip near the angle of the mouth, and fill the aperture with labrets resembling buttons, sometimes made of blue quartz, and sometimes of ivory. Many of them transfix the septum of the nose with an ivory needle. The women are generally tattooed on the chin; and turn up and plait their hair carefully, and are not devoid of pride in their personal appearance. From this circumstance northern navigators justly infer that more deference is paid to them by the men, than usually prevails among semi-barbarous tribes. It is said by Captain Richardson, that the unmarried women among the Esquimaux are modest and decorous in their deportment; but that the married ones allow themselves very considerable liberties, and that, too, with the connivance of their husbands. Yet this reserve, even among the unmarried Esquimaux women, does not exist among the tribes located on the northern coast of Greenland. There both young and old indicated their vicious laxity to the navigators by signs and gestures of the most indelicate and unequivocal nature, and more than once, wives have been known to be offered to the strangers by their husbands themselves, plainly and without disguise, while the woman herself stood by, and freely acquiesced in her proposed prostitution.

The Esquimaux like most barbarians are excellent mimics. They possess the power of imitating the gestures and voices of others with great ability. They also display extraordinary powers of grimace and contortion, and could exhibit themselves in the most singular positions and attitudes. The dress of both sexes is very nearly alike, and consists of a coat with a pointed skirt both before and behind; pantaloons or leggings which extend to the waist; and long boots made of seal skin, and water tight, resembling moccasins. They have acquired considerable skill in the preparation of whale, seal, and deer skins. These they use for various purposes, some as thongs and lines in the capture of sea-beasts, some as harness for their dog-sledges, and some as soles for their moccasins, which are thus rendered water-proof. They have also invented a light water-proof outer dress, formed from the intestines of the whale, which they secure around the top of their small canoes, and which protects them from the waves of the sea. They acquire extraordinary skill in the management of their canoes or kaiyaks, and possess the hardihood of fearless seamen. Their dogs and reindeer constitute their chief wealth, and are in fact quite indispensable to their existence and comfort.

The religion of the great Esquimaux race is a singular subject of inquiry, and yet one which furnishes only the most unsatisfactory results. Their religious conceptions are simple and crude in the extreme. There is but little to know of them on this point; and that little is not to their credit. The most prominent idea in their religion is the belief in witchcraft, and in the agency of evil spirits. They worship demons much more devoutly than they worship God. Cer tain individuals among them profess to possess a great influence over evil spirits. They believe that persons are killed by sorcery; that they are and may become the messengers and servants of the devil; that sorcerers may change the appearance of individuals who are under their spell; and accordingly, sorcerers are themselves a powerful class among them.

Yet the Esquimaux have often become willing and docile converts to the christian faith, as taught them by the Moravian missionaries in Labrador and Greenland. They have readily acquired the art of reading and writing, and displayed no inconsiderable aptitude for the acquisition of knowledge. The language of the Esquimaux is admitted by the most learned philologists to be similar in its structure to the rest of the North American tongues. There seems to be a singular inconsistency between the comprehensiveness and artificial structure of the language, and its resemblance to that of neighboring Indian tribes, and the isolation of the people themselves. Their language does not materially vary along the whole immense extent of country over which their race is diffused; thus furnishing another evidence of the identity and unity of this primitive and singular people.

Yet the Esquimaux are divided into several tribes according to their different locations. Those on the southern portion of King William's Sound, are called the *Tchugatschih;* and they are located between Behring's Straits and Bristol Bay. Further to the north the *Kuskatchewak* reside between the island Nuniwak and Cape Newenham. These are neither nomadic nor given to the chase; but dwell in permanent villages, and have a strong attachment to their ancestral homes. In each of these villages there is a public building termed the *Kashim*, where councils and festivals are held. It has raised platforms around the walls, with a place in the center for the fire, and an aperture in the roof for the escape of the smoke and the admission of light.

The Tchukche tribe who inhabit the shores of the Gulf of Anadyn, seem once to have had possession of the coast of Asia, as far westward as the one hundred and sixtieth parallel. They are divided in the Sedentary, and the Reindeer Tchukche. These are both strong and powerful races, and very much resemble in their appearance the North American Indians. The encroachments of the Russians and Cossacks have driven them back beyond the Kolyma, into the north-eastern corner of Asia; but there they have remained free and unsubdued by their more powerful assailants. This tribe has domesticated both the dog and the reindeer, of which they possess numerous herds. They are skillful traders in furs and walrus' teeth, which they exchange for tobacco, articles of iron, hardware, and trinkets. They frequently travel on their sledges drawn by reindeer, accompanied by their women and children, their arms, tents, and household goods. Their yearly journeys continue for six months, for they make circuitous routes in pursuit of pasture and trade. Previous to the establishment of the Russian Fur company, these people yearly traveled for these purposes over an extent of seventeen hundred miles of North American coast.

Another tribe of the Esquimaux are called the Kutchins, who live westward between the Mackenzie and Behring's Sea. The males possess the average height of Europeans, are well formed, with regular features, high foreheads, and light complexions. The women resemble the men; and Captain Richardson speaks of the wife of one of the chiefs as being so handsome, that in any country she would be considered a fine looking woman. The women have their chins tattooed, and the men paint their faces both red and black. Their arms consist of a bow and arrow, a dagger, knife, and spear. Fire-arms have lately been introduced among them, and are very much prized. Where a man has not been able to obtain a gun, he always carries with him a supply of powder and shot, and for these he obtains a share of the game killed by the possessors of a gun or rifle. This singular expedient exists very extensively among the Esquimaux tribes.

The chief men among the Kutchins practice polygamy, and have two or three wives, and some even five. Very poor men who cannot support a wife remain single. But it is said that a good wrestler, whether poor or rich, can always obtain a wife. In winter the women perform all the drudgery about the house. They collect the firewood, assist the dogs in hauling the sledges, and bring snow to melt for water. They do everything, in fact, except cooking, and that is attended to by the men alone. The women carry their infants, like the rest of the Esquimaux, on their backs in seats made from birch bark, with the sides and back resembling those of an armchair. They even bandage the feet of their children to prevent them from growing, inasmuch as small feet are considered handsome. This custom resembles that of the Chinese, except that it is not confined to the females. The Kutchins are a lively and cheerful people. Dancing and singing are their chief amusements; wrestling and all kinds of athletic diversions are in fashion among them. Their religion also consists chiefly in the belief in sorcery and evil spirits, whom they endeavor to propitiate through their shamans, who profess to be able to communicate with the unseen world, and to possess the power of prophesying future events. When any one of their tribe dies suddenly, or unexpectedly, the event is always attributed to sorcery; and some evil spell is charged against either a member of their own tribe or of some neigboring one. Then blood-money is immediately demanded, and if it be refused, they do not rest until an opportunity is found to avenge the supposed murder by some retributive deed of violence and death. An instance is narrated in which blood money was demanded and received for several years, for the supposed death of a relative who was afterward discovered to be still alive. When demand was again made the ensuing year for the usual payment, three of the party making it were slain in expiation of their falsehood and extortion.

These Kutchins are treacherous and warlike; and generally engaged in hostilities with the surrounding tribes. One half of the population of the Yukon has thus been destroyed during the last twenty-five years. They pass the summer months chiefly in drying the white-fish for winter use. Their wealth consists partly in beads; and to become a chief among the Kutchins, a man must have beads equal in value to the amount of two hundred beavers. In summer when they are traveling they rarely erect their tents. In winter their encampments are usually placed in groves of fir trees, where they either live in huts or in their winter tents constructed of skins with the hair unremoved.

The process of courtship among these people is very simple indeed. The lover goes early in the morning to the abode of the object of his passion, and without saying anything, begins to bring in water; to heat the stones which are used to create steam for their bath; and to prepare food. The inmates then ask him who he is, and why he does this. He states that he wishes to obtain the daughter of the man who dwells there as his wife. If he is not refused, he remains as a servant in the family for a year, and at the termination of that probationary period he receives both a reward for his services and his bride into the bargain. No ceremony of marriage takes place between them. When a man dies, he is mourned by his whole clan. Slavery exists among them to some extent; and those who are in bondage, are prisoners taken captive in war, who are often sold and re-sold by different owners, unless they are redeemed by their own relatives. These slaves have been known to be sometimes sacrificed as victims to the shades of their departed warriors and heroes. They also possess the art of manufacturing various articles of iron ware; an accomplishment which they probably derived at an early period, from their intercourse with Russian traders.

The winter having at length passed away, the travelers who composed Sir John Richardson's company at Fort Confidence, prepared in the ensuing spring to resume their operations. It yet remained their duty to reach Wollaston and Victoria Lands, and thus to complete the search in that direction. In consequence of the forced desertion and loss of the boats of the expedition as previously narrated, it would have beem impracticable for the whole party to accompany those who performed this journey; nor was this in fact necessary; and Mr. Rae, the younger and more robust associate of Captain Richardson, was selected to perform the service which yet remained. The ability and zeal of this gentleman well fitted him for the task. He had already explored the country between Fort Confidence and the Coppermine River during the winter months, for the purpose of ascertaining the best route to be followed in the spring.

Accordingly, in April Mr. Rae, taking charge of the only boat which the expedition still possessed, conveyed provisions, boat-stores, and various other necessaries on dog-sledges, across toward the Kendall River, and posted two men at Flett's Station, together with two Indians, to protect them. Six men composed the crew of the boat under the command of Mr. Rae. Two men were left in charge of Fort Confidence.

Mr. Rae having waited for the breaking up of the ice on the Dease River, hauled his boat thither, on which he embarked on the 8th of June. His ascent of the stream was slow, in consequence of the large masses of ice, some of them miles in length, which impeded his progress. They ascended the south-eastern branch of that stream. On the 17th they passed over the lake from which the river flows, on the ice. It contains some islands and is four miles in width. From this lake they traveled overland for six miles nearly due east, and on the 21st they reached the Kendall River, to which the provisions had been previously conveyed in April. They then descended the Kendall to the Coppermine River.

At this place they were detained by the ice, which was still unbroken, during five days. They then sailed down the Coppermine to the sea; and found a narrow channel along the shore of Richardson Bay, where the ice still lay against the rocks. They proceeded on and rounded Point Mackenzie, and entered Back's Inlet, which was then but partially opened. They soon reached the head of the inlet, and at once sailed up Rae River, which Captain Richardson had discovered the preceding autumn.

For the purpose of examining the country, Mr. Rae followed the river for twenty geographical miles inland. It is very straight in its direction, and flows over a bed of limestone. Its banks are extremely rugged, and sometimes presented precipices 200 feet in height. The party then returned to the mouth of the river. Their position now was 67° 55′ 20″ north latitude. They reached Cape Kendall, where they experienced a heavy thunder-storm, which compelled them to land. On the 27th they continued their course to Cape Hearne. Basil Hall Bay they found filled with unbroken ice from one side to the other. The next day a crack occurred in the ice large enough to permit the boat to reach an island in the middle of the bay. On the north side of this island they found some open water which enabled them to advance two miles further. On the 30th they reached Cape Krusenstern.

This was the most suitable spot from which to desert the shore, and commence the traverse or direct route to Wollaston Land, passing near to Douglass

Island. This circumstance was more fortunate, as the condition of the ice along the shore rendered their further advance in that direction impossible. The party disembarked here and pitched their tents on the top of the cliffs, and waited for a more favorable state of the ice; which had already commenced to break up. Here they were visited by some Esquimaux, who informed them that they had seen several natives of Wollaston Land during the preceding winter, and had been informed by them that no European ships, boats, or seamen had ever visited their country. The situation of the party here was ascertained to be 68° 24′ 35″ north latitude.

The ice in the bay was not sufficiently cleared to permit Mr. Rae to proceed until the 19th of August. Until this period there had been a closely packed stream of ice stretching along the entire shore, and grinding against the rocks as it was driven upon them by the wind. Having pulled seven miles from land and being yet three miles distant from Douglass Island, they were met by a stream of ice so closely packed and so rough, that it was impossible either to pass over it or through it. This compelled the company to return to their former position on the shore. During several succeeding days they poled their way along the beach, and thus advanced a few miles to the southward. On the evening of the 22d Mr. Rae ascended a hill near the shore, and there beheld with a spy-glass nothing in the direction of Wollaston Land but the white ice forced upward by the wind into irregular heaps; while to the east and south-east there was a large space of open water, between which and the ice-bound shore, a vast stream of ice some miles in length was driving rapidly toward Cape Hearne.

There was now no prospect that the sea would open so as to permit the frail craft in which Mr. Rae and his men were embarked to venture across the main to Wollaston Land. Winter was then very near;

and Mr. Rae was reluctantly compelled to give the order to return to the Coppermine River. In ascending this river to the Bloody Fall, the company met the misfortune of losing Albert, their Esquimaux interpreter, and one of the most useful members of the expedition. He was drowned in attempting to extricate the boat from a dangerous eddy into which it had been drawn. The boat was lost with him. They then commenced their journey on foot across the land toward Great Bear Lake, each man carrying a weight of about eighty pounds. After seven days' march from the Bloody Fall the party reached Fort Confidence, whence the expedition had started. They had failed to discover any traces of Sir John Franklin, and had not even reached Wollaston Land, the proposed terminus of their journey, in consequence of the strait being filled with impassable ice.

Meanwhile Captain Richardson and the rest of the men belonging to the expedition, explored Bear Lake and Cape McDonald. They then reached Fort Franklin. The only vestige of the latter which remained, was the foundation of the chimney-stack. Thence they proceeded to Fort Norman. They then embarked on Bear Lake River and descended with the current to its mouth. Retracing the route which they had pursued in their outward journey during the preceding year, the company eventually reached Methy Lake; where Captain Richardson received his first letters from England, which had been brought up from Canada by the governor's canoe, which annually leaves La Chine in May. He arrived at Norway House on the 13th of August, and there the men composing the expedition were discharged. The Europeans among them were sent down to York factory to sail to England in one of the ships of the Hudson Bay company.

Captain Richardson himself returned by way of Boston to Liverpool; and thus ended this additional attempt to discover Sir John Franklin's fate, without having obtained the slightest clue of them; although the plan of search pursued possessed some novel and very considerable advantages in its favor.

The Second Voyage of the Prince Albert in Search of Sir John Franklin, under the command of William Kennedy, in 1853.

This expedition was fitted out for the second time by the liberality of Lady Franklin. The vessel was small, but had proved herself, on a former voyage to the Polar seas, well adapted to the service.* That voyage resulted in discovering traces of the the missing ships at the entrance of Wellington Channel; and on its return Lady Franklin instantly resolved to equip the present undertaking, with hopes of more complete success; and Captain Kennedy was invited by her to take the command.

In May, 1851, the Prince Albert lay in the harbor of Aberdeen ready for sea. Along the sides from the keel to about two feet above the water-line, there had been placed a doubling of planking two and a half inches thick. The bows and stern-posts were sheathed in wrought iron, a quarter of an inch in thickness. Her hold had been strengthened with a perfect labyrinth of cross-beams, for the purpose of better enabling her to endure the immense pressure of the ice. The object of this second expedition of the Prince Albert, was to continue the search by way of *Prince Regent's Inlet*, an important portion of the Polar region, which neither Captain Penny nor Captain Austin had explored, nor any other Arctic voyager previous to that period.

The crew of the Prince Albert consisted of the commanding officer and seventeen men. She was furnished with two large and valuable boats, one of gutta-percha, and the other of mahogany; together

* See page 348 of this volume for the details of this voyage.

with several smaller ones. The vessel was provisioned for two years. On the 22d of May she left Aberdeen Harbor. Lady Franklin was then on board, and as she left the ship after expressing all her wishes and hopes for the success of the gallant crew, was loudly and enthusiastically cheered, as she deserved to be, as she descended the vessel's side to return to the shore. On the 23d of June they made Hoy Sound, and soon reached Cape Farewell. Captain Kennedy had been instructed to examine Prince Regent's Inlet, and the passages connecting it with the Western Sea, south-west of Cape Walker. To the latter point, strong probabilities in favor of finding traces of Sir John Franklin concentrated; inasmuch as it was supposed to be likely that he abandoned his vessels to the south-west of Cape Walker; from the fact that he himself entertained the opinion that an open passage was to be found from the westward into the south part of Regent's Inlet; and because this region of country was known to possess considerable animal life, and he would have the stores placed at Fury Beach soon within his reach. It was also thought that he would have pursued this route, inasmuch as he more probably expected assistance to be sent him by way of Lancaster Sound and Barrow Straits, into which Regent's Inlet opened, than by any other direction.

By the 1st of July Captain Kennedy was in full view of the shores of Greenland. They then presented a spectacle of more than ordinary interest and sublimity. As far as the eye could reach, they seemed a sterile and iron-bound coast, diversified here and there with huge cliffs of rock and ice, ascending sternly into the wintry heavens a thousand feet in height. Often gloomy caverns were seen in the ice which were portals for the discharge of some half-frozen stream into the ocean, filled with small icebergs which were but rolling and tossing in the flood. The vessel soon passed Capes Desolation and Comfort; and by the 8th of July they were three-fourths of their way up Baffin's Bay, and nearly opposite to the Danish village of Upernavick. At this village they took on board six powerful Esquimaux dogs, and sealskin boats adapted to the Arctic regions.

On the 13th, the Prince Albert fell in with the American squadron which had just escaped from their extraordinary drift of eight months in the heart of the pack, through Lancaster Sound and Baffin's Bay. Finding Melville Bay completely closed by the ice, Captain Kennedy determined to attempt a passage further south. After four days of difficult and perilous navigation, they succeeded in effecting an advance of 120 miles through the packed ice, and reached West Water on the 21st of August. This was a very perilous exploit, and is one which has proved the destruction of many a bold adventurer in those seas. The small dimensions of the Prince Albert seem to have given her great advantages over her more bulky associates. On the 26th of August they were off Pond's Bay, and were here for the last time visited by a small company of Esquimaux. The extreme rarity of the atmosphere in these northern climes, was proved by the fact, that the voices of the Esquimaux could be clearly heard as they approached the vessel, at the distance of eight miles.

From Pond's Bay Captain Kennedy steered through Lancaster Sound. On the 3d of September he reached Barrow Straits. At this point he attempted to reach Cape Riley, in hope of there finding traces of Sir John Franklin; but after bearing up repeatedly for the North Land through heavy fogs, snow, and gales, was compelled to abandon the purpose. On the 4th of September Captain Kennedy arrived at the mouth of Prince Regent's Inlet, one of the special objects of his search. He there found an unbroken barrier of ice extending as far down the west side of Prince Regent's Inlet as the eye could see, piled up in dense masses on the shore. The eastern side and middle of the inlet were comparatively open. This state of the ice forbade further progress in the intended direction. They attempted to run into Leopold Harbor, but found that also impossible. Thence they ran down to Elwin Bay to Batty Bay, and to Fury Beach, finding them all closed. They were very nearly involved in the position which had proved the destruction of the Fury—in a narrow lane between the shore and an extensive field of moving ice. Being thus excluded entirely from the western shore of the inlet, they were compelled to sail to the opposite. After making a circuit of some forty hours along a high and dead wall of ice, they reached Port Bowen on the 5th. Landing here, Captain Kennedy found a few traces of Sir E. Parry's party. These were several cairns, a fire-place of stones, pieces of canvas, nails, and broken pipes. There was here, also, a single grave, the lonely resting-place of one John Cottrell, a seaman of the Fury, who was buried in July, 1825, aged thirty-nine.

It was still regarded as of the utmost importance to reach Port Leopold, and there effect a landing. On the 9th having crossed the inlet, and brought the ship to within several miles of Cape Seppings, the southern point of Port Leopold, Captain Kennedy determined to land with the gutta-percha boat, and four seamen, for the purpose of making explorations. He found a narrow lane of water which brought them quickly to the shore. On ascending the cliffs on Cape Seppings, the appearance of the ice was such as to induce Captain Kennedy to conclude that very soon the Regent's Inlet would become clear and navigable. After an hour spent on shore, he prepared to return to the ship, but found his progress entirely cut off by the ice, which, during his delay, had entirely changed its position. Night soon came on. The ocean was covered with huge masses of ice; grinding, tossing and rearing furiously on every side. To attempt to reach the ship then, was directly to court destruction.

They were compelled to draw up their boat on the beach, and turning her over, to prepare to pass the night under her. So intense was the cold that Captain Kennedy was compelled to prevent the men from sleeping during the whole night, knowing that that alone would prevent them from freezing to death. When the next morning dawned, and they looked out on the troubled sea, they found that every vestige of the Prince Albert had vanished.

This position of the captain and his men, was both unpleasant and dangerous. He determined first to fall back to Whaler Point, where Sir James Ross had deposited a store of provisions. They found the house erected by Sir James, still standing, and the provisions in good order, consisting of pemmican, chocolate and biscuit.

It was now the 10th of September and winter was upon them. The only remedy for the lonely exiles, was to make the best preparations possible to pass the winter at Whaler Point, hoping in the ensuing spring to obtain a rescue. It was a sad and sudden termination to the voyage, and they submitted to it most reluctantly. They went to work and transformed the launch left there by Sir James Ross into a shelter, by laying her main-mast on supports at the bow and stern, and spreading over them two sails. This procured them a shelter. A stove was set up in the center of the boat with the pipe running through the roof. This warmed them. They obtained blankets and clothes from the depot left by Sir James; and this rendered their condition more tolerable. Thus their dreary residence in those Polar regions began, with the prospect of a long and increasingly rigorous winter before them. What the final issue might be, they could not predict. Time alone could solve that mystery. The only signs of life which appeared around them, were a few Polar bears and foxes.

Happily an unexpected termination was put to their danger and suspense on the 17th of September, by the sudden appearance of a party of seven men under Mr. Bellot, who had left the Prince Albert in search of the absentees, and had dragged the jolly-boat all the way from Batty Bay. It was the third attempt which had been made to discover and rescue them, by the crew on board the ship. The joy of Captain Kennedy and his men at this sudden deliverance may readily be imagined. They were thus snatched most probably from the jaws of a frozen and mysterious grave which would soon have closed over them.

Five weeks had elapsed during their involuntary absence from the ship, and they seemed to possess the magnitude of years to the despairing wanderers. So far distant were they from the vessel, that it required a journey of several days to conduct them thither. The company then prepared to pass the winter in their present situation. The deck was cleared of lumber and covered with a housing. They then built out-houses of snow for various purposes, for wash houses, for a carpenter shop, and for forges. All the powder on board was taken on shore and buried in the snow. The winter was to be passed in making extensive land journeys in all directions, in search of Sir John Franklin. They prepared a quantity of snow-shoes and winter clothing. As soon as the ice in Prince Regent's Inlet permitted them to travel from the ships with safety, they commenced their explorations.

The first object of inquiry was to ascertain whether Fury Beach had been a point of refuge to any of Sir John Franklin's company, since it was visited by Lieutenant Robinson in 1849. It was also desirable to form a depot of provisions there, to aid in future researches which might be made in the same direction. They followed the base of the lofty cliffs which extend in an almost continuous line from Batty Bay to Fury Beach. The company consisted of five persons including Captain Kennedy. They dragged a sleigh with them, which was no easy task, as the ground was covered the entire way with boulders and large fragments of ice, which had been stranded on the beach by many successive tempests. There were also immense sloping embankments of drifted snow, which lay high up against the face of the cliffs. Their entire journey was performed by moonlight, the sun having entirely bidden them farewell before their departure from the ship.

Sir John Ross had erected in 1832 at Fury Beach, a building which he had named Somerset House. Many hopes centered around this spot, because it was reasonably supposed that if any of Franklin's party had been imprisoned in the Arctic seas, and had ever come near to Fury Beach, they would have repaired to this well known spot, both for shelter and provisions. As soon as Captain Kennedy reached this house on January 8th, he discovered that all his hopes had been illusions. A death-like solitude pervaded the moon-lit and frozen gloom around them. The eye rested on a surrounding waste, relieved by no sign of recent life, cheered by no evidence of the former presence of those whom they sought. The stores which had there been placed were still in perfect preservation. The house itself had become much dilapidated by the severity of the climate, and by the rude salutes of those Arctic storms. The roof was much broken. The inder-staff had been thrown down by the winds, and had been gnawed by the famished foxes. One end of the building was filled with snow. They lighted a fire in the stove which Sir John Ross had once used, and prepared their supper. After spending a few hours in the careful examination of that dreary spot, rendered still more melancholy by the lunar gloom and the disappointment of all their hopes, Captain Kennedy and his men returned after a journey of several days to the ship. No traces of the lost navigators had been seen during this visit to Fury Beach. The state of the weather during the ensuing month, compelled Captain Kennedy to remain in his vessel. There they were nearly overwhelmed by avalanches of snow. There seemed to be but one gale during the winter around the ship; but that gale blew when she came, and continued till she departed. It was dangerous to venture forth even for a short distance; inasmuch as the snow-drifts and the darkness combined, soon involved the traveler in a whirling deluge which rendered it impossible to see six paces off.

A small party were actually lost for a short time, when endeavoring to convey some provisions a short distance from the ship to form a depot. After proceeding a few hours, a furious hurricane arose, which drifted the snow in fearful masses around them. In attempting to cross a bay on their return, they lost sight of the land by which their course was to be guided. Neither sun, moon, or stars illumined the heavens. They knew not which way to turn. They tried the expedient of setting the dogs loose which drew the sledge. They all started off at a rapid pace, and afterward reached the ship; but their gait was too rapid for the men, whom they soon left behind to their fate. They still went on however, sometimes walking, sometimes crawling, sometimes climbing over the immense blocks and masses of ice and snow drifts. At length they reached the powder magazine, and after some further difficulty, they found the ship. Their escape was accidental; for the men had become so benumbed with cold, as to be able no longer to clear their eyelids of the accumulation of snow which had rested on them, and were thus nearly blind.

Thus February wore away, and Captain Kennedy began to prepare for the execution of the chief land journey which had been contemplated by the expedition. The end of this journey was Cape Walker; for it was supposed that if Sir John Franklin had taken his departure for the unknown regions to the west and south-west, he would have started from this point, and not from Wellington Channel.

Five men accompanied Captain Kennedy on this excursion. As far as Fury Beach they were accompanied by seven persons as a fatigue party. Their provisions, clothing, and bedding were drawn on two Indian sleighs by five dogs. They started on the 25th of February, and were accompanied by the whole crew as far as Batty Bay. On the 5th of March Captain Kennedy reached Fury Beach. Here they remained several days, and found the old stores deposited here by Sir John Ross, not only in a state of good preservation, but also much superior in quality to those which they brought with them. These provisions consisted of preserved meats, vegetables, and soups, and after *thirty* years' exposure to the intense climate of the Arctic zone, they were found to be still perfect! The flour had all become caked in solid lumps, and had to be reground and passed through a seive before it could be used; but then it furnished most excellent biscuit.

On the 29th of March Captain Kennedy resumed his march from Fury Beach. He had four flat-bottomed Indian sleighs, drawn by the dogs and men. They proceeded toward Cape Garry over a long route of floes and low-lying points. They uniformly commenced their journey immediately after breakfast, and continued till evening, when a snow hut was greeted, and preparations made to pass the night in it. Their labors were rarely over and repose begun, before ten o'clock at night.

On the 1st of April they reached Creswell Bay, and in the evening came to Cape Garry. They thence proceeded onward to Brentford Bay, where they found a dozen Esquimaux huts, deserted by their inhabitants. Here the party divided for the purpose of exploring several channels of open water which extended toward the interior. Captain Kennedy traveled twenty miles along one of these channels.

From a hill on which he here encamped he saw a broad channel running north-east, which he at first supposed to be a continuation of Brentford Bay. Its great extent however, convinced him that it was a western sea, and that the narrow passage through which he had just traveled was a strait leading out of Prince Regent's Inlet. This being apparently a new discovery, Captain Kennedy called it Bellot Strait, after the second officer of the expedition. This water was afterward discovered to be the northern extremity of Victoria Strait, which Dr. Rae had explored from another direction.

At this point Captain Kennedy determined to proceed in a westward direction, in order to ascertain whether any channel existed there through which Sir John Franklin might have penetrated from Cape Walker.

On the 8th of April he started in pursuance of this purpose. Their progress was slow in consequence of the roughness of the ice. The men became much afflicted with snow-blindness, and were much distressed by the sharp particles of snow drift which were dashed by the furious wind into their eyes. The wide region around them was perfectly level, and Captain Kennedy named it Arrow Smith's Plains. Sometimes the severity of the weather compelled them to remain for several days in their snow-hut. They traveled on for thirteen days without meeting any indications of the approaching sea. This convinced Captain Kennedy that there was no passage by water to the south-west of Cape Walker; and that due north was now the most desirable course to be pursued.

Following this purpose he traveled in that direction for twenty miles over a level plain. On the 24th of April they arrived at the bottom of a deep inlet, which has since been ascertained to be the Ommaney Bay of Captain Austin's expedition. From this point they steered eastward, in order to strike the channel supposed to be to the eastward of Cape Bunny, and by following it to reach Cape Walker.

After three days they came to Browne's Bay. At length on the 4th of May, they approached the bold headland of Cape Walker, for the attainment of which they had endured so much. Here they confidently hoped to find some traces of Sir John Franklin, had he followed the suggestions contained in his original instructions. Captain Kennedy accordingly searched every spot within three miles on both sides of the cape. They followed the windings of the rough ice outside the beach. They examined the base of the lofty cliffs which stretch away northward from the cape. Not a single vestige of the lost navigator could anywhere be discovered.

Captain Kennedy now determined immediately to return to the ship. He pushed directly across North Somerset toward Batty Bay, intending to follow the coast to Whaler Point. This route was double the distance of the one already followed; but it was hoped that perhaps it might lead to some desirable results. On the first day they encamped about midway between Cape Walker and Limestone Island. They passed by Cunningham Inlet, Cape Gifford, and Cape Rennel. At Cape McClintock they found the small store of provisions which Sir John Ross had left there in 1849. On the 15th of May they reached Whaler Point. On the 27th, they left Whaler Point, to return directly to the Prince Albert, and on the 30th their land journey ended by their safe arrival at the vessel.

Various preparations for their departure now occupied the attention of the seamen. On the 21st of July, these were completed; but they found it impossible to move the ship. The ice had congealed firmly around her. The only possibility of releasing her was by sawing a canal through the ice which still obstructed the bay. After the hard labor of a week, a canal half a mile in length, and sufficiently wide to permit the vessel to pass was cut through. This channel was then cleared of the ice by the use of Copeland's blasting cylinders.

On the 6th of August Captain Kennedy and his crew joyfully bade farewell to Batty Bay, where the Prince Albert had remained three hundred and thirty days. In Elwin Bay they were detained a whole week by the compact masses of ice which still obstructed the sea. On the 17th, the ice suddenly cleared away, and they then steered for Beechey Island. At this point they met the "North Star," from England, commanded by Captain Pullen, which had been despatched by the British Admiralty, to pursue the search after Sir John Franklin.

Having completed the object of the expedition, as far as had been in his power, though without any very satisfactory results, Captain Kennedy on the 24th of August bore away for England, leaving the North Star preparing to winter at Beechey Island, and carrying with him the latest dispatches for the Admiralty from Commander Pullen. He wished to touch on his voyage at Navy Board Inlet, hoping to be able to ascertain the state of the stores which had been placed there. Two unsuccessful attempts to accomplish this purpose were defeated, and Captain Kennedy was then compelled by stress of weather, to relinquish that design. On the 21st of September the Prince Albert reached Cape Farewell; and on the 7th of October, she anchored in Aberdeen Harbor. Six weeks had elapsed since the commencement of her homeward-bound voyage. The entire expedition had occupied the period altogether of fifteen months. During their winter stay at Whaler Point, many of the men had traveled two thousand miles in excursions in various directions. The expedition settled the point, that Sir John Franklin could not have advanced by Cape Walker, but had taken the northern route through Queen Channel and Penny Strait; and that traces of his fate could alone be

found from the westward or Behring's Straits. Yet there too, other researches, equally sagacious, persevering and thorough, have all unfortunately proved equally unsuccessful!

ARCTIC EXPLORATIONS; THE SECOND GRINNELL EXPEDITION IN SEARCH OF SIR JOHN FRANKLIN IN 1853, '54, '55, BY DR. E. K. KANE, IN THE BRIG "ADVANCE."

IN December, 1852, Dr. Kane received his orders from the Navy Department at Washington, to conduct an expedition into the Arctic regions in search of the great English navigator. The ship "Advance," in which he had formerly sailed, was placed under his command. He immediately proceeded to select his crew, to equip the vessel, and to make the other preparations which were necessary. His party numbered seventeen picked men, all of whom had volunteered to try with him the perilous vicissitudes of his daring venture. The brig sailed from the port of New York, on the 30th of May, 1853; and in eighteen days arrived at St. Johns, New Foundland. After providing themselves at this place with an additional stock of fresh meat, and a valuable team of Newfoundland dogs, they steered for the coast of Greenland.

The avowed purpose of this second Arctic journey of Dr. Kane was, to explore what he believed to be the probable extension of the northern promontory of the peninsula of Greenland. He also thought that the extreme northern headland of this frozen region undoubtedly contained and would exhibit traces of the lost navigators. He supposed that the chain of the great land-masses of Greenland might extend very far toward the North Pole; that Sir John Franklin might also have been attracted by this theory, and might have pursued this route; and that by a thorough search in that direction, the utmost limits of which had not yet been invaded or explored by his bold and adventurous predecessors, some light might not only be obtained to solve the great enigma which still engrossed the wonder of men, but also new and independent discoveries might be made in that unknown region.

On the 1st of July Dr. Kane entered the harbor of Fiskernoes, one of the Danish settlements of Greenland. This obscure and lonely community is supported by their trade in codfish. The strangers were received with simple hospitality by Mr. Lazzen, the superintendent of the colony. Some fresh provisions were here also obtained, and an Esquimaux hunter of superior skill was enlisted in the service of the party.

Proceeding on from this point, the other Danish settlements of Greenland were successively visited—Lichtenfels, Sukkertoppen, Proven, Upernavick, at the last of which places the first Grinnell expedition of 1851 had rested after its winter drift. At length they reached Yotlik, the most northern point in Greenland inhabited by human beings. Beyond this the coast may be regarded as having been until that period, unexplored. From Yotlik, Dr. Kane steered northward toward Baffin's Islands, which he found then clear of ice; and passing by Duck Island, bore away for Wilcox Point. As he approached Melville Bay he was enveloped in a thick fog, during the prevalence of which he drifted among the icebergs. After a hard day's work with the boats, they towed the brig away from these unpleasant and dangerous neighbors. He then determined to stand westward, and double Melville Bay by an outside passage, unless prevented and intercepted by the pack. In executing this purpose he concluded, in order to avoid the drifting floes, to anchor to an ice-berg. Eight hours were spent in the severe labor of warping, heaving, and planting the anchors. But scarcely had this task been finished, when the attention of the crew was attracted by a loud crackling sound aloft. Small fragments of ice began to descend. The ship became in imminent peril from the falling fragments of the dissolving mountain. Scarcely had she cast off from the ice-berg, when the face of it descended in ruins upon the sea, crashing and roaring with a thunder not unlike that of artillery.

On the 5th of August they passed the "Crimson Cliffs," so called, from the appearance usually presented by their snow-clad summits. Next day they reached Hakluyt Island; which is surmounted by a tall spire springing six hundred feet into the heavens above the level of the water. They soon passed Capes Alexander and Isabella, and thus entered Smith's Sound. Having reached Littleton Island, Dr. Kane determined to deposit here a supply of provisions, and some permanent traces of his route, to be used in case it should be necessary afterward to send an exploring party to discover the fate of his own. The life-boat was accordingly buried here, containing a supply of pemmican, blankets, and India rubber cloth. They endeavored to fortify the precious deposit from the claws of the Polar bear. And here on this lonely spot, the party were surprised to find the traces of Esquimaux life. The ruins of stone huts, and even the frozen corpses of the dead were discovered; and so singular had been the action of the intense cold upon the dead bodies, that though they had probably occupied their cheerless homes for a century, they were still not decomposed.

The 20th of August still found the brig and her gallant crew navigating the dangerous and ice-ladened waters of Smith's Sound. At this date they encountered a storm of extraordinary fury; and made one of those narrow escapes from destruction, which sometimes give an air more of romance than of reality to the adventures of Arctic explorers. In a terrific gale their three hawsers were broken, and the brig drifted with fearful rapidity under the furious pressure of the storm. Only by the utmost heroism and skill was the Advance kept from being dashed to pieces against the mountains of ice which tossed, rolled, and surged around her in the deep. The greatest danger of all was after the storm had partly lulled, when the bergs continued to thump against the floe-ice; and the certainty of being crushed between the two, stared the voyagers in the face. A sudden means of escape presented itself, and with admirable dexterity and promptitude the crew availed themselves of it. A low, water-washed berg at that moment came driving along past the Advance. An anchor was instantly planted in its side and held fast by a whale line. Carried along with fearful rapidity by this gigantic tow-horse, the little brig was drifted out of danger, and once more escaped the impending ruin. She had a close shave of it nevertheless, and would have lost her port quarter-boat had it not been taken in from the davits.

The navigators continued their northern route by tracking along the ice-belt which hugs the frozen shore. On the 23d of August they had reached 78° 41′ north latitude. This placed them further north than any of their predecessors had been, except Captain Parry. During the progress of the journey, the whole coast had been inspected carefully; yet no traces of Sir John Franklin had been discovered. On the 28th of August Dr. Kane determined to send out an expedition from the vessel to make further search, as the condition of the ice prevented the Advance from being brought near to the shore. The whale-boat was chosen for this adventure. They took with them a sledge and a supply of pemmican. The party consisted of seven persons selected from the crew. The vessel was placed under the temporary control of Mr. Ohlsen. The adventurers were provided with buffalo robes, and other necessary means of protection against the extreme cold. Their progress however was slow, not making more than seven miles per day, in consequence of the obstructions of the ice along the shore. Very soon they were compelled to abandon the boat, and employ their sledge. The abrupt nature of the ground over which they traveled may be inferred from the fact, that frequently they were constrained to carry the sledge on their shoulders over precipices and gorges in the ice, and over high and perpendicular knolls of snow.

In this trip the travelers found many skeletons of the reindeer. Dr. Kane ascertained by scientific observation, that the mean elevation of this part of the coast of Greenland was thirteen hundred feet. After five days' laborious travel, he was but forty miles distant from the brig. Here he determined to leave the sledge behind and proceed on foot. On the 5th of September they discovered a bay much larger than any other previously known to extend from Smith's Straits. It was fed by a large river which poured a flood of tumultuous waters into it from the interior of North Greenland. It was fully three quarters of a mile wide at its mouth. The gallant navigators gave it the name of Mary Minturn River, after the sister of Mrs. H. Grinnell. This river was traced for forty miles toward its mouth; and its origin was found to be derived from the melting snows of the interior glaciers.

From his researches in this region, Dr. Kane came to the conclusion that this coast of Greenland faced to the north. His longitude here was 78° 41′ west. After sixteen miles of foot journey the company reached a great headland to which they gave the name of Thackeray. Eight miles further on, a similar eminence attracted their attention; to which they applied the epithet of Hawkes. The table-lands here were twelve hundred feet high. The party continued their difficult and dangerous journey until they reached some lofty headlands, where they determined to te-minate their excursion. These reached an altitude of eleven hundred feet, and overlooked an expanse extending beyond the eighteenth parallel of latitude. The view from this elevation was marked by every element of gloomy and cheerless magnificence. On the left, the western shore of the sound stretched away toward the northern pole. To the right a rugged and rolling country appeared, which ended in the Great Humboldt Glacier. Toward the north-east the projecting headland called Cape Andrew Jackson, appeared; and the vast area between was a sea of solid ice. Farther still, a stream of icebergs presented their rugged and unseemly bulks to the eye of the observer.

Having carefully examined the whole country as far as his glasses would reach, Dr. Kane determined to return to the Advance. Winter was now rapidly approaching, and it was necessary to select some appropriate spot in which the crew and the vessel might pass its long, gloomy, and dangerous interval. For various reasons which need not here be detailed, Dr. Kane resolved to remain where he then was. He had arrived at the conclusion that Rensselaer Harbor would be the most desirable winter quarters; and on the 10th of September they commenced the labors necessary to render their position tenable and safe. They removed the contents of the hold of the vessel to a store-house which they prepared on Butter Island. A deck-house was built on the vessel, in which the different qualities of ventilation, warmth, dryness, room, and comfort, were sought to the utmost possible extent. A site for the observatory was selected. Stones were hauled over the ice on sledges for its erection. Its location was on a rocky inlet about a hundred yards from the vessel, which they named Fern Rock. Preparations were also made, preparatory to the work of establishing provision depots on the coast of Greenland. The advantage of these provision depots will appear from the fact that by their assistance, expeditions of search could afterward be conducted with the use of sledges and dogs. The provisions for the latter, if taken on the journeys themselves, form so heavy a load as seriously to embarrass the movements of the travelers. But when they were released from this labor, these dogs conveyed the sledges and their occupants on long journeys successfully, and with great rapidity on their tours of examination.

On the 20th of September the first party organized to establish provision depots was sent out. It consisted of seven men. A sledge thirteen feet in length, called the "Faith," was filled with pemmican, and was drawn by those attached to it, by means of track-ropes termed rue-raddies, which were passed around the shoulder and under the arms. The intended location of this depot was sixty miles from the brig, on the Greenland coast. As the bold and hardy adventurers started forth, they were saluted with three hearty cheers by their comrades who remained with the vessel.

The life of the party which remained in the vessel was not devoid of incident and interest. They made a desperate attempt to smoke out the rats with which they were infested. To accomplish this purpose, a quantity of charcoal was burnt, after the hatches had been shut down, and every visible crevice had been stopped. A large quantity of carbonic acid gas was then generated, and the crew spent one night on deck in order to give the rats fair play. One or two of the seamen made a narrow escape from suffocation, by venturing during the night into the fumigated portion of the ship. They were also assailed by another peril. A barrel of charcoal by some means became ignited, which had been left in the carpenter's room at some distance from the stove. After some labor and more anxiety, the fire was suppressed before any very serious damage had been done to the vessel. The corpses of twenty-eight defunct rats, of all sizes, ages, and sexes, became the next day the trophies of the successful attack of the crew upon their foes.

By the 10th of October the party which had been sent to establish the first depot of provisions, had been absent twenty days; and their return was anxiously expected. Dr. Kane at length determined to start out in search of them. He traveled with one companion on a sledge drawn by four Newfoundland dogs. He averaged twenty miles per day with this singular team. On the 15th, several hours before sunrise, he perceived on the distant and snowy waste, a dark object which seemed to move. It proved to be the returning depot-party. They had traveled at the rate of eighteen miles per day, and had been twenty-eight days engaged in their laborious expedition. Some of their limbs had been frozen, and they had met with other mishaps, though none were of a very serious nature, and they had accomplished the purpose for which they had been sent out. The greeting which ensued on their return to the ship, was hearty on both sides. They had made the first deposit of provision at Cape Russell. Thirty miles further on, they left about a hundred and ten pounds of pemmican and beef, about thirty pounds of a mixture of pemmican and meal, and a bag of bread. On the 10th of October they made their third and last deposit on an island called James McGary, after the second officer of the expedition. Here they erected a cairn, and buried six hundred and seventy pounds of pemmican, and forty of meat, biscuit, with other items, making in all eight hundred pounds. One incident which occurred during their journey, illustrates very clearly some of the perils which attend Arctic travel. The company had pitched their tent for the night and had retired to rest. It was about midnight. They had been lulled to slumber by the grand monotonous thundering of the neighboring glaciers. Suddenly the floe on which the tent was placed, cracked with a stupendous report directly beneath them. The sleeping party needed no further promptings to bestir themselves. Repeated reports around them gave evidence that the ice was breaking up. The sledge was immediately placed upon a detached piece of ice, and rowed and paddled to one of the firmer fields which remained attached to the bergs. Here they obtained safety until the morning, when they quickly removed from their dangerous position. They eventually returned in safety to the brig.

By the 7th of November, 1853, the darkness of an Arctic winter began to settle down upon them. It was necessary to keep the lamps lit constantly. They had the comfortable prospect of ninety days of darkness yet to come. It was natural that the lonely adventurers should begin to devise some means of amusement, by which they might beguile the cheerless monotony of their existence. A fancy ball was projected, and an Arctic journal bearing the appropriate title of "The Ice Blink," was commenced. Thus the slow and tedious days and nights of their winter sojourn wore on. In spite of the intense cold, Dr. Kane continued to make his magnetic observations in the observatory. When the thermometer stood at forty-nine degrees below zero, and even at sixty-four degrees below zero, he still effected his astronomical investigations and calculations.

On the 21st of January the first traces of the returning light became visible. Its approach was indicated by a beauteous orange tint, which flushed the distant southern horizon. But still, the darkness seemed to be eternal and unvarying. The continued absence of light appeared to affect the health of the party, as much as the excessive rigor of the cold. By the 21st of February the sun's rays became clearly visible, and when March arrived, it brought with it the almost perpetual day which alternately takes the place in the Arctic realms of almost perpetual night. During the winter, nine noble Newfoundland, and thirty-five Esquimaux dogs, which were of the utmost value, had perished. Six only remained out of the whole number which had been taken at the commencement of the expedition; and these were now their only reliance in their future operations.

By the 18th of March the spring tides began to

break and move the massive ice which still bound the Arctic Sea. The ice commenced to grind and crush· the water to dash to and fro; and the vessel to rise and descend in a range of seventeen feet per day. On the 20th a depot-party was sent out, preparatory to the commencement of the operations of the summer. Those who remained in the ship commenced to clean it, to take down the forward bulwarks and to clear the decks. The necessary preparations for inland trips and researches were made; sledges and accoutrements were contrived, and moccasins were fabricated. While these labors occupied their attention, a portion of the depot party suddenly reäppeared at the vessel. They brought back a terrible report. They had left four of their number lying on the ice frozen and disabled, and they had returned a great distance to obtain instant relief.

Not a moment was to be lost. Ohlsen, the only one of the returned party who seemed able to give any information, was wrapped up in buffalo robes and placed upon a sledge. Nine men started out to the rescue. The cold was intense, ranging seventy-eight degrees below the freezing point. The instant the party ceased to move they would have been frozen to death. Violent exercise alone kept them alive. When they ventured to apply snow to their lips to slake their thirst, it burnt like caustic, and blood immediately followed. Some of the men were seized with trembling fits, and some with attacks of short breath. Dr. Kane himself, fainted twice upon the snow under the intense cold.

After a laborious and dangerous journey of twenty-one hours, the lost party were discovered. They were nearly forty miles distant from the brig. Their condition was perilous in the extreme; and the succor did not come a moment too soon. But the rescuers were scarcely better off than the rescued. They were compelled to drag a load of nine hundred pounds upon the sledge; and during their return trip the whole party were in imminent danger of being frozen to death. They could with the utmost difficulty resist the disposition to sleep, which would have immediately sealed their fate. After a fearful journey of several days the party regained the brig; but the sufferings of that terrible occasion were almost beyond the power of imagination. They had traveled about ninety miles; and most of the men had become temporarily delirious; nearly all were frozen in some portions of their bodies; and two of them ultimately died in consequence of their exposure.

On the 27th of April, the time having arrived to continue his researches both after Sir John Franklin and in Arctic discovery, Dr. Kane determined to resume his expeditions. He resolved now to follow the ice-belt to the Great Glacier of Humboldt, and thence to stretch along the face of the glacier, toward the west of north, and make an attempt to cross the ice to the American side of the channel. The object of this bold venture was to attain the utmost limit of the shore of Greenland; to measure the waste which extended between it and the unknown west; and thus to reveal, if possible, some of the mysteries which surrounded the North Pole. The journey was immediately commenced. After many adventures and sufferings which we will not describe, the Great Glacier of Humboldt was reached. A more magnificent object than this does not exist on the globe. It presents a shining wall of ice 300 feet in height, frowning over the frozen sea below, and extends unbroken for sixty miles. It is the great crystal bridge which has for ages connected together the two continents of America and Greenland, and it extends from the sea toward the interior, through vast and unknown regions.

Dr. Kane now determined to organize a double party, in order to ascertain whether a channel or any form of outlet existed to the northern extremity of the coast of Greenland. He was convinced of the existence of such a channel from the movements of the ice-bergs; from the physical character of the tides; as well as from certain and uniform analogies of physical geography.

On the 3d of June one of the parties of exploration set out from the brig. They had a large sledge thirteen feet long. They aimed directly for the glacier-barrier on the Greenland side. Their orders were to attempt to scale the ice and examine the interior of the great *mer-de-glace.*

On the 27th of June one of the parties, directed by McGarry and Bonsall, returned to the brig. Several of them had become nearly blind. After twelve days' travel they had reached the Great Glacier. They found the depot of provisions, which had been deposited the previous season, destroyed by the bears. These brutes had broken open the tin cases in which the pemmican had been deposited. An alcohol cask strongly bound in iron was dashed into fragments; and a tin liquor can was mashed and twisted into a ball. This party of explorers had found it impossible to scale the Great Glacier, and returned to the brig without having effected any results of importance.

The other party, which had been placed under the guidance of Mr. Morton, left the vessel on the 4th of June. On the 15th they reached the foot of the Great Glacier. They steered northward, keeping parallel with the glacier, and from five to seven miles distant from it. The thickness of the ice over which they journeyed was found to be seven feet five inches. They traveled frequently with the snow up to their knees. When they had reached Peabody Bay they encountered the bergs, whose surface was fresh and glassy. Some of these were rectangular in shape and some were square; and their length varied from a quarter of a mile to a mile. The task of traveling over these bergs was full of difficulty and danger. At length they made their way through them to the smoother ice which lay beyond.

On the 19th of June, having encamped, Morton ascended a high berg, in order to examine their future route and survey the surrounding desolation. From this point he beheld an extensive plain which stretched away toward the north, which proved to be the Great Glacier of Humboldt, as it appeared toward the interior, which also fronted on the bay. From this point the advance of the party was perilous. They were frequently arrested by wide and deep fissures in the ice. This difficulty compelled them to turn toward the west. Some of these chasms were four feet wide, and contained water at the bottom. From this point they beheld the distant northern shore, termed the "West Land." Its appearance was mountainous and rolling. Its distance from them seemed to be about sixty miles.

At length, by the 21st of June, the party reached a point opposite the termination of the Great Glacier. It appeared to be mixed with earth and rocks. Traveling on, they reached at length the head of Kennedy channel, and saw beyond that the open water. Passing in their route a cape, they called it Cape Andrew Jackson. Here they found good smooth ice; for during the last few days they had passed over rotten ice, which not unfrequently threatened to break beneath them. Having entered the curve of a bay, they named it after Robert Morris, the great financier of the revolution. On the smooth ice in this vicinity the party advanced at the rate of six miles per hour.

Kennedy Channel here grew narrower, but afterward it widened again. Broken ice in large masses was floating in it; but there were passages fifteen miles in width, which remained perfectly clear. Six miles inward from the channel, mountains rose to the view. On the 22d of June they encamped, after having traveled forty-eight miles in a direct line. They were still upon the shores of the channel. They could plainly see the opposite shore, which appeared precipitous, and surmounted with sugar-loaf shaped mountains. At this part of their journey they encountered a Polar bear, with her cub. A desperate fight ensued, in which the singular instincts of nature were strikingly illustrated, by the desperate efforts made by the poor brute to protect her helpless offspring. Both were slain. A shallow bay covered with ice was then crossed. They passed several islands which lay in the channel, which they named after Sir John Franklin and Captain Crozier. The cliffs which here constituted the shore of the channel were very high, towering at least two thousand feet above its surface. The party attempted to ascend these cliffs; but found it impossible to mount more than a few hundred feet. On the highest point which they attained, a walking pole was fastened, with the Grinnell flag of the *Antartic* attached to it; and thus for an hour and a half this standard was permitted to wave over the highest northern region of the earth ever attained by the foot of man.

They here encountered a cape, and the party desired to pass around it, in order to ascertain whether there lay any unknown land beyond it. But they found it impossible to advance. This then was the utmost limit and termination of their journey toward the pole. Mr. Morton ascended an eminence here, and carefully scrutinized the aspects of nature all around him. Six degrees toward the west of north, he observed a lofty peak, truncated in its form, and about three thousand feet in height. This elevation is named Mount Edward Parry, after the great pioneer of Arctic adventure; and is the most extreme northern point of land known to exist upon the globe. From the position which Mr. Morton had attained, he beheld toward the north, from an elevation of four hundred feet, a boundless waste of waters stretching away toward the pole. Not a particle of ice encumbered its surface. He heard the dashing of unfrozen waves, and beheld a rolling surf like that of more genial climes, rushing and dashing against the rocks upon the shore. This was certainly a mysterious phenomenon. Here was a fluid sea, in the midst of whole continents of ice, and that sea seemed to wash the Pole itself. The eye of the explorer surveyed at least forty miles of uninterrupted water in a northern direction. The point thus reached in this exploring expedition, was about five hundred miles distant from the Pole. Had the party been able to convey thither a boat, they might have embarked upon the bright and placid waters of that lonely ocean. But having been able to make this journey only with the sledge, further explorations were of course impossible. The most remarkable development connected with these discoveries was, that the temperature was here found to be much more moderate than it was further south. Marine birds sailed through the heavens. Rippling waves followed each other on the surface of the deep. A few stunted flowers grew over the barren and rocky shore. The inference which may be drawn from these and other facts is, that this open sea, termed the Polar Basin, stretches to the Pole itself, or at least continues a great distance until its course is interrupted by other projections of the terra firma. These are mysterious inquiries, still the great *desiderata* of Arctic travel; which will remain unanswered, until some more successful explorer, gifted with greater physical endurance, if any such can be, and furnished with ampler and more abundant facilities than any of his predecessors, shall persist in defiance of every impediment in advancing, until he boldly plants his foot upon the very spot now termed the North Pole.

The several parties which had been sent forth by Dr. Kane, to explore the regions just described, having returned, the season of Arctic travel had nearly terminated, and the members of the expedition were about to relapse into winter quarters, with their usual darkness, monotony, and gloom. But before resigning themselves entirely to this unwelcome seclusion, Dr. Kane resolved to make an effort to reach Beechey Island. At this point, already so frequently referred to in the preceding pages, Sir Edward Belcher's squadron was then supposed to be stationed; and from them the American explorers might obtain both provisions and information. Accordingly, Dr. Kane manned his boat, called the "Forlorn Hope," which was twenty-three feet long, and six feet and a half beam. The necessary amount of provisions were placed on board, and the bold venture was undertaken. Sometimes the boat was navigated through the unfrozen channels of water, which intervened between the floes of ice; at others she was placed on a large sledge called the "Faith," and thus transported over the frozen wastes.

This party approached Littleton Island, which had been visited by Captain Inglefield. They here obtained a vast quantity of eider ducks. They then passed Flagstaff Point and Combermere Cape. Then came Cape Isabella and Cape Frederick VII. On the 23d of July they reached Hakluyt Island; and thence they steered for Cary Islands. But on the 31st of July, when they had reached a point but ten miles distant from Cape Parry, their further progress was absolutely stopped. A solid mass of ice lay before them on the sea, extending as far as the eye could reach. This barrier was composed of the vast seas of ice which had drifted through Jones' Sound on the west, and those of Murchison's on the east. The adventurers were now compelled to retrace their way. About the 1st of August they regained the brig, without having met with any accident, but also without having succeeded in attaining the object of their excursion. They found the "Advance" just as tightly wedged into the ice as it had been during the preceding eleven months, with no hope of getting her released. Two important questions now demand-

RICHARDSON & COX SC.

ed their attention. The first was, how they were to pass this, their second winter in the Arctic regions; and how they were to make their escape in the ensuing spring.

Whatever might be the issue of the future, Dr. Kane determined to leave a memorial at the spot which he then occupied, to prove to his successors the fact that he and his expedition had been there. He painted the words "Advance, A. D. 1853–54," upon the broad face of a rock, which rested on a high cliff looking out upon the frozen waste. Near this spot a hole was drilled into the rock, and a paper containing a history of the expedition and its present condition, was placed in glass, and sealed into the cavity with melted lead. Close at hand were buried the corpses of the two members of the expedition who had already ended their toils and sufferings.

The prospect of a second winter amid the eternal snows and ice of the Polar Circle, was not inviting to the adventurers. A portion of them felt convinced of the practicability of an immediate escape to the south. On the 24th of August Dr. Kane summoned all hands together, and clearly stated to them the aspects of the case. He advised that all should remain by the brig till the next spring; although he declared that those who wished to return could make the attempt. Eight men concluded to remain; and nine of them resolved that, rather than endure the miseries of a second winter near the Pole, they would run the risks of an instant attempt to escape. This resolution they made immediate preparations to execute. A full share of the remaining provisions was measured out to them. They were assured of a welcome reception if they chose to return; and they started forth on August 28th from the brig. One of this party returned to the vessel in a few days; the rest wandered for many months, and endured much misery and exposure, before they rejoined their wiser comrades in the brig.

Dr. Kane and the eight men who remained with him, immediately began to prepare for the horrors of the ensuing winter. They gathered a large amount of moss with which they lined and padded the quarter-deck. This expedient rendered their cabin imperious to the changes and the extreme severity of the atmosphere. They stripped off the outer-deck planking of the brig, for the purpose of fire-wood. The chief necessity of the explorers was fresh meat, to guard them against the scurvy. To obtain this food, frequent excursions were made for the purpose of capturing seals. On one of these occasions Dr. Kane narrowly escaped a watery grave. He was at twelve miles' distance from the brig, with a single attendant. The ice broke beneath their sledge, and they were precipitated into the water. After great exertions and amid extreme danger, they succeeded in regaining ice sufficiently strong to bear their weight. They lost their sledge, tent, kayack, guns, and snow-shoes.

At length, by the 21st of October, the rays of the sun had ceased to reach them; and darkness—the cold and cheerless darkness of an Arctic night settled down upon them. They were compelled to confine themselves to the precincts of their gloomy cabin, and waste away as best they could, the slow hours of their long winter. Their only light was an occasional aurora, whose pale, bright arch of brilliant hues seemed to be resting on the distant Pole. The thermometer now ranged 34° below zero. Thus, in this strange monotony of routine and incident, November and December wore away; except that during the latter month, a portion of the party who had deserted the brig on the 28th of August previous, returned to their old quarters. They had suffered much; and had left the remainder of their party two hundred miles distant in the midst of great destitution. The thermometer was then fifty degrees below zero. When Christmas came it was celebrated for the second time by this gallant crew of heroes, amid the Arctic solitudes, with such means as they could command—which indeed were few; and thus ended with them the year 1854.

The three most dangerous and dreary months of the year—January, February, and March—were now before them. During these months it was exceedingly difficult for the adventurers to procure fresh meat, which was their only preventive and cure of scurvy. With this disease every member of the party became at last infected; some so seriously that their lives were in danger. Thus the dreary drama of their Arctic exile dragged on. They waited patiently for the time to arrive when they could commence the necessary preparations for the journey of thirteen hundred miles which they would undertake in the spring. The vessel would evidently remain so firmly fixed in an ocean of ice, that its removal would be utterly impossible. Their return must be effected with the combined use of sledges and boats. Yet before commencing a final retreat, Dr. Kane resolved to attempt once more a northern excursion, hoping that it might result in some useful discovery connected with the object of the expedition.

The region which was yet to be explored was the farther shores beyond Kennedy Channel. The aid of the dogs was indispensable to the accomplishment of this task; and there were but four left out of the sixty-two, which composed their stock when they left Newfoundland. An arrangement was however made with Kalutunah, one of the wandering Esquimaux whom they knew, for the use of his dogs and three sledges. Thus reënforced, Dr. Kane, accompanied by several experienced Esquimaux travelers, commenced his journey. In two hours they reached a lofty berg fifteen miles north of the brig. The view of the channel presented from the summit of this berg was not very favorable. The outside channel seemed filled with squeezed ice; and on the frozen plain beyond, the bergs appeared to be much distorted.

Nevertheless, Dr. Kane resolved to make the venture. They quickly passed fifteen miles further; when the party halted to feed and rest. The journey was then resumed. But unfortunately the traces of a Polar bear soon attracted the attention of the Esquimaux, and the temptation was too strong for famished men to resist. A chase ensued. The animal was quickly brought to bay, attacked, and dispatched. Then ensued another gorge, and after the gorge there necessarily came an interval of repose and sleep.

A sleep of four hours' duration ensued upon the open snow; after which the party arose and resumed their journey. Dr. Kane desired to steer directly to the northward; but his associates declared that to cross so high up as they then were, was impossible. The fate of Baker and Schubert in the preceding year, who attempted this feat, recurred to their recollection, and convinced them that the attempt would be then extremely hazardous. Again was the leader of the expedition fated to experience a disappointment, and to return to the brig without having accomplished the purpose for which he set forth. But before he did so, he embraced the opportunity which was within his reach, once more to examine the Great Humboldt Glacier, one of the most remarkable monuments in nature. The whole horizon before him was bounded by long lines of ice-bergs. They undulated about the horizon, but as they descended to the sea, they resembled an uneven plain with an inclination of about nine degrees, still diminishing as they approached the foreground. Vast crevasses appeared in the distance like mere wrinkles. These grew larger as they approached the sea, where they expanded into gigantic stairways.

The appearance of this Great Humboldt Glacier resembles in some respects the frozen masses of the Alps; and reminded the bold adventurer of many scenes which he had witnessed in the mountains of Norway and Switzerland. The average height of this great glacier along the water's edge was about three hundred feet; and this height was presented by an uniform perspective of sixty miles in length; thus exhibiting one of the most sublime and imposing spectacles which the mind can conceive. The configurations of its surface and form clearly indicate that its inequalities follow those of the rocky soil on which it rests. Having made various observations upon the phenomena connected with this glacier, Dr. Kane resumed his return toward the brig. The company traveled over the frozen surface of the ice to the south of Peabody Bay. The first spot at which they landed was called Cape James Kent. It was a rugged and lofty headland; and it presented in the distance a strange spectacle of a rude surface, covered with millions of tons of rubbish, rocks of every imaginable shape, and slates of immense size and of infinite variety of forms. On the south-eastern corner of Marshall Bay the party found a group of Esquimaux remains, consisting of a few deserted huts and graves. They were the rude and melancholy relics of a race of lonely wanderers who had passed away. These remains were surrounded by the bones of the seal and the walrus, and the dissevered vertebræ of a whale. There were indications that the spot had long been deserted; and yet no changes had been effected by the silent lapse of time in those frozen and primeval solitudes, in the appearance and position of these simple monuments.

This journey was enlivened by several interesting bear hunts; and a few details respecting this Arctic entertainment may here not be inappropriate.

The dogs with which these hunts are carried on, are very carefully trained to play their part. This part is not to attack the bear, but to hinder and impede his flight. While one of these dogs occupies his attention in front, another salutes his hind legs with vigorous bites. This keeps the animal oscillating between several distinct parties of foes; and while he is battling with one and the other, the hunters come up. In the first instance, as soon as the bear sees the approach of the dogs and men, he rises on his haunches, carefully inspects his foes for a moment, and then takes to his heels. As the hunter approaches him, if he is riding on his sledge he loosens the traces of his two foremost dogs, which releases them from their burden, and enables them to attack the bear. Soon after, the rest of the dogs are liberated in the same way. When there are two hunters, bruin is soon and easily dispatched. They surround him, and while one of them pretends to stab him with a spear on the right side, and thus engages the bear in his defense in that direction, the death wound is inflicted on the left by the same weapon. If there be but one hunter, the task is neither so easy nor so safe. The hunter grasps his lance firmly in his hands, and provokes the bear to pursue him by running across his path, and then pretending to flee. When the bear has begun the chase, the hunter suddenly doubles on his track by a dexterous leap; and while the bear is in the act of turning around, he is stabbed with the spear in his left side below the shoulder. If this stab be skillfully executed, the bear is at once disabled and soon expires. If it is not, the hunter has then to run for his life, after leaving his spear sticking in the side of his victim. If the bear gets the hunter in his grasp, he salutes him with divers hugs and squeezes, which are much more vigorous and affectionate than agreeable. He sometimes also uses his teeth. Dr. Kane saw some Esquimaux hunters who had been bitten behind in the calves of the legs; and another who had received a similar salute somewhat higher up.

Having returned to the brig, Dr. Kane resumed his preparations for final departure. Frozen fast as she was in the ice, there was no possibility of removing her. The only possible means of escape was by the combined use of boats and sledges. The party went to work industriously in the manufacture of clothing suitable to the journey. Canvas moccasins were made for each of the party, and a surplus supply of three dozen was added to the stock. Their boots were made of carpeting, with soles of walrus or seal hide, and some had been fabricated from the chafing gear of the brig. Other portions of their clothing were made out of blankets. Every one acted as his own tailor. Their bedding was made out of the woolen curtains with which their berths in the brig had been adorned. These were quilted with eider down, and buffalo robes were added to increase their warmth.

Their provision bags consisted of sail-cloth, made water-tight by the application of tar and pitch. They were of various sizes, so as to be more conveniently stowed away in the boats. The ship-bread was powdered by being beaten with a capstan-bar, and then pressed down into the bags. Pork-fat and tallow being melted down, were poured into other bags as into moulds, and thus left to freeze. Concentrated bean-soup was cooked up and prepared in the same way. The flour and meat-biscuit were protected from moisture in double bags. Dr. Kane's plan was to subsist his party for some time after they left the brig, by new supplies of provisions which he could bring from the vessel by trips with his dog-team.

The means of conveyance which were to carry the company on this long and weary journey, and which were to be carried by them in a great measure, consisted of three boats. These had all suffered very materially from exposure to the ice and the Arctic storms; and were scarcely sea-worthy. They were strengthened and tinkered in every possible way by oak bottom-pieces, and by wash-boards which protected the gunwales and gave them greater depth. A housing of canvas was stretched upon a ridge line, which was suspended by stanchions, and which were fastened over the sides of the boats to jack-stays.

Each boat had a single mast, and it was so arranged that it could be easily unshipped, and carried alongside the boat. The boats were mounted on sledges. The provisions were stored carefully under the thwarts. The boats were to be drawn by the men with rue-raddies, or straps, which passed over the shoulder and were attached by a long trace to the sledge. The philosophical instruments were carefully boxed and padded, and placed in the stern-sheets of one of the boats. Spy-glasses and small instruments the travelers carried on their persons. The powder and shot, which now became of infinite value to them, were distributed in bags and tin canisters. The percussion caps, the most valuable of all, Dr. Kane himself took charge of and reserved.

Having made all the preparations which were possible under the circumstances of the case, Dr. Kane announced to his crew that he appointed the 17th of May as the day of their final departure from the brig. Each man was allowed to select and retain eight pounds of personal effects. The announcement of their final departure toward the south was not received by the members of the expedition with the enthusiasm which Dr. Kane had expected. Some doubted the reality of the journey home; and suspected that it was merely a maneuver to remove the sick to the hunting grounds. Others thought that the real purpose was only to journey further south, whilst the brig was retained as a refuge for them to retreat to; while others suspected that their leader merely wished to reach some point on the coast where he could obtain a rescue from passing whalers, or from some of the English Arctic expeditions which were still supposed to be lingering in those remote regions. The sick among the crew, who had long been accustomed to inaction and indulgence, declared themselves unfit to be removed, and unable to travel a mile.

But in spite of all these obstacles, the resolution of the commander of the expedition was unalterable.

He was determined to commence this memorable journey on the day appointed, at all hazards. At length the day preceding that of departure arrived. The boats were removed from the brig and placed upon the ice. This process seemed to revive to some degree the desponding spirits of the men. The provisions were then conveyed into them; and other necessary transfers were made. After some hours of active operations, the whole of their task was completed; and the men returned on board the brig, in order to spend their last night in that familiar shelter. After supper they retired to rest, in order to recruit their energies for the toils which were to commence on the ensuing day, upon the final success of which their future existence depended.

At length the wished-for moment arrived when the weary adventurers were to take their last farewell of the vessel which had been associated with them in so many vicissitudes and dangers. All hands were assembled together in silence in the winter chamber. The day was Sunday, and the exercises began by the reading of a chapter of the scriptures. Dr. Kane then took Sir John Franklin's portrait from its frame, and enclosed it in an Iudia-rubber scroll. The several reports of inspection and survey were then read, which set forth what results had already been attained, and contained the reasons which induced the commander of the expedition to take the steps which were to ensue. He then addressed his men in reference to the journey on which they were about to enter, explaining its necessity, the method according to which it was to be conducted, and the certainty of final relief and escape which it would bring them, if they resolutely persisted in carrying it out. Thirteen hundred miles of ice and water lay between their present position and the shores of North Greenland. He closed by directing their hopes of safety, not unfitly, to that great Unseen Power who had already rescued them from a thousand deaths, and who would continue to be their very present help in every time of need.

The men responded to the sentiments and purposes expressed by Dr. Kane with more enthusiasm than he seems to have anticipated. They drew up a statement in which they expressed their conviction of the necessity which existed of abandoning the brig; the impossibility of remaining a third winter in the ice; the obligation which rested on them to convey the sick carefully along with them; and their determination to coöperate with their leader in his proposed measures of escape. This statement was handed to Dr. Kane. He also had prepared a narrative of the considerations which induced him to abandon the vessel. This he posted to a stanchion near the gangway, so that it might attract the attention of any one who approached the vessel. The party then went on deck; the flags were hoisted to the mast-head, and lowered again; the men paraded twice around the brig, carefully scrutinizing her timbers, associated in their minds with so many pleasing and painful recollections; and having thus saluted the vessel for the last time, they rushed away over the ice toward the boats, which had already been removed, filled with their cargo, and made ready to commence their homeward journey.

The whole return party consisted of seventeen persons, including Dr. Kane. Four of these were sick, and unable to move. The rest were divided into two companies, and appropriated to the several boats. Dr. Kane took charge of the dog-team, which was to be used for the purpose of conveying provisions from the vessel to the crew, during the first few days of their journey. To the boat called "Faith," McGary, Ohlsen, Bonsall, Petersen, and Hickey were assigned. To the "Hope," Morton, Sontag, Riley, Blake, and Godfrey were detailed.

The first stage of the journey was to a spot called Anoatok, which had been a halting place in their winter journeys. It was a single hut, composed of rude and heavy stones, and resembled a cave more than it did a house. Strange to say, this bleak and forlorn corner of that frozen hemisphere, the gloomiest and most detestable on the whole face of the globe, bore a name which was imposed by the least poetical of human beings, the Esquimaux, which was not devoid of beauty; for Anoatok in the jargon of the shivering natives means "the wind-loved spot." It was perched on the extreme point of a rocky promontory, and commanded a wide view of the icy straits, both toward the north and south.

Dr. Kane had exerted himself to repair the hut, and make it fit to shelter the sick. He had added a door to its broken outlet, and had introduced a stove and stove-pipe. Other improvements had been made. A solitary pane of glass, which once had faced a daguerreotype, was inserted in the door, to give a scanty light. The provisions which had been removed to this place were eight hundred pounds in weight. Seven hundred pounds still remained in the brig, to be removed by successive journeys of the dog-team. The services of these six dogs were indeed invaluable. In addition to all their previous journeys, they carried Dr. Kane to and fro, with a well-burdened sledge, nearly eight hundred miles during the first two weeks after they left the brig, being an average of fifty-seven miles per day.

So feeble and reduced were the parties who dragged the two boats, that they advanced but a mile a day, and on the 24th had only made seven miles. The halts were regulated entirely by the condition of the men who required longer rest at some periods than at others. The thermometer ranged below zero, and the men slept at night in the boats, protected by their canvas coverings. Had it not been for the shelter which the hut at Anoatok afforded, the four sick men—Goodfellow, Wilson, Whipple, and Stephenson—they must have perished. At the time of their removal into it, they were so drawn up with the scurvy that they were wholly unable to move. Yet their delay in this hut was extremely gloomy; for it lasted from the time that they were removed from the brig, until they were carried forward by the sledge to the boats which had been dragged by their respective crews in advance of them. During this interval they were carefully fed and attended by Dr. Kane.

Dr. Kane's visits to the brig from time to time, in order to obtain supplies of provisions, were full of interest to him. On the first of these he found the vessel already inhabited by an old raven, which had often been seen hovering around, and whom they had called Magog. The fire was lighted in the galley, the pork was melted, large batches of bread were baked, dried apples were stewed, and then the sledge was made ready to return with the load. Such was usually the routine of Dr. Kane's lonely visits to the brig. After the first of these visits, when he returned to the "wind-loved spot," Anoatok, with his sledge, he found that the sick who still remained there had exhausted their provisions; that their single lamp had gone out; that the snow drifts had forced their way in at the door, so that it could not be shut; that the wind was blowing furiously through the open tenement; and that the thermometer ranged only thirteen degrees above zero. The invalids were disheartened and hungry. A fire was built with tarred rope; a porridge was prepared for them out of meat biscuit and pea soup; the door was fastened up; a dripping slab of fat pork was suspended over their lamp wick; and then all turned into their sleeping bags, after a hearty though not very savory meal. So overcome were they all with exposure and weakness, that they slept until after all their watches had run down.

Dr. Kane then hurried forward to the sledge party, who had by that time reached Ten Mile Ravine. They were struggling with the deep snows, were overwhelmed with fatigue, and were somewhat disheartened. Although their feet were much swollen, they had toiled that day for fourteen hours. Some were suffering from snow-blindness, and were scarcely able to work at the drag-ropes. In spite of all their toils and sufferings, morning and evening prayers were constantly read by the adventurers. Meanwhile the sledge party advanced slowly toward the south. On the 28th Dr. Kane paid his last visit to the brig. He was compelled to leave behind his collections in Natural History, his library, and some of his instruments, such as his theodolite and chart-box, the useless daguerrotypes, and other companions and mementoes of Arctic toil and suffering. Then he mounted his sledge; gave a last look at the blackened hull and spars of the Advance; fiercely whipped up his dogs in a paroxysm of mournful gloom; and sped away for the last time, over the snowy waste which had been associated with so many recollections. Thus was left behind at last in its frozen bed, the vessel which had been connected with two Arctic expeditions, one of which is the most remarkable on record; and there doubtless she remains, an unseen monument of human enterprise, benevolence, and endurance.

From Anoatok Dr. Kane's next labor was to remove the provisions and men further on in their route. A friendly Esquimaux, named Metek, was sent forward to the next station, with two bags of bread-dust, each weighing ninety pounds. The next station was Etah Bay. About midnight Dr. Kane approached that vicinity. The sun was low in the heavens, and the air around was marked by that peculiar stillness which accompanies the great solitudes of nature. While feeling the oppressive weight of that silence, his ears were suddenly greeted by unexpected sounds of mirth and laughter. He had approached an encampment of the wandering Esquimaux, consisting of about thirty men, women, and children. The cause of their joy was the capture of innumerable birds, called Auks, which they were engaged in catching with nets. These birds, though the thermometer was five degrees below zero, were flying about in the greatest abundance; and the hungry Esquimaux were eating them raw, as soon as taken. He saw two children fighting for an owl, which as soon as captured was torn limb from limb, and its warm flesh eaten, and its blood drunken, almost before life was extinct. This was the spot which these birds mysteriously chose for the purpose of breeding, from year to year; and the Esquimaux as regularly found their way thither in pursuit of them.

The travelers continued their weary march through the snow, dragging their boats after them. Sometimes, when the weather moderated—for it was summer—the sledges broke through. Six men on one occasion were thrown into the water; and the "Hope" was very nearly lost. Help came to them from the Esquimaux at Etah, who sent them the loan of their dogs, together with an additional supply of fresh provisions. The dogs were of infinite service in drawing one of the sledges, upon which the sick men were conveyed. At this period an accident deprived the expedition by death of one of its most useful members. While crossing a tide-hole, one of the runners of the "Hope" sledge broke through the ice. The energy and presence of mind of Christian Ohlsen alone saved her from being lost. By a prodigious effort he passed a capstan-bar under the sledge, and thus sustained its weight until it was dragged forward to firm ice. In doing this his footing gave way beneath him; and he thus was compelled to strain himself. The effort ruined him. Some internal injury had been inflicted by the effort; and he died three days afterward. His body was sewed up in his own blankets, and carried in procession to the head of a little gorge to the east of Pekiutlik, where a grave was excavated in the frozen earth. There his body was deposited with a few simple and appropriate ceremonies. His name and age were inscribed by the commander on a strip of sheet lead; and ere his grave was filled by his comrades, the brief and touching memorial was laid upon his manly breast. A small mound was then erected with rocks and stones over his lonely resting-place; and there now sleep, in that cheerless and wintry tomb, the remains of Christian Ohlsen.

By the 6th of June the party reached Littleton Island. From a lofty height here of some eight hundred feet, Dr. Kane obtained his first view of the open water. His position at that time was 78° 22′ 1″ latitude, and 74° 10′ longitude. So weary were the men of dragging the sledges over the snow and ice, that they wished to take the direct route to the water, upon which they were eager to embark with the boats. But the dangers of the plan proposed overruled their wishes, and the inland route, though longer, was selected. The wished-for water which greeted the eyes of the weary travelers, was Hartstein Bay; and they welcomed it with emotions of rapture resembling those which, as Xenophon records, filled the minds and excited the enthusiasm of the ten thousand Greeks when, after their long and perilous march through Asia Minor, and their escape from the myriads of Artaxerxes, they first beheld the distant waves of the sea whose billows laved the shores of their beloved Greece.

On the 16th of June the party reached the water. It was at the northern curve of the North Baffin Bay. The surf roared sublimely in their ears, and sounded like sweet music after their long and cheerless absence from its bosom. The next thing to be done was to prepare the boats for the difficult navigation which was to ensue. They were not sea-worthy. They had been split with frost, warped by the sunshine, and were open at the seams. They were to be calked, swelled, launched, and stowed. On the 18th the travelers were surrounded by all the Esquimaux who had been assembled at Etah. They had come to bid the strangers farewell, whom they had served to the best of their ability at an earlier stage of their journey. They were indeed a miserable and forlorn race, though kindly and confiding in their dispositions. They received various presents and keepsakes from the travelers—such as knives, files, saws, and lumps of soap. They had been of great service in lending hand-sledges and dogs; in helping to carry baggage and the sick from one station to another, along their weary route; and they parted from the strangers—probably the last they were destined ever to behold in that repulsive clime—with feelings of regret which they did not conceal. Dr. Kane urged them to emigrate further south; for there they could obtain more abundant food, and escape the perils of starvation which constantly surrounded them.

On the evening of Sunday, June 17th, the party hauled their boats through the hummocks, reached the open sea, and launched their frail craft upon its waters. But Eolus seemed determined not to permit them yet to embark; for he let loose his fiercest winds, which began to dash a heavy *wind-lipper* against the ice-floe, and obliged the party to remove their boats back with each new breakage of the ice. The goods which had been stacked upon the ice were conveyed further inward to the distance of several hundred yards. The storm continued to rage, and to forbid them to venture on the treacherous element. At last Dr. Kane saw the necessity of permitting the worn-out men to repose, and in order to do so securely, the boats were removed a mile from the water's edge. The sea tore up the ice to the very base of the berg to which they had fled for refuge, and the angry deep seemed like a vast cauldron, boiling with intense fury, while the immense fragments of ice crashed and rolled together with a sound resembling thunder.

At length the storm subsided, and the troubled sea

became tranquil. The boats were again prepared for embarkation. On Tuesday, the 19th, Dr. Kane succeeded in getting the Faith afloat, and he was soon followed by the two other boats. Soon the wind freshened, and the mariners began their welcome progress homeward; but they had a long and perilous voyage before them of many hundred miles. At length they doubled Cape Alexander. They desired first to halt at Sutherland Island; but the ice-belt which hugged its shores was too steep to permit them to land. They then steered for Hakluyt Island, but had not proceeded far before the red boat swamped. The crew were compelled to swim to the other boats; and the former was with difficulty kept afloat, and dragged in tow by her comrades. Dr. Kane then fastened his boats to an old floe; and thus sheltered, the men obtained their second halt and rest. When they had become somewhat refreshed, they rowed for Hakluyt Island, at a point less repulsive and impracticable than the one attempted the day before. A spit to the southward gave them an opportunity to haul up the boats on the land-ice, as the tide rose. From this the men dragged the boats to the rocks above and inland; and were thus secure. It snowed heavily during the ensuing night. A tent was prepared for the sick; and a few birds were luckily obtained to vary their stale diet of bread-dust and tallow.

On the next morning, the 22d, the snow storm still continued to pelt them; but they pressed onward toward Northumberland Island, and reached it. They rowed their boats into a small inlet of open water, which conducted them to the beach directly beneath a hanging glacier which towered sublimely into the heavens to the immense height of eleven hundred feet.

The next day they crossed Murchison Channel, and at night encamped at the base of Cape Parry. The day had been laboriously spent in tracking over the ice, and in sailing through tortuous leads. The day following they reach ed Fitz Clarence Rock; one of the most singular forms to be seen in that strange clime. It rises to an immense height from a vast field of ice, having the shape of an Egyptian pyramid surmounted by an obelisk. In more frequented waters it would be a valued landmark to the navigator.

Still they continued to toil onward from day to day. Their progress was satisfactory, though their labor was exhausting. Dr. Kane sometimes continued sixteen hours in succession at the helm. But now their allowance of food began to grow scanty. It was reduced to six ounces of bread-dust per day, and a lump of tallow about the size of a walnut. An occasional cup of tea was their only consolation. From this stage in their journey Dalrymple Rock became perceptible in the distance. But the physical strength of the men began to give way beneath their labors and their insufficient diet. At this crisis a gale struck them from the north-west, and a floe, one end of which having grounded on a tongue of ice about a mile to the northward of them, began to swing round toward the boats, and threaten to enclose and crush them. Soon the destruction of the surrounding ice threatened their own. For hundreds of yards on every side around them the ice was crumbled, crushed, and piled in irregular and fragmentary masses. The thunder of the confused ocean of frozen wrecks was overpowering. Suddenly the ice seemed to separate and form a channel; and in that channel, so unexpectedly opened before them, the men rowed the boats with the aid of their boat hooks, and escaped a danger which a moment before seemed inevitable and ruinous. Soon they found themselves in a lead of land-water, wide enough to give them rowing room, and they hastened on to the land, which loomed ahead. Reaching it, they eagerly sought a shelter. The Hope here stove her bottom, and lost part of her weather-boarding. The water broke over them, for the storm still continued.

At length the tide rose high enough at three o'clock to enable them to scale the ice-cliff. They succeeded in pulling the boats into a deep and narrow gorge, which opened between the towering cliffs. The rocks seemed almost to close above their heads. An abrupt curve in the windings of this gorge placed a protecting rock behind them, which shielded them from the violence of the winds and waves. They had reached a haven of refuge which was almost a cave; where they found a flock of eider ducks on which they feasted; and where for three days they reposed from the dangers and labors of their voyage. This retreat they fitly called Weary Man's Rest.

The fourth day of July having arrived, it was commemorated by the adventurers by a few diluted and moderate potations, such as their nearly exhausted whisky flask permitted; and they then embarked and rowed industriously toward Wolstenholme Island. During some succeeding days, they continued slowly to progress toward the south, through the various lanes of water which opened between the belt-ice and the floe. By this time, the constant collisions between the boats and the floating ice had rendered them quite unseaworthy. The ice had strained their bottom timbers, and constant baling was necessary. Their fresh meat had all been consumed, and the men were now reduced again to short rations of bread-dust.

On the 11th of July they approached Cape Dudley Digges; but their progress was suddenly stopped by an immense tongue of floe which extended out to sea for a prodigious distance. They forced their way into a lead of sludge, and attempted thus to advance. They found this to be impossible; and were glad to make their escape from it. Dr. Kane was at a loss how to proceed. He mounted an ice-berg to reconnoiter the surrounding prospect. It was gloomy and repulsive in the extreme. They were in advance of the season; and he discovered that in those waters toward Cape York, the floes had not yet broken up.

They seemed to be surrounded in a *cul-de-sae*, with exhausted strength and food, and no possibility of escaping until the summer had broken open for them a pathway of escape through the water.

Dr. Kane resolved to steer for the rocky shore. Above a narrow ledge of lofty cliffs mounted one over the other to the prodigious height of eleven hundred feet. The waves dashed violently against that ledge; but still it afforded a shelter to the boats. Here they were for the present again deposited; and fortunately a quantity of gulls were found in the crevices of the rocks, which afforded the famished wanderers nutricious food. The glacier which stretched away in front of them was about seven miles across. On ascending the heights above him, Dr. Kane enjoyed a magnificent prospect of the frozen ocean, the *mer-de-glace*, whose glittering surface spread out before and around him. A vast undulating plain of purple-colored ice appeared, extending to the limits of the horizon, resplendent with the varied hues of sun-tipped crystal. This spot, where the wanderers enjoyed so welcome a repose, such nutricious food, and such sublime perspective, they named Providence Halt. Here they remained till the 18th of July.

In resuming their voyage from this point, they encountered an accident which might have proved very serious. When they launched the Hope, she was precipitated into the sludge in such a manner as to carry away her rail and bulwark. They lost overboard their best shot-gun, and an equally indispensable utensil, their kettle which had served them in every possible capacity of kettle—such as soup-kettle, paste-kettle, tea-kettle, and water-kettle. Sailing along they passed the Crimson Cliffs, so named by Sir John Ross. They continued thence to hug the shore. The weather now moderated; and their voyage assumed more agreeable and genial features. The men frequently landed, climbed up the steep cliffs and obtained abundant quantities of auks. Fires were kindled with the turf, and the feasts which ensued were relished with more than an ordinary appetite; and that also the more truly, because the travelers well knew that their good fortune, and their propitious seas and weather, would not long continue. They were now in 78° 20′ north latitude.

On the 21st of June they reached Cape York. Their provisions had now diminished to six hundred and forty pounds, or about thirty-six pounds to each man. The question to be determined was, whether they should delay where they then were for some days until the shore-ice opened; or whether they should desert the coast and venture boldly upon the open water to the west. Dr. Kane ascended the rocks upon the shore, and by the aid of his glass carefully scrutinized the ice. The latter could be seen immoveably fixed to the shore in nearly an unbroken sweep far beyond Bushnell Island. The outside floes were large; and one large lead appeared to the view which seemed to follow the main floe until it was lost to seaward.

Dr. Kane explained to his men the motives which induced him to adopt the course upon which he had determined. The boats were then hauled on shore, examined, and repaired. One of these, the Red Erie, was stripped of her cargo and prepared to be broken up as soon as occasion should require. A beacon was also erected on an eminence, which could be discerned both from the south and the west, surmounted by a red flannel shirt. Under the cairn was deposited a short narrative of the condition and purposes of the party. They then resumed their voyage steering south by west through the ice-fields. For a while they progressed safely enough. But soon the irregularities of the surface, loaded as it was by hummocks and even larger masses, made it difficult to discern the state of the ice in the distance. At length they lost their way; the officer at the helm of the leading boat deceived by the irregular shape of a large iceberg, had deserted the proper lead, and had steered far out of the true course.

Dr. Kane at once ordered a halt, and ascending an ice-berg some three hundred feet in height, he surveyed the prospect. It was by no means encouraging. They had advanced into the recesses of the bay, and were surrounded on all sides by immense ice-bergs and floating ice. So dismal appeared their situation that one of the sturdiest members of the expedition, who accompanied the commander in his survey, burst into tears at the sadness of their situation.

There was but one means of deliverance, and that it behooved them to adopt instantly. They must resume their sledges and retrace their way to the westward. One sledge had already been cut up for fire-wood. The boat Red Erie now shared the same fate; and was laid upon the floor of the other boats. Three days of hard dragging over the ice ensued; at the end of which time they regained the ice-berg which had misled them in the first instance, and had induced them to take a course which had nearly ended in their ruin. From this point made easier by experience, they steered in the right direction into a free lead, and were wafted onward by a friendly breeze from the north.

Another trouble now assailed the travelers, not less important than the one they had just escaped. Their provisions had fearfully diminished, and yet they were hundreds of miles distant from the nearest Danish settlement of Greenland. Their strength diminished in proportion with their food. The latter had become so much lessened, that five ounces of bread-dust, four ounces of tallow, and three of bird's meat, were all that could be thenceforward allowed each man per day. The commander now determined to try the more open sea, as their progress along the coast had been retarded by its sinuosities. During two days heavy fogs impeded their rapid advance. A south-westerly wind brought the outside pack upon them, and compelled them to haul up on the drifting ice. By this means they were drifted with it twenty miles away from their proper course. The labors and toils of the party were extreme and exhausting; and yet they manfully kept up their spirits.

A strange phenomenon now showed itself among them; and one too of ominous import. Though worked excessively they yet felt no hunger. They also seemed to lose their physical strength. The "Faith" also very nearly escaped destruction, by being left behind for a short time. The outside pressure had broken the floe asunder, and the Faith began to float away from them. Her loss would have entailed that of a large portion of the scanty provisions which they still possessed; and would have inevitably sealed their ruin. By the utmost exertions of the men, some of whom seemed nearly thrown into hysterics by her threatened loss, she was again secured.

The situation of the voyagers continued to become more critical. They experienced a difficulty in breathing, and an inability to sleep. Their line of travel lay through the open bay, in the midst of the great ice-drift which hurried from the Arctic climes into the Atlantic ocean. Their boats were frail and shattered, and constantly made enough water to require their utmost exertions in bailing, in order to keep them afloat. Their fresh food had been exhausted for some days; and they suffered from a low fever which prostrated them to the utmost.

At this point of their progress they happily killed a seal which they discovered on a small patch of ice. The first sight of it created the utmost enthusiasm among the men. As the boats silently approached him and before they were within rifle shot, the seal raised his head, surveyed the strangers, and was preparing to dive into the water. The best marksman of the company with their best rifle, had just drawn sight upon the seal; and the lives of the whole party may be said to have depended on the success of the shot. A moment of breathless anxiety ensued; but the skill of Petersen prevailed. At the instant the crack of the rifle was heard the seal relaxed his long body, and his head fell flat on the ice upon its utmost verge. With a loud yell the famished men urged forward the boat with their utmost strength. When they reached the ice they rushed over it, laughing, crying, and brandishing their knives. The unhappy seal was cut into strips before he had fairly time to expire; and was gorging the men with his raw remains. Not a single ounce was lost; the intestines even, were boiled in the soup-kettle; and the cartilaginous flippers were distributed and chewed to pieces with the utmost relish.

This opportune supply of fresh food saved the lives of the party. Their mental and physical health was restored. Several days afterward they killed another seal, and thus each one retained a *mens sana in sano corpore.* On the 1st of August they came within sight of the Devil's Thumb, and were no longer wanderers in unknown regions; but were within the limits of the district frequented by the whalers. Soon they reached the Duck Islands. At length they passed Cape Shackleton, and then steered for the shore of Greenland.

Their long voyage with its infinite anxieties and toils—their perilous adventures amid cheerless continents of ice—their narrow escapes from the mountainous ice-bergs—their sufferings from cold, hunger, and disease—their apprehensions of an unknown grave in the solitudes of the Arctic realms—their doubts of a final happy escape from the innumerable perils, and of their welcome vision of their native land and the firesides of their former years—all these now terminated in eventual triumph and escape. They now shaped the course directly toward the shores of Greenland, which clearly loomed up in their distant horizon. Next day they met the first inhabitant of that world from which they had been so long shut out. It was a Greenlander who, in his small canoe or kayak, was seeking eider down among the islands which stud the coast. They hailed him. One of the men, Petersen, knew him. It was Paul Trocharias. "Don't you know me?" enquired Petersen, as the boats approached. "I'm Carl Petersen." "No," answered the Greenlander, "his wife says he is dead;" and with this response he rowed away from them.

During two days longer they continued to follow the coast, sailing southward. At the end of this time they discerned the single mast of a small shallop, and heard words of mingled English and Danish from the sailors on board of her. They soon discerned that it was the Upernavick oil-boat on its way to Kingatok to obtain blubber. The annual ship had arrived from Copenhagen at Proven; and this was one of the boats which supplied her with a cargo of oil. From the sailors on board the shallop, Dr. Kane first received information of the great events which, during his absence had agitated the world to which he had been so long a stranger; how England and France had combined with the Turk to humble the haughty pride of the imperial Romanoff; and how vast armies were then engaged in mortal strife on the once quiet and fertile plains of the Crimea. For the first time he learned the importance which Sebastopol had acquired in the history and fate of the world, surrounded as it then was with a battling host of a hundred thousand men.

They rowed on. · Soon Kasarsoak, the snow-capped summit of Sanderson's Hope appeard to them, towering above the mists; and as they approached the welome harbor of Upernavick, from which they had issued several years before in the gallant vessel they had now left behind them, they felt as only such men under such circumstances could feel. During eighty-four days they had lived in the open air, tossing in frail boats on the bosom of the angry, half-frozen deep. They were delivered from a thousand deaths, and arrived at last safely at Upernavick, where they were received with hospitality by the charitable Danes, who inhabit that lonely and cheerless outport of the civilized world.

Dr. Kane resolved to embark his party in the Danish vessel the Mariane, which sailed on the 6th of September for the Shetland Islands. They took with them their little boat the Faith, which had accompanied them through so many adventures. They only retained their clothes and documents, of all they had once possessed on board the Advance. On the 11th they arrived at Godhaven, where they found their former friend Mr. Olrik, the Danish Inspector of North Greenland. Here Dr. Kane first heard of the squadron under Captain Hartstene, which had been sent out from the United States in pursuit of him, and learned that it had touched at that spot.

This squadron consisted of two vessels, the United States barque "Release," and the United States steam-brig "Arctic." They had sailed from New York in June 1855, and on the 9th of July they were at Lievely on the coast of Greenland. On that day they resumed their search after the party of Dr. Kane, and sailed for Waigat Strait, intending to touch at Upernavick for information. From Upernavick both vessels stood northward. They soon met the floating ice drifting down; but they persisted in advancing, and thus worked along for forty miles to Wedge Island. Here they were compelled to moor themselves to the bergs, and await the opening of the ice, which had become so compact as to render their immediate advance impossible. After several days the ice opened, and enabled them to proceed. They then steamed to Sugar Loaf Island, and entered the closely packed floe of Melville Bay. By the 13th of August they had forced a passage into the North Water, after twenty-eight days of laborious sailing. They then passed Cape York and Wolstenholme Island. Here hastening on in the steamer, Captain Hartstene visited Cape Alexander and Southerland Island. These points were beyond the reach of the Esquimaux, and might probably contain traces of Dr. Kane's party. They were thoroughly searched; but no evidence appeared that any human foot had ever invaded those frozen solitudes. Thence they advanced to Pelham Point, where they observed a few stones piled together. A party landed here, and beneath this rude monument they discovered a small vial with the letter K. cut in the cork. The vial contained a large musquito, and a small piece of cartridge paper, on which was written "*Dr. Kane*, 1853."

This discovery induced Captain Hartstene to push further north. The ice however soon stopped his progress; and drifting southward with the current, he examined Cape Hotturton and Littleton Island. But no trace of Dr. Kane was found, though in a former letter to his brother, he had expressed his intention to erect a cairn on one of these localities. Fifteen miles north-west of Cape Alexander they discovered a party of Esquimaux, who, three miles distant on the Greenland shore, had a temporary settlement of seven tents, inhabited by thirty persons. Here Captain Hartstene found many articles which had belonged to Dr. Kane's party, and which had been left behind; such as tin pans and pots, canvas and iron spikes, as well as the tube of a telescope which was recognized as having belonged to Dr. Kane.

Captain Hartstene closely interrogated the Esquimaux as to their knowledge of the missing company. From them he learned that Dr. Kane, having lost his vessel somewhere in the ice to the northward, had been at that point with two boats and a sled, and after remaining there ten days had proceeded southward toward Upernavick. With such conclusive evidence before him Captain Hartstene also determined to return southward. He touched at Cape Alexander, Sutherland Islands, and Hakluyt Island. Thence he steered for the entrance of Lancaster Sound, and examined the coast between Cape Horsburg and Cape Warrander. After passing Cape Bullin he found the ice firmly packed, and the vessels seemed frozen into their winter quarters. But after twenty-four hours spent in a laborious attempt to batter their way through the ice they succeeded; and after thus making the circuit of nearly the whole northern part of Baffin's Bay, they returned toward Possession and Pound's Bay. Along this whole voyage they constantly fired guns, burned blue-lights and threw up rockets, with the hope of attracting the attention of the wanderers. They were disappointed however, and seeing no traces of Dr. Kane's party whatever, Captain Hartstene concluded that they had passed through Melville Bay to Upernavick; and he resolved at once to follow them thither.

His conjecture was right. On the 11th of September, as the Greenland vessel Mariane was about setting out from the port of Godhaven, having Dr. Kane's party on board, the look-out man at the hill-top announced the approach of a distant steamer. Soon she came nearer, having a barque in tow; and the immortal stars and stripes floating majestically at her mast-head. Instantly the Faith was lowered from the side of the Mariane, and the party in her pulled lustily for the approaching vessel. All the boats of the settlement hurried after her wake. Presently the Faith was alongside the Arctic; and Captain Hartstene eagerly hailed a little man in a ragged flannel shirt; "*Is that Dr. Kane?*" An affirmative answer was instantly returned by the Doctor himself; and in a few moments the distinguished navigator bounded on the deck of his country's ship; was received with loud plaudits of welcome by her commander and crew; and thus he and his party returned again, as those alive from the dead, to an unfrozen world of civilization, comfort, and security. Dr. Kane's labors had not resulted in the discovery of any traces or remains of Sir John Franklin's party; but it was the means of securing important additions to geographical knowledge, and valuable acquisitions in botany, meteorology, geology, and other departments of science. His researches have left but little to be obtained by any successor in Arctic explorations, however resolute, vigorous, and accomplished he may be. Dr. Kane and his associates returned to New York in the squadron of Captain Hartstene, on the 11th of October, 1855.

www.ingramcontent.com/pod-product-compliance
Lightning Source LLC
LaVergne TN
LVHW021311110826
845150LV00003B/544

* 9 7 8 1 4 2 5 5 5 7 9 9 7 *